At Ground Zero

Young Reporters Who Were There Tell Their Stories

EDITED BY
Chris Bull
&
Sam Erman

THUNDER'S MOUTH PRESS

AT GROUND ZERO: *Young Reporters Who Were There Tell Their Stories*

© 2002 by Chris Bull and Sam Erman

Published by
Thunder's Mouth Press
An Imprint of Avalon Publishing Group Incorporated
161 William St., 16th Floor
New York, NY 10038

Library of Congress Cataloging-in-Publication Data is available for this title.

ISBN 1-56025-427-0

9 8 7 6 5 4 3 2 1

Designed by Paul Paddock

Printed in the United States of America

Distributed by Publishers Group West

Contents

Introduction

Swimming against the tide of survivors seeking secure ground, journalists raced to the World Trade Center on the morning of September 11. Arriving at the scene, these intrepid witnesses were greeted by the collapse of the twin towers and a firestorm of debris so enveloping that breathing, let alone reporting, became a matter of life and death. "If the desire to flee in life-threatening situations is strong, the desire to stay and document is often stronger," writes photographer David Handschuh ("A Lens on Life and Death"), one of the tewnty-five contributors to this volume. "It's not a feeling of being invincible. It's just a need to keep recording the truth."

Handschuh should know. As he was snapping photos of the towering infernos, one of which would end up on the front page of the next day's *New York Daily News*, a "tornado" of debris lifted him off his feet and blew him nearly an entire city block, where he came to rest under a vehicle. After being dragged to safety by rescue workers, he would spend months nursing a broken leg. Far more devastating than the physical injuries were the psychic wounds. Handschuh writes that the images he captured that morning, including bodies hurtling toward the earth, are of such graphic horror that he will never share them with another human being.

Handschuh is the elder statesmen of the contributors to this anthology. With more than twenty years' experience, he had the benefit of wisdom to cope with journalistic challenges the events posed as well as the emotional fallout, which, for many, included flashbacks and nightmares.

Most of the contributors are at earlier stages in their careers, and thus even more vulnerable. Living among economic abundance and peace and security at home, it was difficult for many to imagine the earth-shattering events of September, let alone live through them. Yet to a person, each found their way through the thicket of personal and professional difficulties. They confronted the pain head on by honoring the strength of the survivors who were also their sources.

For instance, sixteen-year-old Alexander Epstein ("Out of the Blue"), a student journalist at Stuyvesant High School, watched the impact of the planes and the buildings' collapse from the window of his classroom. Despite his impulse to see the attack as an unfortunate "mishap," he was sagacious enough to put safety before story, warning his classmates away from the exposure of windows.

Chris Williams ("Facing the Fear"), a student at the Columbia University School of Journalism, watched as reporters put intrusive questions to survivors of the attacks. Some, he felt, went beyond the bounds of decency. By the end of the dreadful week of the suicide airline attacks, he was contemplating a career change, afraid of the reporter he would become. But with the encouragement of a retired nurse who is married to one of his journalism professors, he resolved to do his bit to improve the profession rather than abandon it. Like every writer in this collection—regardless of age—both Epstein and Williams, matured far beyond their years in the succeeding weeks.

Clearly, these journalists are a far cry from the mythologized war correspondent coping with internalized images of suffering and despair through stiff drinks and bawdy jokes. Many contributors discuss the strength they drew from their backgrounds. Jennifer Chen

Introduction

("The Vacation") of Reuters refers to her experience as a correspondent in war-ravaged Asian nations. Christine Haughney ("The Flow of Humanity") of the *Washington Post* invoked her coverage of the verdicts in the trial of Islamic terrorists who were convicted in the 1998 bombings of the U.S. embassies in Kenya and Tanzania.

But even that experience could not prepare Haughney for the post-traumatic stress that many journalists suffered in the wake of 9/11. "I also didn't know how to share with my friends and relatives what I was going through," she writes. "It almost felt like everything I had to say about work was too depressing. When my friends joked that a crushed bag of potato chips resembled World Trade Center victims, I remarked that the remains I saw were far more pulverized than potato chip crumbs. When my boyfriend tried to rent a movie to watch with me, it took three tries to find something that didn't have a plane crash or a terrorist in it."

The *Philadelphia Inquirer*'s Zlati Meyer ("Start Spreading the News") gained perspective through a kind of gallows humor and by recalling the stories of her grandmother, who survived a Nazi concentration camp, and an Israeli friend murdered in a suicide bombing. "My generation seems most affected by—and has best embraced—the American notion of a happy ending," she writes. "My grandparents saw the horrors of international conflict in Europe and Asia, my parents recall welcoming Vietnam into their home with the same ease as Mayberry. Generation Y, including my four younger siblings, has only experienced prosperity, the era of cloying inspirational posters sold in in-flight magazines: 'You can't spell accomplishment with out ".com."'"

The flip side of youth and inexperience is exuberance for the story and a candid, even raw, perspective on the momentous events engulfing New York and Washington, D.C. These intrepid reporters and writers dodged police barricades and falling debris, pitched in on rescue and relief efforts, interviewed shell-shocked survivors, and thereby recorded the events for posterity.

Chris Bull

David Paul Kuhn ("All I Hear Is Silence"), New York correspondent for Tokyo's *Yomiuri Shimbun*, doggedly remained at Ground Zero for over twenty-four hours, sleeping in an abandoned building in nearby Battery Park City. He left only reluctantly, believing that he had no right to be exhausted or upset in the face of such massive suffering.

The *New York Daily News* dispatched Peter DeMarco ("Journey to Ground Zero") to "get as close as you can" on September 15. When he arrived, police had sealed off everything south of Canal Street. After talking his way through one barricade, piggybacking with Tom Brokaw's news crew through another, and disobeying an officer's order to leave the frozen zone, DeMarco finally arrived at the former World Trade Center site to record his observations. "As the sun set, I glanced at a rescue worker who had dragged a chair from the bustle to the river's edge," DeMarco writes. "He began to weep, and I turned away."

For a variety of reasons, several contributors never made it to Ground Zero. Instead, Abby Tegnelia ("Camaraderie and Sorrow") of *New York* magazine, got an equally harrowing assignment: to camp out at hospitals to interview friends and relatives of the dead. Jennifer Smith spent five long months summoning the ghosts of the victims of September 11 for the elegiac "The Lost" section of *Newsday*.

"Writing these obituaries day in and day out didn't seem all that much easier for more experienced reporters," Smith writes with remarkable sensitivity. "Novice or veteran, we were all grappling with the same emotional issues. If interviewing people about September 11 made us relive that day all over again, what must pushing the reset button do for the victims' families whom we prodded to talk?"

S. Mitra Kalita ("Seeking Solace in My Notebook"), a business reporter for the same daily newspaper, did not rush toward the attacks, knowing instinctively that *her* story was in the Muslim neighborhoods of Queens and Brooklyn. There she found a halal butcher who, fearing a reprise of the anti-Muslim backlash that followed the 1993 bombing, shuttered his store early. "Please don't print my store name," the butcher begged her. "I'm just trying to make a living."

Critics lament the drift of mainstream media toward entertainment and scandal, charging that coverage of the great issues of our time languishes. Overnight, the journalistic landscape changed for the better, opening careers and beats to previously unimaginable possibilities.

But even this development pricked the conscience. These writers and broadcasters struggled to reconcile the opportunities this story afforded them with the enormity of carnage and suffering they saw all around them. They recoiled against the image of tabloid journalists forcing microphones and tape recorders into the faces of grieving victims even when they felt obliged to engage is a gentler variation of the same practice.

Heather Nauert ("Have You Seen...?") dreaded live interviews with friends and family of the disappeared. The general assignment reporter at Fox News feared that by encouraging her sources to tell their stories of hope for survivors, she would be complicit in a cruel hoax. Having surveyed Ground Zero herself, she knew that hope had died when the buildings collapsed.

In another brutally honest passage, Michael Howerton ("Witness to Catastrophe") of the *Stamford Advocate* describes sitting in his car, gathering the strength to knock on the door of a grieving family. He recognized the intrusiveness of this aspect of his job. Once inside, he treaded lightly.

Yet Howerton also recognized the benefit of chronicling private pain for public consumption—for himself and, by extension, for his audience. "The desire to sit in those houses is a mix of curiosity, fear, and ego," he writes. "If I can get close enough to study misfortune and calamity, to record the texture and measure the pain, maybe I can inoculate myself from its reach. By being close to the target, I could surely avoid the next strike. It was as if by withstanding the heat from the fire I could prove my toughness, and by watching the victims, learn how not to be burned."

—CHRIS BULL
May 2002

A Lens on Life and Death

By David Handschuh—*New York Daily News*

As *DAVID HANDSCHUH drove along the West Side Highway to the 9:30 a.m. graduate photojournalism class he teaches at New York University, he saw smoke billowing from lower Manhattan. He immediately called the* New York Daily News, *where he is a staff photographer, and headed toward the World Trade Center. There he photographed the previously unimaginable, even for a veteran chronicler of horror: falling debris, flaming buildings, body parts, images that to this day he has never shown another human being. As a second plane slammed into the north tower, he snapped a shot he still does not remember taking. As the first tower collapsed, a thunderous wave of hot gravel and glass catapulted Handschuh an entire city block, trapping him under a car. After rescue workers carried his unconscious body to safety, he became trapped again in a deli as the second tower came down. Handschuh, who broke his leg, was evacuated across the Hudson. His only regret: he had relinquished his camera in the chaos.*

Handschuh has been a staff photographer at the New York Daily News *since 1986. He has been nominated several times for a Pulitzer Prize, and has received awards for his photography from the Pictures of the Year Competition, The New York Press Photographers Association, The New York Press Club, the Society of Silurians, the Deadline Club, and many police, fire, and EMS organizations. He is a former president of the ten thousand-member National Press Photographers Association. Handschuh's photograph of the second plane hitting the North Tower appeared on page two of the September 12* Daily News. *As he was recuperating from his injuries, his graduate course on photojournalism was canceled for the term.*

If the desire to flee in life-threatening situations is strong, the desire to stay and document is often stronger. It's not a feeling of being invincible. It's just a need to keep recording the truth.

It's something I've been doing for more than twenty years as a newspaper photographer in New York City: using my camera to bring reality to the readers.

September 11 was a bit different from the start. Instead of working my usual early-morning shift at 6 A.M., I was scheduled to work Election Day returns, starting at 5 P.M.

I remember waking up that morning and looking out the window and noting what a beautiful day it was. It was the first day of a graduate level photojournalism class I was scheduled to teach at New York University.

Class began at 9:30 A.M. I wanted to be in my classroom, ready, by 9 A.M.

Driving across the George Washington Bridge, I sat in traffic and gazed out at the beautiful skyline. The Empire State building clearly stood out in midtown. The Twin Towers of the World Trade Center held up the southern end of the panoramic view.

I had no idea that in a few hours the city skyline would be dramatically changed and that thousands of families would be ripped apart by a gang of cowards who rode missiles filled with humans.

I was fiddling with the FM radio, the police scanner, tucking receipts and papers under rubber bands on the sun visor in my car while sitting in bumper-to-bumper traffic.

A Lens on Life and Death

Then I looked up.

There was a massive column of smoke coming from lower Manhattan.

The voices from the Manhattan Fire Department on the police scanner in my car were yelling to send every piece of apparatus available to the World Trade Center. My first thought was that some knucklehead had accidentally flown his Cessna or Piper into the building.

I called the office of the *New York Daily News*, told them I was on 14th Street and the West Side Highway, and asked if they wanted me to go. *Daily News* deputy director of photography Michael Lipack, who was running the desk, said to go.

I called NYU and left a message to please leave a note on my classroom door. "Professor Handschuh will be late today due to a news emergency." I didn't realize I would be an entire semester late.

My next phone call was to my home. "A plane hit the World Trade Center. I'm going" was the message I left on the answering machine.

As Fire Department Rescue One rushed southbound in the northbound lane of the West Side Highway, I swerved across the traffic island and followed it on its rear bumper. It wasn't the first time I had followed the big red truck as it raced, with siren blaring and lights flashing, to an emergency.

Their rear door was open and I could see the firefighters as they strapped on their air packs and pulled tools from compartments, getting ready to do battle with the flames and smoke.

We raced down the West Side Highway into oncoming traffic, and several firefighters waved to me out the back door. They recognized me as a friendly face who had covered their heroics for more than twenty years.

Less than two hours later, all eleven of the firefighters on Rescue One would be dead.

I arrived at the World Trade Center at 8:53 A.M. according to the dashboard clock of my *Daily News* car. I remember looking at the clock and praying that many would be spared, hoping that a few people were delayed by voting, or just took a few extra minutes outside to enjoy the crisp, clear morning.

At this point, I felt sure that I was observing a horrible accident. A single aircraft had hit the tower. At this early hour, I don't believe that anyone could have predicted a second jet slamming into the south tower.

I had no inkling of danger and no concern for my personal safety. I just thought I would be recording the largest challenge that the paramedics, firefighters, and police officers of the City of New York would ever face.

Fire department chiefs and commanders with years of experience in structural firefighting and collapse had no clue that both towers would soon be pancaking down. No one standing in the street or arriving soon after had a clue that the beautiful morning would soon turn into a field trip to hell.

And I had no idea that I would be covering one of the biggest stories in the history of the modern world.

There was massive destruction looming ninety floors up, but it was eerie and quiet on the street. In a city in which the curses of cab drivers and banging of garbage cans often serve as a wakeup alarm, it was like someone had hit the mute button in New York.

People were coming to work with their coffee and breakfast in a bag, silently standing and watching. You could hear the flames crackling and the glass breaking. You could see debris falling.

As I turned my camera lens on the flaming north tower, I realized that not all the debris falling to the street was glass and metal. I can't begin to describe what it looked like as some chose to jump to their deaths rather than confront the reality that they were about to be burned alive.

Many photographers recorded images that morning worse than the most horrible nightmare anyone could have.

A Lens on Life and Death

West Street was littered with debris—office papers, broken glass, and body parts: sights I never want to see again. I took photographs that I will never show anyone.

I walked south to the corner of Liberty Street, hoping to make pictures of people leaving the towers. There were few, yet the smoke and flames continued to spread.

People were fleeing the Marriott Hotel. Women ran carrying their high heels so they could run faster. A few were covering their heads with serving trays as they fled across West Street. People were helping others run and avoid the blizzard of debris. Medics were starting to arrive to care for the many who needed medical attention.

The streets of New York's financial district started to resemble Europe during World War II. Cars and vans were burning. Long, shiny limos had three-foot-long pieces of airplane parts through their hoods.

And then came this noise, a loud, high-pitched roar that seemed to come from everywhere, but nowhere. The second tower exploded. In just seconds, it became amazingly obvious that what at first appeared to be a horrible accident was really an act of hostility.

I didn't see the second plane, though I was looking at the tower at the time it hit. I have no recollection of making the picture that appeared on page two of the *Daily News* the next day, a photograph taken milliseconds after the plane hit the south tower.

Taken from street level looking up at the World Trade Center, the photograph is framed by an achingly beautiful blue sky as an ominous black cloud of smoke billows out of the North tower. A brilliant orange fireball spews glass, concrete, aircraft parts, and melting steel.

Time stood still as I documented the horror. But all too soon, it seemed, another loud terrifying noise shook the ground. I looked up as the south tower began to crumble and disintegrate in slow motion.

By instinct I grabbed my camera and brought it up to my eye, but in the back of my mind I heard a voice that said, "Run! Run! Run!" I've been doing this for more than twenty years and I've never run from anything.

Listening to that voice that morning saved my life.

I managed to get about forty or fifty feet and had just rounded the corner of Liberty Street when I was picked up by a tornado of night. It was like getting hit in the back by a wave at the beach. Instead of salt water, this wave was made of hot gravel and glass, cement, and metal. Suddenly, I was flying, with no control of my feet or legs. I had no choice as to which direction I was heading. I was literally flying.

The noise was overwhelming. There was cracking and creaking and things flying. The debris and the choking cloud kept coming. The locomotive-like noise lasted forever and was followed by silence. I don't think I lost consciousness, despite being picked up and thrown almost a full city block, landing under a vehicle and trapped by debris.

I know I was under a vehicle because I lifted my head and hit either a bumper or gas tank. I couldn't breathe, but eventually cleared my nose and mouth of debris.

I thought I was going to die, scared and alone, facedown in the gutter of a lower Manhattan Street. I reached for my cell phone to call home and tell everyone that I loved them, but it was gone. My pager was gone. My glasses were gone.

But somehow I had held on to my cameras. And in those cameras were two disks, with a total of 180 images recorded on them. Those two small disks held millions of pixels of history.

I started calling for help and was soon answered by words that I will never forget. "Don't worry, brother. We'll get you out." Firefighters call each other brother. The moment I heard those words, I knew I would be OK. The men and women I've photographed saving lives in New York City for twenty years were there to save *my* life this time.

A Lens on Life and Death

My guardian angels, I later found out, were Lt. Tom McGoff and a team of firefighters from Engine 217 and Ladder 131, Brooklyn. They dug me out of my tomb and went off in search of others more severely injured. I later learned that two firefighters from Engine 217 lost their lives that day, most likely after saving mine.

Another team of firefighters, led by Phil McArdle of the Hazardous Materials Unit, picked me up minutes later and carried me a block to a delicatessen in Battery Park City.

Shortly after leaving me on the floor of what they believed to be a safe place, the second tower collapsed, causing the facade of the deli to collapse. We were trapped again.

There were fifteen grown men inside: medics, cops, and firefighters who were holding on to each other for their lives. Some were calm. Others were crying or screaming, with just the desire to live. And there was my coworker, fellow *Daily News* photographer Todd Maisel, who ran after a team of rescuers carrying an injured victim to safety. Todd was in shock, realizing that the victim he had photographed was me.

I gave Todd my cameras and equipment to take into the office. He then photographed me lying on the floor of a deli, injured but alive.

I don't know how long it was until the dust cloud from the second collapse subsided. "We're getting you out of here," my guardian angels said. Using small hand tools, sheer strength, and the will to survive, they broke through the debris that was trapping us.

Three rescuers, EMS paramedic chief Charlie Wells, a police officer, and a firefighter, carried me to an NYPD Harbor boat.

I was strapped onto a backboard and placed on the front of a boat with an injured police lieutenant, a firefighter, and a few walking wounded. We headed across the Hudson River toward Ellis Island.

It was an amazing boat ride—beautiful blue sky, bright sun shining on my face. Under different circumstances it was the perfect weather for a Hudson boat cruise.

David Handschuh

Every wave we hit sent shocks of pain through my body and brought me back to reality. We were in the shadow of the Statue of Liberty, upon which is written the words:

> Give me your tired, your poor,
> Your huddled masses yearning to breathe free.

And I'll always remember the image before me as I squinted to see without my glasses: smoke rising from the World Trade Center, a symbol of New York, a symbol of the United States, a symbol of the American economic system—in ruins.

And I didn't have a camera.

The Flow of Humanity

By Christine Haughney—*Washington Post*

Throughout 2001, CHRISTINE HAUGHNEY of the Washington Post *covered the repercussions of international terrorism. She interviewed families and loved ones of the victims of the Pan Am flight that exploded over Lockerbie, Scotland. She covered the testimony of people wounded in the U.S. embassy bombings in Tanzania and Kenya. On September 11, terrorism struck at her own doorstep for the first time. She detailed the World Trade Center bombings and their aftermath, learning first hand the terror experienced by her sources.*

A Boston area native, Haughney, twenty-eight, joined the Washington Post *in May 2000, covering New York. Her coverage of air quality in the Ground Zero area spurred an internal Environmental Protection Agency investigation on how the federal body provides information to the public about air quality following national disasters. A graduate of Wellesley in political science, Haughney also earned a master's from the Columbia Graduate School of Journalism. She has interned for the* Wall Street Journal *and worked for the* Mobile Register *in Alabama, where her reporting on a drug raid on the home of a bed-bound grandmother attracted national attention. Despite losing her own home to a fire in 2001, Haughney still lives in New York City.*

For me, the story of terrorism began on a January morning, 2001, eight months before the attacks on the World Trade Center. It felt like weather suitable for a judgment day—blustery and dark. As an editorial aide in the *Washington Post*'s New York bureau, I had been hired to help cover breaking news events and write features in the New York area. This morning I was assigned to interview relatives of the victims of the 1988 Pan Am Flight that exploded over Lockerbie, Scotland.

Before dawn, these families silently herded into the federal building in downtown Manhattan to witness by satellite television the verdict against two Libyan men tried in a court in the Netherlands. At 6 A.M. , about a dozen relatives emerged from the building to offer sound bites on the one intelligence agent who had been convicted. At that hour, the only light came from camera flashes.

In my eight months reporting for the *Washington Post*, I had interviewed loved ones of murder victims, survivors of sexual assaults, and participants in other gruesome cases. The same thread of grief and anger ran through every story. It seemed that my interview subjects' grief turned to anger over time. When these victims' relatives, mainly graying parents and articulate siblings, lined up to deliver their comments to a pack of flashing cameras and barking reporters, I expected them to have put their tragedies behind them. It had been so long since they lost their loved ones.

A dozen years had made these relatives more articulate. They could offer informed sound bites about the progress their victims'

The Flow of Humanity

group had made on airport security. They sternly warned the Bush administration to treat Libya as a "rogue nation."

But their grief also felt very fresh. Some families described their children like they were alive as investment bankers, lady-killers, and actresses. Within minutes, they broke down and wept. They confessed how the crash led to divorces, depression, nervous breakdowns, and family infighting. One mother carried a frayed photograph of her son and repeated that he should have just called her for the money to take a different flight home.

"You can't believe the sorrow and horror families go through," said Jack Flynn, who lost his son, John Patrick Flynn, returning from Syracuse's study abroad program in London.

"You never get your kid back. You don't get your kid back."

I couldn't imagine twelve years of grieving. I couldn't understand why these seemingly polished families had not come to terms with their emotions. Their grief felt so deep and infectious, I felt uncomfortable being close to it. I wrapped up my reporting and left.

That morning was my first lesson in the difference between covering terrorism in the courtroom and living through it in the city I consider my home. Before the Lockerbie verdict, I could leave behind my stories of horror and woe when I clicked the send button.

The terrorism trials I would cover in the ensuing months also would be easy to walk away from each time I left the office. Covering a terrorist attack in New York City would prove much more difficult. The sights I lived through and the people I interviewed during the World Trade Center attacks don't leave me.

On the last day of May I was dispatched to cover the verdict in the trial of four men convicted in the 1998 bombings of the U.S. embassies in Kenya and Tanzania. Outside of the federal courthouse in downtown Manhattan, I met more victims' relatives—articulate and informed speakers who still had spent years processing their pain. Again I recorded their stories and ran back to the bureau to file my story.

But with this verdict, the trial had only begun. I was assigned to cover the second phase, in which the jury had to decide whether two convicted terrorists should be sentenced to the death penalty. Over the next five weeks, I spent time with victims' relatives, survivors, and the convicted terrorists. Each morning I had to return to the same courtroom with them. They became the familiar faces of my daily routine.

Throughout the hearings, it took both prosecutors and defense attorneys about 20 minutes to read the 224 names of mostly Africans and several Americans killed in the attacks. So the jury could not overlook them, they repeatedly ran through the names during the trial. Prosecutors displayed photographs of these victims with their spouses and children.

Susan Bartley lost her husband, a consul general, and her son, an intern at the embassy in Kenya. She described the adventures of a foreign service family. She then talked about starting over without her husband and son. From snoring to good-bye kisses, she missed everything about her husband.

"There is no written formula to begin my life without my husband," she said.

I sat through testimony from some of the forty-six hundred injured victims from the attack. They described a beautiful day clouded with choking smoke. They talked about running through darkness and fumes to escape the collapsing embassy. And they talked about how they struggled to overcome these memories.

Lydia Sparks lived in eight countries during her husband's sixteen-year career with the Foreign Service. At the United States Embassy in Nairobi, she was working as the warehouse manager when the attacks took place. She described how shards of glass from the bombing cut her body from head to toe. It took eight or nine operations to remove glass embedded in her eyes. She still has nightmares about people she knows who died and how she could not even bear the sights and sounds of a fireworks display at her high school's homecoming. She only relived the death and destruction all over again.

Another survivor, fifteen-year-old Sadeeta Patel, had been passing the embassy in a school bus on his last day of school when the building exploded. He was brought to the same hospital where one of the convicted terrorists had gone for medical help. Patel had lost the vision in his right eye. He couldn't play cricket or read anymore. Yet he spoke calmly about the experience.

During this trial, I learned about the effects these attacks have on rescue workers. Channa Commanday, a family nurse practitioner, testified about caring for the hundreds of victims at a local hospital. Three years later she could not erase the images of "a sudden wall of broken bodies." She described a decapitated man walking behind her shadow. She said she couldn't forget the pale green hospital hallways smeared with blood.

"The only screaming has been in my heart," she said.

In these trial phases, I also saw accused terrorists for the first time. Two convicted terrorists, twenty-four-year-old Mohamed Rashed Daoud Owhali and twenty-seven-year-old Khalfan Khamis Mohamed, were close to my age. I wondered what path had led these men—shackled at their hands and feet and surrounded by guards—to this courtroom. A jury found Owhali guilty of driving the truck and tossing grenades at embassy guards in the Kenya attack and Mohamed guilty of helping deliver the bomb that tore through the embassy in Tanzania. Both men, I learned, were followers of Osama bin Laden. Owhali had been such a good soldier in one of his camps that he was introduced to bin Laden himself. In photographs, Owhali smiled like I do in photographs. I watched him each day as he scribbled notes and whispered to his attorneys. When his attorney asked the court to sentence him to life in prison rather than the death penalty, I tried to picture him existing behind bars for the next half century. In the words of his attorney, the young man did not know what lay ahead of him.

Christine Haughney

In July, I was able to hear these terrorists speak at the trial of Mokhtar Haouari. He later was convicted of helping Ahmed Ressam with a plot to blow up Los Angeles International Airport. For the first time Ressam spoke publicly about bin Laden's camps in Afghanistan. There he learned "how to blow up the infrastructure of a country."

With chemicals he had bought in garden shops, Ressam described in a faint voice how he had put together 120 pounds of explosives he planned to detonate in a car outside of the Los Angeles International Airport. He spoke about learning how to pump gases into the air vents of government buildings and to kill puppies with cyanide and sulfuric acid.

Even though I listened for hours about how terrorists planned to blow up the United States, I never imagined they could carry out their diabolical plans. They were like many of the seedy characters I covered in drug trials. They didn't seem menacing or effective. It was another fascinating trial. My friends joked that I was spending time at the courthouse with the latest "men in my life."

On the morning of September 11, I was eating a bagel in my Brooklyn apartment when I heard on the radio that a plane had hit the World Trade Center. Within minutes, my pager began to buzz. It felt like the standard routine of covering breaking news in New York. I grabbed a notebook and ran to the train. I brought a cardigan sweater with me in case I had to work late.

A few minutes after nine o'clock, I arrived one block from the World Trade Center complex and gazed up at the smoking tower. Victims dressed in black were falling from the tower like blackbirds. "Five, six," the woman standing next to me counted them. I didn't want to believe they were people. I pushed toward the building until a policewoman stopped me.

"Stand back, the building is going to go."

I looked for a police officer who would let me through. But another policeman and a national guardsman blocked my path. I

The Flow of Humanity

tried to work my way around to the base of the tower. I got mad at myself for not switching to the N or R train, which stops closer to the World Trade Center.

Pushing to the front of the crowd, I interviewed soaked and shocked Port Authority workers who had just escaped from the tower. I pestered them for their names and job titles. Then I heard what sounded like thunder. I turned around and looked up. The World Trade Center was falling.

As this metallic cloud enveloped me, I decided I couldn't report until I could see. As I ran north, I tasted the World Trade Center on my lips. I remember thinking it was a good thing I was a runner to outdistance a falling skyscraper. I heard a woman cry "Lord Jesus, protect us." I watched people pull out umbrellas to protect themselves from the raining soot. I remember thinking it was a good thing I bought platform shoes with treads so I could run faster. I told myself I had to make myself run faster because I had to mail my sister's birthday present. I felt like crying and I told myself that grown-up reporters don't cry. Just run until you can see.

I made it to the Brooklyn Bridge. I interviewed people—well-dressed businessmen and women also covered in ash. I interviewed Morgan Stanley employees who described the ceiling collapse above them and the elevators blowing up before they could board them. Some people shouted at me. "I'm not talking to the press. I just ran for my life." One Morgan Stanley worker pointed to the second burning tower.

"The story is back there," he said.

As I walked back across the Brooklyn Bridge, soot covered New Yorkers shouted at me, "You don't want to go back there. You don't want to do that."

As I neared the edge of the Brooklyn Bridge into Manhattan, I bumped into a firefighter covered in silvery soot. He had thick gray debris clinging from his ears and arm hair like cotton. He said he had been lining up dead and burnt bodies at the foot of the first tower when it fell. He had lost his partner and his fellow fire-fighters when he ran for his life. He told me not to go back into Manhattan because the buildings were only beginning to topple.

"When you see the cops running you know you got no chance."

He started to cry. I tried to give him my cardigan so that he could wipe his face.

I then joined the crowd streaming over the Brooklyn Bridge and searched for a phone to call in my interviews. I found a synagogue and asked to use theirs. My editor, Alan Cooperman, told me to file my story, go to a hospital to interview doctors and injured patients, and then get back to the bureau in midtown Manhattan. I told him that Manhattan was blocked off. He said to do whatever I had to to get there, even if it meant walking.

Ever the dutiful reporter, I asked a hot dog vendor to point me to the Long Island College Hospital to find out how many wounded patients had arrived. Outside, there were more reporters and doctors than victims. I chatted with an ambulance driver shuttling back and forth between Ground Zero and the hospital. He agreed to give me and another reporter a ride into Manhattan. I climbed into the back of the ambulance littered with open syringes and streaked with blood. We rode over the Brooklyn Bridge and he let us off near Building Seven.

It was 12:15 and I walked through blocks of sandy remains. I walked by a discarded sandal, tufts of pink fiberglass, and thousands of burnt statements from the bank where my close friend had just quit her job. It was silent except for the distant chatter of police officers and photographers. I was so close to the collapse that there was nobody around to interview. A photographer pointed me to a block littered with plane limbs. But he said that police had stopped letting reporters down there. He also said that the photographers who walked down that street were too traumatized to talk about what they saw. At the end of this day, I had to be able to describe this for a story.

The Flow of Humanity

Without anyone to interview, I had my first moment to wonder if my family and friends were safe. I tried to remember what time my boyfriend Mark, who takes the PATH train from Hoboken, had said he planned to go to work. I wondered if the fire had extended to the buildings of my friends who worked at Goldman Sachs and the New York Stock Exchange. I was so close to the collapse that there was no line at the pay phone. I tried to call Mark and I couldn't get through to his cell phone. I left a message on my parents' answering machine and asked them to try to call him.

Then a policeman directed me north. The Solomon Smith Barney building—Building Seven—was about to collapse. This time I followed his directions. I walked up Church Street and asked for the nearest hospital. I arrived at St. Vincent's near Union Square and listened to the press briefings across the street from the hospital. My editors had asked me to get interviews with some of the injured. I thought of the wall of bodies that arrived at hospitals following the embassy bombings. But this time there were few survivors to interview. There were more families searching for their relatives who worked in the towers than there were survivors.

I finally found fourteen-year-old boy Isaiah Lopez. He had run to find his mother when he heard that the towers had been hit. He received seventeen stitches on his left hand when he was cut by a piece of glass. He spoke as calmly as the boy who was injured passing the embassy in Kenya in his school bus.

"I see a guy with a half an ear," he said. "I see people jumping from the buildings."

Nearly twelve hours after the attacks began, I had trouble remembering the name of the hospital from which I was reporting. A cashier in a drugstore told me that I looked very tired. Each time I sneezed on the train, passengers moved away from me. Soot rose from me like a cloud. I licked metallic dust off my lips. My neck itched from fiberglass needles.

That night I stayed at a Hilton Hotel in midtown because I wasn't sure if I could get back into Manhattan in the morning. I found my boyfriend, who works in finance, perched on a couch in the hotel lobby. On his walk to the PATH train in Hoboken, he noticed that the towers were smoking and had taken a bus into Port Authority Bus Terminal instead of the train through the World Trade Center. He had spent the day in midtown calling my bureau to find out if I was safe. He helped me wash debris from my ears, chatted about the attack's effect on the global markets, and fell asleep.

I stared out from my hotel room window at the twinkling sky-scrapers. I wondered if they too would fall. I tried to keep my eyes open as long as I could to make sure they were still standing. I didn't sleep.

Early the next morning I was sent back north of Building Seven to interview local residents and rescue workers walking out of the smoking pile. From four blocks north, I stared down at the crum-pling building, which had eight floors left and smoke seeping from where its windows once stood. The streets were covered with sandy silt and charred legal documents. Over the din of passing trucks, residents described to me the "flow of humanity" that once passed through this neighborhood. They pointed out the local public schools and community college that had turned into command cen-ters for government agencies. They talked about losing the shops where they bought their clothes and contact lenses. It was the first of many times I would hear younger New Yorkers talk about missing the World Trade Center's Warner Brothers store.

"This is just a beautiful area and to see it like a war zone is dev-astating," said Rob Koppert, who lived four blocks north.

All day firefighters from the entire region grimly walked out of the smoldering site. They talked about passing parked fire engines that were still running even though all of their crew had died. They described walking among pocketbooks and body parts and burning flesh. They all said they could do little to help anyone.

The Flow of Humanity

As I continued to interview these firefighters, it registered how different if felt to live through a terrorist attack rather than cover testimony about one. It didn't matter how many hours of trial testimony I sat through or how vividly the attacks were recreated. It was nothing like running from crumbling towers and inhaling acrid smoke. It was nothing like interviewing heartbroken firefighters. These experiences don't go away when I file my articles. There is too much tragedy to process.

A week after the attacks, I went to Battery Park City to cover the return of residents to their homes that had once sat in the shadow of the towers. As I walked through the Broadway Nassau subway station to change trains, workers in face masks directed me out of the station. The fruity stench of decay had grown so powerful that transit workers had to seal off parts of the station. When I made it outside, all I could smell was the endless smoky stench of burning metal, an odor that lingered for months.

When I arrived at the towers, I convinced a sweet and frazzled resident named Jeannie Kaplan to let me follow her into her apartment as she picked up her belongings. She agreed on the condition that I help her carry some clothes out for her husband and two sons. When we walked into her apartment, the power had been out for a week and the stench of rotting steaks and lemons was overwhelming. As Kaplan searched through her room for her clothing, I took notes about her children's nursery. Her two- and three-year-old sons shared a room that overlooked the Trade Center. Behind her sons' beds and rocking horse rose the smoke from the towers. I noted the objects left behind—Batman costumes and toothbrushes, a stuffed toy named Pepper, toy cars.

For the next four months, I wrote or contributed to more than thirty stories relating to the World Trade Center attacks or the anthrax scare. Most stories required me to return to Ground Zero or revisit that day. I found myself thinking about the logistics of death all the time—from trying to find out the best estimate of the number of dead people to how unhealthy it might be to inhale the fallout. The week after Thanksgiving, a crane operator from Ground Zero gazed at me as if he were spooked. He then told me I looked like the first corpse he had pulled from the World Trade Center pile, a girl about my age and size. As dozens of reporters who had come to New York to cover this tragedy left, I couldn't get away from it.

Like many reporters covering the World Trade Center attacks, I had some minor ailments. My eyes grew so infected with debris that I had to take antibiotics and wear glasses for a couple of weeks. Like most New Yorkers, I had a steady stream of nightmares and restless nights that left me cranky and overtired. I tried to exercise myself into sleeping better. I tried to overwork myself into sleeping better.

I also didn't know how to share with my friends and relatives what I was going through. It almost felt like everything I had to say about work was too depressing. When my friends joked that a crushed bag of potato chips resembled World Trade Center victims, I remarked that the remains I saw were far more pulverized than potato chip crumbs. When my boyfriend tried to rent a movie to watch with me, it took three tries to find something that didn't have a plane crash or a terrorist in it. I wept when a waitress brought me the fish entrée I ordered with its head intact. I covered my eyes until my boyfriend cut off the fish's head and hid it in the breadbasket.

In many ways I cut myself off from my friends. In the first weeks after the attacks, I didn't return their phone calls because I didn't want to spend time inside on the phone talking about work. In many cases I just assumed they couldn't understand what I had seen. The same friends whom I used to joke with about the "boys in my life" said they missed their social planner who organized our plans every Friday night.

Each week my parents would call and ask me what else I was covering besides the World Trade Center attacks. I would tell them that it was all I wrote about. My sister wrote a paper for her high

The Flow of Humanity

school religion class about how helpless her sister felt since the attacks. I think she could articulate how I felt better than I could.

My boyfriend received the brunt of my sadness. He tried to cheer me up. Every week he bought me two large bouquets of brightly colored flowers; one for my office and one for my apartment. He surprised me with front row seats to *The Producers*. He bought me endless sweets: chocolate truffles and chocolate cupcakes with sprinkles. He offered to pay for me to take a fiction writing class so that I could write about something other than the attacks. For Thanksgiving he flew us to Paris and he was concerned I would always be this emotional and sensitive about my work. I wasn't as cheery as before. He couldn't understand the depths of my sadness about the tragedy I had witnessed.

Sometimes it felt easier to connect with my sources. I found myself having endless talks with Tribeca residents and rescue workers about running from the debris and watching people fall from the towers. I had a long conversation with a veteran soldier from the war in Kosovo who understood what death smelled like. He told me someday it would get easier and that I would be able to take my hand off of my nose. I never wanted to reach that stage.

I feel guilty that I hadn't pushed ahead farther toward the towers on September eleventh. I thought of the reporters who were at the base of the buildings. I wished I had been like the journalists who hadn't run until they could see. If I hadn't run could I have better chronicled what happened? I told myself I wouldn't be able to do my job if I had put myself in any more danger. It made me feel better when senior *Washington Post* reporters consoled me that this story wasn't usual journalism. It seems so difficult to balance getting a story with protecting yourself enough to get more stories in the future.

The biggest lesson I have learned from this experience is not to judge how people process tragedy. Just like I didn't understand what the people from my articles had gone through in the

Christine Haughney

Lockerbie plane crash and the embassy bombings, I can't expect my boyfriend, family, and close friends to fully understand what it was like to live and work through the World Trade Center attacks. There's something comforting in that they don't share these recesses in my heart.

Start Spreading the News

By Zlati Meyer—*Philadelphia Inquirer*

Armed with a hard-boiled humor forged from realism, journalists like ZLATI MEYER faced September 11 with a cynical certainty that the sobriety of September 11 would eventually pass. In the first days after the attack, Meyer watched television and Internet news that dwarfed even the voluminous coverage of the Gulf War. She gained a semblance of perspective by recalling the story of her grandmother, who survived a Nazi concentration camp, and an American friend killed in a suicide bombing in Israel. In the wake of September 11, the Philadelphia Inquirer *reporter interviewed Tara Bane, still hoping her husband who worked at the WTC had survived, and Rhonda Forest, a med student who arrived at Ground Zero in time to drag bodies from the rubble. But it wasn't long before Meyer's paper returned to covering stories that only the worst terrorist attack on American soil could make look ordinary: the campaign for Philadelphia school privatization, a rabbi who murdered his wife, and the convicted cop-killer Mumia Abu Jamal's fate.*

Meyer, twenty-seven, is alumna of Boston University and the Columbia Graduate School of Journalism. She taught print journalisn at Hunter College and worked for United Press International in New York, the Staten Island Advance, *and Court TV before joining the* Inquirer. *Her writing has appeared in the* Boston Globe, *the* Christian Science Monitor, *the* New York Post, Business Week, *and* New York *magazine.*

I'm waiting for the September 11 mattress sale.

That's what will happen to that date in a few decades. Think I'm nuts? Ask World War II veterans how they feel about Memorial Day serving as the starting point for Hamptons fun, rather than as a salute to fallen military heroes.

I can see it now. On the fiftieth anniversary, Elton John will be commissioned to write the day's "anthem." Picnics will sprout in parks across the nation. Hallmark will create a line of cards, saluting this occasion with the same reverence as National Secretary's Day. Cub reporters will whine about being assigned to cover September 11 memorial ceremonies, just as journalists of today loathe writing about graying Labor Day parades. A Hollywood hotshot with a titanic-sized ego will direct the epic story of that tragic day, starring Jonathan Lipnicki as the nostalgic octogenarian and Tori Spelling's granddaughter as the beautiful female lead.

That's how I fear September 11 will end up, a white line outlining this, the corpse of American freedom. Perhaps, I will push the events of September 11 to the back of my mind, to the morgue, where horrific stories this reporter has had to write are kept on ice indefinitely. Maybe I'll only trot out the memories when one of my grandchildren return from school, assigned to ask old-timers what they were doing the day "September 11" stopped being just another date.

My story will be rather unglamorous: When I first heard the news, I chuckled.

Start Spreading the News

Sick, I know.

But I instantly thought that either (1) some moron from 1010 WINS crashed a helicopter into the skyscraper, because he was too busy coming up with an annoying drive-time phrase, an heir to "bumper to bumper," or (2) this was a John John redux. Perhaps Matthew Broderick got a pilot's license off of Page Six's radar screen and crashed a *Producers*-funded Cessna into a floor of nice Jewish boys who became accountants, insurance company executives, and traders, not actors.

On September 11, the world was just beginning to wake up, unlike when word of Pearl Harbor and John Kennedy's assassination spread. I was driving my Ford Taurus (the "mobile media mobile" complete with New York press plates, a spare pair of comfy shoes in the trunk, three map books, a phone charger, and an amazing ability to pick up New York radio stations from a few dozen miles away) from my West Philly apartment to the *Philadelphia Inquirer*'s Bucks County bureau, where I had been working for a year and a half. I had lived and worked in New York City for five years after graduating from college and continued to race up the New Jersey Turnpike almost every weekend to trade the City of Brotherly Love for the one That Never Sleeps. I sped for the last ten minutes of my twenty-eight-mile commute, anxious to do what anyone weaned on MTV would want to do next: Turn on the TV.

In front of the antennaed god, I then stood transfixed, thinking something that any rabbi I had encountered during my ten years in parochial school would shudder about: This was the Second Coming.

This was not going to be the slow news day I had prayed for. That afternoon, my bureau mates and I had planned to fete a departing colleague. My primary assignment was to cover a preliminary hearing for a man who faced the death penalty for allegedly murdering his wife in their McMansion the night before she was scheduled to meet with an attorney to discuss securing a restraining order against her allegedly abusive husband. My "civilian life" daily planner offerings included: drop off a roll of film at Eckerd, 5 P.M. Haskelovich *bris,* 8:30 P.M. appointment at Sal's Salon.

10:33 A.M.: An HR department e-mail commanded everyone to wear company ID badges at all times and guard personal and company property "as best as possible." 10:54 A.M.: My then-boyfriend e-mailed to say his office in Chicago was closing. 12:02 P.M.: A company-wide e-mail dismissed all nonessential employees. 1:33 P.M.: The Editors-That-Be had mapped out the Wednesday edition—though the newsroom had been buzzing for hours. Those of us who worked in Bucks County felt a particular connection to the tragedy, because this slice of southeastern Pennsylvania is home to many businessfolk who commute daily to New York.

E-mail became the medium of choice during those first few panicked hours and days. Cell phones weren't working in New York. Novel newsbites crossed millions of cyber-synapses to spread new information, promoting wild, sinister theories. News Web sites were jammed, thanks to the zillions worldwide who wanted to follow the saga from their desks at work, school, or home. But television—the medium I craved as soon as I had heard the news early that Tuesday morning—fought hard against its younger sibling by offering nonstop coverage, which challenged reporters to find a steady stream of witnesses to retell their accounts, producers to scramble for articulate, telegenic professors to give play-by-plays, and production assistants to type up new spools of Chyrons at record speeds. This cubed the sophistication level of the Persian Gulf War, the only other American conflict I recall.

In what is now the war on terrorism, it's my age bracket's time to shine. The old guys may cling to the anchor chairs and mastheads, but the chance to cover this on the home front—and it is a true battlefront, unlike in the 1940s and 1970s—is open to anyone and everyone. Allowing coverage to all has the potential to make us a great generation, though I'm reserving judgment for the time being.

Start Spreading the News

While the rest of America was gorging itself on every gruesome detail of the attacks that insane morning, I was forced to endure information anorexia. I wasn't immediately dispatched to help with the September 11 effort, as I had previously been assigned to cover suspected killer James Sparacio's preliminary hearing. It was hard to concentrate even on a sensational killing. The suspense crescendoed as the district justice painstakingly assured the parties that Sparacio would receive a fair trial. When the hearing finally ended, the three other reporters and I rushed out of the small courtroom to find out what we had missed. Everyone in the small lobby was buzzing about the fall of the Twin Towers. I felt like I did the night the final *Seinfeld* episode aired and I was assigned to do a story on those people who weren't watching it.

As the credits rolled, so did I. My first stop—eight hours before my scheduled appointment—was Sal's Salon in wealthy Yardley Borough, a quaint beauty shop that was busy during the lunch hour. The co-owner, Arlene Latigona was quite a yenta. Sal's managed to attract the kind of clientele you'd like to have in your school district; according to Latigona, an ambassador's wife often popped in for some "maintenance." Latigona didn't even have to leaf through her mental Rolodex for some material. Her son had escaped from one of the towers. She quickly switched into the drama queen role, bustling about the salon, answering the phone with her dye-stained hands, checking on customers and lamenting her status as a "neurotic mother" like a Royal Shakespeare Company pro.

Though Latigona had nothing to worry about, the juxtaposition of reporting on the largest terrorist attack in U.S. history not too far from Ground Zero while a dozen women waited to have their hair styled, nails lacquered, and legs denuded was the start of a sickening, saddening feeling that would only continue to grow in my heart as the country began to recover.

From Sal's Salon, I was off to go door to door to get comments from people somehow connected to the attacks. By this point, we'd received word that Victor Saracini, the pilot of the plane that had crashed in western Pennsylvania, was from Lower Makefield, Bucks County. I immediately set off trying to find folks who knew the doomed aviator, but the streets were quiet, schools, libraries, and stores shuttered. After all, metro Philadelphia was in the crosshairs of the terrorist attacks with New York to the north, Washington to the south and Shanksville, Pennsylvania, to the west. The closest I got was a Newtown Borough shopkeeper whose children attended the same church group as the Saracinis and a Yardley native whose last-minute plans prevented him from boarding a hijacked jet—and who had cheated death less than a month earlier when he managed to prevent a serial pusher from shoving him in front of an incoming subway train.

The miles on the Taurus's odometer ticked off quickly; I zipped around the eastern swatch of the county, hunting for reactions, colorful tidbits of human emotion to splash across the broadsheet in black and white. As the only non-caffeine drinking journalist on the planet, I can only point to naturally-occurring adrenaline as the source of my energy. As it coursed through my body, I had no time to ponder what was going on in the macro sense of world order. The blinders I slapped on kept me focused on getting the story. I forgot to eat and use the bathroom all day—between working the phones, popping out of my cubicle like a groundhog to glance at the TV, and typing.

I turned to the Internet in my hour of need to send an e-mail to the newsgroup my West Philadelphia neighbors had created a year before. In retrospect, the tone indicated that I had morphed—temporarily, at least—into one of those evil journalists who stick microphones into victims' faces: "I regret that it takes a tragedy to send this e-mail. If you know—or know someone who knows—who works in the Twin Towers, pref. a Philly/South Jersey native or someone with a connection to this region (i.e. a student, like you), please, please, please contact me immediately." I netted a neighbor's

Start Spreading the News

brother, a volunteer firefighter in New Jersey, who was helping out, and a family friend's buddy, a Twin Towers escapee. But as the news media has evolved from war to war, the journalist's tool this time around would, like the medium's essence itself, morph at record speed—a lesson I learned a few weeks after the country cast off its sackcloth and washed the ashes from atop its head.

And so, a few years after critics raved about the realism of *Saving Private Ryan*, we had our own ravaging imagery to watch over and over and over (and in the case of CNN, and over and over and over). Sans John Williams soundtrack, the talking heads, trotted out by all the networks and cable news channels, droned on endlessly. I recalled the year I had spent abroad between high school and college in Israel, where news of this sort came almost nightly—the same bloody images, the shell-shocked survivors, the politicians' grandstanding. It was a feeling that would creep into my unconsciousness repeatedly as September 11 receded into our collective memories, especially those of us not in the now-missing shadow of the World Trade Center.

Of all segments of the American population, my generation seems most affected by—and has best embraced—the American notion of a happy ending. My grandparents saw the horrors of international conflict in Europe and Asia, my parents recall welcoming Vietnam into their home with the same ease as Mayberry. Generation Y, including my four younger siblings, has only experienced prosperity, the era of cloying inspirational posters sold in in-flight magazines: "You can't spell accomplishment without '.com.'" My fellow Gen-Xers, the ones whose names are compiled into those annoying "35 under 35" lists, have witnessed the ebbs of the Bushes, the flows of the Hollywood-inspired Ronald Reagan and Bill Clinton. I watched as Reagan galloped us through an era when manliness was measured by shoulder pads. Sure, Bush the first reigned during a slow period, but as a youngster, I saw what I thought was the quintessential "happily ever after" under Clinton.

With Bush the second, seventies babies, like me, are back at the nadir, watching our Internet friends file for unemployment and trade in Manolo Blahniks for Candies. My sister and three brothers can't recall a time when a cable bill was considered less important than a heating invoice.

Ours is the first generation that has no context for war. The children of the 1950s and 1960s had their parents to explain what was going on halfway around the world. We twenty- and thirty-somethings are too old to turn to Mom and Dad for answers and those who are parents have no model on which to base the explanations we give the children. We have had so much practice ignoring conflict. (Our method? Skip cover stories, give a bit more to UNICEF on Halloween, and wait for the documentary to premiere on the History Channel.) In this post-Somalia, post-Bosnia, post-Chechnya era, we are suddenly not able to change the channel. And because this is the first new-media war—to borrow a device of the SATs we took not long ago, the analogy, Vietnam: Television:: Afghan conflict: Internet—we must process information for both ourselves and those who look up to us, as fast as DSL can.

But by the time I was handed names of victims' families to phone later in the week, I was no less prepared to make the sickening calls. By the second one, though, I'm embarrassed to say I had perfected my opening line: "Hi. I'm Zlati Meyer calling from the *Inquirer*. I'm hoping I haven't reached the right (insert last name) residence." Unfortunately, they all responded that I had, though I really wished they hadn't. That first day wasn't as bad as it could have been. There was still hope that people had survived. That spouses had stopped for a cup of latte at a nearby bodega and arrived at work late. That sons and daughters working in the upper floors of the towers hadn't called home yet, simply because the airwaves were too jammed by the buzzing of cells. That sweethearts and best friends had missed their flights.

By Wednesday afternoon, the wheels had been WD40-ed. A

Start Spreading the News

fellow reporter forwarded an e-mail from Temple University's media relations staff, offering up experts on force and diplomacy, national security, economic impact, and psychological aftershocks. The lead editors had set up communal electronic files to save phone numbers and other contact information. It was back to News As Usual.

As the week progressed and the body count and New York City mayor Rudolph Giuliani's take-chargeness skyrocketed, the calls were harder to make. Hope had died. The only waiting at this point was for identification made from charred remains. No good-byes. No open caskets. Better tell the kids.

Of all those I spoke to that first week, the most poignant conversation wasn't with the relatives of Fairless Hills, Bucks County, victim Donald Jones, who worked for Cantor Fitzgerald, or the two University of Pennsylvania med students who sped to New York that first day to help out at Ground Zero, only to find few living to help and settled, instead, on dragging dead bodies out of the way.

The individual who got to me was Marsh & McLennan executive Michael Bane's widow, Tara. The art therapist from Lower Makefield, Bucks County, is twenty-nine years old. Just three years older than I—and much younger than most of the *Inquirer*'s staff—Tara Bane had to face pain I couldn't even dream of. When her husband set off to work that morning to his office on the one hundredth floor of Tower One, it was any other Tuesday morning. I have since seen her on the local news repeatedly and her quotes in coworkers' articles, but I still remember our conversation, before the singsong of her voice became a dirge, when she said, "I'm praying, just hoping that he's found. I've been hearing the stories and apparently some aren't true, which makes me sick. I'm hearing stories of hope."

I didn't cry then, though. I took in those horrible images, digested them, and spat them out in time for my next assignment.

31

The picture of the bodies jumping out the windows was certainly upsetting, as is The Photo every tragedy seems to produce—the gun held to the Vietnamese soldier's head, the *Challenger* exploding thousands of feet up in the blue sky, the tailpiece of Pan Am 103 jutting out of the Scottish landscape, the sooty Oklahoman firefighter carrying a child's body.

Perhaps it was my sense of humor that enabled me to deal with this head-on; think gallows humor. To me, comedy deserves its channel and everything can be boiled down to a zinging punch line for a Conan monologue. I admit to laughing at the jokes borne of previous tragedies that preyed on celebrities' untimely deaths and the NASA tragedy. Hell, "going postal" is an acceptable phrase now.

What clawed at my core was a single word, the very building blocks of my media mason trade. The mal mot was "dead."

Those in control of Ground Zero and many of us in the news business were using more upbeat phrasings to describe the people who had been in the World Trade Center. The favored term was "missing." Sure, we had seen the planes hit, the buildings implode, but this is America, land of the euphemism. If we have "gasoline transfer engineers," we can refuse to come to terms with the massacre in lower Manhattan. The first post-September 11 Friday night, I attended services at the University of Pennsylvania Hillel House, a block away from my apartment. The undergraduate who delivered the short sermon said the word so starkly that it jabbed me in the heart, which had for the previous eighty hours been working on automatic pilot.

Part of me felt as if I had been through this before. In April 1995, a friend of mine died in Israel, the victim of a suicide bomber. That was three years after I had spent a year studying and touring in the Middle East. I knew about terrorism—saw the burned-out vehicle carcasses littering the sides of highways, came late to events after nervous bomb squads cordoned off bus terminals to blow up unclaimed suitcases, visited cemeteries that were home to as many young soldiers as old gin-rummy players, sat on buses beside Uzi-carrying, khaki-clad warriors as old as I, learned to distinguish between an Arab and an Israeli license plate, jumped at the sound of a car backfiring.

This was real. This was war. This was in my America. I didn't feel safe. Even Isaac Asimov's imagination couldn't have cooked this up.

As the grandchild of a Holocaust survivor, I had grown up with stories about war and enemies and knowing that when my grand-mother referred to her time in "the camp," it wasn't a Native American-named retreat in the Poconos. I have been taught to understand ethnic hatred. I capitalize the first letter of the word "holocaust." That feeling of being under attack was genetic and our DNA was programmed never to wear red, white, and black together and to always have a valid passport. My grandmother, who lost everyone in the flames of Auschwitz except one sister, constantly bemoans the fact that she had nothing to bury, no gravesite to visit, no tombstone on which to place a small rock, according to Jewish custom. I viewed the emotions of the three thousand-plus victims' families through this foggy prism, for this was the American holocaust.

That Al Qaeda's missives are always laced with anti-Semitism and anti-Israel vitriol hardens my heart even more. That the attacks took place days before one of the most important holidays on the Jewish calendar, Rosh Ha Shanah, made the prayers, recited at the Wailing Wall in Jerusalem, one's living room, or anyplace in between, even more earnest. To those who fled to the comforting shores of the United States, whether at the turn of the century from Europe or from the former Soviet Union a few years ago, this was a nightmare revisited. The streets once fabled to have been paved with gold were covered in ash, twisted metal, and human remains. The post-Holocaust refrain "Never again!," chanted with the rev-erence of an ancient prayer penned by Talmudic scholars, began to ring hollow. Senseless attacks on thousands of victims? *Those don't belong here. They're scenes from the Polish countryside and swastika-decorated German offices.*

Words journalists usually saved for Middle East coverage now described events in American history. Suddenly, the *New York Times*'s A section took on a new meaning for me. And newspaper sections that showcased the New York-Washington-Shanksville victims' obituaries enable me to follow that other survivor catchphrase, "Never forget." The photos of the innocent nine-to-fivers and plane passengers made the trauma all the more searing than the mental snapshots offered up by my grandmother, who has nothing left from her home other than a pair of Auschwitz-issued shoes.

But slowly things went back to normal, especially in areas not near the crash sites. Philadelphians had their own issues to worry about—the trial of a rabbi accused of murdering his wife, whether the state would take over and privatize the Philadelphia school system, the return of suspected murderer Ira Einhorn, the long-awaited opening of the Kimmel Center for the Performing Arts, local elections, convicted killer Mumia Abu Jamal's fate. Unlike our New York, Washington, and western Pennsylvanian brethren, we had nothing physical to remind us of the destruction—no gap in our skyline, no gaping hole in a building, no crater in a country field.

For a journalist like me, assigned to pick apart that fateful day and hunt for "impact stories" stemming from its aftermath, this was one news piece that didn't end when I zoomed away from my office after deadline. Covering the case of a father who sexually abused his daughter presented fewer problems; that wasn't the sort of thing people chat about at parties. September 11 was the hot topic from September 12 until today, egged on by e-mails with more "forward"s at the top than recipients. A few of the ones I received from Internet-dependent friends soon after the Big Day indicated a return to New York's natural state of rudeness and one-uppence

Start Spreading the News

("Frankly, I find your lack of responsiveness unappealing and insulting . . . not really interested in your 'dating sagas' as you like to say. I've got enough drama in my life for both of us . . . this time it's not a joke," read one Midol-lacking e-mail a Manhattanite friend sent me on October 5.) Most e-mails, however, proffered nothing more than pathetic September 11 humor—links to cheesy Web sites featuring a South Park-inspired Colin Powell and President Bush grooving to "The Banana Boat Song," an attachment featuring the rebuilt Twin Towers with a third one extending above the other two to flip Osama bin Laden the bird, bad poetry (It was a perfect day the visibility was great/Maybe too great/Perfect day. Perfect sky. Perfectly horrible), and really bad jokes (The prime minister of China called President Bush to console him: "I'm sorry to hear about the attack, it is a very big tragedy, but in case you are missing any documents from the Pentagon, we have copies of everything").

Back to Old Media. There was the newspaper's B section to fill up, so in addition to the post-9/11 stories, on September 19, I wrote about how twenty years after the U.S. Environmental Protection Agency accidentally mislabeled a toxic waste dump safe, a mistake unearthed by two Bucks County Erin Brockovich wannabes, the landfill was added to the Superfund site. The following month I authored stories about a husband and wife running against each other for township supervisor, what motivates the seemingly petty power struggles in small municipalities, volunteer baby cuddlers at an area hospital, resolving an election tie, business consultants who specialize in helping family-owned firms, and the increasing number of school districts hiring PR firms to manage their public images.

Yet the topic of September 11 seemed to seep into seemingly unrelated articles, too, like my profile of thirty-two-year-old gossip columnist Coleen Christian, who talked about the unofficial embargo on rumormongering after the tragedy, and a feature about

Zlati Meyer

Muslims celebrating Thanksgiving and Ramadan simultaneously for the first time in over three decades, a quirky overlap of the lunar and solar calendars. The events of that fateful fall day also inspired me to recast a story about volunteerism—though there was a spike in the wake of the terrorist attacks, traditional service clubs, like Kiwanis International, are seeing a dip in membership.

To come up with story ideas, I thought of questions I would have; for example, how do parents explain this horrific incident to children, especially those who embrace video games' and cartoons' explanation of "non-permanent death." My story about how to help the youngest Americans cope was published on September 24 along with a sidebar listing helpful Web sites for parents. Civic-journalism advocate Jay Rosen would be proud. Are people, questioning their own mortality, trying to get pregnant with more urgency? Are folks anxious to get life insurance and draw up wills? How is the redirecting of money to September 11 charities negatively affecting old 501(c)3 standbys and small, community not-for-profits? How has the fashion industry adjusted to wartime?

I wrote about how the events that changed our nation still ring in the hearts of those who live in the cradle of liberty. Yes, (215), not just (212), was deeply moved. I covered a parade commemorating the victims and saluting those fighting in Afghanistan, an afternoon orgy of red, white, and blue; the all-day vigil reading of victims' entire obituaries; and Operation Flour Power, a local school district's effort to bake 2,001 dozen cookies, for soldiers stationed overseas. Profiles included interviews with Christopher Love, an ironically named local software engineer who e-mailed Saddam Hussein in English to ask that he work with President Bush to fight terrorism, and surprisingly received a condolatory response from the Iraqi president (a story that prompted queries from various news outlets around the country), and with New York City firefighter-cum-comic John Larocchia, who helped organize a Bucks County comedy show to raise money for his squad, which lost eighteen members on September 11, leaving forty-eight children orphaned.

Trend stories were also easily generated. Of those that made it through the editor's sieve were an examination of how tourist spots in southeastern Pennsylvania and South Jersey, nestled between a security-enhanced Philadelphia and a scarred New York City, are reporting boosts in attendance, as Americans avoid air travel and steer clear of large cities. "I know airports are doing everything they can for security, but they can't handle everything. I didn't want to be worrying about that on my wedding day," said Nashville's Leigh Ann Villanueva, who together with husband Tony drove twelve hours to honeymoon at the Caesars Cove Haven in the Poconos after canceling their trip to Jamaica on September 12. Another, which sparked the attention of PBS's *Frontline* producers, was the tale of Philadelphians participating in a twenty-four-hour-a-day Psalms vigil, called *shmirah*, at the makeshift September 11 morgue on Manhattan's East Side. The nonstop recitation is done until the deceased are buried to honor the souls. Since the piles of body parts stored there include those of Jews (regardless of religious observance), someone must do the *shmirah*. The cops and medical staffers who sit near there during breaks are in awe, because here are clean-cut young women and men spending their nights and weekends concerned about the victims. In their hands weren't the day's *Wall Street Journal* or Broadway *Playbill*, but copies of an ancient book written when "Random House" meant "any tent."

But one might argue that their prayers also are for the soldiers fighting in Afghanistan, avenging those killed in the twin towering infernos—young men and women whom we may have sat beside in a college class or danced with at Webster Hall, like Pfc. Kristofer Stonesifer, twenty-eight, and Spec. Jonn J. Edmunds, twenty, the first two combat-related casualties of the U.S. war on terrorism.

Their Black Hawk helicopter crashed in Pakistan on Friday, October 19; the military released the news two days later on the

Sunday I was writing the "bright" about Christopher Love. The weekend editor called (that fast, internal phone ring always means trouble when it jingles so close to the end of an eight-hour shift) and informed me that Stonesifer was a Bucks County native and we needed family reaction. Information provided by his father, Ric's, fiancée landed on A1. But when I showed up at his ex-wife's house in rural northeastern Bucks County after ignoring all speed limits in an effort to reach the unpublished address before the obtrusive TV trucks, the man I believe was Ric Stonesifer said only, "You've got to be kidding." His voice was filled with rage, because I was trying to get a quote, as he was trying to get a grip, having only had an hours-long head start in the grieving process. Like an FBI agent, I stayed in my car on the road staking out for an hour to see if anyone else would pass me to head up the winding lane to the house of mourning. Nothing. The following morning when I returned, the man said, "Stay away," and slammed the door in my face. A first for me.

The younger Stonesifer, sadly, also made the war ours. He fought for a country he'd lived in for less than three decades. His images of war come from Oliver Stone, Steven Spielberg, and Michael Cimino. His was a face unlined with the woes of unpaid bills, aging parents, and post-Depression era angst. He used high-tech equipment, but was doing the exact same thing fighters did in his native southeastern Pennsylvania roughly two centuries earlier: Fight for the United States' freedom.

Stonesifer had his Ground Zero, though a world away from where Americans pay homage to bin Laden's victims.

I haven't been to lower Manhattan since the catastrophe.

I have no plans to go.

It's something I don't want to see, in the same way I have zero desire to travel to Vietnam or visit World War II concentration camps. When I drive on the Brooklyn-Queens Expressway on my way to Manhattan, I don't allow myself to turn to the left to sneak a peak at the altered skyline.

Start Spreading the News

Most people haven't embraced this philosophy. New York City officials erected observation decks for passersby to watch the huge cleanup effort. Has this sacred spot in American history, our Achilles' heel forever, become the latest tourist trap? When will Starbucks open a store there?

Perhaps it's denial.

But I think it's my reality.

No jokes here.

Diary of Disaster

By Nick Spangler
—Columbia Graduate School of Journalism

For many ambitious reporters, September 11 was the ultimate challenge. NICK SPANGLER arrived at the World Trade Center within minutes of the first attack. Defying police orders to evacuate the area, he approached the burning towers, avoiding the debris of the collapse by ducking into a Starbucks. Emerging from the protective confines of the café, he witnessed a scene seemingly ripped from a Bosch painting: ash-covered fire men and women searching abandoned buildings, a severed leg wrapped in burlap, uneaten meals covered in thick, beige dust, the collapse of WTC 7. When he sat down to write that night the horrible images were still vivid, and words describing them flowed easily.

Spangler, twenty-five, is a student at the Columbia Graduate School of Journalism. Before enrolling at Columbia he was a bike messenger in Manhattan and a sports reporter for the Southampton Press.

I won't forget the sound the plane made, heavy and rasping. It flew over my head and into the north side of World Trade Center One and then it vanished. I could see only smoke and a hole.

8:46 A.M.

I was outside P.S. 89 on Chambers and Greenwich tailing a city councilman on the third stop of his election-day campaign when the plane hit. "Put the babies in the school, get them inside!" somebody shouted.

I started running. It took me perhaps two minutes to get to the great square off Church Street still bounded by those massive towers. Millions of documents floated in the sky. There were sirens almost immediately but there was no one to stop me and I wanted to get as close as I could. WTC 5, on the north side of the square, was ringed by a ledge about six feet wide and I used it for cover. Fist-sized chunks of concrete and long strips of steel and tiny pieces of glass were hitting the ground beyond the ledge. Three building maintenance guys and a cop came out. We told each other what we had just seen and then when we saw the bodies falling we were rendered inarticulate. "Jesus Christ oh Jesus Christ!" someone said. At some distance falling debris can be mistaken for bodies but I can say this with absolute certainty: I saw two bodies fall and I saw four that had already hit. I saw one fall on the opposite edge of the square, arms out and legs straight. I heard it tear through the roof of a bandstand and I heard it hit the ground. Closer to me I saw a woman hit the concrete.

Nick Spangler

At nine A.M. WTC 2 got hit. There was that same rasping sound and a crack at impact. The others left. I stayed and when the glass came I pressed myself against the wall and covered my face with my left arm. I heard the glass tinkling around me and soothing music coming from speakers above me and I thought there was a time when I could have chosen to escape.

A/C ducts were dropping all over the place but the glass abated. I could see the dead woman in front of me; I knew that she was a woman because she was wearing a skirt (sea green) and I could see her legs. From about 150 yards away, I could see her blond hair but not her face. I thought if I could edge around the corner I could get much closer to her and still be protected by the ledge but the second I made the turn I became terrified and had to back up.

At 9:15 a man came sprinting out toward me. "What are you doing here?" he asked. I showed him my press pass. He pulled out a badge, smiled and said, "Mine's bigger than yours." He was FBI. "This whole area is a crime scene and it's still dangerous out here, man. Just back up across the street." He made the turn I couldn't and he was gone.

I figured I'd retreat and then try to get into the complex from the south side. I ran through the deserted farmer's market and got under the ledge of WTC 2 on Liberty Street. Debris was still falling. Something hit a stoplight and it bounced crazily but did not fall. It was getting hard to breathe. A policeman across the street yelled at me. At 9:25 I saw fifteen to twenty-five firemen cross the Liberty Street walkway toward WTC 2.

Two policemen escorting a television camera team came to get me. We walked back east toward Church. They went inside WTC 2 and told me to leave. I showed them the press pass and argued that cameramen shouldn't have special rights. They didn't buy it.

I waded through ash, rubble, and paper to what looked like a medical staging area. I ducked under the tape and was confronted immediately. I showed the pass. This time, it worked.

Diary of Disaster

"We need triage now!" someone shouted. There were women in tears. I saw raw flesh on the side of a woman's face. I saw people dripping blood.

I spoke with a man named Reyher Kelly who had been on the seventy-eighth floor of WTC 2 when the plane hit. "We had just seen the explosion," he said. "We saw people fall out. I was getting into the elevator when it hit us; the explosion just knocked us down. I was just going for air and light. I jammed my hand in the door and got into the stairs with some people. It was just carnage on the seventy-eighth floor. There were bodies just lying there, arms. There was a person decapitated ten feet away from me. It took us about thirty minutes to get down. We saw some firemen on the twentieth floor, told them to go get those people."

Bill Hay was in WTC 1 on the fifty-fifth floor giving a lecture at the World Trade Institute when the plane hit. "The building started to rock," he said. "I thought it was an earthquake. I looked out the window, saw all the debris falling and just left my laptop, my billfold, passport, plane tickets. It's all gone." Coming down the steps he saw injured people, too many to count. Some were badly burned. Somebody told him the first plane was a 767 Boeing.

Alan Mean was trying to get out of WTC 2 when the plane hit. "I took the elevator down," he said. "It crashed, caught on fire." An EMT was tending to him, fiddling with the buttons on his shirt. "My leg is tingling," he told her.

I ran into the same policeman who'd been yelling at me. "Hey!" he grabbed me by the neck. "You didn't hear me? What are you doing in here?" There were two cameramen and at least one other reporter in the area. I showed him my press card. He took it. "This doesn't mean shit," he said, pocketing it.

I was escorted out. The area was flooded with police funneling all the civilians uptown. I figured I'd turn on Vesey, go a few blocks east before dropping downtown and doubling back. Windows were shattered on both sides of the street. Somebody must have been hit by the glass; there was a little puddle of blood and some crimson napkins in the gutter by the curb.

10:00 A.M.

I didn't make it far. There was a roar like being next to a jet engine and I thought another plane was headed for us. I was wrong. WTC 2 collapsed of its own accord around 10 A.M. People screamed and ran past me. It became a stampede. I joined. A cloud rolled out toward us; we were actually racing it: heavy, suffocating dust and grains of something hard and sharp. We ran up Park Row. I got caught, tried to hold my breath and find a doorway while I could still see.

Somebody opened the door. It turned out to be a Starbucks. There were about twenty people inside. The store manager told us all to drink and handed out bottles of spring water, offering juice instead if we wanted it. The windows turned opaque and we heard things bouncing off the glass. The manager told us all to get into the basement. "Does anybody need anything? Is everybody all right here?" he asked.

We crowded into the basement. A woman in a Starbucks apron was sobbing uncontrollably. Someone she knew named Aaron worked in the towers. The phone rang. The manager answered. "Hello, Starbucks Coffee." The district manager was on the other end. He told us to leave the store. A woman took the phone and told him we weren't going to be leaving for a while. We stayed for twenty minutes, until the air outside cleared and city buses started evacuating people.

10:27 A.M.

I walked back down Park Row. I was talking to a policeman at the Broadway intersection when WTC 1 came down. I heard the roar and saw the cloud swell again. This one carried more debris than before. I ducked back into Starbucks fast. Not everybody had left and together we watched it get dark again outside. Something smashed the front window and somebody yelled a warning as the glass shattered. The store filled with dust and we retreated to an upstairs bathroom. We flushed our eyes and nostrils under the faucet.

The only family I have left in this city is my aunt. She runs a nursery school at 15 Dutch St., not far from the trade complex. I called her at home. No answer. That meant she was almost certainly at her school and I was worried. When it cleared outside I took the only cloth I could find, a rag used to mop up coffee grinds, rinsed it in water and tied it around my head so it covered my mouth and nose. I headed down to Fulton and made the turn onto Dutch. I got to number 15 and they buzzed me in. My aunt was there and she was OK. I grabbed her and pressed my face into her hair.

I couldn't stay and I told her that. I took a Teacher's Roll Book because my notebook was full and when I left she was sitting with her teachers and the children in a circle on the rug. Somebody was playing a guitar.

11:00 A.M.

The sun was barely visible. People were moving in twos and threes towards the river; we were shades, soundless. I went into a deserted Green line station at Two Federal Reserve Plaza. The lights were on and the Metrocard machines still worked, blinking through the dust. There were no footprints but the ones I left.

At the corner of William and Maiden I passed bubbling fountains, phones dangling on their cords. A man in a bandanna and sunglasses was photographing an abandoned stand of dusted bananas and plums and nectarines. Up close I could see around each at the bottom a narrow bright ribbon of flesh where the dust never touched.

11:10 A.M.

I heard a man scream somewhere south of me. I ran toward the sound. Cedar and Pine were empty and a bank guard on Wall Street had heard nothing. I have no idea what happened to that man.

I cut across Trinity and ended up at the corner of Greenwich and Rector. The cops were evacuating a stream of office workers in single-file. They ignored me.

A fireman handed me a pair of masks to replace my rag. I walked north toward the wreckage of WTC 2 with a fire company doing a building sweep. Here the street signs were coated and illegible; the trash and rubble drifted four feet deep. We passed a three-car pileup, windows blown out on every single one.

11:25 A.M.

We heard a rapid series of explosions in the distance. Gas, said one of the firefighters. They were about to search a building that was cleared hours before. It made no sense to them to look again but one said "We gotta do what Cap says" and that settled it.

I wanted to see the World Financial Center and the west side of the Trade complex. It took a while to get there, picking my steps through the wreckage on West St. It got worse farther north; outside the World Financial Center it was all wreckage, and sometimes I had to climb.

11:30 A.M.

What is chaos?

WTC 2 blown to bits, ripped apart. An eggshell-thin frame above a mass of rubble covering most of a city block. Steel girders three feet thick, obscenely contorted.

NYFD, NYPD, ATF, Customs, Secret Service, EMT, Hatzoloh (the Jewish volunteer ambulance service), Parks Department, men in camouflage, canine units. Smashed and upended trucks, engines, ambulances, police cruisers. Sirens, more machinery. A crushed Mercedes-Benz convertible in flames. Reams of documents shuffled out more or less evenly over everything.

Diary of Disaster

I took a photograph for four men who wanted WTC 2 as a back-drop. Everybody was doing it. Kodak disposables were popular.

I saw a piece of somebody's leg get wrapped in burlap and left beneath a defoliated tree.

West St. underneath WTC 1 was the staging area for the first response team. It was annihilated when WTC 2 collapsed. Many of the men that arrived within minutes of the first explosion were missing, buried sixty-feet down in the rubble. The chief was one of them. Rescue 1 and 2 were gone. Nobody could find the EMTs first on the scene. The 279 Company's truck was relatively intact but the 279 Company was missing.

The number of missing firefighters alone was put at one hundred to three hundred. Nobody could say for sure because many of these men were working out of company. Some were headed home, some were on vacation, when they got the call or heard about the disaster on the radio. They headed back, met up with their own companies when they could, formed new ones when they had to, used borrowed equipment if that was all to be had.

Noon

They'd been working for three hours. It was difficult to get bull-dozers on the site to clear workspace. It was hot and a hard wind blowing off the river kicked up the dust and ash. The men were coated in it and the rims of their eyes were red. The masks everybody wore filtered some but not all of the dust and clogged eventually when moisture turned the dust to silt.

Firemen (and it was almost entirely men that day) are tough and they're trained to work in conditions that are literally lethal. Every one of them must know it's going to happen sooner or later to somebody; but nobody's ever prepared when it does.

"Scottie and Mookie went in there. Anybody seen them?"

"Where's Bobby? I ain't fucking leaving until they find Bobby."

"Head count. Fucking head count, NOW!"

Nick Spangler

I spoke with a firefighter who was inside WTC 2 when it collapsed. "I will never forget that sound," he said. "You just heard the building come down. A huge whoosh, and then it was just blackness. We had fifty firemen in there and a lot of us had our gear off." One man was partially buried. "We didn't leave. We stayed to cut him out. There was a second collapse and we lost him."

3:00 P.M.

When a team formed to clear the north tower of the World Financial Center, I followed. The massive dome of the foyer was intact; the marble floor was slick under the ash. There were more documents. The windows on the west side were blackened. Those on the east were blown out. They were double-paned. I explored the second floor alone. Reception: phones off the hook, milk shake on desk, computer monitor on floor. Vase of flowers upright and intact. Gym: rows of treadmills and Stairmasters, heavy bag, dumbbells. More documents. Everything uniformly beige in the dust. Again I felt the powerful swell of unreality: too perfect, an artist's project, life-size in papier-mâché.

I caught up with the firemen on the fourth floor. They split up, working in pairs, keeping constant voice contact. I followed them into rooms with Styrofoam coffee cups left on desks, donuts on paper plates. In fifteen minutes, the men checked every single room, closet, and cubicle on the floor, breaking down doors when they had to.

5:25 P.M.

WCT 7 caused a commotion when it collapsed around 5:25. For the next two hours I watched the rescue work. I tried to call my editor on a pay phone and watched a man next to me hang up and start sobbing. I got my eyes flushed out twice and saw huge men hooked to oxygen tanks weak and sprawling like babies. I talked to a man from Ladder Company 134 in Queens. He began his day getting his

Diary of Disaster

son dressed and packed for his first day of prekindergarten. "You know what? Fuck this," he said. "Just fuck this."

On the train ride uptown I was covered in the dust and my eyes were so full of the junk I could hardly see. People stared and somebody asked me if I was OK. I am pretty sure they thought I'd been trapped, that I'd escaped.

I carried with me three things that I'd snatched at random from the blast site: a memo from Matthew to Jeff about Karen's secretary, the front page of a report on Telecom Strategies for the New Decade, a photograph of a mustachioed man in a tuxedo at a podium. They stink of burnt plastic and there's still enough dust on them to make my skin itch when I handle them.

September 11 was one of the most democratic and liberating events in memory for those of us in the news industry: disasters, by definition violent and random, often are. By being lucky and working hard you could put yourself in the middle of the biggest story in the world, no matter what you were doing before. The demand for information was instant, intense, and overwhelming.

But people are rarely comfortable with those who gather such information, sift it, and weave it into stories as others mourn. The activity seems morbid and profane. If it is practiced with ambition and satisfaction, it seems sick.

There is the girl who called me a vulture; there is the psychologist who believes if I am not in shock, I must be in denial. The normative assumption is that a moral person will be either immobilized or repulsed by a holocaust.

It was quite the opposite with me. I spent twelve hours downtown reporting, headed back to my apartment on 120th St., had some drinks and a shower, and wrote without interruption until afternoon the next day. Most of the time the experience of writing for me is plodding, uncertain, something to be dreaded; but that night the paragraphs came easily and I knew they were good.

I cannot think of a way to say this that is not perverse but I felt an intense passion in the hours after the holocaust, an exaltation. I felt alone at the center of the world; all details became crucial and iconic. I tried to record absolutely everything. My own importance in the world was suddenly magnified, or I felt it so. I fed on the destruction around me.

When the feeling was gone I missed it: a pretty average reaction, I'm told. Everyday life is a lot of what that day was not: tedious, lonely, filled with vacillation and spent mostly trying to satisfy a few very base appetites.

I wrote this about a week after the attack:

I believe that our present way of life ended in those minutes or hours. The American ethos—the way we see the world and our place in it—fractured and will perhaps have to be discarded. That is the dressed-up, smoothed-over analog of seeing planes vanish into buildings and people coming down from the sky. I think it is proper and honest to say I wanted to experience that for myself and communicate it with as many others as I could.

The passage looks dated to me now, in late December. It was written when we thought the death toll was counted in tens of thousands and there were armed Guardsmen posted on the subways and street corners of Manhattan.

Our way of life did not end so much as it was interrupted; and if there is such a thing as an American ethos, it has not been significantly altered. There are those relative few whose lives bear the permanent bloody brand of that day but most of us continue to be shaped by much more banal events.

A communal, truly epoch synecdoche has been taking place ever since the first images of that day were widely disseminated; the reality of that day has been reduced to the image of a plane falling into a building, a building falling down.

That, in retrospective, is as good reason as any for running toward the towers and not away from them. The particulars of the

Diary of Disaster

experience are what keeps it from being eroded by the rest of life and I had to be there to get them. If I were the sort of person that did not care about the particulars or trusted others to get them for me I would probably not have chosen reporting as a career.

Seeking Solace in My Notebook

By S. Mitra Kalita—*Newsday*

While many reporters rushed toward the burning buildings in Manhattan on September 11, S. MITRA KALITA, a business reporter for Newsday's *New York City edition, interviewed residents and business owners in the Muslim neighborhoods of Queens and Brooklyn. Fearing a reprise of the anti-Muslim backlash following the 1993 bombing of the WTC, a halal butcher shuttered his store early that day. A hijjab-clad woman described being treated like a terrorist. And a drunkard who saw Kalita entering a Middle Eastern market cursed at her. Two days later Kalita profiled a Muslim-owned deli serving the rescue workers at Ground Zero.*

Before and after September 11, Kalita, twenty-six, endeavored to cover the South Asian and Arab American communities. Since joining Newsday *in the summer of 2000 she has covered the city business beat, focusing on small businesses, immigrant entrepreneurs, and the airlines industry. She is at work on a book about immigrants in suburbia told through Indians in central New Jersey. Kalita (www.desiwriter.com) previously worked as a reporter at the Associated Press. She has interned at the* Wall Street Journal, *the* Baltimore Sun, *and the* Patriot Ledger *in Quincy, Massachusetts. She sits on the board of the South Asian Journalists Association.*

I was getting my teeth checked.

On the morning of September 11, 2001, I sat in a dentist's chair. Earlier that day, I had seen on the morning news that a plane had crashed into one of the towers of the World Trade Center. I still have no idea what caused me to click off the TV. Perhaps it was the year I spent as a wire reporter in suburban New Jersey where plane accidents seemed as common as car crashes. But dismiss it I did—*probably a Cessna or a student pilot*—and I walked the two blocks from my apartment to the dentist.

"You hear about the plane crash?" he said.

I nodded, silenced by the gloved fingers in my mouth.

"Terrorism," he declared. "It's definitely terrorism. Two planes? Too much of a coincidence."

Two planes? I sat upright, practically banging my head on the lamp attached to my chair. *Terrorism?* That's not what the morning news had said. And there had just been one plane a few moments ago.

"That's right. You're a reporter," said the dentist. Then, calling into the hallway for his assistant, "Get the radio in here."

In came the radio and a stream of static and information. Two planes into two towers. The mayor on the scene. United Airlines. American Airlines. Pentagon struck. More hijacked planes possibly in the air. Landmark buildings from Empire State to Sears Tower evacuated.

As we listened, the dentist gently pushed me down and continued

53

his work. When he left for a moment, I again sat upright and looked through the door. In the examining room across the hall, the assistant listened to the latest on a black-and-white portable television tuned into a Spanish station. I tried to follow, having learned the language in the three years my family lived in Puerto Rico.

The assistant came running into my room. "It fell down," she cried. "One of the towers fell down."

My hand flew to my mouth and I stood. I started to shake. In came the dentist.

I sat back down. The phone rang. It was the dentist's wife.

"I'm not coming home," he said into the phone. "I'm fine."

His gloved finger entered my mouth again. At almost the same time, we spoke.

"I can't do this."

"I'm not going to do the cleaning."

"I have to go."

"You're too much on edge."

I ripped the blue paper bib off. I fished my reporter's notebook out of my bag and ran out the door. I stopped shaking.

In Jackson Heights, the section of Queens I call home, the calm, tree-lined streets I'd walked minutes before were suddenly marked by chaos and confusion. Passersby puzzled over their now non-functional cellular phones. Lines at the pay phones were a half-dozen people deep. Commuters were turned away from subways. Passengers from nearby LaGuardia Airport bussed in. Parents brought children home from school and daycare early.

I interviewed all of them. Rather, as many as I could, in Spanish, English, some broken Hindi, and Bengali. Suddenly, it felt like every life skill I'd acquired, every story I'd ever worked on, converged.

There was Jimmy Van Bramer, a candidate for New York City Council, who kept campaigning, unaware the primary scheduled for that day was about to be canceled.

There was Diana Goldberg, a social worker from Arkansas,

waiting to go home when her plane was abruptly disembarked. "They were saying we should get as far away from the airport as possible," she told me. "Maybe the airport will open in an hour."

There was Lea Perrera, a Brazilian immigrant here just two months, who held her son's hand as she walked him home. With Spanish the only language we had in common, she told me how he kept asking her where the fire was. "I don't know what to tell him."

Then I entered a halal market, a shop selling meat slaughtered according to Islamic law.

It was still early and no one had assigned blame yet for the morning's events. Nonetheless, the butcher braced himself. He shook his head when he saw my face, the same shade as his own, and said sadly: "I just hope this isn't like 1993."

That of course was the year terrorists exploded a bomb underneath the World Trade Center, failing to topple the towers but killing six people. My mind flashed back to my junior year of high school. It was the first year my best friend, the daughter of Pakistani immigrants, was trying to cover her hair with hijjab. She struggled with the decision, and it was not made easier by the fact that stereotypes of Muslims as fanatics and terrorists were being invoked. By senior year, my friend had abandoned the hijjab.

I interviewed the butcher, who didn't want to say much once he discovered I was a reporter. He planned to close his shop. He feared retaliation from the ignorant. He wanted his wife and children to stay indoors.

"Please don't print my store name," he begged. "I'm just trying to make a living."

Across the street from the meat shop, a group of Muslims clustered around a street vendor with a radio. "It's just like Oklahoma City all over again," said one. "They're going to blame us right away."

"Maybe it was an accident," said Nozmur Chowdhury, a Bangladeshi immigrant who couldn't get to his job at a hotel. "They haven't done an investigation yet."

Here was my story.

I hadn't yet talked to an editor and my cell phone still wasn't working, so I got in line at the pay phone, interviewing those waiting around me. On an earth-shattering story like this, reporters essentially feed their notes to a fellow reporter on the other end of the line. Luckily, I reached Katia, a fellow business reporter and my closest colleague at *Newsday*, read her the quotes I already had, and told her the story I planned to report.

"Is anyone already doing it?"

"Not like you will," she said, then yelling decisively into the newsroom, "Mitra's going to Muslim neighborhoods to get reaction."

"Good idea," I heard an editor respond.

Journalists of color, like myself, enter the newsroom knowing our jobs will always go beyond gathering the day's news. We represent. We remind. Yes, we advocate.

In my case, my entry to journalism had everything to do with my skin color. It was 1993 and I was a sixteen-year-old with no career plans. Rider College was running a summer boot camp for minority youth in New Jersey who were interested in journalism. I needed something to occupy July since I couldn't get my driver's license until August. I applied and got in.

It wasn't until a cafeteria conversation a few days before school ended for the year that I felt the first of many uncomfortable moments as a minority journalist. We discussed our summer plans as high school juniors in suburbia do—tennis camp, scholars programs, jobs at the mall, stints as ice-cream scoopers.

"I'm doing a minorities journalism workshop," I said.

My redhead friend stopped before taking a bite of her rectangular pizza. "A *what* journalism workshop?"

"Minority."

"You qualify?"

"I guess so." Then more firmly, "Yeah, Indians are minorities."

Seeking Solace in My Notebook

The redhead shook her head and didn't say anything. She didn't have to.

I left the lunch table early that day and went to the library. I tried to name an Indian—any Indian—who was a reporter. I couldn't.

On September 11, subways had stopped running, and cabs were nearly impossible to hail. Jackson Heights houses the city's largest shopping district for South Asians; Indians, Pakistanis, and Bangladeshis all work side by side. While interactions remain remarkably harmonious, occasional tensions do arise. I stayed in my neighborhood for a good part of that morning, talking to all groups about the potential repercussions. Many merchants shuttered their shops, mostly out of respect, but some out of fear.

"I hear they're cheering on Atlantic Avenue," accused one Indian immigrant, a Hindu, who works in a jewelry shop.

Atlantic Avenue runs through Brooklyn and boasts the city's largest strip of Muslim retailers selling religious artifacts, books, scarves, and clothing. I knew my day's reporting would eventually take me there. First, though, I headed toward Steinway Street in Astoria, a fledgling Arab neighborhood.

Once there, I stopped first at a Middle Eastern grocery and deli I'd been to before. Before I entered, a drunkard swaggered down the street.

"We need to get them," he slurred.

I looked at him.

"What are you looking at?" he said. He muttered, but I distinctly heard him say "Muslim" and "bitch."

I rolled my eyes and walked inside. The cashier, a woman who wears hijjab, had heard him too. So had a grad student who sat at the counter eating a meat pie. The owner, a mustachioed man who emigrated from Beirut, looked distressed.

"We are so sorry," he said. "Are you OK?"

Before I could introduce myself as a reporter, the owner and his cashier had put me into a chair and handed me a just-warmed meat pie and a cup of mint tea.

"I'm fine," I mustered in between bites and sips. "But I'm here to check on how you're doing."

And so went most of my interviews, filled with fear of what was to come and sadness for what had already happened. I made my way down Steinway Street, stopping at a travel agency, a mosque, Moroccan restaurants, and Egyptian cafés where smoke from cigars, cigarettes, and shisha pipes swirled.

"A lot of people are scared, but we have no time to grieve and cry like everybody else," said Ali El Sayed, owner of the Kabab Café. "Because everybody's categorizing us."

By late afternoon, I knew it was time to get to Brooklyn, but cabs appeared even harder to hail.

Determined to keep interviewing, I approached a man on the corner. We started talking. His name was Faysal. He was from Algeria. He drove a limousine.

"How much you want to drive me around for the day?"

"You won't be able to afford it."

"One hundred bucks OK?" I asked, with more than a hint of desperation.

We talked as he drove. I got my first update in hours from the car radio. I didn't pause to think about my friends who worked downtown. I just kept interviewing. I didn't stop to call my mother. I just kept asking questions.

As the car passed the Manhattan skyline, we grew silent. I stared at the plumes of smoke. I turned away . . . toward Faysal to ask him another question.

The summer of the journalism workshop did more than jump-start my career. At the impressionable age of sixteen, I discovered a job with a mission. I formed relationships with aspiring black, Latino, and Asian reporters as we talked late into the night about combating ignorance through education, interviewing minorities for more than stories about crime, holidays, and religious festivals. We threw around all the clichéd sayings I would be hearing for years to come. We wanted to cover communities from within. We wanted to give voice to the voiceless. We really meant it.

Indeed, it took being a reporter to discover my cultural identity. Religion never played a big role in my home; my father is Buddhist, my mother Hindu. We lit incense, worshiped icons, and prayed at births, weddings, and deaths. As a child in Puerto Rico, I also remember going to Catholic church with my neighbors. My brothers and I put our shoes out for gifts on Three King's Day and took part in paranda, a ritual that mimics Joseph and Mary's search for lodging. As a teenager in New Jersey, I attended so many bat and bar mitzvahs that I learned parts of the Torah. And my closest friend in high school was a Muslim Pakistani-American, in spite of the warring homelands of our parents.

When it came to our rearing, my parents weren't overbearing or strict like some families we knew. We had no curfew. We weren't forced to take Indian dance, language, or religion classes. There were no expectations of arranged marriage. Instead, my parents chose subtle methods to ensure we had some ties to their birthplace. At home, we speak Assamese, a northeast Indian language. Bookcases fill every room, boasting the Bhagavad Gita and biographies on Gandhi. But there's also black literature and the Bible, Kahlil Gibran, and *The Satanic Verses*. I awoke on weekend mornings to the strains of Indian music and the smells of curries and fried breads. But my mother also makes better platanos than samosas.

Every day as a reporter, I translate worlds, including my own. September 11 was no different.

On the way to Brooklyn, we passed hundreds of New Yorkers forced to leave Manhattan via bridges and tunnels. These were people whose knowledge of city geography was its subway map. For many, that city ended at Manhattan's borders.

I asked Faysal to stop at an ATM machine inside a gas station. There, I met two distressed-looking women who lived in Brooklyn, frantically calling their friends with cars to come get them.

"Forget it," I said. "I can take you as far as Atlantic Avenue."

Once we let them off, I called the office to "feed" once again. I would be working with our religion reporter on the Muslim story and was told to call her once I felt I had enough in Brooklyn.

The stores I hit on Atlantic Avenue voiced similar concerns to those in Jackson Heights and Astoria. But there is no Muslim monolith. To be sure, everyone denounced the attacks, but I encountered varying levels of patriotism and sympathy for the U.S. government. Some merchants had "Defend Palestine" slogans posted in their stores. Others had bumper stickers that warned, "Anyone who wishes to keep his dignity should give up disputation." Another read: "The worst of provisions for the hereafter is aggression toward people."

When I came upon a woman who wore hijjab' and a weary expression, I think I knew I had enough to call in the article.

"Today, people say 'terrorist' and they turn and look at me," she said. "The ignorance that dwells within people's minds, you cannot account for. I want to get out of here before nightfall."

I called in my final feed and left before nightfall as well. It's not that I was scared, but I felt an urge to be in the newsroom, see familiar faces, get a feel for the other aspects of this story.

On my way back to the office, my cell phone rang. I had forgotten it existed.

It was Aabir, a family friend I'd known since he was a toddler, calling from Washington, D.C. "Where are you?" he said. "My mother called me and said your mother called her and that she can't get in touch with you."

My mother.

Seeking Solace in My Notebook

"I'm fine," I said. "I gotta go though. I'm in the middle of reporting."

I dialed the number to my parents' home. "Ma, it's me. I'm fine." I could tell she'd been crying. For my sanity, I remained a reporter, not her daughter.

"OK, I gotta go. I'm still working. Call everyone and tell them I'm fine."

My cell phone now functional, I checked my messages—more than a dozen. I returned none.

Back at the office, I read the stories I had contributed to: stranded airport passengers, subway riders, closed businesses, and the city's Muslims. I talked to colleagues about the stories they had been working on.

What to do now?

"Go home," said the metro editor. "It's almost midnight."

It took a newspaper to make me cry.

On the subway to work on September 12 I read the coverage of what had happened. I started to shake. Then I came to these words, an e-mail sent from a worker in the World Trade Center after the first plane crashed: "I don't think I'm going to get out. You've been a really good friend."

Alone on the subway, I sobbed.

I paused to look up at a man seated near me. Despite tears in his eyes, he said nothing. I looked around the subway car and saw that everyone else's eyes were filled with tears or blank stares. It was silent.

And that's how the next few days stayed. Silent. Sorrowful. Sullen. Those of us in the newsroom remained on virtual autopilot, scrambling to keep up with the barrage of breaking news.

I felt conflicting loyalties. I wanted to continue covering the backlash. But early in my career, I set rules. To avoid being pigeonholed, I paced articles about South Asians with articles about other immigrant groups or subjects. As a business reporter, I had also carved a beat at the paper out of the city's moms and pops, just as likely to be called Ma and Baba, Ami and Abu, Ima and Aba. I also was responsible for some airlines coverage, namely the businesses dependent on them for survival. They included taxi and limo drivers, parking garages, and cargo handlers—all industries heavily dominated by immigrant workers. And I knew the World Trade Center's death toll included many Bangladeshi dishwashers and cooks and waiters at Windows on the World. Would their obituaries be forgotten among the bond traders and bankers?

Everyone was suffering. The question was where to begin. My editor, accustomed to helping young reporters prioritize, advised me to take it one story at a time.

On the Thursday after the attacks, I ventured into the area immediately surrounding the World Trade Center for an article that would end up being about a deli—owned by a Muslim—where all the rescue workers had been eating.

I've never seen a war zone, but I imagined this came close. An acrid smell of smoke and dust and devastation in the air mixed with the salty smell of the nearby South Street Seaport. Parked cars covered in dust and soot. Pedestrians walked around with masks, tissues or T-shirts covering the lower halves of their faces. Again, I turned to interviewing to avoid facing it.

After my interviews, I headed north to catch the subway home. Curious about what the disaster area actually looked like, I took an inside route.

As I approached Ground Zero, I craned my neck to see where the twin buildings had once towered and only saw smoke. I heard a shout, "Everyone, get away!" National Guardsmen in green camouflage uniforms started to run, joined by police officers. Then I saw people who looked like me, civilians, running but turning back to look occasionally at where we were running from. Apparently the Millennium Hotel, next to where the Twin Towers had stood, had shifted.

Seeking Solace in My Notebook

I looked down at my notebook, still in my hand. I searched inside my handbag for my cellular phone. *Should I call my editor? My parents, to say good-bye? Would I be OK?* When you run from a building, you wonder where to turn, inside another building or far, far away. You wonder if it'll hurt when it all ends. You wonder if someone will find you.

I ran. Once safely on Manhattan's East Side, I started to interview people.

Perhaps it was the only way a reporter could deal with tragedy, as a news event. Don't get me wrong: I tried to humanize and empathize. I patted arms when people cried. I gave directions and even rides to the stranded. I lent quarters for phone calls.

But there seemed to be no end to the suffering. Everyone in this city has a story to tell.

I've talked to business owners who've lost everything, to Wall Street analysts too traumatized to work, to superintendents taking care of pets whose owners never returned home. Their stories will take years of telling; it's more than I can ever write in a single lifetime, but I can try.

On the Friday night after the attacks, while out surveying the city's subdued social scene, a woman I was interviewing suddenly turned to me and said: "I hope you don't mind me asking. How are *you* doing?"

I didn't know what to tell her.

That sleepless night, I pondered her question. It was the first time someone had turned the questioning on me. I had successfully been avoiding friends and family, saying I was too busy reporting to talk.

I was scared. I was angry. At the terrorists, yes, but also those who perpetuated ignorance and questioned some of their fellow Americans' intentions. After September 11, I confess I cringed at the sight of an American flag because I never knew if its display was motivated by patriotism or fear.

S. Mitra Kalita

Sometimes, I dream of life before September 11, 2001. I thought I was too fat. I wondered who would marry me. I honked at slow cars on the highway.

Slowly, those trivial feelings are returning. Still, it will never be the same. Even now, the enormity of that day hasn't quite sunk in. The search for meaning in all of this is much too much to bear.

So I pick up my notebook and keep going.

All I Hear Is Silence

By David Paul Kuhn—*Yomiuri Shimbun*

DAVID PAUL KUHN, a reporter for the New York bureau of Tokyo Yomiuri Shimbun, *the world's largest circulation daily, arrived in lower Manhattan just as the second tower collapsed into a blinding fog of debris. Disembodied torsos and limbs flashed in and out of sight. As the cloud dissipated, Kuhn could see fine particles dusting everything, like snow in September. He met an African immigrant ready to pull a trigger to defend America, his adopted country. Firemen sprayed woefully inadequate streams of black water onto the inferno that would burn for months. Kuhn stayed at Ground Zero until Wednesday afternoon, sleeping in an abandoned building in nearby Battery Park City. When he left, he did so reluctantly, believing that he did not have the right to be tired or upset in the face of such massive suffering.*

Kuhn, twenty-four, went on to cover numerous World Trade Center-related stories, anthrax, and the crash of American Airlines Flight 587 in Rockaway, Queens. He is a University of Wisconsin, Eau Claire, graduate who double majored in journalism and comparative world religions. While an undergraduate, he interned at Time *and* Money *magazines. After graduation he traveled throughout Southeast Asia and Europe. He then moved to New York, becoming the fourth generation of his family to live in the city. He is currently completing a novel based upon his travels.*

All I hear is silence. It's a haunting reminder. The dead can't talk. They seem to exist in the static, on my tape between interviews from September 11, 2001. When the silence passes there is interview after interview, person after person failing to convey what they saw, felt, and feared. I come back to that long hush. The tragedy only makes sense there, in the abyss of that static. All the terror from that morning stays where words have no place. Listening to the silence, as the tape reels forward, the memories rush through me. People are running through darkness. Towers are falling, vanishing into rubble. The ground is shaking. A tremendous rumble is heard. The smoke is suffocating. The air is full of ash, flakes dropping from the sky like dead snow. Then, there is only gray. The silence reminds me of that gray, and walking over unfathomable graves, past the overwhelmed. I saw crushed worlds. I remember how sunny it was that morning and how downtown New York became one color, an off-white world of ash. It was when America divided into two histories for me—before September 11 and after. It was when history became a part of me and for the first time the American experience became mine. But, when it happened it was none of those things. It was all too fast, too chaotic, and too new to be comprehensible.

I was in the middle of it all. When you're in the middle of it all you have no perspective, no ability to step back and understand what is going on. I had no idea what was going on. All I had were confused vignettes. I couldn't even get my mind around the fact

All I Hear Is Silence

that the twin towers were gone. I hadn't seen them hit by the planes. I hadn't seen them fall on television. I hadn't seen anything but chaos. How does one write about chaos—chaos that turned to tragedy and clear objectives? It seems everything has already been said, or written, or heard, or seen live on bloody CNN. I picture the word "live" at the corner of the screen and talking heads pontificating shortly after the towers had fallen. I had no tolerance for the talking heads in the months after. They were all egos. I think about the image of the *Hindinberg* crashing when I think of the World Trade Center now. I think of the black-and-white airship smashing into the ground and the massive fire consuming it until there was nothing. I think of that cracked, panicked, powerful voice saying, "Of all the humanity." Was there a voice like that on September 11? I feel guilty even writing that date. It seems prostituted by now, some ploy of propaganda or day to say where we were and what we felt. I care little of what others felt who weren't there. I care little for how I felt. I don't deserve to feel anything because I was only there. I lost nothing.

Today, when I return to Ground Zero I see commodities—the commercialization of tragedy. It is now the number one tourist site in the city and T-shirts are being sold by the dozen. There is a sign directing tourists to the nearest pub. Tragedy for sale. It's the American way, I guess. Even worse are the anniversaries where the cable news channels have to show us those towers falling again and again and again. Then there are the New Yorkers who will compete with stories, each trying to one up each other on how they experienced September 11. I am often silent. I don't want to reduce that day to a bullet point on a résumé. But it's not people's fault. We're raised to believe we are the sum of our experiences, when in reality we are the sum of our choices. And, when I reflect, what is saddest is how the dead had no choice. Those who were high in the towers were going to die. Then there were those who risked death, the "heroes." I struggle with that word. We are whores with words like "hero", using them too much to be true. If there were heroes that morning, they were all the people that helped. It was the closest most had come to hell and the rescue workers were struggling for life, to save lives, in an ashen world.

How far away hell seemed in the early morning of September 11. It was warm, the perfect autumn day to be barefoot in Central Park. New Yorkers were voting in the mayoral primary. I was on the subway heading to work when the planes hit. It was just after 9 A.M. when I got out at Rockefeller Plaza, and I saw people standing around a television, mesmerized by the screen. I saw what they saw, smoke trailing off the towers. Rushing to my bureau in the Associated Press Building, I spoke with my editor. I was twenty-three and about to cover the largest story in decades for the largest paper in the world. It was a Japanese daily and I had been covering hard news for them for only a few months.

No one wanted to head south. I offered one cab driver fifty dollars, but he refused. I finally caught a taxi to my apartment in the East Twenties, ran up the stairs, and grabbed my Rollerblades. With a bag full of notebooks, my shoes, and a tape recorder over one shoulder and my camera bag over the other, I skated down Second Avenue. It was empty except for the occasional police car, racing by with siren blaring. I was riding the sound of those sirens and the smoking towers in the distance.

I skated faster than I ever had. I hit City Hall, only blocks from the World Trade Center, and maneuvered around the fleeing crowd. I saw thousands of people covered in ash crossing the Brooklyn Bridge. Survivors filled the streets. The exodus north had begun. The first tower had already fallen. I continued south and barely noticed the frightened faces. I was looking toward the cloud. I wanted to be there. Then I heard a rumble and the ground trembled. People stopped walking and ran for their lives. They had been running for their lives all morning. There was a new black cloud.

All I Hear Is Silence

It rushed toward us, thinning before my eyes. People were running out of it, appearing from nothing at all. Everyone was gasping for air. That's when I stopped skating south. I was only blocks from the tower that had just fallen. But I never saw it come down. I was too intent on the cloud from the first collapse to look up. I tried skating away but the ash was so thick that my wheels could not move. I went to a doorway, covered my mouth, and waited for the cloud to fade. People ran by me and only parts of them were apparent. I saw twisting torsos coming in and out of the cloud, until it was so thick, so all-encompassing, that there was only gray.

Time passed and so did the density of the cloud. A policeman handed me a gas mask. He told me the area was "frozen," meaning even my NYPD press pass did not allow me to be there. The police didn't want the press there and journalists like me relied on the confusion to stay in the area. Walking north I passed a woman whose black dress was covered in dust. She sat on the curb coughing, looking down at her high heels. To the right of her was a policeman. Back stepping in disbelief, he held his arms over his head as he looked south. Like all those walking out of the haze, he had glazed eyes. But except for their shock, those before me seemed OK. Those who were not OK were somewhere in that gray, somewhere down the street.

The streets had emptied. The last wave of people had passed. I looked south but could see nothing. The air was still heavy. Suddenly, it seemed like winter. There was something cold and quiet and the falling flakes of snow seemed dirty and dead. The ash beneath my feet would give with each step. I reached down and touched it. I let it fall through my fingers. Thinking of what made up that ash, I shivered. I thought of Elie Wiesel's novel *Night*. It was his first night in Auschwitz and he was writing about what he felt. "Never shall I forget those flames that consumed my faith forever . . . never shall I forget those moments that murdered my God and my soul and turned my dreams to dust." I had memorized those lines in high school and they lived that morning. *This dust was too thick to be from human remains.* I told myself that. And, the dust was everywhere, a mixture of debris and paper blanketing downtown New York. My city looked like Pompeii, or some postapocalyptic shadow of Manhattan. I still could not believe the towers had fallen. Intellectually, I knew they were gone, but there was too much smoke to get a clear look. Nothing was clear. And, as we all come to learn in tragedy, a gap exists between understanding and reality. A gap only filled by time.

New Yorkers were accustomed to looking up and seeing those towers. They were as constant as anything could be. As a boy, I remember how fast the elevator was that took you to the top. Up there, I was too scared to stand at the edge. Years later, in high school, I kissed a girlfriend named Felicia for the first time beneath the World Trade Center. It was in January, on one of those warm New York winter nights when the sky glows a deep blue. My last time there was only weeks before September 11. I was meeting my cousin and his wife from Battery Park City at the plaza between the towers. We were heading to a party in Tribeca. It was quiet that night as I waited for them on a cement bench. Soon I decided to lie down, folding my hands behind my head I stared up at the fully lit towers as they broke the night.

I was like many people that day, anchoring myself to some memory of what was already gone. I skated to the south side of the towers. I went up a small incline and saw a young couple. They weren't covered in soot like the rest of us. I asked them the usual questions. "Where were you? What did you see? How do you feel?" They were students and told me that when the towers fell they were in an NYU dormitory that was locked down. They had snuck out and kept on asking me where they should go to donate blood. *How should I know?* But they asked me because I was not shaken. It was past 11 A.M. and there were two types of people now down there—the people fleeing and the people with some task,

All I Hear Is Silence

some reason to be rational. My reason was journalism. It's easy to be collected when you're hiding in duties. This couple was looking for a duty. He said, "I'm O negative. We heard on TV they need blood." Something in his voice and the very center of his eyes affected me. He was like a deer that gets his hoof caught in a trap. The same way a deer will gnaw his own foot off without reason, determined to free himself of the metal clamps, this young man was going to donate blood.

That morning people wanted to feel useful. Anything was better than being another victim. Some spoke nonsensically, bordering on hysterics. All that kept them from crossing over to fits of tears and rage were their self-appointed missions, no matter how important or how unneeded.

It was time to call my editor but my cell phone could not get a signal. Finally, I found a working pay phone, called my bureau, and dictated quotes to another reporter. I was so involved in the quotes and getting back to the scene that I forgot to ask what was happening in the rest of the world. *What else had been hit?* I was reading powerful quotes, words that consumed my every thought. They were conversations directly with people's souls. Journalists usually speak to people on the surface. Often, it's the way they want to sound. But in tragedy the masks are off and people say what they feel, because what they feel is everything at that moment.

"I was terrified, terrified, I thought the world was ending."

"How angry are you?" I asked an African immigrant who was beneath the towers when they fell.

"Very, very angry, even to pull a trigger. I'm not from here but I'll go to war. To see people dying, man, they don't know nothing, they just working for a living, you know what I mean? Jumping. They had no choice, man. God bless America." He struggled to speak, half panicked and half enraged. He was my first September 11 interview.

"Why did you say God bless America?"

"They lost a whole lot of important things, documents, human lives. The World Trade Center is the most significant feature. So, I think God bless America and put everything back again."

Like this man, everyone down there was most haunted by the jumpers. It was already rumored a fireman had died after being hit by one. Another couple jumped holding hands. They fell some eighty floors never letting go. *God, they never let go.* I spoke to people unable to escape the sound of the jumpers hitting the ground. They said it was loud and when the impact was heard everyone froze. Others could not get rid of the sight of bodies bouncing off the pavement. I imagined what would bring someone to step over the edge. *What was it like up there to make jumping the better choice?* It seemed to be the very death of hope. But now, hope was everywhere. People were on missions. Everyone wanted to save someone.

Whenever I left people I would say, "Be safe." Everyone spoke like that. *It must be how people speak in war.* I continued on to the collapse, hoping to see the rescue effort firsthand. Standing a block from the rubble a fireman told me, "Once you make your way over there you'll see, when you see a half body in front of you, you'll see what I saw." He was in the north tower when the south tower fell. His eyes were red. I didn't know if they were red from what he saw or the chemicals in the air. Our eyes stung. It smelled like burnt rubber mixed with sulfur and smoke. It was a smell that would linger for months.

I was still on skates and in order to make my way through the debris I had to walk with them, as if they were shoes. It was like using ski boots on a balance beam. I stood off to the side and looked at the rubble. There I saw an arm without a body. It was partially covered. *Was it even there at all?* I imagined it was from one of the jumpers. There was still a haze over the debris and in my mind as well. Those minutes were confused, too surreal to fully grasp. Every so often the wind would clear the air. I thought of the scene

All I Hear Is Silence

in *Life Is Beautiful* when the fog thins and hundreds of limp bodies, piled upon one another, appear out of nothing. But I never saw a body. The dead were buried under thousands of tons of concrete and steel. I recall one fireman walking over that steel. He was mumbling and I couldn't understand him. He kept on saying something as he shook his head. Then I understood him.

"I've lost my whole company." Over and over he mumbled, "I've lost my whole company."

I moved a few blocks away from the rubble so the police wouldn't notice me and escort me out. Many journalists had already been forced to leave. I wandered several blocks north, there were few civilians left. The scattered refugees remaining either intended to stay or had somehow missed the exodus out. Some of them were confused. They walked without intent until someone directed them. The yellow tape was up. Thousands of police were bringing order to the area. Firemen fought the flames, flames that would burn longer than any other fire in American history.

And, a lot of people were dead. More than at Pearl Harbor they said, but we didn't know how many. I was told numbers from 5,000 to 20,000. No one knew how full those towers were. I tried to have perspective. Even if it was 20,000 people, Vietnam had killed nearly three times that—58,000 dead Americans. But that was over a period of years. I remembered once hearing over 50,000 people had died in a single day of combat in WWI. Yet, none of those happened in minutes. Only Pearl Harbor came to people's minds, but as horrible as it was, it was a military strike. These were civilians. This was America's Hiroshima, America's Dresden. This time someone did it to us. Yet, to be fair to history, we were not at war on September 10. So people compared it to Pearl Harbor. They used numbers to show the value of the tragedy. If it was bigger than Pearl Harbor, it was worse. But for me, it was the very immensity of those numbers that kept the tragedy from becoming personal. I couldn't relate to something so immense. It was like thinking of the Holocaust without thinking of my great-grandfather, whose name I bear.

I heard scattered radio reports about the Pentagon being attacked. It was past noon and as far as I knew, what was happening in downtown New York was happening across the United States. Rumors abounded. A third plane was on the way. Terrorists had attacked San Francisco. The Pentagon was destroyed. The president was missing. Dick Cheney was in charge of the federal government. *Were we at war?* It sure looked like it. Cars were reduced to frames, entire sides of buildings gone, and little explosions were heard as frequently as fireworks on the Fourth of July. Everything burned. Not just the wreckage or our eyes, but our skin as well. It stung from the fiberglass in the air.

Still on the West Side, I skated north to speak to more civilians. Instead I found empty streets. It was the eeriest sight yet. Scattered pieces of paper blew in the wind and everything was white—the cars, the buildings, an empty baby carriage on the edge of a curb. I imagined the mother in Picasso's *Guernica* lifting her baby from its carriage and running for their lives. The ash was haunting. The emptiness was haunting. This place had always been alive, always vibrant. Now, nothingness. And with all the emergency personnel already downtown, for a moment I swear to silence. It was like walking out of a bomb shelter and discovering World War III was over.

People were still crying. Firemen lined up by a phone near the West Side Highway, calling their families to say they had survived. One of them told me how it felt to speak to his mother. Everywhere, people were declaring life. Some were angry; some upset; some in shock; some wanted to go to war; some wanted to go home; but they all knew they were alive, as only survivors do.

There was now a triage on the West Side Highway. As the afternoon progressed thousands of firemen sat waiting for their turn. I sat with them. I wanted to talk to them without a pen or tape recorder. I took off my Rollerblades and stashed them beside a

All I Hear Is Silence

building. All I had were dress shoes to put on. I watched the firemen. I wanted to look at them, eat something, and get some rest. They didn't want to rest or eat or be still at all. They wanted to fight the fire and rescue their brothers. It was like tours waiting for combat in Vietnam, except everyone wanted to go. They wanted to feel necessary. They wanted to save someone. They wanted for it all to be worth it. But as the hours progressed and fewer survivors were found, the firemen were forced to recognize what they could never admit—the missing were gone.

There was one fireman leaning against a wall. His head was cradled in his left hand and his right hand held a cigarette. His orange pants were dirty and discolored. They were pulled down below his knees so he could cool off. Wearing his FDNY blue T-shirt and shorts, his left knee was up against his chest. His face was covered in dust. He sat there, on the ground, and I wondered whom he was thinking about.

I learned later that television reporters were saying morale was high. A lie. Morale was low. Many of the firemen felt low by early afternoon. It was not that they were cowards, not at all. They just couldn't believe how much they had lost. Firemen, policemen, emergency medical workers—they are not the iron heroes out of comic books. They are mostly from working-class families. Many were young like me, and all are very human.

They now had time to reflect upon what had happened. They asked about the missing, was Jim dead from this company or Darren from that precinct. They embraced one another, as only men of war do. They kept looking up, telling one another "they're gone." Each person had a story. They passed rumors off one another to figure out what was fact. Their faces were pure Hemingway. They were returning from the Great War and part of them had been left behind. Their expressions were a mixture of sadness, disbelief, and total firmness of self. And for whatever sadness they felt, the firmness was winning. One can't mistake that for morale.

No one was happy or in high spirits. There was no spirit, only instinct. But it was a hell of an instinct.

We knew other buildings would fall. Every so often areas were evacuated. I went on the roof of a building in Battery Park City to see the destruction from above. Standing some thirty stories up, I trembled. *Could this building fall?* That day nothing was certain. The most certain things in New York had fallen. Anything could fall after that.

When I looked down at the ruins I saw clouds of smoke, piles of rubble, and thousands of rescue workers. It seemed synchronized from above. The walkway leading to the World Financial Center was smashed. I looked to where the Twin Towers once stood and only spines of steel remained. The cars and people looked like toys. I thought of playing war as a boy when tragedy was abstract and I could have fun with war. I took some pictures and walked back downstairs to call my bureau. There was no light in the stairwell. It was frightening. *It must have been like this in the World Trade Center. Craving light as if it was life itself.*

The building had one of the few phones that worked in Battery Park City. It was one of those cheap push button phones that don't need electricity. None of the buildings had electricity. I was talking to a fellow reporter at my bureau, twenty minutes past 5 P.M. That's when 7 World Trade Center fell. It plummeted and another cloud of smoke shot up from the ground. I hung up and sprinted up thirty flights of stairs to see the destruction from above. The cloud grew and people ran like ants from a fire. All the firemen on the West Side Highway stood up at once. *It was happening again.* But this wasn't the Twin Towers. No one was inside.

I descended and sprinted across the West Side Highway. In the confusion I reached the base of the structure and stood while firemen tried to drown the flames. The hoses got stuck and could barely reach the rubble. The water was black and the air heavy with

All I Hear Is Silence

dust. I couldn't see beyond the fire. Between piles of steel littering the street, the ground was soft and thick, coated in a mud of debris. You couldn't walk without stepping in a puddle or tripping over steel. Then the haze cleared and only a pancake of steel and concrete remained. And there was nothing above the ruins. Emptiness. Only sky where the World Trade Center had been. It was like seeing no pyramids in Egypt or no Eiffel Tower in Paris. We rely on these structures. They symbolize what all humans crave, permanence. But they were gone and so was everyone left inside. Firemen worked tirelessly to extinguish the flames, as the hours progressed and evening turned to night. Security had tightened by midnight. The air remained thick; the smell was even thicker. Police arrested a few civilians still in the area. I was by the fire, where there were no cops. The firemen tolerated my presence, as long as I didn't get in the way. I didn't. They had erected a flag at the base of the ruins. It stood large on a mound of rubble. Lit by the truck lights, the night's shadows fell over parts of the flag, as it blew in the wind.

I returned to Battery Park City around 2 A.M. On the phone my editor said I could leave but I wanted to stay. I slept on a couch for a few hours in an abandoned building's lobby. It was a sordid sleep, the waking type. I arose at dawn, threw some cold water on my face, and walked back out to the West Side Highway. My skin still burned as I walked along the Hudson River, looking over to New Jersey. The sun had barely risen and its orange glare was visible off the water. Battery Park's often cool morning wind blew off the river. Police were sleeping on benches. Scattered cartons of food littered the area. I heard seagulls and turned back toward the water. They flew like nothing had changed. I took a deep breath. *Yesterday happened.* I walked on to the pile, as the ironworkers were calling it. The firemen's ranks had thinned and the National Guard had arrived in force. Security was the priority. I was an outsider, maybe the only journalist around, an alien among these men and women. Those awake looked worn, a little bit beaten. No one wanted to admit it. "No one could beat our bravest," they said. But heroism is not black and white. The rescue workers were inspirational because of their humanity, not in spite of it.

There was still hope. The rescue workers tried to find any reason a person could survive. Some said there could be space in the underground food court; others speculated that firemen could be caught in pockets of air between steel beams. Every doctor, fireman, medic, volunteer, ironworker, and policeman refused to give up. They were united by solidarity, a collective determination to deny death. But they were also sad and entirely humbled. The aimless still walked that way. And hundreds were ready for their shift. I sat with a busload of firemen waiting to go back to the front, back to Ground Zero. Time would prove their dedication. They would dig through the nights, through the rain, deep into the rubble. I would speak to firemen a week later in that same spot. They were less hopeful but still digging. They would dig for months. They were digging anywhere but into themselves. Anything was better than sitting around thinking about it. They wanted to do anything but think about it. They knew the only thing that saved them was chance.

I would leave Ground Zero much more slowly than I had entered it. It was the afternoon and another warm autumn day. I walked up the West Side Highway holding my bags and Rollerblades, still unable to get my mind around the tragedy. I passed the press line. Cameras were everywhere. Journalists waited their turn to enter the scene. I saw a press pool heading south, escorted by police. I continued north and saw thousands of New Yorkers cheering the rescue workers. Women were on their boyfriends' shoulders, children were in front of the crowd so they could see, and the waving of flags seemed necessary and sincere. It began to hit me how big all of this was. Two women came up to me.

"Are you okay, were you in the towers?" they asked. "No, I'm fine, I'm a journalist." *Was I allowed to be upset? No, I'm a journalist.*

All I Hear Is Silence

But I was not upset. It still was not personal. I was only numb. They must have seen that I was numb.

When I returned to my bureau I had little to say. Colleagues asked what I had seen, if I had nearly died. I didn't have the words. I had to see a photograph, one image that captured all the tragedy. I still had not seen the planes hitting the towers or the towers fall. It came on the television. I froze. It suddenly seemed like a bad Hollywood movie. Planes get hijacked, crash into towers, towers crash into the ground, thousands die, and people search for the survivors. I was sick. *Is this what it would become?* It was too horrible for Hollywood, too real, too fresh, to be recreated for years. Were the hijackers horrible? Could I call them evil? Was this evil, is anything evil anymore, or do we explain away all that is bad? The nineteen terrorists were evil, their cause meaningless beside their act. They had attacked the innocent and the very psyche of the world's city. With all the gray of that day, what was good and bad was absolutely clear. But the tragedy was still not as clear. The worst things exist beyond the mind, where only our souls exist. This was one of those things. I did not want anyone to cheapen that. But September 11 was already beginning to be cheapened. The television news played background music and used dramatic lighting as people spoke about the tragedy, calling it the worst day in the history of the world. I wanted to scream. *Why couldn't people just let it be as it was, let it be really horrible? Why do we have to use words like Holocaust or Pearl Harbor at all? Why is it a competition?* I sat at my desk imagining what it was like, sitting on planes as your future crashed into a skyscraper. After that, I couldn't stand to see the towers fall again. I still can't. *Mourn the dead, not the towers.* I typed in my notes and my reporting became part of a larger story. I was anonymous and maybe it was better that way. I checked my e-mail and sent a mass message to say I was OK, after which it was time for me to go home. I got up and left, with my skates in hand and my bags over my shoulders. They were covered in dust. Inside them were handfuls of ash, along with a book with an airplane on the cover that I'd found underneath the rubble. I also had a check I had uncovered. The address was 1 World Trade Center.

It was past dusk and I was home. Setting my bags down I felt as if I hadn't slept for weeks. But first I would eat. I walked up Third Avenue to my favorite sushi restaurant. It was raining out and thousands of New Yorkers filled the streets. People didn't want to be alone in their apartments. Near the armory, television crews interviewed those who passed by. Posters of the missing were up. Hundreds scattered across my neighborhood—on store windows, TV vans, the sides of streetlights. I walked to a phone booth and looked at several. I looked at their eyes and held them, trying to find something intense. One girl was described as quiet and another guy was said to have a scar on his shoulder. I read who was looking for them. There were words of total desperation. I felt so badly for the mothers. There was a poster up of someone my age. He had black hair and brown eyes. He looked so full of life. It was the first time I saw myself in the dead. I stood there quietly, alone. The rain rolled off the poster, blurring the ink. I composed myself but he was still dead. They were all dead. Everyone was hopeful that night. But I was not. I had been there. I knew better. If there was a poster up, they were dead.

From Nightmares to Redemption

By Petra Bartosiewicz—*New York Observer*

Like many late-rising reporters on September 11, PETRA BAR-TOSIEWICZ of Brooklyn found herself trapped outside Manhattan when the city suspended subway service. Shortly after the attacks, this New York Observer *writer rode her bicycle to the Brooklyn Bridge, circumvented a police roadblock, and pedaled into downtown New York. On the evening of September 12, she was among the first journalists to enter Ground Zero, spending the night with rescue workers amid the rubble. When journalistic instincts told her she had to get into the restricted area, Bartosiewicz helped distribute bottled water, taking notes on what she saw every step of the way.*

Bartosiewicz, twenty-seven, is a 1996 graduate of the University of Virginia who covers city affairs for the Observer. *She has also written for the* Atlantic Monthly Online. *Her diary of her activities in September reveals both the pervasiveness of the destruction in the city and the possibility of redemption.*

Notes from September 12, 10 P.M:
The masts on the boats in the harbor by the Winter Garden swayed gently in the breeze. A cold wind swept in from the river, kicking up white dust (trees, garden shrubs, all covered in thick ash frost). Further inland, opening into a gaping wound, the rubble slowly ascended to a twisted smoking pile, and girders stood like bombed out cathedral walls framing the main rubble heap where the search for bodies was led. A steady buzz of helicopters flew overhead and police cruisers floated on the river.

In the end, it came down to a piece of plastic yellow police tape stretched across Greenwich Street, two blocks from the World Trade Center. I crossed it. And on the night of Wednesday, September 12, I entered the blast zone, Ground Zero, just after dark.

I hadn't planned to come here, but after two days of reporting in the city, feeling aimless wandering between morgue and hospital, I'd found myself traveling farther and farther south. A press pass had gotten me through all the checkpoints until the final one. Beyond this line, no press were allowed. And so I made a decision—or rather, succumbed to an impulse. Backing away from the flashing lights and perimeter guards, I looked around and saw a dusty case of water bottles sitting in a darkened vestibule nearby. Hoisting the water to my shoulder, I walked back to the police line, lifted the tape, and headed south, not looking back.

From Nightmares to Redemption

No one noticed, no one stopped me, and so I continued, down a block lined with buildings turned ghostly white with ash, handing water to soot-covered firefighters and police officers until the box was empty, and I was standing before the rubble of what had been the World Trade Center.

I was in Ground Zero. But now, standing at the base of this canyon, staring at the utter blackness, the busted windows, the concrete and steel beams chewed to frayed cloth by the blast, looking up to see shards of glass clinging feebly to window frames above my head—I wanted to *run*.

And I almost did. For a long while I shook so hard that the few photographs I took would later come out as nothing more than a series of dark blurry streaks. But gradually, the fear faded, as if I had passed through to the other side of some sinister membrane, and my eyes took on a new focus. All around, arc lights illuminated a debris field filled with fatigued engineers pointing out the collateral damage to surrounding buildings; firefighters on extension ladders spraying impossibly small arcs of water onto the hissing mass; groups of rescue workers sweating and stripped to the waist; police officers digging through the rubble. Grimy, exhausted faces, vacant eyes, every one of them, but none afraid. And beyond it all, the city's lights twinkled from what seemed like a thousand miles away.

Why did I stay? No one had assigned me here. Should I have felt guilty, a trespasser? At times I did—I felt like a parasite. But journalists were not the story, and wallowing in self-doubt, worrying whether one had the right to be there, was useless. Watching the events unfold on September 11 was overwhelming to the point that there was nothing to do but record what you saw as best you could. And so I spent that night among the scorched heaps, climbing the rubble till dawn, handing out water, scribbling pages of notes, and talking with the rescue workers. The reason to go there, to see the destruction firsthand, was to feel the event as palpably as one who witnessed only the aftermath could. And then, simply to write it down. There was no such thing as absolute accuracy or objectivity, and the greater point of writing it all down would become clear much later.

Shortly after 9 A.M. on September 11, my head still wet from the shower, I heard a hushing distant *boom* over Brooklyn, followed by the wailing of fire trucks. I thought nothing of it. A minute later, my mother called from Washington, D.C., to ask if I was all right. "Look out the window," she said. I pulled back the curtain to reveal a clear view to lower Manhattan: a crystalline morning, a man tarring a neighboring rooftop, his back to the city.

Two smoking towers.

I called the office to tell my editor I'd be late. The subways were closed. I packed a bag with spare clothing, flashlight, pens, my lunch, and hopped on my bicycle, hoping the Brooklyn Bridge would still be open. What were my profound journalistic thoughts at this moment? I was praying I'd brought my press credentials along. Arriving at the base of the bridge, all was chaos: people flooded in from Manhattan, some sobbing, others with hollow blank eyes; everyone covered in white dust. A police officer next to me listened to his radio. "They've hit the Pentagon," he announced to no one in particular. The police wouldn't let anyone across the bridge, credentials be damned. I rode around in circles for a few minutes until I remembered a second staircase onto the pedestrian walkway. It was unguarded, and so I ascended, bike over shoulder, and rode against the tide into downtown Manhattan shortly after the collapse of the second tower. F-15 fighter jets screeched overhead; smoke and dust were everywhere.

I write for the *New York Observer*, a Manhattan weekly chronicling New York's wealthy and elite. On September 11, primary election day (a scheduled Democratic mayoral runoff was quickly canceled), politics and politicians, money and power, seemed irrelevant.

From Nightmares to Redemption

The *Observer* was scheduled to go to press that evening and our reporters were sent out to cover the hospitals, the morgue, and City Hall. We had one day to rewrite nearly the entire paper. But what sense could we make of anything beyond that two towers had fallen, and untold numbers were dead? None.

Prominent editors-in-chief across the city declared that irony was dead.

When I descended from the Brooklyn Bridge to City Hall, survivors of the collapse, caked in white, most with their shoes missing, were still staggering out of the haze. A lone television truck was parked by the mayor's office.

A young man named Adolfo Rodriguez was looking for his father, Alexis Leduc, a forty-five-year-old maintenance supervisor who worked in the towers. "My father called at 8:45 when the first plane hit the other building. He said, 'I'm OK, if anything, beep me.' I'm already guessing now he's badly hurt, I can't think he's dead." Months later, I found Mr. Leduc memorialized in the *New York Times* "Portraits of Grief" series.

City comptroller Alan Hevesi, a mayoral candidate, arrived downtown shortly after the collapse of the towers, riding a squad car into the city from the polls in Brooklyn, and went immediately to donate blood. I asked him a few questions, watching over his shoulder as carbine-toting U.S. Marshals patrolled the Federal Courthouse. "They must die, the people that did this," he said, looking at the sky.

The periphery of the blast zone was two blocks from where the comptroller stood. Black firefighters' shoes were lined up against a wall; firefighters arrived on commandeered city buses. There were no more trucks available. There were too few dust masks to go around.

"I keep hearing badge numbers over the radio," said one police officer with black streaked cheeks. "No one's answering."

Further uptown, across the street from a blood bank, Governor

George Pataki was giving an impromptu press conference to a lone journalist. He took a call on his cell phone from the vice president and then turned to his aides and gravely relayed a message. Where was he when he heard of the attacks? In his limousine, he said, riding into the city. His face was stretched taut like paper.

As dusk fell on the city's makeshift command center at the police academy in midtown, I watched as Mayor Giuliani swept past with his entourage. The mayor, covered in dust, was returning from Ground Zero. His mouth was turned down, his eyes were stricken: No one spoke.

I biked back to Brooklyn at midnight on September 11. The streets were barren, the air thick with dust. As I approached the Brooklyn Bridge again, a city engineer flagged me down. "Better get out of here," he said. "The air's full of asbestos."

At home, I collapsed into bed, not even bothering to turn the lights on, only to find the sheets were covered in shards of glass and dusty debris. I had left the window partially open; the dust cloud from the towers had passed through here too.

When I awoke at dawn the next morning, I had forgotten the day before. Then the local radio station began playing a somber peal of church bells. I made coffee, packed my bag, and returned to the city.

Notes from September 12, 8 a.m.:

Smoke plume rising from WTC site (like a purple rat's tail) into distance of Staten Island. South City Hall Park, blanketed in ash like snow—plants white. Court papers, invoices, a chef's hat. City Hall Park fountain still running. Firemen lugging hoses, dust everywhere—ash several inches deep. Trash everywhere. Silhouette-black-clad group of firefighters heading south on West Broadway, against the sun. Dust masks, rubber gloves, water bottles, a box of Entenmann's cake.

From Nightmares to Redemption

• • •

Arriving in the city early on September 12, another incongruously beautiful day, I felt a perversely peaceful solitude in walking the debris-strewn streets around lower Manhattan. Aside from rescue workers, firefighters, and police, few people were around. But there was something equally awful about standing, voyeur-like, with nothing but notepad and pen in hand, watching others work. Observing the events from the sidelines did not feel like a neutral position.

Yet, in the adrenaline-soaked hours of the days following September 11, I suddenly felt I understood why war correspondents haul off to killing fields with rucksack and pen. Perhaps an encounter with the realities of such work—a night spent clinging to the side of some cursed bullet-riddled mountain in Afghanistan, or a long-stretch of mind-numbing inaction, cold, fear, or hunger— would have quickly cured me of that sentiment.

But certainly there were times after September 11 when I wished that I worked for a daily paper instead of a weekly. With the rest of the media reporting aggressively on every conceivable angle surrounding the attacks, there were no scoops or newsbreaks for the *Observer*. Instead, our editors told us to think ahead, attempt to contextualize the events, find the themes and stories that had not yet been covered. But it would be a long time before I felt able to find any broader perspective beyond the immediacy of the events.

When the dust finally settled over Manhattan several days after September 11, what was left were two Ground Zeroes: one, a physical scar, a smoking crater of twisted girders, rubble, ash, and bodies, and the other, its spectral sibling, a temporal space from which unspooled the stories of each individual who was there, who saw two towers fall, who loved someone who had died. I did not feel the right to grieve then, nor now; I was not in the towers when they were hit, I did not know anyone in the towers personally, I was not part of the rescue effort; I wasn't even in Manhattan when the towers collapsed.

Now, six months later, I feel light-years from the immediacy of the events of that day. All around, the political, industrial, and commercial machines, briefly stunned into silence, have shifted into motion again, and even the least-hardened cynic can point to the signs of a return to pre-September 11 normalcy: The family of a doomed passenger aboard the September 11 flight that crashed in Pennsylvania is seeking to copyright his last fighting words, "Let's roll." Internecine squabbling over who will control the reconstruction of the World Trade Center site has erupted among the city's development elite. Several employees of the New York City Port Authority have been charged with stealing from a September 11 relief fund. And Hollywood, too, has recovered from its brief moral quandary, releasing its first big budget war epic since the attacks, *Black Hawk Down*, a high-gloss piece of wartime propaganda. Watching a formation of eight Black Hawk helicopters skimming in silent predatory flight over shark-infested waters off the coast of Somalia (a doomed mission), we should raise a fist in the air and cheer for the good ol' USA, and we do.

And yet the emotional core of that day remains, untouchable, still smoldering. Riding the N train through lower Manhattan—just below where the Twin Towers once stood—the Cortland Street station is still roped off with pink plastic police lines. Plywood boards posted on the platform bear the spray-painted warning: DO NOT STOP HERE.

Notes on the night of September 12:

Just after midnight, the first body of a New York police officer was found. All New York City police officers in the vicinity immediately ran to the site. The area was quickly cordoned off and police called in the Honor Guard to bring out the body of one of their own. Officers watched briefly, then left the scene with numb eyes and returned to work. There was no time to grieve.

From Nightmares to Redemption

• • •

Several weeks after the attacks I met a man named Richard Ostrander, a burly welder from Pennsylvania. He'd driven into the city in the aftermath of the attacks to volunteer his services and made his way through the gauntlet of police lines outside Ground Zero. He ignored officers who told him to go home. They threatened him with arrest.

"Arrest me then," he challenged, and kept walking. He made his way to the heart of the rubble field, and there he remained, cutting steel and girders. At first, he'd drive the four hours it took to get home and spend the night with his wife and children. Later, he stayed near the rubble, sleeping on Red Cross billets, on cots, on chairs. The night I saw him, he was on his way back to the National Guard Perimeter at Chambers Street, returning from a bender of beers and bourbon, his first drink after an eleven-day stretch.

"I burn steel," he told me, "and that's what I'm doing here." He was wary of story-hungry journalists. "You guys aren't telling the real story down here," he said. "We aren't heroes. There aren't any heroes here. The firemen aren't heroes, the policemen aren't heroes, the construction workers aren't heroes. They chose this life, this is what they do, this is their job. They chose to put themselves in danger. You go ask that cop, right now, right there, ask him if he thinks he's a hero! Go ask him!"

After September 11, the media seemed possessed with a desire to tell every story, to cover every angle. For weeks the newspapers and television were a deluge of information: personal tragedies, business failures, lives sent into a tailspin, a fearful nation, an angry nation. But the impulse to tell all ultimately waned—people needed to move on, and there was only so much to say. In the end, very little of what was said approached, could approach, the thing itself.

Seasoned editors and writers quickly recognized this. Within weeks, irony was declared reborn—a miraculous resurrection.

Time stood still, briefly, and the dust cloud that rose up from the towers, blotting out all other events for days, weeks, eventually passed.

But things were not the same as before. For several months I kept a bag packed with Ground Zero helmet, boots, a sweater, flashlight, and dust mask, ready under my desk at the office. The normal rhythms of work returned, but like a twisted mask, slapped on slightly askew. For weeks our city editor wrote of little else than the firefighters.

Now, the story is no longer September 11. The physical scar that is Ground Zero will soon be erased, replaced by new buildings and new commerce, and a memorial. We move on, but for those who were there, who saw two towers fall, who loved someone who died, their stories have rippled out from this space, forever expanding, affecting us all.

Those stories, I think, will be told for a long time to come.

Six months after September 11, I'm dreaming of riding in a car with someone I don't know, along a tree-lined stretch of highway. Perched high in the trees are Easter baskets the size of cars, wrapped in pink cellophane and brimming with candy.

"Stop," I instruct the driver. "Let's take a look."

We pull over and descend off the road to one of the trees. At the base of a soaring old oak are three white rabbits. My companion's white poodle begins jumping all over them, slobbering and whimpering. The rabbits glance at each other, smiling, lock arms, and begin singing in unison: "We are not afraid. We are not afraid. We are not afraid." A fat gray-haired hippy grandmother appears and explains the baskets are gifts sent to us New Yorkers, from people all over.

The next night, I dream of another car ride and another companion I can't place—this time we're plowing through a blizzard. A deer approaches and begins butting its head against the windows.

From Nightmares to Redemption

What appear at first to be curious nuzzlings become sharper and harder, until I'm yelling frantically to my companion to move on, *move on*! It's going to break through and kill us.

The first dreams in the weeks after September 11—a plane careening out of the sky, teetering past buildings, a plume of smoke rising over the horizon, a fire I could smell but never find, a mausoleum encountered in the middle of a forest clearing, filled with deer staring out at me with silent black eyes—brought me no closer to understanding.

Journey to Ground Zero

By Peter DeMarco—*New York Daily News*

By the time the New York Daily News *dispatched PETER DEMARCO to "get as close as you can" to Ground Zero on September 15, police had sealed off everything south of Canal Street. After talking his way through one barricade, piggybacking with Tom Brokaw's news crew through another, and disobeying an officer's order to leave the frozen zone, DeMarco finally arrived at the former World Trade Center. He spent the day interviewing the workers and volunteers at a site he came to see as hallowed ground.*

A newcomer to New York, DeMarco, thirty, joined the afternoon Express *edition of the* Daily News *after earning his master's degree from the Columbia Graduate School of Journalism in 2000. Raised in Lynnfield, Massachusetts, DeMarco attended Tufts University before working at a variety of Boston-area papers. When the* Express *folded in late September 2001, DeMarco returned to Boston, where he writes part-time for the* Boston Globe *and drives a snow plow during the winter for his father's business.*

My assignment was simply to "get as close as you can." And the more I thought about it, the more it terrified me.

Around 3,000 people had died in the collapse of the World Trade Center, but in the four days that followed, a mere 108 bodies were recovered. The rest were buried, or dismembered, their unidentifiable carnage scattering several blocks like a Civil War battlefield, or had simply disintegrated in the tremendous heat inside the combusting towers. It would be months before the last bodies were found.

And this is what I was supposed to "get close" to.

Other reporters were also assigned to Ground Zero, but I was the rookie. Having been at the *New York Daily News* one year and one week, I was still relegated mostly to phone work and copy rewrite. I had yet to explore a murder scene or view a deadly accident—the bread and butter of the country's number one tabloid. My biggest exposé had been the disappearance of the Rocky the Raccoon balloon in the Macy's Thanksgiving Day Parade. So when the city editors asked for volunteers to work that Saturday, September 15, I jumped.

Daily News staffers had reported from Ground Zero every day since the terrorist attacks, including that Friday, when President Bush made his first visit. But by Saturday the military and New York Police Department had barricaded streets within about a mile of the Trade Center to keep the public away—a buffer area that became known as the frozen zone. I arrived at Canal Street, the northern border of the zone, fifteen blocks north of Ground Zero, at 6:45 A.M. and quickly learned that the press were not being allowed in. Police guarding Church Street told me to go a mile north to the Jacob Javitts Convention Center to get clearance; police blocking Broadway said I needed to go a mile east to police headquarters near the Brooklyn Bridge; cops at three other intersections didn't know where to send me—except away.

I phoned an editor and two reporters, but they had no advice on how to go lower. I interviewed a few people leaving the frozen zone—a construction worker and a woman with long black hair who had handed out water bottles to firefighters for the Salvation Army—and kept walking, hoping to find a way in. In Chinatown, two cops in a parked cruiser were letting residents pass south of Canal to get to their homes, so I approached them.

The driver grunted when I explained I was from the *Daily News*, but his passenger, a white-haired sergeant, had a newspaper (albeit the competition) in his hand and warmed to me. Soon he was out of his cruiser, describing the inner workings of the frozen zone in impressive detail. I told him he would have made a great reporter (hey, he might have), and sure enough, he let me by.

From there I picked my way down empty streets, avoiding security forces, until I reached the intersection of Chambers and West Broadway. Four National Guardsmen and aluminum traffic barriers blocked West Broadway to the south, and six cops guarded Chambers Street to the west. *End of the line.*

For two long hours, I didn't move, keeping my notebook hidden while talking with Red Cross workers and an occasional firefighter filtering out from the blockade. My hopes began to fade when, suddenly, my misery had company—or so it seemed.

A man in a black jacket and baseball cap and a woman in a tan coat carrying a small television camera strolled down West Broadway and up to the National Guardsmen. I spied a press pass dangling around the woman's neck and chuckled to myself. *Didn't they know the media weren't supposed to be in this far? They're going to be kicked back to Canal Street.* At least *I* had tried to be somewhat secretive about my presence, I thought.

But after a brief conversation, one of the guards turned and led the pair past the barrier. They were getting in.

I seethed. *Who were these people? How could they just walk through?* I decided that if they were getting in, I was getting in.

With my chin forward, I crossed the intersection and strode toward the remaining guards, careful to avoid eye contact. Yanking my press pass out from under my shirt, I picked up my pace so it appeared I belonged with the other reporters. My heart pounded, my underarms sweated, my mouth was dry—but I kept walking.

They're going to stop me. They're going to stop me.

I felt light-headed and nauseated. But the guards didn't seem to be paying attention. I reached the barrier—still nothing. I stepped through and kept walking, expecting at any moment they would come after me. But they never did. Just like that, I was in.

I am not entirely proud of the way I reacted to the tragedy on September 11, at least not personally.

Professionally, of course, it was the biggest story of my generation and my first opportunity to make a significant contribution to the paper.

Until then I had been writing for the *Daily News Express* edition, New York City's first afternoon paper in a decade, a throwback to the days when the morning's news was in readers' hands for the commute home. To allow time for printing and distribution, stories had to be finished by noon, requiring an early start to my day.

I was eating oatmeal at my desk shortly after 8:46 A.M. when photo editor Mike Lipack turned up the volume on one of the police scanners. There was a fire at the World Trade Center. Moments later a reporter called saying he thought he had just seen a plane hit one of the towers. My editor, Bob Kappstatter, clicked the office television to CNN to see video of smoke pouring out the top half of one of the towers. We would later learn that a hijacked American Airlines plane from Boston had crashed into it.

Kappy turned to me. "Start typing," he said.

With no more facts than what was being reported on television, I wrote, "One of the World Trade Towers was hit this morning by an airplane that apparently veered off course or lost control." The sentence lived for ten minutes, until the second tower was hit and I started over. Then the Pentagon was attacked. Within an hour I had written four leads; by 10:30 I had written eight, the last describing the horrifying collapse of both towers.

Working furiously, I didn't dwell on what was happening. My heart raced, my palms sweated, I pounded the save key every other minute—but I felt little sadness for those who had perished. At one point my father called from Boston, his voice cracking with emotion. He had heard that 50,000 could be dead and didn't know if I was alive.

"I'm fine, Dad. I'm like a mile away from it," I said, slightly annoyed. *Didn't he know I had a deadline?*

About 10:30 A.M., because of all the chaos, the afternoon edition was canceled for the day. J. K. Dineen, my friend and fellow *Express* reporter, and I were told to go to police headquarters and stand by for official statements, which was fine by me. Though my story would not be published, I would finally get to see for myself what was happening out there.

We barreled out of the *Daily News* building on West 33rd Street and found people huddled around parked car radios like World War II. Streets were closed, subways shut down, and there were no cabs, so J. K. and I had to walk more than three miles across the island to headquarters. Thousands streamed from the downtown as ambulance and fire truck sirens screamed in all directions. Smoke, drifting eastward to Brooklyn from the Trade Center, cloaked the skyline.

Journey to Ground Zero

Four ash-covered men sat on the steps of St. Bernard Church on West 14th Street, and J. K. and I gave in to our curiosity and stopped to talk. One man's brother-in-law was on the ninety-fourth floor of the first tower when it was hit. Between prayers the man was calling his brother-in-law's cell phone, but he could not get a connection. We moved on, without it dawning on me to say a prayer, too.

Hundreds were mobbing St. Vincent's Hospital in Greenwich Village to give blood, and a man began yelling for people with O-positive—the universal donors—to begin a separate line. It was my blood type, but I didn't stop.

J. K. and I split up after learning police headquarters had been sealed off, and I headed closer to the tragedy, reaching a triage center at the corner of North Moore and Greenwich streets. For the first time I was scared of what I might see, but it turned out no injured had arrived. There was a more pressing issue, though. Seven or eight blocks down Greenwich Street, the No. 7 World Trade building, a smaller, forty-story structure, was on fire. The street was closed; the building was going to collapse.

At 5:30 P.M. there was a rumble. The building's top row of windows popped out. Then all the windows on the thirty-ninth floor popped out. Then the thirty-eighth floor. Pop! Pop! Pop! was all you heard until the building sunk into a rising cloud of gray that began creeping up Greenwich Street like a slow-moving tidal wave.

En masse, everyone on the street, including the doctors, ran like hell. I ducked around the first corner I saw, breathless, but the wave of debris died out blocks before the triage center. The No. 7 building was much shorter than either of the Towers, and its downfall, thankfully, was not deadly. Still, seeing it go gave me a strange rush of adrenaline.

No patient was ever brought to the triage center, which seemed odd at the time, and at 9 P.M. the doctors and medics folded up the beds and went home. I left, too, and as I walked east through the

West Village, I passed by an old fire station. The lone engine was gone from the garage, and the firefighters' lockers were open, their shoes and belongings strewn across the cement floor. A lone dispatcher sat in his booth. He was the only company member left.

"I can't talk to you now," he said to me. "We lost a lot of guys today."

As I emerged from the firehouse, a man stepped out from the darkness. His blond hair was slicked back, his metallic tie and shirt, fashionable. In a soothing voice he explained he was from a TV newsmagazine and did I know anything about the fire station?

His cameraman set up for a shot in front of the empty firehouse. With them was a volunteer firefighter from Pennsylvania who had videotaped the rubble up close and was lending his bootleg footage to the show.

The dispatcher charged from the station, angrily ordering them away. *Insensitive tabloid reporters!* I thought.

But in all the excitement, had I been any different?

Four days had passed since September 11, and here I was, on the inside of a police barrier, with a view of the No. 7 building again, now just a mountain of debris on West Broadway a few blocks away.

I caught up to the woman in the tan jacket, who lagged behind her partner and the guard.

"Excuse me, Miss?" I said, with my best take-pity-on-me face. "I'm with the *Daily News.* I've been waiting two hours to get in. Can I ride in on your coattails?"

She looked me over once, and nodded OK.

We walked a few more steps before I asked whom she was with. "NBC," she said.

"Really? Wow," I said, honestly impressed. "But how did you get in? They're not letting anyone in?"

"Well," she replied, "we wouldn't have got in if it weren't for Tom."

Journey to Ground Zero

I looked confused, so she pointed to the man in the black hat. And there, walking five feet in front of me, was Tom Brokaw.

My jaw slackened, but this was no time to fawn. The guard escorting the group would assume I was with NBC—Why else would I be there?—and if I was with NBC, I wouldn't need to introduce myself to Tom Brokaw. My best course of action, I reasoned, was to say nothing and appear preoccupied by my new surroundings.

The landscape indeed had changed dramatically. Buildings were blanketed in gray soot, trash and debris blew across the pavement, burying parked cars to their wheel wells, and traffic lights were off. Nothing moved, like a war zone in the quiet aftermath of gunfire.

Our group walked past Warren Street, Murray Street, Park Place, and Barclay Street, finally joining together at Vesey Street at the rubble of the abandoned No. 7 building. Its forty stories had been reduced to a fifty-foot-high pile that spilled onto the street and half buried an overturned hot dog cart. A lone pretzel hung from a hook in its glass case, as if time stopped when the building came down.

A firefighter walked by, and Brokaw asked him a few questions. Breaking my silence, I asked one as well. Brokaw looked at me squarely for the first time, and I imagine he could only have been thinking, "Who the hell is this?" But he did not blow my cover, and for that alone, I will be a fan for life.

After about five minutes the National Guardsman, in a southern accent, suddenly announced, "OK. Tour's over," and began to usher our band back toward the police barriers. *How could we be leaving when we just got here?* I thought. I expected Brokaw might ask to see more of Ground Zero, but he seemed content with just a peek of it. And I certainly couldn't say anything.

One of journalism's most important ethics is to be truthful when asked about your identity, and I had taken pains to do so during my journey. True, I had walked past the National Guard barrier under

NBC's umbrella. But we were all journalists, and though I wasn't a famous news anchor, I had as much right to enter as they. But now, I faced a dilemma. What if, without physically or verbally resisting, I just didn't follow orders? What if I moved away from the group, and no one stopped me? What if I didn't leave until someone *made* me leave?

I slowed my pace. No one noticed. I lagged further behind the group, and still no one noticed. When I was almost a full city block behind, I stopped and ducked down an empty street.

I got about fifty feet before I heard the voice.

"You're not supposed to be here," said the police officer, walking to me. "And you weren't supposed to be with them, either."

I tried to hide my shock. *How did he see me? Where did he come from? Was he going to arrest me?*

"No problem, officer," I squeaked.

Lowering my head in subservience, I turned and walked in the direction of the barrier, not daring to look him in the eye.

It was over, I thought. If I was lucky, the guards at the barrier wouldn't arrest me. But they'd probably confiscate my press pass. I berated myself. *Why hadn't I moved faster? Why hadn't I broken away from the group sooner?*

Warren Street, empty and inviting, was directly to my left, so I asked myself the question once more.

How badly did I want the story?

Like the Grand Canyon, the Roman Colosseum, or St. Peter's Cathedral, the size of Ground Zero was at first overwhelming. It seemed to be all around me, and its scope belittled me.

The towers' 220 stories seemingly had been run through a gigantic office shredder, reduced to mountains of concrete slivers, tangled wires, steel, pipes, rebar, office chairs, computer monitors, papers, and other bits and clumps. Like a cauldron, the mass smoldered in places, and though it was midday, the fallen debris had formed pockets as dark as caves. At least a half dozen wounded office buildings encircled the ruins, comprising an area as large as the downtown of most cities. Chunks were torn from them and their windows were smashed by the thousands. And somewhere, unseen, were the remains of nearly three-thousand men, women, and children. But I did not immediately think of those who had perished. I was too in awe, and too amazed that I had made it there.

My wonder turned to confusion when I tried to make sense of what I saw. It was difficult to tell where the buildings had stood, and whole street sections were buried. If there was an order to the rescue effort, it eluded me. Standing on the corner of West and Vesey Streets, I was surrounded by regiments of police, firefighters, FBI agents, FEMA agents, phone company employees, Salvation Army volunteers, and hard-hat steelworkers who were either coming or going, removing debris in five-gallon buckets, or just standing around baking in the hot sun, dodging the convoys of construction trucks passing through. There were hundreds, maybe thousands of people at Ground Zero, and though occupationally diverse, there was a sense of a common purpose. It had been just four days since the collapse, and there was still a chance someone could be trapped alive.

I soon became aware that I was doing nothing but standing and gawking and became paranoid someone would notice I didn't belong. I drifted into a group of idle volunteers, avoiding conversation and hiding my notebook.

What was I doing here? Where are the other reporters? I felt alone and scared. Police were everywhere, more than I could count, and I was only a few feet from the command center tent, filled with dozens more uniformed officials. Gradually I made small talk with some volunteers, discovering that most had yet to help out because the New York City firefighters refused to end their shifts on the pile. But I was too nervous to talk to the real rescuers, too nervous to leave the cover of the group. In two hours I barely wrote a word in my notebook, and had moved no more than one hundred feet. Self-doubt and panic returned, as if I were outside the police barrier on Chambers Street again. *Could I do this?*

And then, a marvelous thing happened: I saw someone I knew. The Salvation Army worker with the long black hair I had met at 7 A.M. on Canal Street had returned to Ground Zero and was coming my way with water for the troops. I leafed through my notebook and found her name: Michelle Castellano.

"Hey, it's you," she said, handing me a bottle.

I had spoken with her for no more than five minutes that morning, but I greeted her like family. It was a relief not to be so alone anymore! She stopped and described all of Ground Zero to me.

"But why don't you just see for yourself?" she said. It was the push I needed.

I drank my water, and, following her advice, worked my way westward to the entrance of the American Express Building, whose spacious, marble-floored atrium had become an operations center filled with medical supplies and a food line. Outside, the café tables in Cove Yacht Marina, on the Hudson River, were piled with everything from batteries to eight sizes of jeans—a flea market for rescue workers in need of supplies. Stacks of plywood and other construction materials cluttered the promenade while wagons of hot food were unloaded from a docked cruise boat. An army of dirty, tired firefighters flowed through the marina, peeling off their jackets, sitting down to eat, getting a massage, visiting the makeshift chapel, or merely grabbing some office furniture from the building, finding some shade, and trying to sleep.

I took out my notebook and began to meet Ground Zero's people: a chaplain from Oklahoma City who had counseled disaster workers at the Alfred P. Murrah Federal Building; canine handlers from New Jersey who said their dogs were weary from all the dead scent; a young, lanky firefighter who, in his eighth week on the job, was digging through the debris with a two-foot spade as the lead man on a bucket brigade; another firefighter, from Brooklyn, convinced someone was waiting to be rescued in one of the towers' protective elevator shafts; a young couple, former Manhattan dot-commers, who were turned down as volunteers but snuck into Ground Zero on a boat at 2 A.M. so they could help anyway.

In the marble-floored atrium I met Angelica Sage, a forty-five-year-old florist from San Diego who was in New York City for a convention the day of the attacks. With her Salvation Army tag hanging off her gray sweater, she warmly greeted firefighters at her coffee stand, ignoring their filth and their drained expressions. "I got the beans from Starbucks. Got 'em just for you," she would say, with a wink. When a firefighter looked like he needed it, she would give him a pat on the arm, or a hug.

Sage had cracked only once in her two days at Ground Zero. She had served coffee all night, making it "stronger and stronger and stronger" to keep the men going. At 9 A.M. the building abruptly lost water pressure, and there was no water to brew with. When the next group of firefighters came, she had nothing for them and screamed for water before going off to calm herself. "I felt I had let them down," she said.

Later I asked a woman handing out medical supplies how she was able to cope working within constant view of the disaster. "I come here to do my job, then I go home and cry my eyes out," she told me. "But you don't cry here."

It was a good rule, in theory. But even in the marina, which was shielded from the debris by a building, there was no escaping the pall of death. Dusty windows were inscribed with the names of dozens of missing firefighters, and shrubs were littered with hundreds of office papers blown from who knows what floor. On the walls of one area were taped thank-you notes from children. American flags, tall buildings, rainbows, and hearts were written in crayon, along with words like "We love you" and "You are our heroes." Every so often a firefighter would stop to read a few, breaking away as tears welled in his eyes. As the sun set, I glanced at a rescue worker who had dragged a chair far from the bustle to the river's edge. He began to weep, and I turned away.

Working twenty straight hours and sleeping in the hallways of abandoned office buildings, going without showers or even running toilets, coughing from the bad air, and ignoring every impulse to openly grieve—none of these things mattered to the people working at Ground Zero. "I'm going to stay here until they find him. He'd do the same for me." "What can we do on the outside that can be as important as what we're doing here?" "There's got to be hope. It's just too many men to lose." These were their mantras. For all the evil that had caused the collapse of the World Trade Center, here, in the aftermath, was a counterforce of incredible humanity and self-sacrifice, a force that derived its strength not from the victory of finding survivors, of which there would be no more, but instead from the simple act of trying.

The rescue workers and volunteers' cause was almost sacred, and, after time, I desperately yearned to join their circle. But I could not. I was invited to sleep overnight in corridors with volunteers and told I could walk on the actual debris pile if I just helped bring water bottles to firefighters. I would have been handed a special green pass allowing instant access to Ground Zero on the next day just by saying I was a volunteer. I passed on every offer. For one thing, it wouldn't have been ethical. But more than that, as New York City mayor Rudolph Giuliani remarked, Ground Zero was a hallowed place, and there were certain boundaries within it that, as an outsider, I felt I dare not cross.

I resolved, instead, simply to do the best job I could do, not just as a reporter for the *Daily News*, but as a witness to the rescuers' heroism. I wrote down every word, every action, every story I was told. I became a sounding board for grief—they couldn't tell a fellow worker, but they could tell me—and let one woman cry on my shoulder. By the end of the day, I had worked nineteen hours,

Journey to Ground Zero

without lunch or dinner, and I was exhausted, like everyone else at Ground Zero. In that, at least, I took solace.

Throughout the day I had phoned in my interviews and observations to the rewrite desk, and finally, around 9 P.M., I was given permission to go home. I had been the only reporter from the *Daily News* to make it to Ground Zero; the paper would send someone else in the morning. Good job, they said.

Still, I lingered. About 11:20 P.M. I found myself staring straight at the debris of the towers, lit up like a ballfield at night. A few dozen firefighters stood and sat next to me, most of them waiting for their turn at the bucket brigade. Everyone was beat, dazed.

Ground Zero's giant crane began to lift—it had something big—and from the rubble emerged a fire truck.

The truck rose straight into the air, some twenty or thirty feet above the pile, where it dangled in the darkness, and every worker stopped to watch. Its ladder section had been crushed, as if a giant foot had stepped on it, and the cab was bent to the left, as if its neck had been broken. All of the windows were missing, but the truck was not charred. It was a brilliant red and white, and on the passenger door of the cab, painted in gold leaf, were the letters "FDNY Ladder 18."

Methodically and carefully, the crane swung the truck over cleared ground and gently lowered it behind a row of dump trucks. A large, crème-colored tow truck backed up to the fire truck, and, minutes later, started to pull forward with its haul. A large group of firefighters standing directly in the tow truck's path parted to let the vehicles squeeze by—so close the men could have reached out and touched them. The tow truck drove at a crawl, and the red and white corpse moved slowly past the men, holding back tears.

And then, without a word being spoken, the firefighters reached up, took off their helmets, and placed them over their hearts.

Ladder 18 slowly passed into the blackness, and in a moment, was gone.

Peter DeMarco

Silently, the men returned their helmets to their heads, and their eyes to the pile. And the night's work went on.

I had now seen all I could hope to see at Ground Zero, and so, I headed for Canal Street, where I had begun my journey at dawn. Frequently, I looked back at the shining glow of the debris pile, growing smaller and smaller as I gained distance. I passed several police checkpoints along the West Side Highway. No one questions you when you *leave* Ground Zero. At Canal Street, thousands of people stood on the curb, waving American flags and cheering wildly for the occasional rescue worker or fire engine that emerged from the frozen zone. I veered off a few feet before reaching the crowd, fearing they might mistake me for one of the heroes.

Postscript: Peter DeMarco fed information to four rewrite editors at the Daily News *while at Ground Zero, but they were so overwhelmed with material from other reporters working on other stories that only a fraction of what he told them was printed. The main Ground Zero story contained a single sentence about the fire truck. Also, DeMarco's name was mistakenly left off the story. Two days later, on September 17, the* Daily News's *afternoon* Express *edition was canceled, in large part because of the economic downturn caused by the attacks, and DeMarco was laid off. He submitted stories to the main edition for another two and a half weeks until the freelance budget was cut and he was let go for good. His last assignment was covering Mayor Rudolph Giuliani on primary election day.*

He would like to dedicate this story in memory of New York City firefighter Steve Mercado.

A Detoured Commute

By Jill Gardiner—*Staten Island Advance*

For reporters at the Staten Island Advance *like JILL GARDINER, the most deadly attack on American soil since Pearl Harbor was a decidedly local story. Two hundred ninety-one residents of the sixty square mile island perished on September 11. At night, Manhattan resident Gardiner slept on the pullout couch of her childhood friend Jennifer Boltuch. During the day, in borrowed clothes, she wrote memorials to victims, a feature of the paper that would run for three months. Eventually the* Advance *wrote 218 obituaries. Over the next months, Gardiner attended morning funerals at which hundreds of firefighters formed human walls of grief. She investigated the fate of dozens of working-class Mexican Staten Island residents who had worked at or near the site.*

Raised in northern New Jersey, Gardiner, twenty-six, graduated from the University of Wisconsin, Madison, in 1998. She covered education for a small newspaper in rural Wisconsin before moving to New York City, where she earned a master's degree at the Columbia Graduate School of Journalism in 2000. She joined the Staten Island Advance *three weeks later. Gardiner describes how covering Staten Island's grief and resilience sealed her respect for the borough dominated by strip malls and military veterans.*

When the first of the World Trade Center buildings collapsed, I was standing at the gateway to safety: The Staten Island Ferry Terminal. With my hands overhead, I darted toward the underbelly of a docked boat, just blocks from where two jetliners had slammed into the city's tallest skyscrapers. The deckhands lowered the ramps by clutching the cables with sturdy grips and forcing the attached pulleys into motion. Within seconds the accordion-style gates opened and five thousand frenzied people flooded onboard.

In the middle of the pushing and shoving, a blond woman with glassy blue eyes stood perfectly still, as if in a daze. With tears spilling down her cheeks, she stopped and asked me whether it was safe to board the boat. Amid chaos that felt like a detonating minefield she was afraid the boat, sailing through the New York Harbor to the land of civil servants and cul-de-sacs, would be a target. She was alone and anonymous like everyone. I didn't know how to respond and I don't know what she ultimately did. But I boarded.

As a reporter for the *Staten Island Advance*, a newspaper with a circulation of about 90,000 that covers the city's smallest borough, my job drastically changed on September 11. I had been hired as a general assignment reporter in June 2000 after working for a small newspaper in Wisconsin and then earning a master's degree in journalism. I began writing about health and medicine about six months into the job, but after the Trade Center attack responsibilities blurred. The court reporter left her post to help report on

A Detoured Commute

the chaos in Manhattan, the real estate reporter put aside development stories to cover impromptu candlelight vigils, photographers spent hours searching for Staten Island families in the city, and somehow the paper got published. Nothing had prepared me for this assignment.

The Island lost almost three hundred current and former residents, many with spouses or partners and young children. They left behind thousands. And the *Staten Island Advance*, the lifeline of the community, documented as much as it could with a staff of about thirty news reporters.

As I made my way to the middle of the ferry that morning, looking for a seat, I didn't know the extent of the damage or that Staten Island would be so grotesquely wounded. The bright orange life vests, which are usually stored under the wooden benches, were already being passed around. The mass exodus from lower Manhattan had begun and we were among the first to escape.

The camaraderie was strange; it seemed like we were off to see fireworks or a ball game together. Passengers who usually ignore one another other for a newspaper or book banded together. They sandwiched onto benches, huddled by the concession stand, and crowded onto the deck, crippled with fear, unsure whether they would get home.

The boat pushed away from the tip of lower Manhattan, enveloped in a plume of thick, gray dust. When it emerged, everything came into focus. At the ferry terminal we had craned our necks to see what was happening. We had been too close to the epicenter to have a vantage point. On the boat what the entire country was watching on television came into view. The difference was that we could also smell it and taste it.

We watched the north World Trade Center tower burn like the wick of a candle. The other one had already collapsed. We stared out the windows in horror, oblivious to the imposing statue on the right or to the mass migration over the Brooklyn Bridge to our left.

Everyone seemed to be praying for safety, too nervous and helpless to move.

The ferry was at mid-harbor when the second building fell. I'm sure some knew then, in their gut, that they had just lost relatives, friends, and neighbors. From the window on the boat it looked like a massive pile of ash and dust had been dumped from the sky. The building had vanished as if part of a warped magic act. The boat, usually the artery connecting work to the familiar landscape of home, had suddenly taken on a new significance: the shuttle to safety.

Ferrying between Manhattan and home is a daily ritual for thousands of Staten Island residents. With almost half a million people, the island could easily be a city in any other part of the country. But in New York, it feeds off the easy commute to Manhattan, the international financial capital of the world. Those who call it home see it as a refuge from Manhattan's towering buildings, sky-high rents, and exhausting bustle.

On any other Tuesday morning, the boat would have been empty heading in this direction, with the exception of the crusty old man who regularly coerces passengers into a shoe shine, a handful of stragglers, and the lawyers going to court on the island. This ride was different.

I was sitting next to Mark Cannon, a forty-two-year-old prosecutor at the New York Sate Attorney General's Office, who is a part of the large, and exclusive, club of native Staten Islanders. With sandy, auburn hair and broad shoulders, Cannon was levelheaded and quickly became my confidant. I contacted him three months later to meet for breakfast and rehash our shared experience.

"I've been taking that ferry since I was five or six years old and I've never seen anyone put on a life jacket," Cannon told me as we ate in a deli on the bottom floor of his office building on Broadway, cater-corner to the Trade Center site. "I remember feeling like a sitting duck and thinking they were going to blow up the boat, that it

A Detoured Commute

was a floating coffin and that they were going to take out all of us in one shot."

I agreed. The situation was unthinkable, petrifying. The woman sitting directly across from me was frantic. Her hysteria seemed to weigh the boat down as we sloshed through the water, counting down the minutes. A business executive in the next aisle stroked the ropes on her life vest vigilantly until the boat began moaning, the way it does when being docked. As we arrived on shore I took out my notebook and leafed through the quotes I had gathered. I scribbled a lead, trying to capture the magnitude of the situation, but ended up rewriting it later.

It was impossible to believe I had been in my apartment on East 28th Street in Manhattan an hour and a half earlier drinking tea and eating a fruit yogurt for breakfast. I left for work at 8:30 and had been driving south on the FDR Drive, the highway that runs along the East River, when the first plane hit. Within seconds police cars of every kind, fire engines, and rescue vehicles were racing past me, sirens blaring. I had an unobstructed view of the north tower, which was billowing thick black smoke and engulfed in flames, through my windshield. I exited immediately and parked my car in a lot on Pearl Street, six blocks east of the Trade Center. If I had continued over the Brooklyn Bridge I probably would have reached my desk before the first collapse. But instead I ended up at the ferry terminal running for my life.

When the boat docked on Staten Island around 10 A.M. it was clear we were no longer in danger. Mark Cannon and I exhaled and parted ways. He went home to his wife and children. With the smoldering skyline to my back, I ran to my newspaper's small Borough Hall satellite office.

With my family calling to make sure I was safe and my editor pressuring me to file, I quickly pounded out a twelve-inch, first-person story. As an afternoon newspaper, we were able to publish the news in our first edition, probably the only paper in the city to do so. My story ran on the front page under the headline "On the Scene: Panic and Fear" with a photo taken from the roof of the paper's main building. An editor had ripped apart the original front page, laid out the new version, and sent our draft of history to the presses.

I went back to the ferry terminal with two coworkers and started what would be an all-consuming assignment. For the next five hours, hundreds of people, including many who had never been to Staten Island, evacuated the city by boat and ended up in the borough they knew only as the butt of jokes—most about Fresh Kills Landfill, the largest garbage dump in the western hemisphere.

Staten Island had become a sanctuary for those who had just seen hell. Nobody cared about the stench of trash wafting through the air on the other side of the island. They were happy to be out of Manhattan, far from the trendy restaurants, multimillion-dollar business deals, and smell of death. Meanwhile, doctors, nurses, police officers, and paramedics turned the landmark terminal into a triage center and prepared a makeshift morgue at a ballpark next door. But the wounded never showed and the bodies they expected were never recovered.

Hundreds of local families held out hope as they waited for spouses, parents, children, brothers, sisters, cousins, and friends to come home. Many stayed up all night waiting for the phone to ring. The people they loved most had vanished. It was incomprehensible. They had dry cleaning to pick up, gym memberships to renew, and families expecting them for dinner. They had weekend plans, vacations, and theater tickets. They were young and their final moments were too haunting to visualize. How could they be gone?

The final death count on Staten Island came to 291, including 78 firefighters, two Port Authority officers, one police officer, and more than 200 bond and stock traders, financial analysts, and Trade Center employees. There was also one Staten Island resident killed on United Flight 93, which crashed in Shanksville, Pa.

A Detoured Commute

The *Advance* began running victims' photos the day after the attack and continued for the next four months. On October 6, the paper was wrapped in a special-edition slip, the kind tabloids use for World Series issues. It contained 240 head shots of victims and the headline "Taken From Us" in fine black letters. A purple-and-black bunting ran along the top edge.

The service the *Advance* provided by eulogizing the Staten Island dead was indispensable. It was the only local source of information, the only place readers could find out which of their neighbors were gone. The *Advance* has always been an institution on Staten Island. It gives residents a collective identity and provides them with a voice in a city that does not always pay them much attention. Reporters there write about everything from cancer clusters and hospital conditions to traffic and real estate developments. As a result, Staten Island's politicians and power brokers have become accustomed to answering questions and taking their community's concerns seriously. The paper is an integral part of that community cohesion.

Though part of New York City, Staten Island often feels as if it's in a different time zone. It is largely working class, a place where firefighters and police officers live on almost every block and where generations of families go to the same high school. It's where kids play in Catholic school sports leagues, where war veterans outnumber subway riders (there is only one train line), and where residents erected American flags as soon as the towers were hit. It has its own colleges and universities, its own hospitals, its own zoo, its own mall, its own performing arts center, and its own problems. And, yes, it lives in the shadows of the other more urban and eclectic boroughs.

Mark Cannon, the prosecutor I befriended while fleeing from Manhattan, has strong ties to the place. His native-Islander status, which goes far in the borough and is not extended to anyone who was not physically born there, meant he knew dozens of victims.

Some were from his days at Monsignor Farrell High School, others from playing basketball or attending church.

"Mike Fiore, John Fischer, Tommy Hannafin. I played ball with some of these guys all of my life," he told me. "There were so many firefighters in my neighborhood and so many kids in my sons' classes who lost fathers."

Until I began working at the *Advance*, I had never been to Staten Island or known a community like it. It lives up to its reputation as the city's strip mall capital and it has more than its share of fast food restaurants, electronic stores, nail salons, and mobsters. But after the attack, it displayed more heart than any community I have ever known and showed incredible compassion and poise. Residents began dropping boxes of bottled water, Gatorade, socks, and medical supplies at the ferry terminal for rescue workers on the other side of the harbor hours after the attack. Support groups were operational within weeks and residents attended funerals for victims they did not know. The devastation its residents suffered was sickening. And reporting their stories gave me a newfound respect for the island.

In the days after the attack, *Advance* reporters fanned out all over Staten Island and Manhattan, waiting at area hospitals, sitting with families in their worst hours of agony, and creating lists of the missing. We ate meals in the newsroom, napped on the bathroom couches when we became sleep deprived, and produced story after story. Many of the editors made their careers there and are part of the community fabric in the same way the pizza places and Lions Clubs are. They know every back road, every humdrum organization, and every good restaurant. It was no surprise when their newspaper became the procedural clearinghouse for the community until the Family Assistance Center was set up in Manhattan.

In the four months after the attack, we wrote 218 tribute obituaries, similar to the "Portraits of Grief" in the *New York Times*, but longer and more detailed. The newsroom became the hub of information for everyone on the Island. Readers dropped off pictures, called to find out about funeral schedules, and confided in reporters. As we wrote, ferries shuttled relief rescue workers into Manhattan. Boats coming back brought those who had been searching for survivors. They were dazed and barely able to muster words to describe what they had seen.

Civilians on the Island were in limbo, home from work but trapped in an eerie in-between period. The only bridges linking the sixty-square-mile island to the rest of the world—the Verrazano-Narrows, the Goethals, the Outerbridge Crossing, and the Bayonne—were essentially sealed off by security checkpoints.

For the week of September 11, I stayed with Jennifer Boltuch, a childhood friend from New Jersey who was living with her fiancé in the West Brighton section of the borough. They pulled out their couch, gave me clothes, and fed me. In exchange, I made sure their friends' names were added to the victim list, something I would have been sure to do anyway.

One of their close friends, Jason DeFazio, a bond trader at Cantor Fitzgerald, had been married two months earlier. My friend's fiancé, Joseph, was in the wedding. Like Mark Cannon, Joe Crescitelli grew up on Staten Island. He played ball there, attended Curtis High School on the North Shore, and had dozens of local affiliations. Every morning during my stay, one of his friends would come by with a couple of coffees, each with the right amount of milk and sugar, and a copy of the *Advance*. They would sit around the glass dining room table looking at the paper to see if they recognized anyone, just like our readers were doing all over the island. And each day, I would lie in bed awake, having worked until three or four o'clock in the morning, listening as they reminisced about people they had known for years who were now dead.

Some of their friends were firefighters, others were part of the fraternity of securities traders—many were the first in their families to wear a suit to work. Almost all were male and came from blue collar backgrounds. Despite the salary disparity, firefighters and securities brokers are cut from the same cloth on Staten Island and often move freely between the two professions.

For months after the attack reporters at the *Advance* covered heartbreaking firefighter funerals (many of the civilian ceremonies were done in private). The ceremonies were ornate, complete with Scottish bagpipe bands and Fire Department motorcades. Until the Trade Center attack, these funerals were held only for isolated tragedies. Afterward, they became commonplace.

An aerial view of the borough would show churches peppering the landscape, usually empty, but filled by converging residents from nearby neighborhoods on Sundays and holidays. After September 11, these patterns became muddled. Churches everywhere became magnets for mourners all over the island, any day of the week. I covered Tuesday-morning funerals where more than five hundred uniformed firefighters formed a human wall outside a chapel, standing at attention as the pipes skirled "Amazing Grace." The coffins, draped in American flags, were often empty because remains had not been recovered. The mayor, the governor, the fire commissioner, and dozens of elected officials attended each one in some combination. Distraught family members read eulogies. Some did not have the tears left to cry. They looked empty and hollow.

At each funeral, I sat in the last pew and took notes. By the time I left I was usually wiping away tears. It was impossible to remain indifferent, even though as a reporter I had learned to sever myself from many emotional subjects. That professional code was not applicable anymore.

At firefighter Frank Esposito's funeral, the fire commissioner handed Dawn Esposito her husband's helmet as hundreds of officers saluted her and an engine carrying the coffin rolled away. I kept his Mass card in my desk for months and then brought it home to save.

A few days earlier Captain William O'Keefe had been

A Detoured Commute

remembered. His teenage daughters, Kaitlin, sixteen, and Tara, nineteen, had clutched to their mother as they walked out of the cathedral in tears. The horror of the individual grief and the collective nightmare had to be documented. The *Advance*, naturally, had taken on the role.

Of the stories I wrote, some stand out more than others.

John Talignani, the Staten Island resident killed on United Flight 93, hated flying. He was on his way to a funeral for his stepson, who was killed in an automobile accident in San Francisco a few days earlier. He hadn't flown in years and was scheduled to meet his other two stepsons in California. Instead, they had to mourn the loss of both their brother and father.

Neil Dollard, a native Staten Island resident who had recently moved to New Jersey, prepared a sautéed spinach dish and a homemade tomato sauce the night before the attack. He was a twenty-eight-year-old bond trader at Cantor Fitzgerald. He had planned, in a week's time, to visit his family in Italy with his girlfriend. Like the others, he never came home.

The undocumented Mexican immigrants, working as dishwashers and cooks at Windows on the World, the restaurant at the top of Tower One, also never returned. Members of the Mexican community on Staten Island could not agree on how many were killed. Estimates varied wildly; some told me none of the workers lived on Staten Island, others insisted that at least a dozen from the borough were killed: no one could connect me with their families.

Like undocumented immigrants in Seattle, San Francisco, or St. Louis, illegal residents on Staten Island are often hesitant to come forward for government assistance—even when it comes to something like prenatal care. That ideology held true after the attack too. Local Mexican community leaders, officials at the Mexican consulate in Manhattan, and others told me that getting the families to come forward for emotional and financial help was a real challenge. I never did get an answer to my question.

Jill Gardiner

Though the *Staten Island Advance* may not be a big name off the Island, it covered the biggest story since Vietnam in the area that claimed the highest concentration of fatalities. The community devoured everything that was written and the pool of possible stories was endless. A few months after the attack, the Poynter Institute, a well-respected media organization, posted September 11 covers from hundreds of papers around the world on its Web site. When I discovered it, I scrolled down unsure if the *Advance* would be featured. Sure enough there it was. I was thankful that someone thought to include it.

The Vacation

By Jennifer Chen—Reuters

Former resident JENNIFER CHEN returned to New York City on September 10, there for the first time since she had joined Reuters in Singapore thirty months earlier. She awoke in her friend Siobhan's apartment to the sound of the first plane crashing into the Twin Towers. After watching the second tower crumble, she headed south. Passing shell-shocked survivors fleeing north, she was reminded of refugees she had seen while visiting war-torn Indonesia and Sri Lanka. On Wednesday, she reported to Reuters' New York office, where she was assigned to cover what had become of Asian and Asian-American businesses that had been located in the World Trade Center. Chen dreaded returning to Asia for another assignment. She knew she would be forced to defend America against charges that it doesn't care about the down-trodden, is too arrogant to learn about the rest of the world, and was not justified in unleashing bombing campaigns in the devastation that is Afghanistan.

Born in Connecticut, Chen, twenty-eight, was educated at Cornell and the Columbia Graduate School of Journalism. She lived in New York for four years before moving to Asia. Today Chen is a general news editor for the Associated Press in Bangkok, Thailand.

The morning of September 11, I was lying awake in my friend Siobhan's apartment on the corner of Christopher and Washington near West Street, around twenty blocks north of the World Trade Center. It was my third day back in America after having spent nearly three years in Asia, where I've been working as a journalist.

The sky was cloudless and deeply blue in a way you seldom see in Southeast Asia, where the hot tropical sun blanches everything.

I was lying awake thinking how strange it seemed to be back in New York, secretly longing to return to Asia as soon as possible. New York with its harsh, fast rhythms was unbearable compared to the languid pace of life I've grown accustomed to in Southeast Asia. Even the conversation of my friends seemed unreal—full of references to the latest places, books, and films. I'd forgotten these were important when you lived in New York. In my mind, I was in Thailand—Chiang Mai in the north to be exact—chatting in pidgin English and Thai with an old woman who sold drinks by the side of a temple. She poured a Coke into a plastic bag and ladled in some ice while trying to speak to me in Mandarin. The back of my shoulders and neck were hot from the blazing sun.

Then there was a whine, and a muffled thud. A few moments later, I heard sirens race downtown.

I thought it was a massive car accident. Suddenly, Siobhan burst in. A plane had crashed. Into the World Trade Center. And you could see it from the fire escape.

The Vacation

We pried open the window of her studio and climbed onto the fire escape, her in work clothes and high heels, me, bare-footed, in pajamas. Below, people gathered in knots of two or three. Traffic stopped and men and women hung off the windows of their cars, shouting and pointing. A woman stumbled up the street, sobbing.

Siobhan had quicker instincts than I. She climbed back into the apartment and turned on the television to New York One, the local twenty-four-hour news station. After gaping at the tower for a few seconds, I, too, climbed back in.

For the next hour or so, we took turns watching the news and climbing onto the fire escape. When the second plane hit, the people on the street shrank back and gasped.

"Fuck," a man screamed from his pickup truck, stopped at the corner. Others gestured at him, telling him to move his car so the ambulances and fire trucks that were weaving their way downtown could get by.

When the second tower collapsed I looked at Siobhan, who was already in tears and frantically trying to locate her boyfriend, who worked near the area.

"I have to go down there," I told my friend

I thought of that moment with something akin to shame later. As an aspiring journalist, I had reacted slowly, stupidly, merely blinking at the unfolding scene. I hadn't grabbed my notebook and rushed out. I hadn't called the Reuters bureau in New York— located in a mammoth building in Times Square, and filed head-lines. I sat there, in my pajamas clutching a pillow, only every now and then climbing back onto the fire escape to gaze dumbly at the burning towers and the billowing smoke.

But when the day was over, and the streets below 14th were empty save for rescue vehicles, I was more ashamed of how I had left Siobhan, whom I've know since college. She and I had been roommates for two years at Cornell, and then lived together for four years in New York. We used to joke that in some states, we would be common-law spouses.

No words of assurance or comfort, just a flat, "I have to go down there," then dressing, digging out a notepad and pen and charging out the door.

"Jenn went into reporter mode," I heard her tell others later. There was a note of disbelief in her voice. I tried to apologize.

"Don't worry about it," she said.

But it stayed with me for a long time.

Before I left the apartment, I called another old friend, Jonathan Landreth, who was then working in the Reuters bureau in New York.

"Where are you now?" he asked.

"Near West Street," I answered.

"Walk down there. Call in what you see," he said in his calm measured tones. Even during this moment of chaos and confusion, Jonathan—who I always secretly regarded as a *dage*, or big brother, in Mandarin—kept his wits about him, and was able to help me keep mine.

As I turned the corner to West Street, I saw the masses of people walking away, fleeing north, toward safety. They seemed to move in slow motion, as if they were walking underwater. In the movies, you always see people running from disaster, screaming. These people moved deliberately, with a purpose, but not in a hurry.

Four ambulances roared up the street. It finally hit me that many people had died or were dying. I wondered whether I could do it, whether I could go down there and see mangled bodies, pain, death, destruction. *I can't, I can't, I can't*, I said to myself between sobs. I kept walking.

Scores of teenagers passed me, joking and laughing, happy to be out of class. Men in business suits gathered around phone booths, patiently waiting their turn to call home.

A man walked past, covered in dust with muddy tear streaks on his face, blood oozing from his forehead, and his shirt in shreds.

The Vacation

In my three years in Asia, I'd never reported in a war zone. I never felt any strong desire to do so. I have many friends— reporters, cameramen, photographers—who have lived and worked in Cambodia, Indonesia, and East Timor. Occasionally, in a bar in Bangkok or Jakarta, someone would nudge me and point toward a middle-aged man clutching a drink.

"Covered the Vietnam War," the person would whisper. "Been rotting in Asia ever since."

Predictably, the journalists I know who have been to war zones are a hard-bitten lot. The reporters are quick with sarcastic barbs and have a bit of a swagger. The cameramen and photographers pop pills and scoff at how their agencies send them on hostile training courses—where they were kidnapped by former British commandoes in the English countryside to prepare them for the worst in Sierra Leone or Afghanistan—five years too late.

The closest I had ever come to a war zone was in Sri Lanka, where my boyfriend, Simon, and I had decided to go on holiday one year. There, the government and the separatist Tamil Tigers have been fighting for years in a conflict that has claimed more than 64,000 lives. The Tigers are particularly well known for their suicide bombers, who are often young recruits with explosives strapped to their bodies. Many places of incredible beauty in Asia— Sri Lanka, Kashmir, the Malukus in Indonesia, and the southern Philippines—are also places where war has been waged, fiercely and for decades.

The American journalist Robert Kaplan once wrote that you know you are in a country where there has been a civil conflict because the roads are terrible. In Sri Lanka, especially north of the capital, Colombo, the potholes were two feet deep and five feet wide. Cars drove into them, not over them.

But despite the sandbagged guard posts around Colombo and eighteen-year-old soldiers saddled with huge automatic weapons, I never felt any real danger from anything or anyone. The most terrifying experience I had there was sitting in the front seat of a minibus with an amphetamine-pumped driver who was trying to negotiate the roads with a steering wheel bigger than he was, and whose idea of fun meant playing chicken with large trucks. "Stay away from the public officials," Simon and I joked. The Tamil Tiger suicide bombers had a penchant for blowing themselves up while standing next to government officials.

On September 11, in New York, at home, I was walking past fleeing people. Refugees. They were people I had walked by every day when I was living in New York: high school kids in baggy hip-hop pants, commuters from Connecticut and New Jersey, women in smart black pantsuits, men in blue shirts and pinstripes. This is not East Timor, I thought. Not Kalimantan. Not Sri Lanka, Cambodia, or Vietnam. This is New York. This city is supposed to be safe. Secure. Home.

Jonathan, who spent the next week or so pulling twenty-hour days, told me later that Reuters had sponsored a counseling session for journalists covering Ground Zero. The following week at his apartment in Brooklyn Heights, I told him it struck me how unprepared the journalists were who covered the disaster. They were financial reporters and society columnists. Certainly not war tourists running around in flak jackets with the visa stamps of the great shit holes of the world on their passports.

He told me of one reporter who had covered Bosnia and West Africa. "It's different when it is home," the reporter had said.

"He didn't need to say anything else," Jonathan said, and we both sat in silence for a few moments.

I interviewed a man who had turned to gaze upon the wreckage of the buildings and the great plumes of smoke and dust. He spoke calmly, gesturing with his hands to show how the towers had disappeared. For twenty years, he had worked across the street from the World Trade Center, commuting from New Jersey.

The Vacation

"Is the PATH train open? I guess I should go back," he said absently. My hands shook as I jotted down notes.

I needed a phone to file, but didn't have a cell phone with me, and the booths around me were taken. So I ran into the nearest store. "Sorry," the owner said, shaking his head. "Another reporter is using the phone."

The next open shop also had a line of people waiting to use the pay phone. I begged the owner to let me use the store phone. He took me to the back room.

After several attempts, I got through to Jonathan. Before he finally picked up, I looked around and realized that I had stumbled into a porn store. The shelves were lined with videos showing buxom blondes displaying ample amounts of cleavage and bending over tantalizingly. I was standing next to a rack of dildoes.

"I'm in a fucking porn store on West Street surrounded by dildoes," I said to Jonathan. We both laughed, allowing ourselves to relish the one ludicrous moment of the day. *All hell is breaking loose, and I'm in a goddamn porn store.*

Back on the street, people flinched when a fighter jet zoomed above their heads. They thought they were under attack again. I headed south.

A black car with shaded windows came to a screeching halt at the corner of West and Leroy Street. A window rolled down. "Get the fuck out of here quick," a man in a suit with dark glasses shouted at us. "There are going to be gas explosions."

Everyone scattered. Months later, a friend of mine, a former journalist based in Jakarta who now works for a risk consultancy group, described the moments before something catastrophic might happen as "terrible, terrible clarity." Your brain moves more deliberately. Time itself slows down.

When that man shouted from the car, my thoughts became clear—*Get out, and you will be upset about it later.*

There would be more moments like that in the following days:

Jennifer Chen

The bomb scare in the Condé Nast building, next to the Reuters office in Times Square. The bomb scare in JFK as I waited for my flight to Tokyo.

A few weeks after September 11, I found myself in the back of a taxi in Singapore, where I worked then as a regional economics reporter for Reuters, feeling heavy-hearted and bewildered.

That day, on September 11, I never made it to the devastation. A police officer turned me back, and Jonathan urged me to return. Later, he told me how worried he was for me, still jet-lagged, still disoriented from my return journey. Welcome home.

That night, I called Simon, my boyfriend, who is a freelance journalist in Jakarta. Two months before, we had broken up, and communication between us was fraught and difficult.

He was still asleep when I called from Siobhan's balcony. In New York, the air was acrid with smoke and debris. They had already closed most of lower Manhattan to traffic, and it was quiet in the streets below save for the occasional siren. After a few awkward pauses, I said to him quietly, "Do you know what has happened here?"

"Of course I know, Jenn . . . I was thinking of you," he said tensely.

I wept after I hung up. All I wanted was for someone, anyone, to tell me it was going to be all right.

The following day I turned up in the Reuters office, asking how I could help. Partly because I spoke Mandarin, and partly, I privately guessed, because I was Asian-American, one of the editors quickly corralled me into calling Chinese, Taiwanese, and Japanese companies that were in the World Trade Center and finding out many people were missing.

After hearing strung-out reporters slam down telephones and mutter cuss words, I was glad that the editor had assigned me this

The Vacation

task. I've learned that impatience and curt questions get only polite resistance, or, worse, blank stares and stubborn silence from Asians.

The Japanese consulate provided me with a list of companies that had been located in the World Trade Center with the number of employees and the number that were missing—a little under one hundred. Many of the firms were branches of large brokerages and other financial services firms.

In contrast, many of the Chinese- and Taiwanese-run businesses were small and immigrant-run, which meant phone calls to both the consulates and community groups. These were neither multinational conglomerates nor large securities firms. These were small import businesses run by workers who toiled and sacrificed until they had enough to rent an office or retail space in the World Trade Center. Mr. Chen's computer parts store. Mr. and Mrs. Lee's gift shop filled with lacquered boxes and copies of the terra-cotta warriors in Xian, China. Even if they escaped, hours of work and their life savings lay under the rubble. For many Chinese, it was just as disastrous to lose their business.

My parents had arrived in America from Taiwan nearly thirty years ago, and if the people out on the street were those I passed by every day while I lived in New York, these people were the ones I grew up with.

There was a company in the World Trade Center that was owned by a Mr. Chen, who had another firm somewhere else in New York. When I called information, the operator asked, "Ma'am, that was in the World Trade Center. Do you still want that number?"

After work, I met up with Siobhan and my friend, Phil Oxenstein, at the Corner Bistro in the West Village. As we walked back home, we passed a disheveled black man in a battered fatigue jacket, preaching about Sodom and Gomorrah. When he saw me, he paused, and then said slowly and ominously, "The problem with this country is that we let in too many goddamn foreigners."

Before I left New York in September, a friend—a reporter for *Newsday*—asked me what I disliked most about of the United States now that I had lived abroad for a few years. "We don't know enough about the world," I replied without hesitation.

On the night of September 11, a few friends gathered in Siobhan's apartment to watch the news. "We should just bomb Afghanistan," said one of them. She was a self-proclaimed liberal, well traveled for an American, having spent time in Italy and India, from which her parents hailed. A few days later, she noticed passersby were giving her and her brother dirty looks, mistaking their Bengali features for Middle Eastern ones.

In my travels throughout Asia, I have met Canadians, French, Germans, South Africans, Indians, Italians, Israelis, Dutch, Japanese, Taiwanese, New Zealanders, Malaysians. Loads of Brits and Australians. They were of all races and ages and economic backgrounds.

While I have met other Americans who work in Asia, I have never met another American while traveling. This despite the fact that in many countries anyone carrying an American passport can stay for sixty days without a visa.

It was for this reason—the very plain fact that it is said up to 70 percent of Americans do not have their passports—that I dreaded returning to Asia. I dreaded defending American foreign policy because I knew there were plenty of examples of U.S. policy going horribly wrong, or displaying nothing more noble than arrogance and chauvinism. Especially in Southeast Asia, where one only has to go to Vietnam, Cambodia, and Laos to see what the Americans left behind.

I dreaded accusations that Americans can ignore the deaths of seven thousand Indians in an earthquake, but expected the world's sympathy when it came to our own because I knew some Americans had no idea where India, let alone Gujarat, was. When I moved to Asia, I'd had people at home ask me if Taiwan was the same thing as Thailand, if Singapore was in China, whether I've taken the train from Singapore to Indonesia, and whether they spoke Chinese in the Philippines.

Even when I argued against that comparison, saying the earthquake in Gujarat was a natural disaster as opposed to the murder of thousands in the World Trade Center, I would still get retorts:

"What about Bosnia? What about East Timor? Americans didn't give two shits about those places."

"Doesn't matter because Americans are still arrogant, and still think they are the center of the universe."

Or worse, because I shared the sentiments behind this comment: "That doesn't mean the Americans should bomb Afghanistan."

When I returned to Asia, I wanted others to see September 11 as something terribly unique. To keep the pain and the devastation of that day intact and whole. For me that was a way to honor the dead and New York. Interpretation, I thought, would distort it. But no event as enormous as the destruction of the World Trade Center can ever escape interpretation.

And no nation as admired and reviled, both in extreme fashions, as America could expect to mourn its dead quietly and humbly.

A few months later, I met a remarkable Filipina woman, Ping. For nine years, she has lived and worked in Singapore as a maid, sending all the money she earns back to her two sons in her village near Zamboanga, which was in the southern Philippines, where U.S. troops are now stationed to help the Philippine government fight Muslim rebel groups.

Nothing about Ping's sweet and gentle demeanor hinted at the harshness of her life. When she came to Singapore, her husband abandoned her and her children and took up with another woman, with whom he had another family. Her village is poor, and has been caught up in the government's three-decade-long battle with Muslim insurgents who kidnap villagers for ransom.

One day, while walking through the village center with her youngest son, then six years old, she stopped to chat with a friend. When she turned around, she couldn't find the boy. After desperately searching for him in the shops, she found him lying in the street, bleeding and unconscious. A car—which in her village probably meant somebody with more money and power than she—had struck him and driven off.

Though he survived, and has recently entered university, Ping was still haunted by the accident. "I just turned around, and he wasn't there anymore," she told me, her eyes tearing at the memory.

And that's what happened to us on September 11, on a mass scale. We turned around, and the World Trade Center and over three thousand people had disappeared.

But what Ping's story revealed to me is that for so many, too many, people in the world, such disappearances are a part daily life. Loved ones can be, and are, snatched away. Thousands can disappear and chaos often reigns over law and order.

September 11 didn't set America apart. It meant that we've joined the rest of the world.

Earlier in March, Simon traveled out to Ambon, in the Maluku Islands in Indonesia—better known as the Spice Islands, where the Dutch, Portuguese, and English fought over the right to trade nutmeg. Three years of sectarian violence in Ambon and the surrounding islands has left 5,000 people dead and 500,000 others as refugees.

I felt a twinge of panic when the *Christian Science Monitor*, for whom he was writing, gave him the green light for the trip.

"Call or send me a text message when you get there, and every few days," I said to him, trying not to sound too worried.

A month before, the *Wall Street Journal* reporter Danny Pearl

The Vacation

was murdered while reporting on a story in Pakistan. He was a friend of a friend, and I remember hearing stories about him and his wife, Marianne.

Before Danny was murdered, Harry Burton was killed in Afghanistan. He had been a friend of Simon's in Jakarta, and an acquaintance of mine as well as a colleague at Reuters. He and three other journalists, including Reuters photographer Azizullah Haidari, were shot dead by bandits on a lonely stretch of road. Aziz, who was Afghani, was returning to Kabul for the first time in twenty years.

One of Simon's predecessors, Sander Thoenes, had covered Indonesia for the *Christian Science Monitor*. He was murdered in East Timor in September 1999, when a U.N.-sponsored referendum for independence for the tiny former Portuguese colony led to a bloody rampage by pro-Jakarta militias.

Since September 11, the deaths of working journalists have hit increasingly close to home. While September 11 affected journalists in New York, the conflict in Afghanistan meant that a number of Asia-based journalists were being flown in to cover the war, and they were people that I knew.

A recent report by the Committee to Protect Journalists said a total of thirty-seven journalists were killed worldwide in 2001, compared with twenty-four who were killed in 2000. I didn't want Simon to be next.

Nonetheless, after September 11, I could no longer justify what I was doing as a financial reporter in Asia. While being a financial reporter was never the end game for me, I'd grown comfortable with it. It paid well, and provided just enough intellectual stimulation to keep me going.

After September 11, and particularly after a visit to Indonesia—a place where I've come to feel a mixture of love and exasperation—I found myself sitting at my desk at work trying to think of less hackneyed ways of talking about the financial markets and bracing myself for chats with analysts and dealers about the ways the already rich could grow richer. *What on earth was I doing?*

Recently, I quit my job at Reuters. I joined the Associated Press in Bangkok. There I'll be a general news editor and will eventually return to the field. This time I hope I'll be better prepared.

As It Became Ground Zero

By Stacy Forster—*Wall Street Journal Online*

STACY FORSTER sat at her desk at the Wall Street Journal Online *when she heard a deep rumble and massive collision of steel and concrete. Out the window of the* Journal's *Liberty Street office, she saw flames engulfing the top of the nearby north tower of the World Trade Center. Stepping into the unfolding disaster, she encountered airplane seatbelts and a severed arm, not to mention dozens of terrified eyewitnesses. As both towers pancaked, she twice fled clouds of dust, evacuating to New Jersey, where the* Wall Street Journal Online's *backup offices were being established. As she undertook the grim task of reporting on the aftermath, Forster endured a two-hour commute to the* Journal's *new building and long, exhausting hours. To get through this trying period in her life, she depended on the support of her colleagues.*

Before joining the Journal, *Forster, twenty-nine, worked for a think tank called the Project for Excellence in Journalism in Washington, D.C., the Clinton/Gore reelection campaign, and the White House Office of Political Affairs. She holds a master's degree from Northwestern University's Medill School of Journalism and has reported for the Dow Jones Newswires in Dublin.*

On March 11, 2002, six months after the disaster at the World Trade Center, I was in Greencastle, Indiana, talking to students at my undergraduate college, DePauw University.

A former professor had asked me months earlier if I would come talk about my job, but when I sat down to write my speech, I knew I had to talk about my experience on September 11. After my speech, a current student approached me. "Why did they send *you* out to cover it, if you were a financial reporter?" he asked.

On September 11, it didn't matter. I was there and able to report. I had been working for the *Wall Street Journal Online* for a year and a half, writing about online brokerage firms and Internet investing. It was my first job out of graduate school. In early 2000, I thought I'd end up at a medium-sized newspaper covering local issues, like city hall or education. But then Jason Anders, a friend from DePauw, encouraged me to apply to the online *Journal*—where he worked. To my surprise, I got the job and found myself moving to New York.

The summer of 2001 was a long one for me. I had been working for the *Wall Street Journal Online* for a year when I survived a round of layoffs in March. Afterward I remained anxious about my job security and the faltering economy. As a business reporter, I knew that the drumbeat of stories about downsizing could spell trouble for me, too. What's more, the managing editor of the online edition had been replaced at the beginning of the summer. I had little contact with his replacement, Bill Grueskin, who had joined us from the print side of the *Journal*, and I was confused by the

As It Became Ground Zero

contradictory messages my editors gave me. As my frustration mounted, communication fell off. I was miserable.

My friends from work kept me sane. Since moving from Chicago a year and a half earlier, my social life had largely centered around my colleagues. Our crew spent many evenings under the patio umbrellas outside Foxhounds, the watering hole in our World Financial Center (WFC) building. From the patio we could see the Hudson River to the west and were just across the street from the World Trade Center. Those nights were opportunities to dissect our work and rehash the day over plates of nachos and chicken fingers.

Still, I wanted a change. After Labor Day, I was determined to start fresh. I set up a meeting with Bill to get a read on what he thought I should cover. Our conversation relaxed me immediately. He was bursting with ideas for the Web site and proposed a new role for me as a general assignment reporter. He wanted the staff to produce fresher content throughout the day, and for the Web site to be more vibrant. He thought my ability to produce on deadline would be better used in that capacity.

On the morning of September 10, he sent me an e-mail inviting me to his office. Just like that, idea became reality. I was a general assignment reporter. I would report to a new editor, Terri Cullen, whom I trusted and had seen as a mentor in the newsroom. For the first time in months, I was happy. That night, I called my parents and told them about the meeting. I couldn't contain my excitement. "Things could not get any better," I told them.

For about twelve hours it was true.

The next day, I was at work earlier than usual, reading the paper before turning on my computer. Erin Schulte, who writes the daily stock market update, was chatting with me about the sleek black wraparound dress I had just broken out for the fall. Our conversation was interrupted at about 8:45 A.M., midway through my breakfast cup of blueberry yogurt. I heard a deep rumble and then the crunch of metal. The windows rattled, even more than they would when a fierce wind whips against the building.

Everything seemed to freeze for a moment and the scene felt strangely serene. From my desk on the eleventh floor of the WFC, I had a good view of the lower corner of the north tower. Papers fluttered to the ground. I leaned over and saw flames engulfing several floors high in the north tower. My coworkers quickly rushed to my window. For a bunch of journalists, they weren't very eloquent. One by one, they all blurted out the same thing: "Oh my God, the World Trade Center is on fire."

Our editors conferred quickly to decide how to handle the story—did we think it was bigger than it really was because it happened across the street? No, Wall Street would definitely be affected, which made it news, they decided. Sophie Hayward, an editor who had joined WSJ.com just a few weeks earlier, was updating the Web site and news editor Tony Robinson sent through a bare-bones story about an explosion in the World Trade Center. It may have been one of the first published reports of the disaster because of our proximity to the scene and ability to publish instantly. Erin updated the market story to reflect that the explosion would likely have an impact on stocks that day.

I grabbed my reporter's notebook, cell phone, and purse. "Be careful," one of my coworkers, Michael Bragitikos, warned me as I dashed out. He treats me like a little sister, so I thought he was being overprotective and sort of laughed at his caution. Dave Pettit, the deputy managing editor, chased me to the elevator and gave me quick instructions: Gather color. The newswires will get the facts, so talk to people who can describe the scene.

To get to the World Trade Center from the World Financial Center I walked across an enclosed pedestrian bridge overpassing the busy West Side Highway. I was the only person heading toward the Trade Center. At the bottom of the stairs, I saw debris scattered across the familiar street. The man who sold newspapers on the sidewalk was gone; his stacks of papers were on fire. Another man sold fruit; he was gone, too, but his fruit cart was toppled over, its umbrella mangled. A campaign worker who had been handing out fliers had also fled.

As I made my way across a parking lot, I tried to piece it all together, but it wasn't adding up. *Was it a fire? A bomb?* Glass, luggage, a seatbelt, mangled pieces of metal. The debris was smoking and a car was on fire. But the streets were remarkably quiet. I was momentarily confused by what I thought was restaurant trash— *was there a Dumpster nearby that had exploded, too?* Then, I saw a severed arm. I was looking at pieces of human flesh.

I reeled—for a split second. I knew that I could—and had every right to—freak out, break down, throw up. But losing it wouldn't help me accomplish anything, whether it was talking to eyewitnesses or crossing the street. With every step, I needed to look down to find a clear path. I took a deep breath. Then I moved on.

People were gathered in front of the Amish Market across from the south tower of the Trade Center. "Did anyone see?" I asked. "I'm a reporter and I'm trying to figure out what happened." No one responded. They simply looked skyward at the burning building. It wasn't until I was about a half block south that I found someone coherent. The man told me he had been walking toward the pedestrian bridge when he heard what sounded like a sonic boom, and then metal crashed down around him. "I was lucky," he said, shaking his head in disbelief.

People talked about a plane, and my first thought was that a small plane had accidentally crashed into the building. But it didn't make sense—what were the chances that I had stepped over one of the few seatbelts that would be on a plane that size? I took a step back and felt something squish beneath my heel. I cringed then looked down and was relieved to see it was only part of a sheaf of papers that had fallen to the street. Behind me, a police officer was closing off the street with yellow crime tape. I maneuvered around a barrier to get to the other side, out of the way.

What happened next is still a blur. I didn't look up. I didn't realize that a plane was flying directly over the street on which I stood and was about to crash into the south tower. I just heard a deafening whine followed by an explosion. The Deutsche Bank Building at the corner of Cedar and Washington Streets, one block south of the World Trade Center, was behind me. It had a small overhang under which I ducked to take cover. A man and woman joined me there, and we pushed ourselves against the marble wall, listening to the crash overhead and watching shards of glass and metal fall like hail.

I tried to determine how safe my position really was. About fifteen seconds later, the man told the other woman that it was safe to move farther away from the building. I followed them down Washington Street. When I turned to look back about two blocks away from the south tower, it was as if someone had taken a can opener and wrenched a hole in the side of the building. You could see the silhouette of an airplane slanting to the left.

Still expecting to file quotes, I kept questioning eyewitnesses. Many of the people streaming onto the streets had evacuated from the Trade Center. They were upset, but said people had been relatively calm as they hurried to get out. People were incredulous, wanting so badly to deny that the crashes had been intentional. I asked people what they saw, what the planes looked like. "Was it a commercial airplane?" I wanted to find someone like my brother Sean, a pilot for Mesaba Airlines, a commuter service in the Midwest. He can identify models of aircraft at a glance.

As more and more people told me the planes had markings similar to American and United Airlines, I started to worry about Sean. He certainly hadn't been on either of those planes. But people on the street were saying they had heard other planes were hijacked and missing in other parts of the country. Please don't let him be flying today, I thought.

My cell phone wasn't working—everyone else on the street was also trying to make calls. I found a pay phone and got in line. After telling Dave Pettit at the office that I was all right, I started dictating quotes. I don't know how I managed to read anything I had written down. When I looked at my notebook later, I couldn't recognize the shaky handwriting and notes scrawled across the lined pages.

I could hear the keys clicking away on the other end of the line as he took notes and filed them to editors in Brussels, who were about to take over the publication of the Web site. My quotes soon made their way into the stories on the Web site, adding eyewitness accounts to the details that were being published. Dave told me the newsroom was being evacuated and our staff would regroup at the intersection of Albany Street and the Hudson River, which was about three blocks west of me.

Because some streets were now blocked by emergency vehicles, I had to walk several blocks south before I could go west to the river. I moved slowly, asking questions of people huddled in the streets. But I couldn't find two people who could provide the same description of the second plane. Someone pointed out a four-foot-wide airplane tire that had crashed on a corner four blocks south of the Trade Center. I ran my fingers over the Goodyear logo and thought about how easily it could have crushed someone waiting for the WALK sign.

After I found my colleagues, I learned that Dave, Tony, and other top editors were already on a ferry to New Jersey to set up an emergency newsroom. It was almost 9:50 A.M., and I had been outside for about an hour. Those of us who remained were clearly shaken. My friend Jason from DePauw had also been reporting down on the street about a block west from where I had been. He watched the fruit seller return to collect his fruit cart just before the second plane hit. He also watched people trapped by fires jumping from the top floors of the Trade Center; he stopped counting them after fourteen. We decided to go to technology editor Tim Hanrahan's apartment in Battery Park City, about six blocks south of the Trade Center. Tim and Erin were already there, planning to use his phone and computer to stay in touch with the Brussels bureau. We headed back east one block and turned to go south in front of Foxhounds, four blocks from the Trade Center at Albany Street and South End Avenue.

Then thunder sounded. *What were we hearing? Another plane? A bomb?* We all ran.

Moments later, a cloud of dust caught up with us. First we headed south one block, then turned west to run toward the river. Even my high heels didn't slow me down. The dust storm obscured buildings, the water, and even the sun. At the corner of West Thames and the Hudson River, now six blocks away from the Trade Center, someone directed people into a Battery Park City apartment building. I stood outside, helping people with baby strollers hoist them over a railing. I wasn't sure I wanted to go in.

I joined six of my colleagues inside, including Bill, the managing editor, and his wife and young daughter. We still couldn't get calls on our cell phones, but I could tell from messages streaming into my voice mail that my family and friends were trying to reach me. I huddled with people around a small radio and learned the Pentagon had been hit by a plane and that another had crashed in Pennsylvania.

We were herded outside yet again when security guards decided the building might not be safe. Moments later, the second tower collapsed. But I don't remember hearing it fall. Jason turned around and asked, "Do you think you can run again?" I decided I couldn't run with the Coke I had bought from a vending machine. I stopped to throw it away, as if someone would care if I had tossed the can on the ground.

I couldn't get out of New York fast enough. The thousands of people gathered at the southern tip of Manhattan could have been the next target of a terrorist attack. I finally got a call through to my parents in Eden Prairie, Minnesota, a suburb of Minneapolis, where

As It Became Ground Zero

I had grown up. Sean picked up the phone. He lives a few miles away from them, and was at the dentist when he heard a radio report about the plane crashes. He had visited me two weeks before and used my office to store his luggage while sightseeing. Knowing I was so close to the World Trade Center, he rushed to my parents to see if they had heard from me.

Instead, he tried to calm my dad, who was watching CNN with the phone in his hand, hitting redial over and over only to get my cell phone's voice mail. "We've been trying to call you," Sean said somewhat sternly.

"I know," I told him. "I couldn't get through." I asked him if he knew what was going on. Those of us in the middle of the chaos knew less than people hundreds of miles away who were watching on TV.

At the time, my dad was on his cell phone talking to my mom. She's an elementary-school teacher and spent the morning worrying about me while balancing a classroom full of kids.

Eventually, all kinds of boats—police boats, ferries, tugboats—started pulling up to the side of the South Cove of Battery Park City. I thought the "women and children first" rule was something that existed solely in movies like *Titanic*. I was wrong; police were not allowing men to evacuate across the Hudson to Jersey City, New Jersey. Sophie and I and two other editors—Jessica Braun and Jenny Reisinger—left Bill, Jason, and another editor behind.

Bill's wife and daughter had crowded onto a boat before the second building collapsed. He asked me to try calling her cell phone to tell her he was all right and say he would try to find them when he could get on a boat. Businessmen in dust-covered suits joined emergency personnel to lift us over the harbor wall so we could board a tugboat painted with bright green shamrocks. The men on the tugboat heard the news while eating their breakfast and came to see if they could help. Sausage was still sitting in a skillet on the stove in their galley.

Stacy Forster

As they lifted me over the wall, I looked down at the dress Erin had complimented earlier. It suddenly struck me as funny that I may have been dressed right for the after-work meeting I had planned, but not for what I had done that morning. Jenny was behind me in line, but almost left behind when the police declared the boat was full. I went back to be sure she came aboard.

We spent several hours at Our Lady of Czestochowa, a Catholic church in Jersey City, attending a mass and talking to other evacuees. Our group of four was finally able to contact our editors at about 3 P.M. The New York office was likely destroyed—or at least uninhabitable—but the Web site had to be updated. Dave asked us to get to a makeshift newsroom at a Dow Jones complex in South Brunswick, fifty miles away from New York. The trouble was we had no car, trains weren't running, and major roads were closed. Jessica Braun's mom and brother had left their home in New Jersey to try to pick us up. We had a vague idea of where they were, but didn't know if we'd be able to find them.

We hitched a ride from a member of the church, but could only get to one side of the Hackensack Bridge out of Jersey City. Our driver wouldn't be able to get back if he took us across, so we walked the half mile across the glimmering water. Jessica's family met us halfway. Her mom gave us big hugs on behalf of our own worried parents. We went to their house briefly, then hit a Target for some new clothes and essentials for the night. It was about 7:30 P.M. when we reached Dow Jones.

About ten coworkers were already there, struggling to publish the next day's paper to the Web site. We also updated "The Aftermath of Terror," the newly created section devoted to news of the attacks. Our computer technician was literally wiring computers together as people arrived, tearing down cubicle walls in an unused corner of the building. As soon as a computer was hooked up, we'd fill the seat to prepare stories for the site. The computers kept crashing. Work was slow. I got a rush course in publishing stories

As It Became Ground Zero

directly onto the Web site, not normally a reporter's responsibility. Sometime after 1 A.M. they told us to leave and get some sleep.

The only place where Dow Jones could find rooms that night was at the Peacock Inn, a bed and breakfast in Princeton, about fifteen minutes away from the office. Erin and I flopped onto twin beds. She and Tim had made it to Dow Jones by about 10 P.M. after a trip like ours—by boat, train, and borrowed SUV. She too had been on the street reporting and was haunted by the images of people falling from the sky, trying to escape the raging flames.

When we got to the B&B about 2 A.M., we flipped on the TV to watch—for the first time—the scenes of the day. But as I tried to fall asleep, the real-life images kept me awake. I numbly watched television until the Tylenol P.M. I had taken kicked in. I started to drift off, but the wail of sirens on the news kept me awake. The day's soundtrack itself had been one of nonstop sirens. I finally clicked off the TV, but the rumble of trucks outside was hardly more comforting.

The next morning, work provided some solace. New York and all that was still unfolding there seemed far away. Amazingly, the print version of the *Wall Street Journal* came out. It was a riveting edition. The staff of the print newspaper had, like us, scrambled and worried about the safety of coworkers and sources who worked in the Trade Center. The printing press was in South Brunswick, and a backup newsroom was created for them, too.

We didn't realize how comforting it was for readers to see the newspaper on September 12. Our subscribers wrote and called in appreciation. Some were surprised that the paper had been able to publish at all without access to its main office. After watching the horror of September 11, picking up the *Wall Street Journal* the next morning reminded many readers that perhaps the world hadn't changed as much as they feared.

As the online staff, we didn't have the print *Journal*'s luxury of a single evening deadline. The Internet was the most reliable way to get information that day, and readers flocked to our Web site. The content, usually available only to paying subscribers, was offered free of charge. Readership for the lead story about the attack was two and a half times what it had been for a story earlier in the year about a surprise interest-rate cut—the most widely read piece on the site during the first six months of 2001.

Even as we struggled with balky computers and networking problems, we produced some amazing coverage. On September 12, Michael Broadhurst, an assistant news editor, took a list of World Trade Center tenants and created a chart on the Web site with information about the employees of the companies in the buildings. Within minutes of publishing it, e-mail flooded in with updates from readers.

I stayed in South Brunswick for three days, but it felt like more. The days were long, punctuated by outages of the computer system. Nights were spent talking and drinking at the Peacock. Everyone piled into the room that Erin and I were sharing. We scrounged up a bottle of vodka, and Tim and Erin made a run to the WaWa convenience store for orange juice. To forget the violent images, and for lack of anything better to do, we drank and half watched the parade of experts on CNN. Nothing made sense.

I was in no hurry to return to my home in Park Slope, a quiet neighborhood in Brooklyn. I wasn't sure what to expect or that I even wanted to be there anymore. As other coworkers made their way down to the New Jersey office, I was relieved I hadn't been forced to take the subway and trains like them. I dreaded seeing the MISSING signs that I knew would be plastered on storefronts in my neighborhood. I worried that I had left my air conditioner on when I left on the morning of September 11. I also couldn't stop thinking about how different the world had been the last time I was in my apartment, and how carefree I had been on that last morning before heading to work in Manhattan.

But we couldn't stay away forever. On Friday morning, Erin got on the phone and located a rental car. I roused Jenny.

As It Became Ground Zero

As the car neared New York City, I didn't want to look out the window. The eleventh had been a perfect early-fall day—like summer, but with a hint of crispness. The sky had been the clearest blue I'd ever seen. By Friday, it had turned cold and rainy, as if to reflect the city's mood.

One look at the skyline made my McDonald's lunch sit heavily. A dark cloud of smoke hanging over the hole where the World Trade Center once stood hammered home the point that the landscape—for me, for the city, for the world—was permanently changed.

I'm emotional—I cry when I'm upset. But I hadn't cried all week. At least not until the car crossed over the Verrazanno Bridge from Staten Island into Brooklyn and I caught a whiff of the acrid metallic odor that came from the still-smoldering buildings. President Bush was speaking on the radio. Trucks heading back to Ground Zero to cart away debris lumbered past us on our left. Right then, as it all swirled around me, I broke. For the next few minutes, I sobbed.

After a week surrounded by my coworkers, Erin dropped me off at my apartment and I was alone. I realized that the last time I had been by myself was on the street south of the World Trade Center. I had intentionally surrounded myself with people all week. I was quickly uncomfortable in my little studio apartment. But I was also relieved to finally return home to my peaceful street lined with classic Brooklyn brownstones. I was on edge every single time a military jet on patrol flew low over my neighborhood.

I spent the rest of the afternoon on the telephone, just for distraction and company. I wanted the cocoon of my coworkers. In a few short days, they had become my best friends. We were a team, never traveling more than a few feet from each other. Once we left the Peacock, our firsthand September 11 experience isolated us, and it was hard to talk about some things to family or friends who hadn't been there. Although we had watched some of the nonstop news about the tragedy, we had trouble stepping back and seeing the events from a wider perspective. "You have no idea how big this is," Sean told me on the phone that afternoon.

I was surprised to discover that New York, known for being impersonal and brusque, had sprouted a new sense of community. That evening, from my apartment windows, I saw people streaming down the sidewalk toward a major street in my neighborhood. I followed them and soon found thousands of people holding candles and waving American flags. Some groups broke into song: "The Star-Spangled Banner" and "America the Beautiful." Neighbors hugged and mingled.

Long red trucks from the local fire company blocked the street, and neighbors lined up to shake the hands of the firefighters inside. Eleven members of a neighborhood fire squad had been killed in the World Trade Center, and restaurants and shops were accepting donations for a relief fund. A bookstore's windows had become a bulletin board filled with notices about donation drives for the rescue efforts and stoop sales (the urban equivalent of a garage sale) for firefighters' families.

As a transplanted midwesterner reluctant to move to the Big Apple, I was comforted by what I experienced that night. All over the city, similar gatherings were taking place. It was as if the city's collective attitude—the swagger that makes New York bold and vibrant—was being asserted all at once.

At work, our ordeal was just beginning. The rapid relocation has evolved into a months-long stint in New Jersey. My weeks center around going to and from South Brunswick, stuffing and unstuffing a backpack for a couple of nights at a Radisson hotel across the highway from Dow Jones. If I'm starting from home instead of the hotel, my day begins with a groan as the alarm blares at 5:30 A.M. I'm out the door at 6 A.M., walking to downtown Brooklyn for some fresh air to wake me up before I hop on a van for the fifty-mile trip to Dow Jones.

As It Became Ground Zero

My life is largely on hold. When I swung by a friend's party on New Year's Eve, she couldn't stop saying how surprised she was to see me because I had been so out of touch all fall. When I'm with old friends, often the only thing I find myself talking about is my relocation or the awful commute. September 11 taught us how fragile life is—*why am I spending it working?*

But that's when I get angry with myself. I hate being so annoyed by our displacement. I'm usually able to squeeze the best out of the worst situations. Compared to thousands of other people, I am lucky. I am OK. Dow Jones has been supportive, picking up the tab for all expenses we've incurred because of the displacement and providing resources to make the whole experience more bearable.

But it's hard to remember that every day. Sometimes I want to sell all my things, buy a car, and take off for Wyoming. I don't know what I'd do there, but working at a ski resort seems like a good alternative.

My parents have become the unfortunate recipients of much of my pent-up anger. They encourage me to turn my thinking around and be positive. "Change the tape in your head," my mom says. And she's right. I can't change the situation. I can only change how I react to it.

As another transplanted midwesterner, Erin understands. She grew up in a small town in South Dakota. In the days after September 11, the two of us fantasized about packing up a U-Haul and moving back west—maybe to Colorado. We didn't want to be reporters anymore; we would do anything to get out of New York.

Other coworkers have become closer, too. Before the disaster struck, Sophie and I didn't know each other well. Now, I'll always remember her on September 11, darting around me on one corner while outrunning the cloud of the south tower. She instantly became part of my personal history. Jenny and I were good friends and lived near each other in Brooklyn. When we were caught in the cloud of dust, she had trouble breathing and thought she couldn't run any more. I turned and told her to keep moving, that we'd be fine. Since the fall, we've had countless talks about what "fine" means and how close we are to that point.

About three months after September 11, the old Foxhounds crew all stayed in New Jersey on the same night and had an impromptu reunion dinner. Over our meal, we laughed at how we used to think we'd just be working in New Jersey for a couple of weeks. We had no idea that the cleanup would take so long, or that there was so much damage to our former office. The debris that landed in the *Wall Street Journal*'s office had been filled with asbestos and the company would have to rip out each floor and rebuild them from scratch. Every piece of paper was being cleaned with a vacuum. All this has put off a return to the World Financial Center for at least nine months, maybe more.

Since that dinner, I've mulled over what I did that morning on the street outside the World Trade Center. Instead of writing about the decline of trading online, for example, I spend part of my day tracking events in the Middle East and Central Asia and updating an interactive map.

On the eleventh, I knew immediately that I was in the middle of the story of our lifetimes. As I raced across that pedestrian bridge and caught a glimpse of a dozen fire trucks already lined up alongside the north tower, I was determined to witness the scene and report on it. People who know me well knew to be worried. Allison Sharpe, one of my best friends and former roommate in Washington, D.C., predicted how I would react. "I know Stacy is out on the street reporting," she told another friend as the events unfolded. "She ran out of her building to get closer."

That's why I got into journalism in the first place—to be at the front of the line for new experiences. Some of my editors say I was one of the first reporters on the scene—if not the first. But I struggle with how to describe that feeling. It's not right to say it was exciting or invigorating. I was drawn to it, but I certainly didn't enjoy it.

As It Became Ground Zero

Michael Broadhurst put it best: It's a matter of balancing your feelings as a journalist with your feelings as a human being.

Most journalists, I suspect, would feel the same way. A few days after the attack, Jason Fry, an assistant managing editor at WSJ.com who hadn't yet made it to work that day, grilled me about what I'd seen and heard. Finally he admitted he was somewhat jealous to have been safe in Brooklyn rather than in lower Manhattan.

Still, it wasn't what I expected when I took a job covering markets and online investing. I never imagined the high heels I wore at my desk would become an impediment. I had never read about plane crashes and wondered what the debris looks like on the ground, still smoldering. I never wondered how millions of tons of concrete and steel could be reduced to particles of dust in seconds.

But following my speech at DePauw, another student asked me if I would change anything about what I did on September 11. I thought about it for a moment and realized that the day, the experience, is now part of who I am. I said no.

"Have You Seen . . . ?"

By Heather Nauert—Fox News

HEATHER NAUERT, a general assignment reporter at Fox News in New York City, had spent enough time at Ground Zero to know there would be few survivors. But she also had to interview the families of victims, many of whom still held out hope. Nauert grappled with ethical questions about whether she was exploiting her subjects, her responsibilities to her viewers, and her ambivalence over furthering her career at a time when so many people were suffering. Viewers across America saw her question the tearful and trembling Joe Scharf about his missing brother John. They heard Melissa Bouveais describe how her cousin, Richard Bosco, had shown up on an inaccurate list of survivors on a Web site.

Before joining Fox, Nauert, thirty-two, spent nine years in Washington, D.C., as a political consultant and freelance writer. In 1998 she became an on-air political analyst for the Fox News Channel in Washington, D.C. In 2001 she received her master's degree from the Columbia Graduate School of Journalism.

The morning of September 11, I walked into the New York newsroom of the Fox News Channel at 9:04 A.M. It's always a noisy place to work, but not because over one hundred people work in one large, open room. It's because there's a television set on every desk and they're all tuned to the Fox News Channel, where I'm a reporter. But something was very different this morning—people shouted, they walked faster, and the volume on the televisions was turned up much louder than usual. Normally subdued colleagues yelled orders and they moved with greater purpose and precision. I knew something big had happened. I stopped a producer running out the door. "What's going on?" I blurted. She paused.

"A plane hit the World Trade Center."

How quickly things change. Just a few days earlier, I was reporting on the missing Washington, D.C., intern Chandra Levy. Now more than ten thousand people in New York were feared dead. In an instant, I was reporting on the biggest story since Pearl Harbor.

I hurried to my desk, recalling the man who had recently parachuted onto the Statue of Liberty. This was probably just another stunt we'd air live until our directors bored of it. My colleagues and I checked our TV sets and pagers and read wire reports. Katie, the producer I work with, buried her face in her hands and cried; her family was visiting from California and planned to tour the World Trade Center that morning. No one knew where to begin. All we knew was that our 5 P.M. show, *The Big Story with John Gibson*, was off the air and that the attack would be covered live throughout the day. At 9:06 A.M. another plane hit. The wires reported that the FBI was investigating possible hijackings. It all happened so fast.

I called a terrorism expert to ask who he thought was responsible. "Are you available for a live interview?" I normally don't book live guest for our daytime news segments, but today was different. Our roles were pared down and everyone pitched in to help. I pulled all the research I could find about the World Trade Center and terror groups, printed it out, and stuffed it in my bag. I took off my high heels and put on loafers, hoping I'd get sent out to cover the story. I felt helpless in the newsroom, watching everything unfold on my eight-inch TV. I wanted to go to the site, get close, and see what was happening, but the more senior reporters had it covered.

Midmorning, our building, located a few blocks from New York's Times Square and Rockefeller Center, was evacuated. Then it was locked down. The only people here were Fox News employees. Our basement newsroom became our bunker—without windows or any idea what was going on outside. There could have been mass chaos on the streets above and we wouldn't have known it. The thought was creepy.

The Trade Center buildings crumbled, the south tower at 9:59 A.M., the north at 10:28 A.M. Like millions of other people, we watched it on TV. When the first building came down, we gasped and some of us cried. The buildings' collapse cut off the television broadcast signals that were transmitted from the World Trade Center. This blackout made cable channels like ours even more important since so many viewers were counting on us to bring them the story. It was tough to get an outside phone line, so everything we knew about the attacks we learned from our reporters, from what we could see on TV, and what we read in wire reports. My husband, Scott, got through by phone. Like many others in New

"Have You Seen . . . ?"

York City, he had watched the World Trade Center burn from his midtown office before his building was evacuated. He wanted me to come home.

"This is my job," I said. A few hours later, I was sent into the city.

I had always known a tragedy would force me to cover a big story fast. Reporting on the World Trade Center certainly qualified. But an uncomfortable thought nagged me. Covering a disaster, no matter how terrible, could be my break.

For the first day I followed Mayor Giuliani, walking thirty blocks with Katie to reach his makeshift emergency command center on the East Side of Manhattan (the permanent one was destroyed when the World Trade Center fell). The city streets were empty, but the bars and restaurants seemed full. I was glad I had changed shoes and grabbed a few extra notebooks. When we arrived, police barricades blocked the street, and cadets guarded the building. The block was lined with stretchers, waiting to transport victims to the hospital across the street. We finally entered the command center, passing Mayor Giuliani and Governor Pataki.

"People want to hear from our leaders," I said to the governor.

"No comment now." His flack blurted out, "We'll talk in an hour." But the stunned expression on the governor's face mirrored the shock everyone felt.

I snuck into the war room, where city agencies had set up posts and asked a few questions, but it wasn't long before another flack threw me out. We sometimes call them "flacks." Usually their job is to help get the information you need for a story. More often than not, they stonewall by trying to keep you away and avoiding your questions, even at a time like this.

Across the street at the hospital, I could see doctors waiting by their makeshift MASH unit. There weren't any patients. The doctors said they had initially treated a few people for simple injuries, but that most of the victims were "probably gone."

The assignment desk dispatched me to St. Patrick's Cathedral, where a prayer vigil was being held. They wanted live reports. Since I couldn't get a taxi and hitchhiking didn't work, I ran another thirty blocks to get there. About 8:30 that night, my husband, Scott, rode his bike from our West Side apartment to meet me (virtually all public transportation had stopped). I had forgotten to check in with him during the day, and he had gotten worried.

"Are you OK?" he asked.

I apologized, "Sorry I forgot to call." We sat on the steps of this beautiful Fifth Avenue cathedral and talked about the day. I told him about the empty hospital. He told me about his colleagues from the investment bank Morgan Stanley who worked in the Trade Center. (Later we learned thirteen of them were killed.) Although we talked, I was distracted by the demands of my job. It hit me that Fifth Avenue is usually a very busy street, but tonight it was eerily quiet—New York had become a ghost town. Normally you can see the Trade Center from Fifth Avenue. Now it was gone. Hopping on his bike to go home, Scott shouted, "be careful." I dismissed his admonition, thinking how tame my day had been in comparison to that of so many others. The reports I was scheduled to give were all preempted by breaking news, so I was sent home.

To prepare for the next day's assignment, I called the live desk. It's staffed twenty-four hours a day by producers who track breaking news, then send reporters, cameramen, and other producers to the scene.

"What do you need me to do?" I asked, hoping that I'd get sent out the next morning. "The morgue," the desk producer dryly answered. Even though it was late and I had an early call the next morning, I couldn't stop watching the news. The telephone seemed to ring all night.

"It's been like this all day," Scott explained. Friends we hadn't talked with in months called to find out if we were okay. Scott wondered if the client he was supposed to meet the next morning was safe. (He worked on a top floor at the Trade Center.) Scott made me a late dinner, which was unusual; he works in finance and is usually the one working very late at night. This week would be different. The stock market closed for the first time since the Depression, his company received numerous bomb threats, and some of its employees died at the WTC. His office closed for the week. My job, on the other hand, was just kicking into overdrive. I told him I would be working long, strange hours. Our first wedding anniversary was less than two weeks later, and I hoped that we would still be able to go away to celebrate it. I fell asleep exhausted, and a few hours later Scott woke me. I had to get to the morgue early.

I filled a large bag with supplies: water, granola bars, makeup, a subway map, and extra cash. It was dark and quiet when I left at 3 A.M. The subway was running, but I was the only one on it.

When I arrived at 4 A.M. on September 12, Chelsea Piers (normally a skating rink) was buzzing with volunteers. Rescue workers were receiving medical treatment for burns and smoke inhalation. Later, they were sent back to the World Trade Center site to continue looking for victims. Only rescue workers were emerging from the site for treatment, and doctors said that wasn't an encouraging sign. While the triage unit was busy, the morgue sat empty. At 5:30 A.M., I began my live reports. I interviewed rescue workers and medical volunteers until late morning. These were my first live reports since the attacks occurred the day before.

The live desk sent our crew of five, which consisted of a cameraman, soundman, producer, and two satellite truck engineers as close to the site as we could get—about twenty blocks away. At this point, the police turned us back. The cameraman, soundman, and I decided we could get closer on foot, but eventually we split up. When I got about four blocks away, I was again turned back by police. But before I left, I saw crumbled buildings, crushed metal, burned-out cars, and lots of ash. It was obvious very few could have survived that collapse. But thousands of families did not share my realization. Or they refused to. They believed their relatives were still alive, either waiting to be rescued from the rubble or wandering the streets in a daze.

When I arrived home on September 12, Scott was waiting for me. He had watched the news coverage on TV all day. "How did it go?" he asked when I opened the door. "Are you OK? Did you see the site?" He was clearly upset, and kept saying, "all those people." I avoided the obvious "I'm lucky to have you" conversation people sometimes have after hearing about a terrible accident. Instead, I hugged him.

"I'm fine, just tired. I want to go to bed." I was covered with soot and worn out. "Good night. We'll talk in the morning." He was disappointed, but I didn't have the energy to talk.

The morning of September 13 came too quickly. I was up at 4 A.M. to cover the story at the newly established family center. Instead of visiting all the area hospitals in attempts to find missing relatives, families were now being asked to come here. Thousands of people would eventually go to the center to check consolidated hospital survivor lists. Most people, however, were not lucky. They had to file missing persons reports with police officers. I needed an angle.

There was one I didn't want—interviewing the victims' families. I didn't want to be the movie caricature of a pushy, ruthless reporter. "Excuse me, sorry to bother you. I'm a reporter. . . ." before shoving my microphone into the face of someone who just learned their friend had died. In light of the September 11 devastation, I thought it would be insensitive to intrude on people's grieving by asking for interviews. I also knew something that most of the families didn't want to acknowledge, that the chances that anyone had survived were slim. I didn't want to exploit them.

My first live shot that day was scheduled for 8:20 A.M. I arrived two hours early. Across the street from the family center, I noticed a group of reporters surrounding someone. I squeezed in hoping to catch a briefing. Instead I found thirty-something Ron Fazio asking for information about his father, missing since the attack. Ron Sr. had worked for the insurance company, Aon Corporation, on the ninety-ninth floor of the south tower. Ron Sr. had called home after the first airplane hit. As Ron Jr. spoke, I hung on every word; no one interrupted him. His father had said that he saw fire and debris falling from the neighboring building but that he was safe. He had planned to leave, but saw something approaching: a second plane flying toward his own building. His phone line went dead. He had not called back.

Ron Jr. looked desperate. His eyes were red and on the verge of tears. "Do you know where he is?" he pleaded. *What could I possibly say? Dead?* I was stunned. His was the first personal story I had heard. Previously, I had only heard bystanders' accounts. Now, a stranger was telling me about his father's final words to his family and asking for my help. I kept thinking about my own family and imagining how I would feel if our roles were reversed.

It wasn't my place to tell Ron Jr. about the empty hospitals or about the doctors and rescue workers or that it looked like nobody had made it out alive. Who knows, maybe his father had made it? I felt helpless, knowing that I could only dampen his hopes. A few reporters started to delicately pepper him with questions. I mustered one: "What's the company doing to help?" I don't remember his response, but our eyes locked for a minute and mine welled up with tears. I looked away and noticed that other reporters had begun to cry too. I had to walk away. I wondered if American reporters had ever covered a story like this, a story that we were this closely tied to. I was sucked in. After all, many of us knew people in the buildings and families who were missing loved ones.

I was frustrated. It was before 8 A.M., and I had already cried. I knew this day was going to be tough. I took a deep breath and said aloud, "I have to get through this. I'll deal with my feelings later."

A few minutes later, Verna Nesbitt walked up to me. She clutched a photo. Her voice was determined. "I'm looking for my brother-in-law, Oscar," she explained as she showed me his wedding picture. They all called it "looking for." Everyone there was looking for someone—someone who hadn't come home—someone who was probably dead. She asked me to put his picture on television. I reluctantly agreed and grabbed our camera crew. We still had time before our first live report, but I decided to get her story on tape just in case we needed it later. I kept the questions informational and did not ask how the family was holding up. With the camera rolling, I asked what she had learned from city workers inside the family center. She sounded disappointed and said, "They're going to put his picture in their database. I asked if I could see the list of names from the morgue. They said that's not available yet."

Oscar had worked for the New York Department of Tax and Finance on the eighty-sixth floor of the south tower, the second building hit. Verna said he obeyed the directive from World Trade Center personnel announcing that the building was safe. He was last seen comforting a coworker. Like Ron Jr., Verna thought I could help her.

I went to our satellite truck to take a deep breath and prepare for my 8:30 A.M. "live shot." I touchedup my make up and combed my hair. I couldn't bear to wear a suit. It seemed inappropriate. Comfortable shoes and a jacket and T-shirt were more appropriate, given the situation, I thought, but other reporters were done up in suits, stockings, and high heels.

The crew I was working with had driven in from the Midwest the night before. They're based in Chicago, but when the attack took place, they packed their cameras, equipment, and enough clothing for a few weeks and hightailed it to New York. Dutch, the audio guy; Sven, the cameraman; and Ruth, the producer, met me at the satellite truck Fox hired immediately after the attacks. It was filled with high-tech equipment that enabled us to give live reports and beam them via satellite to our studios. When we file reports, they're done on tape and the stories are edited later, but when something big happens, we "go live" and work out of satellite trucks to speed the delivery of news.

Earlier that morning, Dutch and Sven had staked out a spot in the small, crowded media pen police had constructed. Cameramen from other news agencies were trying to nudge us away from our position, but our guys kept pushing them back to make sure we didn't lose it. As it got closer to my first "hit," I hooked up the audio cords and my earpiece, and waited in front of the camera for my turn. I could hear our other reporters giving their live reports: one at Ground Zero, one at a hospital, another at JFK Airport, someone else at the Pentagon. Someone in the control room in New York told me that I was next. It was 9:05 A.M.

The anchor introduced me. "Good morning, John. We're at what's being called the 'family center' on the East Side of Manhattan. Families who are missing relatives from Tuesday's attack are being asked to come here to fill out paperwork that authorities say could help them identify survivors and victims. Families are being asked to fill out a missing person's report and to talk with police detectives to give a physical description and details about the person's last known location." Two minutes later, I finished, disconnected the cords, and walked away in search of coffee and any new information to use for the next live hit an hour later.

I discovered that prior to that day, many families had searched every area hospital to try to find their missing person. Now, with the family center available, they were checking hospital lists here as well. I called the assignment desk to discuss my next live report. I told my colleague Todd Ciganek that people were starting to line up outside the family center. Some were asking me for information. I told him that they all seemed distraught. Some pleaded, "Please, help me find my brother. I know he's there waiting to be rescued."

Their stories and appeals were compelling, but I still didn't want to interview them. I knew I eventually would have to. I asked him if he wanted me to and he said what I suspected, "Yes!"

He was right that personal stories were good television and would bring the story home to people far from New York. Since this was only my fifth day doing live shots I wanted to have something compelling to present. But I also felt uncomfortable as more families approached me. They all wanted to talk, to put their family members' pictures on television. Those who didn't stayed across the street behind police barricades.

Most families had printed fliers containing detailed information about the missing person. One said: *John Scharf, 29 years old, tattoo on arm, American eagle.* John served in the U.S. Marine Corps. His older brother Joe brought the flier to me and asked if I would interview him. I did, holding up a photo of John in front of a large Las Vegas hotel. Joe told me about John's last phone calls: one to his fiancée and one to his father. Joe stood well over six feet and had a large, muscular build. Nonetheless, he trembled and started to cry. Watching him fall apart shook me. I finished the interview and wished him luck. This time, the crew was fighting back tears too.

I felt guilty putting Joe on the air, letting him describe John's physical characteristics and cite the private words of that last desperate phone call. I had a hard time looking him, or any of them, in the eye. I called the assignment desk to explain, "It just feels wrong. Most are dead."

Even worse was that despite the buildings' collapse and the fact that families hadn't heard from their relatives in two days, they remained so hopeful. Joe Scharf insisted, "If anyone made it, it's John." Others said this too. I was only encouraging their false hopes.

Yet people clamored to be interviewed. Some waited an hour and a half for my next live shot, just for a chance to tell their story on television. Others pleaded to be put on. Friends persisted, "Her husband's a firefighter, he's missing. Please put her on TV." Some came back every day to ask if I would put them on television again. When I finished the interview, they'd walk to the next camera and repeat the same routine. Some would later tell me about all the interviews that they had done: Canadian radio, Australian TV, NBC, you name it. Sometimes I would slip, even on live television, saying things such as, "Your brother sounds like he was a good man."

Anthony Gardner, the brother of a missing man, sharply corrected me, "He *is* a good man."

"Excuse me," I said, feeling awful.

I called Todd at the assignment desk again. He explained that with six thousand people feared dead in the attacks, it would be impossible for people around the country to comprehend just how many *lives* had been lost. "This is a human story," he said, "people need to understand that." By interviewing these people, he said, I could "bring home" the real tragedy to those who didn't lose someone in the attacks and to those who only saw it on television. This sounded logical. After all, it had only been after meeting the families and people who had lost loved ones that the magnitude of the tragedy had hit home for me. He added, "This is why we're here—to do this public service." I agreed and felt confident that I was doing the right thing.

After our phone conversation, I asked families how they felt about being interviewed. Many explained that being on TV meant they were doing everything possible to help find their loved one. Some claimed they accomplished more by talking with me than by simply staying home. Others hoped someone in our viewing audience would recognize the missing person. These reasons made sense to me, and I had a new enthusiasm for my job and felt as though I was contributing in some small way.

As I interviewed one man, he gave out his mobile telephone number for people to call if they had information about his missing sibling. Moments later, his phone rang. I spoke on camera while he answered the call. "Thank you very much," he said and hung up. He turned back to me and explained, "That was someone calling from Texas to say they're praying for me and my family."

"What does that mean to you?" I asked.

"It's keeps us going." Even though he didn't know the person on the other end of the phone—it was a viewer watching him live on Fox—it was an emotional moment and it illustrated the power of the television medium. Todd was right.

I tried to tell each person's story with compassion and professionalism without being too sappy, sensational, or cold. I was never sure whether I was striking the proper balance.

Stories of the missing people are truly remarkable. I interviewed the nephew of Abe Zelmanowitz, a man who stayed in a WTC building because he wouldn't leave his wheelchair-bound friend. I interviewed a woman whose sister lost her husband. That sister couldn't come to the family center because she had just given birth. The new mother and her doctor named the baby Hope, because they hoped the father would eventually come home.

During a later live shot, I reported that a Web site had been set up to list survivors. There were 14,000 names on it. I said that this information might be useful but that the site was voluntary and that its information should be independently verified. I turned to interview Melissa Bouveais, who was looking for her cousin, Richard Bosco. He had attended a September 11 meeting at the firm Cantor Fitzgerald. Cantor Fitzgerald had lost about seven hundred employees and numerous visitors. Melissa held up a photograph of Richard. Trying to make it personal, I asked, "How are you all doing?"

"We're doing as good as we can," she replied. "We're here hoping to find reassurance that he is OK because he came up on a Web site."

"We're hearing that this Web site may have some good information, but that others are saying it's not reliable," I said. "What did your cousin's wife say when she read his name on it?"

"Her reaction was her prayers has been answered, so we came to Manhattan to bring him home. Now there's some doubt that we'll find him." Our time had run out, so I thanked Melissa and signed off.

"Again, families are bringing a lot of information here, hoping that it will help them find their missing relatives. Back to you." I looked away, shaken yet again.

By my next live shot, I had collected dozens of the fliers that families had printed. This time, I fingered through them to show just how many people were missing. I was in the midst of interviewing a woman when a man grabbed my arm, screaming, "He's OK, they found him. He's on a list!" The list was a Web site posting names of people recovering in area hospitals. The family jumped and screamed, then left. I was left to explain that the online lists were not always reliable. I never heard from the family again.

It's now clichéd, but the missing people and their loved ones came from all walks of life. Hagee Abucar, an elderly Indian immigrant, was at the family center filling out the missing persons documents for a young stockbroker who employed him as a dogwalker. The broker didn't have any living relatives, but Hagee acted as his family. He was difficult to understand because he had a thick accent and he seemed nervous about being on TV. But at the end of the interview tears welled. "God bless America," he said.

It struck me that before the attack, the missing had all been full of life, making plans to buy a house or start a job. The photos that their relatives had brought to help identify them were of their happiest of times: at a wedding, on a night out with friends, holding a newborn baby, or cooking at a summer barbecue. I didn't know these people, but I caught glimpses of their personal lives and met many of their family members and friends.

As the week went by, my family in the Midwest said I looked exhausted on television. I did look terrible. I showed empathy to the families but at home I had no energy or emotion for Scott. All I could say was, "I don't want to talk about it."

I just wanted sleep. He would cook me dinner or visit me at the family center but I didn't have much to say. I didn't even want a hug. When he stopped by the family center, I didn't show him much affection because of the families nearby. I didn't want them to feel sad about what I had and they were missing. At home, I couldn't cry. He advised me, "You have to talk about what you're going through. What you've seen is horrible. It's so sad." But I felt completely numb.

"I'm too tired." I unwittingly shut him out.

At the time, I didn't realize that this was everyone's tragedy—including his, although it feels strange to even think this, since we didn't lose any family members or each other. When you're reporting, you know intellectually that you're nothing more than an observer. But with an attack as horrifying as this, it's virtually impossible not to get sucked in. I kept thinking about all the people I had met who were my age, women who were planning weddings and looking for their missing fiancés. Our similarities also made their tragedies hit closer to home.

My company offered us access to grief counselors, but that seemed silly to me. I didn't lose a family member. I just covered it. Even if I wanted to, I was too busy working. Although I don't regret not seeking counseling, I wish I had realized then that even though reporters are supposed to distance themselves from a story, that doesn't necessarily work when you're covering something horrific in your own backyard. You can't help but internalize the images of death and destruction.

I covered the two family centers for nearly two weeks. During that time, I witnessed the mood shift from frantic and hopeful to anger and depression. Eventually, families didn't want to talk to the press anymore. Instead, they would swiftly walk by clutching plastic grocery store bags or duffels. I suspected that they contained the personal effects that the police had asked them to bring—a hairbrush, razor, or toothbrush—personal items that could provide a DNA sample for body identification.

On my last day of covering the family angle, I was assigned to the mayor's makeshift command center across town. There, it was all business, no emotion, just paid staff doing their jobs. This was a stark contrast from the emotional story I had just left.

After working two weeks straight, I was given the weekend off. Scott and I left New York City for the first time since the attacks. We returned to the small, rural town where we were married one year before. Along the way, we noticed American flags painted on barns and draped over front porches. At one high school, students were painting an enormous flag on the lawn—it must've been the size of a football field. It was comforting to know that people hundreds of miles away from New York City shared our grief. Once I was away from the city, I was able to talk with Scott about my work and the sadness I felt about the loss of life. I was thankful for having that weekend to reconnect with him and think about how fortunate I was to have my life and him.

Months later, I still think of the people I interviewed, how they're doing. I've gotten in touch with a few, just to check in.

Since then, I've interviewed a woman who lost her fiancé in the attacks. I've interviewed many widows and mothers who lost their adult children. Recently, I met two women in their early thirties who were pregnant when their husbands died on September 11. Since then, they've given birth—one to a girl, the other, a boy. Most of the stories that I cover today are about the war, airline security, or bioterrorism, but every single one is related to September 11. Before, I covered Chandra Levy or stem cell research. On November 12, 2001, I covered the New York crash of the American Airlines' flight 587. Covering this crash was banal compared to covering the attack on the World Trade Center. Prior to September, I worried about how I'd handle reporting a plane crash. Sadly, I can say, it was unemotional. If I ever cover a tragedy again, I'll know my baptism by fire prepared me for it. I'm hoping that the worst is behind us all.

Learning to See

By Cindy Schreiber
—Columbia Graduate School of Journalism

For CINDY SCHREIBER, a student at the Columbia Graduate
School of Journalism, reporting is a calling. To her husband's dismay,
she traded a high-paying Wall Street job for thousands of dollars in
tuition costs and the opportunity to become a working journalist. Five
weeks into the semester, two planes crashed into the World Trade
Center. Schreiber rushed to the scene. Despite a series of mishaps and
mistakes attributable to her inexperience, she got the story (reproduced
here), gaining the confidence that she had made the right career move.

Born in Jersey City, New Jersey, Schreiber, thirty-two, grew up in
Hasbrouck Heights. She graduated from Columbia University in 1998
with a bachelor's degree in literature. Before enrolling at the Columbia
Graduate School of Journalism, she worked at Newsweek and as a
financial editor at Morgan Stanley and J.P. Morgan. She and her husband live in the East Village of Manhattan.

My college adviser didn't take me seriously when I told him I wanted to be a reporter. The only thing he asked was whether I read the op-ed page in the *New York Times*. I didn't even know what the op-ed page was. All I could think of was how at home we read the *New York Post*. My father used to tuck the paper under his belt to keep warm in the wintertime at the bus stop. But with my credibility already in question, I didn't tell my adviser that. Yawning over the piles of add/drop forms and registration requests on his desk, he seemed as unimpressed with me as I was.

My first job out of college was as a trainee in the manufacturing and distribution department at *Newsweek* magazine. I ordered software and laptops for the reporters, but on Saturdays I tagged along with anyone in the department who would allow it. I learned the basics of magazine production, everything from how to write a cover message to the printer to how color was created on the page. My dream was to learn how the magazine came together from back to front. I was on track, though, for a career in production. My only chance of becoming a reporter seemed to be journalism school.

A lot of people say journalism doesn't require a degree. But I felt I needed one. I worked full-time as a secretary to pay my way through college, and I worried that no one would take me seriously as a reporter. I didn't have any clips. I hadn't worked on my college newspaper, or even my high school one. Thinking journalists were elite, I basically had an inferiority complex. Even though I thought I could do it, I didn't see a reason why anyone else would.

Cindy Schreiber

Applying to journalism school felt like going to a party full of exceptional people you don't know. You're confronted by theology majors from Oxford, interns from the *Cape Times*, or maybe a group of speechwriters for the first lady. Meanwhile, I worked as an admin in a regional sales office. Retracing my life, I tried to find what made me qualified to be at that party. I don't come from a highly educated family, although my sister and I graduated college. I haven't traveled much. My hometown, Hasbrouck Heights, once distinguished by its mullets and shopping malls, is not much to write about, either. I started to bore even myself.

In the end, childhood seemed like the most interesting part of my life, so I wrote a thousand words about 1974, when I was four. The essay was mostly about neighborhood life: little boys running over birds with their bicycles, mysterious recluses and battered wives. It wasn't really about me.

Three months later, I got a very light, letter-sized envelope in the mail from Robert Mac Donald, the admissions director at Columbia. It was a form rejection letter, except for one sentence underlined in blue ink. He wrote that I needed a year or two more journalism experience and to reapply. The blue ink, a personal touch, convinced me there was still hope, and I set out to fulfill his request in earnest.

I found my first editorial job three months later. It was not for a magazine or a newspaper, but a Wall Street firm. In 1999, J.P. Morgan hired me to edit a weekly equity-research report for its institutional clients and to produce a daily technology report based on early-morning news. I couldn't believe they were paying me to do something I enjoyed so much. And it paid well. I went from secretary to editor overnight (after four jobs, twelve temp assignments, and six years of night school). A year later, I was writing company profiles for Morgan Stanley and preparing a new application to Columbia.

Sitting at my desk at work last May, I got a call from Mac

Learning to See

Donald. He offered me a spot for the fall semester. Without hesitation, or even talking with my husband, Ken, I left a well-paying Wall Street career to pay $30,000 tuition with only the hope of becoming a reporter. I practically floated the rest of the day.

A good reason to become a reporter is to change the world. I just wanted to learn and write about it. But, as one of the speakers said at school orientation, there isn't any other profession where, every day, you get to listen to a complete stranger tell you the single most fascinating story of their life. It just makes me want to cry every time I think about it.

Every week in Reporting and Writing I, the foundation course at Columbia Journalism School, my professor assigned a slug, or heading, for our stories. For the week of September 10, the slug was "in the bunker." To prepare, my teacher asked us to read a story about a reporter who lived under fire with three Israeli soldiers guarding a settlement in Palestinian-controlled territory.

My professor said we probably wouldn't find stories as dramatic as that on our beats, but to try to find a character that was experiencing some kind of struggle. My beat was Coney Island, Brooklyn, which I chose because my professor encouraged us to show initiative by covering neighborhoods far away from campus. He mentioned his best student a couple of years ago and how she picked Coney Island, the last stop on the F train. I wanted to be like his best student.

For the article, I found a woman whose daughter had been raped by a drug dealer in the stairwell of the Gravesend Houses, a housing project where they lived. She was in the process of suing the city. I met the woman at the Stillwell Avenue subway station when I was interviewing commuters about their thoughts on the primary. She agreed to an interview, but didn't have a phone. In order to arrange a time, I'd have to come knocking. On September 8, I met a group of ten-year-olds from a local political club who were passing out campaign fliers in her building. I was glad I didn't have to enter the building alone. Going door-to-door, floor-to-floor, I found her apartment. The woman and I arranged to meet there the next Tuesday for the interview.

When I went to bed on September 10, I was scared to go back on my own the next morning. I prayed no one would notice me poking around for information. My husband, Ken, kept saying I was an "idiot" to go into a building by myself where I know a woman was raped in broad daylight by drug dealers who continued to threaten her and her family. The woman, he reminded me, was afraid to talk about it. But I thought it was a great story, as close to "in the bunker" as I could get in the United States. I decided to focus on the promise, not the danger. Otherwise, I might as well have quit, canceled my student loans, and gone back to Wall Street.

The next morning, the phone rang just after 9 A.M. My sister Barbara was screaming, "Where's Ken? Where's Ken?" I didn't know what she was talking about. I told her he was at work, and she started crying, "Where? Where? Turn on the TV!" CNN showed the World Trade Center on fire. Ken works at the mercantile exchange, which stands right near the towers. My sister kept crying and screaming, but I wasn't afraid for my husband's safety at all. I told her he was fine and that I had to go. She thought I hung up the phone so that I could track down Ken. But the only thing on my mind was getting downtown as fast as I could. An hour later, after I had already left and Ken had gotten home, Barbara called again. She couldn't believe I was not there, and neither could he. Because I have driven them both crazy at times with my nervousness— wearing seat belts in cabs, swathing myself in sunscreen, refusing to sign tax returns without every single receipt (dull, remember?)— they were sure I wasn't anywhere near the World Trade Center. But staying home that day, to me, felt riskier.

Seeing the images on TV, not knowing what would happen next—reports hadn't yet confirmed it was a terrorist attack—I knew only that I had to get there fast. I didn't wait for the news because no one knew what was going on. I wanted to see for myself. I took a quick shower, grabbed my tape recorder, and ran out the door.

I got on the R train at 8th Street and Broadway. Sitting on the train, I saw a woman with a tape recorder and microphone at the end of the car. The conductor announced that the train would bypass City Hall and Cortlandt Street. Three women in their sixties got angry because they had an appointment at City Hall and didn't know how to get there. There was some talk about how the towers and the Pentagon had been attacked. When the train started moving, everyone offered one another detour directions. I traced the subway map with my fingertip, trying to figure out how to get to the World Trade Center from Canal Street. None of us had a clue what was happening down the tracks before us. The Cortlandt Street station had collapsed.

When I got out at Canal Street, a flood of people was walking north on Lafayette Street. I was so confused about what direction to take that I asked a young man, dressed in a suit and tie, which way downtown was. He pointed in the opposite direction and said, "But you don't want to go down there."

It sounds melodramatic. Growing up, I thought that nothing ever happened in my lifetime. Nothing really big. But walking down Lafayette Street on September 11, full of people heading north as I headed south, the world was changing before my eyes. I think reporters head to places everyone is running from out of a simple need to know—not so much for their bosses or their careers, although that's part of it, but mostly for themselves. It's a kind of driving curiosity—not morbid, not noble. You can't not go. Everything else seems less real than what you're running toward.

The best thing I can compare it to are the grainy newspaper pictures printed the next day in the *New York Post* and the *Daily News*. I remember looking at the black-and-white images of firemen leaning against a fire truck, with that look in their eyes that they've been somewhere you haven't. They reminded me of the photographs of World War II that I grew up on, portraits of soldiers and survivors. I might as well have been looking at the pictures in a history book in the library, but they were in that day's newspaper. In a way, the men in them seemed dead, like it happened a long time ago. Their faces showed how permanent and fleeting life can be. I wanted to understand what it meant.

As I neared City Hall Park along Centre Street, I started seeing people in the crowd covered in dirt. At first, they came one by one with smudges of brown or white dust on their clothes. Then I saw an entire group covered head to toe in white powder an inch thick. Emerging from this cloud of particles, they staggered in horizontal rows across the sidewalk. Their faces were blank. They didn't scream or even talk. I don't remember hearing any sounds at all, and it was only afterward, in the ambient sound of my tape recording, that I know how loud it really was. Turning on my tape recorder, I walked up to each person, introducing myself as a student reporter. "Can you tell me what happened?" I asked.

Almost everyone stopped to tell me their story, which, under the circumstances, I couldn't believe. One man told me he walked down eighty-one flights with a co-worker from Bank of America. Another man, covered in white dust, worked across the street from the towers and described how his entire office shook. A woman told me she saw people trapped underground behind locked gates at the 1 and 9 train station (according to an officer, they got out). They each stopped to be interviewed, just yards from this huge dust cloud.

I walked up to a man dressed in a suit and asked him to tell me what he saw. He pointed with his right arm to the north tower and said, "You see that? I've got a thousand employees up there." I asked him his name, and he said Howard Lutnick. He said he

Learning to See

worked for Cantor Fitzgerald. I asked for his phone number, but he waved me away in either disgust or despair. That night, I learned he was the company's chief executive, and that nearly seven hundred people who worked for his firm died that day, including his brother.

Then I felt a vibration and heard a deep rumble. Everyone started running up Centre Street. I ran straight ahead into the middle of the street and stopped in my tracks. Everyone looked behind them at the plume of smoke in the sky. The north tower was gone.

Court officers and federal marshals directed everyone north. At the time I didn't realize there were no police officers there, but I should have. The police had rushed to Ground Zero, and twenty-three lost their lives that day. A WABC-TV news van was parked at the corner of Worth and Centre Streets. I asked the crew if I could stand near the van, because the court officers were evacuating the area.

I never felt entitled to go where no one else was allowed. But wearing the shoes of a reporter gives you a sense that you belong exactly where you don't belong—that it is your job to be behind government lines. You have to obey the law, but you can at least fight with conviction to stay. But you also have to make sure you are worthy to be in that place. As a novice, I was feeling my way through the situation. I should have focused on a specific question and sought answers. But I didn't know where to begin. Instead, I focused on details and hoped they would add up to something.

And that's when John Costanza approached me and asked where he could find information about survivors. He had mistaken me for a real reporter. I wasn't one, yet. If I had been, maybe I would have realized how powerful his story was. His wife, he said, worked in the World Trade Center. In a quiet voice, he asked me the questions so many others would soon be asking: Where could you go to find out about loved ones? Why wasn't anything set up for the victims' families? Why weren't the phones working? I should have stayed with John that day, searching for the information he needed and reporting on how it could or could not be found. Concerned with the possibility that news would break, I missed the significance of his story. John, in a way, encapsulated the entire tragedy. No one was in the bunker—facing the struggle of a lifetime—more than he at that moment. Staring into his eyes, I failed to see it.

And after asking dozens of people whether they were able to contact their families, I started thinking about Ken. I called him from a pay phone and he was fine, but very angry. It was bad enough I was going to a public housing project that day, he said, but this was too much. How could I have left the house without knowing he was okay? Without letting him know I was OK? It never dawned on me until I called him, because I never stopped to think about the danger for either one of us. I had to be there. That's all I was thinking.

The day after, I set out for St. Vincent's Hospital. On the way, I spotted a Greek Orthodox priest walking out of the 8th Street subway station. Draped in black robes, he swept down Broadway like the image of death itself. I asked him if I could follow him downtown. We walked through Soho together to the barricade at Canal Street, where photojournalists snapped pictures of him. I didn't have a police press pass, and it was only because of him that the police let me through. In fact, a Greek Orthodox cop personally escorted us into Stuyvesant High School, where a triage center was forming.

Doctors and nurses in surgical-green scrubs transformed Stuyvesant's hallways into a makeshift emergency room. Except for a school-newspaper clipping framed behind a glass trophy case, the school showed no signs of American high school life. Below front-page clippings from the *Spectator*, hand written paper signs were

Learning to See

taped to the wall. They read "Wound Care," with black arrows pointing down to tables stocked with iodine, gauze, and latex gloves.

I introduced myself to a doctor. When I asked if I could go to Ground Zero with his team of nurses, he said not to identify myself as with the press. The first thing they teach you at Columbia Journalism is never to lie about who you are. I walked with his group with my press identification tag from Columbia displayed on a silver chain around my neck.

Along the four-block walk, National Guardsmen in green camouflage and black berets guarded the open spaces where secretaries and brokers had eaten their lunches two days before. A white Starbucks coffee cup lid, a torn piece of yellow foam cushion, and office papers with black type looked eerily up at me from the street.

On a cement island at the intersection of Vesey and West Streets, the doctors and nurses gave eyewashes to the workers. We canvassed the area, from one rescue volunteer to the next. At first, they were very hesitant to have their eyes washed. But soon, firefighters, carpenters, and ironworkers began lining up one by one, lifting their heads to the sky. They blinked as salt water ran down their cheeks. The doctor asked each man his name and where he was from, probably just to see if they were coherent. I didn't ask any questions. I didn't know what the rules were. Asking questions might have gotten me kicked out, maybe even arrested. But asking questions would have helped me to understand. At the time, I thought it was important just to observe. Looking back, I know that was not enough. Anyone can be a witness; a reporter asks questions and gets the answers from other people's perspectives.

My professor calls it "fearlessing." It's a term Mormons use for walking up to strangers on the street and talking to them about the church. The best example of journalistic fearlessing at Ground Zero was a reporter who had a way of taking out her notebook from beneath her jacket, crouching beside one person after the next and getting their stories down in her notebook. She had been at Ground Zero since the previous morning, and told me she had slept on the street. To me, she represented all I hoped to become: tough, skilled, and resourceful. In a word, fearless.

A flurry of black and yellow jackets charged past us—firemen yelling that another tower was collapsing. We ran as fast as we could in different directions. I fell into a three-inch-deep puddle of wet cement and debris and the entire contents of my bag—my notebook, tape recorder, and camera—spilled. When I hit the ground, my wedding band slipped off my finger. Afterward, a fireman took me back to the site and helped me search for my ring in the mud. All I could find was my red reporter's notebook, floating in the debris.

I was completely covered in wet cement and bleeding from my arms and hands. As I walked away from Ground Zero, firefighters directed me to the triage center. The doctors gave me an eyewash and warned me not to put my contact lenses back in: asbestos in the air could burn my corneas. It was getting dark, and I couldn't see anything. I walked home, unable to even read the street signs.

The West Side Highway was lined with tractor trailers stacked with boxes of supplies and equipment. The trucks stood still in the traffic, so I tried to count all the boxes on one of the trailers. I counted twenty cardboard boxes with black 3M logos written on the sides. I noticed a man leaning against the cement barricade along the highway, and I asked him what he was doing. He was a truck driver delivering supplies to the rescue workers. He must have noticed the blue surgical mask around my neck covered in mud, because he walked back to his truck and grabbed me a good white mask.

I have no idea what I looked like. I was covered in dried cement from head to toe. The back of my left arm was bleeding and white gauze covered the palms of my hands. And suddenly a gaggle of reporters surrounded me.

Within seconds, microphones were in my face. The huge eyes of news cameras disoriented what was left of my already blurry world. The reporters asked me to climb over the highway divide, so they could steady their cameras. Before I knew it, I was staring at the ground, trying to keep the light out of my eyes and give an accurate report. But I didn't know if it was Tower 5 that had collapsed or even if it had collapsed. Worst of all, rather than reporting the news, I was becoming the news.

The sun had set. Turning the corner east on Christopher Street, I heard a crowd clapping and, without my contact lenses, I couldn't see any faces. I passed a blurry candlelight vigil in front of a red firehouse, but the memorials were all but invisible. People could see me, but I could not see them. In a way, I felt like I was in front of the news camera all over again. It was like walking through an invisible world.

From the moment I woke up on September 11 to that moment in front of the firehouse, there were people right in front of me that I could not see—John Costanza, the firemen, my husband, even myself. My eyes were fine, but my perspective was shifting. Truthfully, if I learned anything in those days, it was that the World Trade Center rubble was no place for beginners. It took a real professional with a lot of experience to get the story. But you have to start somewhere. And for me, both literally and figuratively, it was Ground Zero.

In the Bunker—class assignment
Faces, blank and covered in ash, emerged from a choking cloud of dust this morning onto the siren-filled streets of lower Manhattan.

"You see that?" asked Howard Lutnick, chairman of bond-trading firm Cantor Fitzgerald. "I've got a thousand employees up there," he said, pointing toward a blazing hole at the top of One World Trade Center minutes before the tower collapsed.

This morning, terrorists hijacked two Boeing 767 passenger jets, crashing them into the 110-story twin towers of the World Trade

Center. American Airlines Flight 11, carrying 92 people bound for Los Angeles from Boston, crashed into One World Trade Center at 8:45 A.M. Eighteen minutes later, United Airlines Flight 175, carrying 65 people, also bound for Los Angeles from Boston, crashed into Two World Trade Center, which collapsed at 10 A.M. The collapse of One World Trade Center followed 29 minutes later.

"The whole building shook," said Anthony Christopherson, who said he heard "a shudder" and what sounded like an explosion before he escaped down the stairs of Two World Trade Center from his Bank of America office on the eighty-first floor.

Plastered in white ash, Lou Epstein said he was working at his desk in a building across the street from the World Trade Center when he heard the explosion.

"I went outside and the papers were flying down from all over like confetti," he said.

A few blocks north of City Hall Park, at the corner of Worth and Centre Streets, court officers and U.S. marshals kept the crowd moving north in anticipation of another attack.

"You got 26 Federal Plaza, you got the courts, you could do a lot of damage in this area," said one court officer, who did not want to be named.

Without pay-phone, cell-phone, or subway service, people gathered around a WABC-TV crew van to watch the news.

"It looked like nuclear winter," said reporter Anthony Johnson. "We were right on the block when the first tower came down . . . all of a sudden we heard this rumble, like an earthquake. The next thing you know this cloud, a plume of smoke thirty stories high, started coming right at us." Johnson said he and his two-man crew ran for cover in a nearby store.

Donna Hendricks, a PATH-train terminal supervisor at the Port Authority, said she was able to evacuate train passengers and Port Authority employees who were underground when the first plane hit One World Trade Center.

Learning to See

"We heard a big boom and then I started smelling gas. So I told my employees to get out," said Hendricks, her black hair covered in white ash.

Outside St. Vincent's Hospital on West 12th Street and Seventh Avenue, Dr. Leonard Bakalchuk told reporters the first wave of patients were people who managed to escape before the buildings collapsed. He said the most serious injuries were burns to the skin and airways, as well as penetrating wounds to the chest and legs. The doctor confirmed three deaths at the hospital as of 7:45 P.M.

"We are used to all kinds of things at St. Vincent's Hospital," Bakalchuk said. "But this is our city—you look down the street and the buildings are gone."

Father Lloyd Prator of St. John's Episcopal Church said he arrived at St. Vincent's Hospital just after 9 A.M., but spent most of the day working alongside Emergency Management Services personnel on the street. The priest said he gave blessings to police officers and firefighters, as well as last rites to two dying firefighters.

"It was an honor to be able to minister to some of the finest people in New York," Prator said. "It's a blow to the whole city."

Listening Back

By Beth Fertig—WNYC Radio

For journalists on September 11, it was an all too familiar and terrifying zigzag. BETH FERTIG, a reporter for WNYC Radio and a contributor to National Public Radio, dashed toward the World Trade Center from her Greenwich Village home to report firsthand on the attacks. When the first tower collapsed shortly after her arrival, she turned around and raced for her life toward the relative safety of Foley Square, a few blocks north. In the meantime, though, she managed to record the rumbling sound of the building's collapse on her minidisc recorder. Within twenty-four hours, the recording was broadcast on NPR affiliates across the United States.

Fertig, thirty-six, has deep roots in the city that came under siege. She was raised on the Upper East Side before moving to Great Neck, Long Island, at age ten. A graduate of the University of Michigan who majored in English, she also earned a master's degree in social sciences from the University of Chicago. Before joining WNYC full-time in 1995, she worked for a chain of weekly newspapers in Boston. In 2001, she was awarded the prestigious Alfred I. DuPont-Columbia Journalism Award for a 2001 series on the Edison vote, a proposal to privatize five failing New York City schools.

Back in January, some of us at WNYC took turns listening to air checks from September 11. Few of us had had a chance to hear our own work from that day because we were each so busy. So when we finally got the chance, months later, we marveled at our colleagues' professionalism. Despite the horror unfolding and severe technical constraints, we generally kept our cool and kept our listeners abreast of the latest developments. Our reporters on the scene recounted every detail at Ground Zero, from the discarded shoes, abandoned by people running in fear, to fire marshals washing in a fountain. Yet we could also hear ourselves struggling—as though we were learning as we went along. Sometimes our sentences rambled. We sounded disoriented and made a lot of umms and pauses. Other times we just didn't know what to say. After I played my recording of the first building collapse, I actually said: "It seems to be a lot calmer, thankfully . . . I'm just glad to see there isn't any more disaster right now."

Listening back, I cringed at how inept I sounded, moments after being so professional. But September 11 wasn't like any other new event. Those of us on the scene had to describe the indescribable. Often, we were our own best sources. As my colleague Amy Eddings put it, "It took me several minutes before I stopped looking for an 'official' to interpret what I was seeing for me." When the towers fell, we had to describe what we had seen in real time, even though it was unclear how or why they had fallen. We often had less information than our colleagues and producers in the studio, because we had no sources other than the terrified bystanders around us and our own eyes. And the nature of what we were witnessing was so upsetting, we had to constantly battle our own emotions. This didn't always make for the best reporting. But it produced riveting radio that captured the anxiety and drama taking place all around us.

Like every reporter in town, I did not wake up ready for tragedy. It was primary day and I planned to cover election night. I was sound asleep at my apartment on Thompson Street in Greenwich Village when the first plane hit. Minutes later my phone rang and I was shouted awake by my news director, Kevin Beesley. I was more annoyed than anything else. "They sure picked a great day," I growled, sarcastically into the phone, unaware that it was a real emergency. A few weeks earlier, someone had flown a parachute into the Statue of Liberty. *Had a small propeller plane bumped into one of the towers? Did they really need to wake me for this? Couldn't they send someone else?*

Kevin's voice was urgent, and as a former television news producer who worked in Jerusalem and Afghanistan, he doesn't panic easily. So I knew this was serious. I just didn't know how serious. I jumped into the shower. Then my boyfriend called.

"Are you watching this?" he asked.

"I know!" I said, getting out of the shower. "A plane hit the Trade Center. I'm on my way."

"I think you should turn on CNN!"

I ran into the living room and turned on my television. The towers were burning. *Oh my God!* I started to panic, so I turned off the television and ran back into my bedroom. I threw on the black pantsuit I was planning to wear to cover the primary. I knew something terrible was happening. But I was still thinking about what I was supposed to be doing that day. Maybe I'd still cover the election after I was done with this fire at the Trade Center. *Would I have time to vote?*

Listening Back

I sprinted downstairs with my knapsack full of gear—the same equipment I always take to work. A microphone, minidisc recorder, headphone plugs, and notebooks. As soon as I got outside, the enormity of what was happening hit me. My walkup building is a mile north of the World Trade Center, and Thompson Street was filled with people staring south, watching the Twin Towers burn. It was a surreal vision like something out of a Magritte painting. Blue sky, silver towers with orange flames shooting out of big black holes. Now I really began to panic. I dashed to the Bleecker Street subway.

When the train pulled into the Brooklyn Bridge-City Hall station I saw scraps of paper and ash floating everywhere. I ran into the Municipal Building, where our station is located, but the twenty-fifth floor newsroom was empty. Two WNYC managers ordered me back downstairs. The building had been evacuated and our morning news anchor, Mark Hilan, was on the air alone. On the ground floor I ran into Betsy Gardella, a WNYC executive, who pleaded with me to persuade Mark to leave. She was understandably worried, but I told her he was doing the right thing. We owed it to our listeners to stay on the air.

Clearly, I knew what the news anchor should do. But I had no idea how this radio reporter should proceed. Kevin had told me to track down the mayor or the police commissioner. But I didn't know where they were or if another reporter had already made it to the World Trade Center. Kevin and the others from our newsroom weren't around. There was total chaos outside the office building. My cell had no signal. There were long lines at every pay phone.

I looped behind the Municipal Building to Police Headquarters only to find it evacuated. Across the street City Hall was being evacuated too. A cop told me the mayor had gone to his command center at 7 World Trade. "But you didn't hear it from me," he said. "Be careful. There's lots of glass falling. You could get hurt."

I had to get to the World Trade Center. I had been putting it off.

Beth Fertig

I'm terrified of fire. My house in college almost burned down after an incident involving a light bulb and my roommate's bathrobe. Even if the flames would be too far away, I knew I'd be surrounded by casualties. I found WNYC's program director, Dean Cappello, standing outside the office building. I told him I was going down there. "Don't do anything crazy," he warned.

My heart raced as I pushed through the crowds lining Park Row. Thousands of people poured from the World Trade Center. Gawkers mixed among them. Like a fish swimming upstream, I slowly made my way south. I was afraid. But the whole situation was so strange; I felt more like a character in a disaster movie than a journalist. I envisioned myself as an actress playing a journalist like Téa Leoni's role as a television reporter covering the asteroid bound for earth in *Deep Impact*.

I got as far as the traffic circle at the southern edge of City Hall Park when I was stopped by a police officer. She wouldn't allow me any closer and said it was for security reasons. I displayed my press pass and microphone, arguing that I needed to find the mayor and get to the Trade Center. "We don't know what's going to happen next," she said, sternly. "I'm trying to protect your life." Then—as if on cue—the south tower collapsed. I couldn't believe it. The building came down so orderly, floor by floor, that I presumed it was a controlled demolition. I hoped that it was. *Maybe they got all the people out and now they're bringing the building down to prevent any more casualties.*

The rumbling was deafening, like an overhead train. I held out my microphone. "The building's falling," I yelled over the roar. I described the huge cloud of smoke, and then joined thousands of people running for their lives. I headed back around City Hall Park, running up Park Row. A thin African-American man stood outside J&R Music and Computer World screaming, "Oh my God!" He spoke for us all. I tried to interview him, but he became incoherent, moaning and muttering. I followed the mob north.

Listening Back

Horns honked as emergency vehicles raced toward the towers. Police officers told people to head north and east. I gasped for breath, holding my microphone out to collect the sounds. Back at the Municipal Building, I saw my colleague Marianne McCune. She had just hitched a ride with a bicyclist in order to get to Manhattan from Brooklyn because the subways were down. She was now preparing to go to the towers, with her microphone out. "Don't go down there!" I shouted. She turned on her recording unit and asked me what I had seen. I spoke quickly, in a rush of words, about the building collapse and the smoke. Then I cried.

Marianne and I were a sight, walking arm in arm away from the Trade Center carrying our microphones. I felt useless, aimless. Marianne and I sit right across from each other at work and we'd gotten to know each other pretty well over the past couple of years. We would share bits of our personal lives in the morning, and then share M&M's in the afternoon. Often, we'd still be at our desks late at night, too. I'd be obsessing over which piece of an interview to use in a feature story, while Marianne would be hunched over her Macintosh computer, searching for the perfect sound effect to use in one of her reports. We had an easy admiration for each other's professional compulsions. Now, we had to depend on each other— and neither one of us felt very professional that morning. Marianne says she felt like she was starting from scratch—as though she had never even been a reporter before, because she was so unsure about how to proceed. Here we were, one block away from our office building, and we couldn't get in because it had been evacuated. We needed to get on the radio to describe what had happened for our listeners, but my cell phone wasn't working and there were still huge lines by the pay phones. Then, by some miracle, Marianne's phone picked up a signal. She got through to the anchor, Mark Hilan, and passed me her phone.

"I don't know if I can hook up a headphone to play this," I told Mark. I fumbled with my digital recording unit and described my day to kill time. Then I played my recording into the phone through a tiny portable headphone. "The building is falling right now, people are running through the streets, smoke is everywhere," I heard myself screaming.

I couldn't hear Mark's faint voice over the din of sirens. He had broken away from NPR's coverage of the attacks in order to provide more news from New York City. He cut to Amy Eddings, another reporter, with riveting tape of folks who had seen the plane crashes. While I was on hold Marianne scanned the hundreds of people standing around Foley Square watching the cloud of smoke. They were staring in disbelief, and some were covered with white concrete particles and ash.

Amy finished playing her tape, and was describing the chaos and devastation she had seen. She said people had left behind tennis shoes, dress pumps, and duffel bags scattered everywhere.

"Let's go back, if we can, to WNYC's Marianne McCune or WNYC's Beth Fertig to hear what they can tell us," Mark announced.

It was my turn to provide some other perspective. Thankfully, Marianne had found a young man. She whispered his name, described where he worked, and stuck him next to the cell phone.

"Mark, it's Beth in Foley Square with Marianne. Marianne was just rounding up people who were eyewitnesses to the explosion and also to the two planes going through. I'm here with Denny Sito who works across from the World Trade Center."

I passed the phone to our witness, not knowing whether he understood he was about to go live on the air with tens of thousands of listeners. Denny took the phone and calmly began telling his story.

"I got off the E train at approximately nine o'clock and there was huge confusion over what was going on," he explained. "All of a sudden a massive crowd of people running toward us, people getting off the train. So we got off the subway track and walked up and all of a sudden I saw Tower One, half of it, the top of the building on fire. At approximately 9:05 as the fire was progressing, I saw people jumping off the tower. Literally jumping off the tower without any ground support whatsoever. It was not a pretty sight. Five minutes after, I heard a rocket sound or jetliner literally hitting Tower Two. The explosion was so massive that while I was standing in front of it, if I didn't run away it was literally a life-or-death situation."

I was in awe. Of this witness and of Marianne for finding him. But now the phone was back in my hand. Mark was talking.

"We can recap for you very quickly here the reason we are here. Beth, if you'll hold on just one moment. Two planes crashed into the World Trade Center earlier this morning and one of the towers collapsed into the street, below. The upper third to upper half of one of the two towers, we're told it's World Trade Center One. President Bush says it's an apparent terrorist attack, witnesses telling of bodies falling from the 110-story towers and people jumping out. WNYC's Beth Fertig is near the scene. Beth, what do you want to report at this moment?"

Oh no! I've got nothing to add.

"Uh, it seems to be a lot calmer thankfully," I fumbled. "That's all I can really say from here at Foley Square. Everybody's still looking at the scene ahead of us, which is just unbelievable. The southern tower is down, the northern tower still standing although burning, uh, and I think most of the sirens have gotten wherever they were heading at this point so I'm just glad to see that there isn't any more disaster right now."

There was a long pause. *Please let me get off the phone!*

Mark jumped in. "Beth, we are coordinating at the studios trying to make sure we get as many people who saw this or experienced it or whatever."

Then I started thinking like a reporter. *Just tell them what you know.* I remembered the police I'd seen evacuating the area.

"I assume we should tell people all of lower Manhattan has

pretty much been evacuated right now," I said. "Police are telling people go north and go east. Get away from the area. City Hall is closed. Police Plaza is closed. Our office building, the Municipal Building, is closed. I can't tell about these courthouses, some of them seem to still be open but it's hard to tell . . ."

It wasn't great, but at least I sounded confident now. I had some facts to provide our audience. Mark must have picked up on this because he kept me on the line. He asked if I could see anything left of the southern tower, which had collapsed.

"No, I can't, Mark. I can't see it at all. There's a building blocking my vantage point."

The federal building blocked our view. Smoke was everywhere. For all I knew, a few stories might still be standing under the thick black cloud. Mark asked me about the north tower. "Can you still scc flames?"

"There are flames," I said, watching the building. I tried to stick with what I knew, but I couldn't hide my emotions. I gasped at the sight of one tower where there used to be two, and even that tower, with its upper floors consumed in flames, was hardly the tower I knew. "It's totally obscured by smoke. Marianne and I are trying to watch it. And what's so incredible is these buildings are a fixture of the New York skyline. You're used to seeing them there. To look over the top of these buildings and not see the two Twin Towers or only part of one, as a New Yorker it's like a piece of your life has vanished, not seeing these buildings here."

Finally, I had been personal and coherent. Mark continued to recap the events with aplomb. He mentioned the crash at the Pentagon, the evacuation of the White House. Then I heard a rumbling. "Mark, there's another sound," I said, breaking in "Something is happening. There was a big sound. We don't know what this is."

But I did know. I knew before I even looked up. It was the same sound I had heard before. "We can see the video in our studio,"

Listening Back

Mark said, urgently. "It appears the remainder of the World Trade Center has collapsed to the ground!"

"We're in the worst place we can be, Marianne, we can't see a thing," I blurted out, not knowing we were still on the air.

"WNYC's Beth Fertig and WNYC's Marianne McCune are on the street below trying their best to give you as much of a vantage point as they can from where they are." Then me, "It's gone, it's gone."

"You can hear Beth Fertig in the background," said Mark. "Are you saying it's gone?"

"It's gone, it's gone," I answered. "All we see is smoke, the smoke is moving, and there's no tower standing there anymore. We don't know how much of it is left."

Marianne pulled eyewitnesses to the phone. One guy had run down eighty-seven flights of stairs. After his interview, the cell phone finally died.

We continued interviewing from Foley Square. Even though we were no longer live, we knew we would use the stories later. And it gave us something to do. I felt calmer holding the microphone and interviewing people. Marianne has told me she was dumbfounded. She describes it as shock with a sense of doom. But in hindsight I remember her as the calm one. She got me through that morning. We thought like a team and reminded each other how to do our jobs—by describing what we had seen and by interviewing the witnesses. We also warded off each other's sadness.

The stories that morning were horrible, poignant, and human— sometimes all at once. We saw fire marshals washing themselves in the fountain at Foley Square. They were covered with the ubiquitous white powder created when the towers collapsed. I didn't know how to approach them so I joined another reporter already questioning them. A fire marshal named Michael Smith described trying to help people when the tower came down. He had seen people burned to death. "It's like a war zone. People were injured

189

everywhere," he said. He lay down by the fountain with a wet towel over his face. I didn't want to press him further, so I turned to the others. There were three fire marshals at the fountain. They said there were originally ten in their group. They didn't know if their colleagues were dead or alive.

Someone attended to a crying pregnant woman. She didn't want to be recorded, so I left her alone. I felt conflicted about interviewing traumatized people. They didn't need me asking, "How does it feel?" Then again, my job was to inform the rest of the city what was happening in lower Manhattan. Television could show them the burning towers. But radio would give voice to the tragedy. I just didn't want to make things any worse by making them relive their horrors. I spotted two women crying on the steps of a building on Worth Street. Approaching gingerly, I asked what happened. They had been inside one of the towers but didn't want to talk. Another woman, who was trying to help them, suggested they speak on the radio so their friends and family would know they were all right. *Good point. I'm glad she suggested it, and not me.*

The women opened up. "I just heard an explosion," one of them began, wearily. Her name was Loretta Williams. "Everything collapsed. I went down the stairs and I felt the shaking again." The woman next to her was also crying but she declined to speak. Loretta said they were both shaken up. I asked her to describe what she saw inside the towers. "Couple of people were burned," she said, "Their skin was coming off." My stomach turned. I kept my eyes on her face and concentrated on her words. I thanked her for speaking with me.

Marianne had been interviewing someone else nearby and spotted some emergency workers treating people in the street. They told her about a triage center in the city's Department of Health, just around the corner. We went inside and found doctors and nurses handing out orange juice and water. I was so thirsty from smoke and exertion that I took two cups. The health department workers were wearing big white T-shirts emblazoned with an image of what had been the city's greatest threat before that morning: the West Nile virus mosquito. It must have been the closest thing to a uniform they could find.

Marianne and I knew we needed to get back on the air. We had recorded incredible stories. We asked the health department spokeswoman if we could use her phone. Leading us upstairs to the press office, she allowed us to sit at one of the desks.

We finally had a working telephone, but we needed a bigger set of headphones in order to play our recordings into the mouthpiece. The tiny earplugs I had used outside weren't adequate. Fortunately, someone at the health department loaned us portable headphones. We called WNYC. Marianne and I were sounding professional again. By interviewing as many people as possible on the scene, and at the health department, we had found a role for ourselves. We were still hesitant to speculate about anything we couldn't confirm with our own eyes—including the precise cause of the disaster. But we had plenty of other dramatic material to draw upon.

"The department ambulances are bringing people from the explosion, crash, whatever we're calling it," Marianne said, during her first update from the health department. "We were speaking to some people in the building when the explosion happened and emergency workers. One emergency worker told me he was rescuing people after the first explosion and when the second building came down there was so much dust in the air he couldn't see a thing and he was saved by the flash of a photographer's camera. That's what gave him enough light to get out."

Chilling images like this painted a picture. So did the tape. When it was my turn to speak, I played my interview with a survivor I'd met in the lobby of the health department.

"This is Charles Diaz, a captain with the Sanitation police who responded to the scene after the planes hit the building and then found himself a victim of all the chaos that was going on and was

191

injured," I explained, setting up my interview. Then we heard from the captain.

"There were people injured all over the place. Crying for help, screaming for help. We couldn't see in front of our faces, total darkness like the sun was covered over."

Fertig: "It looks like you might have broke. . ."

Diaz: "Yeah, I think I broke my wrist or my arm, I don't know which one yet."

Fertig: "Yeah, it looks like you have quite a sling with tape and a ruler."

Diaz: "Yeah well they don't have anything here so I just taped it up."

Fertig: "Is this where they're bringing people who were injured?"

Diaz: "Everybody around here yes, it's like a triage area."

Fertig: "What I can't imagine is how many people were hurt or killed. Do you have any sense of?"

Diaz: "No, no, I have no idea."

Fertig: "Did you see a lot of people . . ."

Diaz: "I saw people buried. Crawling out of the rubble like I was."

Marianne and I stayed at the health department for an hour or two. We also played our interviews for National Public Radio so listeners across the country could hear what we recorded. Marianne gave live updates for NPR's newscasts and afternoon programs. Somehow we each managed to call our families. Thankfully, my parents had been listening to the radio and knew I was all right. I kept it pretty much together when I spoke with them. I didn't cry until I put down the phone. Speaking to the people I loved, not just an anonymous audience of radio listeners, made me feel more vulnerable. I wasn't a reporter covering a tragedy. I was another human being affected by it. Marianne and I split up for the rest of the day. The health department told me Mayor Giuliani was on his way to a makeshift command station at the police academy in midtown. It was a surreal two-mile walk.

Listening Back

The trains were down. People filled the streets, staring south at the big cloud of smoke, which looked like a storm cloud gathering over Lower Manhattan.

I reached the mayor's command center before his news conference, and wound up doing live interviews with NPR and WNYC from a fax phone because there weren't enough telephones for all the reporters. "The number of casualties will be more than any of us could bear, ultimately," Giuliani announced. I felt like crying during his press conference. This was the part in the disaster movie when we rally behind our leader and defeat the enemy—a monster on a rampage, a terrible storm, or the aliens. But at that moment, we had no idea what was happening next. While it was comforting to see the reporters I'd worked alongside at City Hall, it was also disorienting. We were all transplanted into the same awful, unfamiliar territory. *Everything you know is wrong* popped into my mind. It was a song by a band called Christmas that I used to play at my college radio station.

In one morning, an unforeseen event had drastically reshaped the city. Our world now revolved around a place that no longer existed. And that loss created a new vocabulary as well as a new map. First we had, "The site of the World Trade Center." Eventually, "Ground Zero."

But at that moment, in the mayor's command center, I clung to the familiar and comforting. And in a room full of city reporters, this meant black humor and sarcasm. We joked that Giuliani planned the whole thing to ruin the election so he wouldn't have to leave office in January. We also speculated about whether a bomb had brought down the towers. None of us knew that flaming jet fuel and the impact of the planes could cause so much damage. Mostly we traded war stories about where we were that day. Being with the press corps again distracted me from thinking about how many people had died, and how horrible their last moments must have been.

Later, I caught a bus to NPR's midtown bureau. That's when I learned about what happened to my radio station. Starting at around 5 P.M., I had trouble getting through by telephone. At first I thought it was just the fax phone I was using. But it turned out WNYC's phone lines had died. And that made it impossible to broadcast from our studios. We were saved by a skeleton crew of producers and engineers who had already gone uptown to NPR and put together a makeshift on-air studio in someone's office, using a portable mixing board and microphone. From here, we were able to keep our station on the air.

WNYC is an unusual station because we broadcast on both AM and FM. We had already lost our FM signal because the transmitter had been on the North Tower of the World Trade Center. We were now left with just AM. It wasn't long however before we lost our AM signal, too. Normally, we beam the AM signal from the Municipal Building to a dish on the World Trade Center, which then sends the signal to our AM transmitter in New Jersey. When the towers fell we relied on a backup system. A high-quality phone line that carried the signal out to the transmitter. But by early evening, that connection broke down too because of damage to Verizon's downtown phone network. For a few frightening hours we had no signal on either AM or FM. I was working at the NPR bureau and heard all of the engineers scrambling to find a solution. Eventually, one engineer in New Jersey drove to the transmitter and established a new connection the old fashioned way. He unscrewed the earpiece from a regular telephone, and literally connected the copper phone wires to the AM transmitter. We could now send our signal over the phone directly from NPR's bureau. Sometime around three o'clock in the morning I heard the engineers cheer. We were back on AM! The result sounded thin and tinny. But we were broadcasting again. Later, NPR drove a satellite truck up from their Washington headquarters to help us establish a better AM signal.

While all this was taking place, Mark Hilan and Amy Eddings

decided to camp out in the downtown studios in case we were able to restore the phone lines and broadcast from there again. Having defied an evacuation order, they were afraid to leave—fearing they wouldn't be allowed back in. They ate whatever food they could wrestle out of the vending machine, and stayed warm under the blankets used to cover the station's baby grand piano. By the next day, though, it was clear we would have to keep broadcasting from NPR's office because our phones still weren't working. We stayed there for two weeks.

While Mark and Amy were holding the fort at WNYC's studio in the Municipal Building, I spent my night at NPR's bureau finishing a feature story with the tape Marianne and I had collected downtown. I left work at around 5 A.M. Wednesday morning. Only then did I allow myself to release my emotions. Manhattan was closed to traffic south of 14th Street so I walked from there home to Thompson Street. I stared at the place in the sky where the towers once peeked over the Washington Square arch, formerly my favorite view. I felt lonely and horrible and the tears started pouring down my face. A few doormen saw me, but the only person who said anything to me was a homeless man outside Washington Square Park. He asked me why I was so upset.

"Look behind you!" I yelled.

"So," he said, "it's not the end of the world."

Everyone at WNYC has a breakdown story. For most it came at the end of a grueling shift, when they had time to think about what had happened. What surprised me was how many of my peers, like me, questioned their journalistic performance. A few even felt guilty. Could they have done more? In retrospect, that makes sense. September 11 was my most humbling experience. In the weeks afterward, I met journalists from numerous news organizations. We invariably swapped stories. Some asked where I was with just a hint of professional competition. The mere mention of which cross streets one had reached triggered the outlines of a mental map to determine who was closer. When a bunch of reporters crowded around a radio correspondent as he told them his dramatic life-threatening story, about how he broke his way out of a store when a tower collapsed you could hear them thinking, *I wish I had that story*. But other times the competition could be more blatant. On September 12, a reporter from another radio station asked me, "So have you cried on air yet? I have." I was flabbergasted. "No, is this a contest?"

In the weeks that followed I became angry. Angry at the way my city had changed. Angry at how many people had died for no reason. And angry at the changes in my job—working nonstop on weekends, a pager going off at all hours. *What's next? Powdered sugar on a subway track posing as anthrax? People getting sick by opening mail?* And when we started bombing Afghanistan, I was angry with the protesters on both sides; I didn't agree with any of them. It wasn't World War II and it wasn't Vietnam, either.

I was also angry with the people who could escape September 11. People who worked in midtown, far away from Ground Zero. They didn't have to smell the sour smoke every day and see the ruins on their way to work. *How dare they get on with their lives?* I felt like my boyfriend was living in some other world because he worked at a bank in midtown. He did his best to understand, even waited up for me in my apartment when I'd come home in the middle of the night during those first few days. But when he respectfully declined my suggestion to visit Ground Zero, I felt angry with him—even though he was perfectly entitled not to see it. He'd had enough. Unlike me, he actually knew a few people who died in those towers. But I still had this strange desire for everyone else to see what I'd seen. Otherwise, I feared, September 11 wouldn't be real.

Sometimes I wanted to stop being a reporter. This was more than I had bargained for. Six days after the tragedy, I was allowed two days off. I'd been working almost continuously since the eleventh and eagerly anticipated the break. I hoped to catch up on my sleep. But instead of feeling relief, I just felt worse. I went to synagogue to celebrate the Jewish New Year and started crying even before I even got there. On my way, I'd passed my local firehouse and found out that they lost almost a dozen men. Later I tried to distract myself. I went to a clothing store, but the whole idea of shopping seemed trivial. I left in shame. As the night wore on, I became anxious. *Could I return to work?*

But when I woke up the next morning, I felt strangely energized. Maybe I needed that "breakdown" time to reflect, and to absorb what had happened. Maybe I had gotten a little of the grief and anger out of my system. As I left my house with my recording equipment and microphone, preparing to interview immigrants from Pakistan and Afghanistan, I realized I was doing something familiar. I could listen to other people and report on their stories. I could turn on my equipment, scribble into my notepad, and do my job.

A Fireman's Son

By Matthew J. Malone
—Columbia Graduate School of Journalism

Many journalists reported and experienced September 11 simultaneously. Hearing the news, MATTHEW J. MALONE, at the time a student at the Columbia Graduate School of Journalism, raced to the closest train station, which happened to be in Mineola, Long Island. With city-bound service cut, he could not find his way to Manhattan. To secure interview subjects, he waited on the platform as survivors of the attacks returned to Long Island. Rail cars delivered stunned, soot-covered passengers. Malone, the son of a fireman, soon realized that dozens of firefighters had died in the collapse. He recalled watching his father douse a blazing car before it could explode. Newly aware of the dangers his now retired dad had faced, he reflects on his family and his long-repressed fears about his father's dangerous profession.

Before graduating from Columbia this year, Malone, twenty-eight, co-founded and edited the satirical thelongpoint.com, and wrote for Aspen Magazine, *an insider's look at the famous resort. Today, he and his wife, Melissa, live in New York City with their dog, Allie.*

I grew up near the train station in Mineola, New York. My family lived in a cookie-cutter house, three blocks from everything and close to nothing. The town is indistinguishable from many other Long Island neighborhoods, one-story shops with forgettable architecture and neighbors who always remember. If you drive around and read the signs, you'll see that that Mineola is the county seat. I'm not sure what that means, but I can't help but wonder who approved such an auspicious appellation. County seat or not, life proceeds slowly here. Everything is regular, even, like the coming and going of the train.

I feel like I've waited for that train most of my life, at railroad crossings, on the platform, in a car waiting to pick someone up. It is as familiar to me as the scar on my finger, as my mother's voice. If I think hard I can hear its ferocious rumble, its piercing horn, its weary hiss as it stops at the platform. I can smell the stale beer, the coffee, and the pulpy scent of newspaper. I can see my neighbors coming home from work. Mineola is a commuter town, thirty-five minutes from Manhattan. As E. B. White said, towns like mine give New York City its tidal restlessness. We come in and take its money and head back home. The train puts food on the table.

But sometimes the train brings grief, too. It is the same line on which Colin Ferguson shot six people in 1996, staining the windows with blood. On September 11, I suppose the faces in the windows looked the same, just as indescribable as the day Ferguson raised his gun. But soot on the windows. Planes as bullets. The train rolling on.

Matthew J. Malone

On September 11, I will head to the train station to write a story.

That morning, I wake up a bit late. I check my cell phone messages. My aunt. *Are you OK?* My wife, Melissa. *Call me.* I dial seven digits and the world changes: "Are you OK?" Melissa says. "Turn on the TV."

So I stand there watching CNN, the towers burning. How stupid I look, there in my pajamas, pulling up spoonfuls of Raisin Bran as the city explodes. The day's *New York Times* is on the counter, with a fresh fold and news that is so stale, so insignificant. I look out our front window in Roslyn Heights, New York, thirty miles from the World Trade Center, searching for smoke.

The towers in flames, jet fuel burning, people jumping, I get dressed quickly and grab my flimsy student press pass and arsenal of sharpened pencils. I head out the door and the day overtakes me. The sky is painted a rich cornflower blue; the air is cool and sweet; the sun is burning. It is too beautiful, too perfect. Now I'm suspicious of sunny days.

I race through town toward the train station. The damn stoplights are still slow. Gas is still expensive. The shops still look somber: the variety store, the Duane Reade Drugs, the Silver Dollar Bar. I pass St. Aidan's, my grammar school; it looks smaller, more forlorn, every time.

There are people walking around town. They must know what's going on; I wonder why they're outside running errands. But I guess that's what you do when you can't *do* anything, go to K-Mart and check out the blue light specials. *Got to get my oil changed. Pick up some Charmin at the grocery store. See if I know anyone who died today.*

My mind drifts back to the burning towers. I just passed them in my car last week on the West Side Highway, craning my neck to see all the way to the top. I remember the last time I went inside, years before. I had dinner at Windows on the World with my then-girlfriend and her parents. I was about nineteen. I wore shorts, which weren't allowed, so I had to put on a pair of busboy's pants I got from the maitre'd. Ordering a fancy dinner in borrowed, tight white pants. I ordered filet mignon, as did someone else, but they pronounced it in proper French. My face blushed, the borrowed pants felt tighter.

The time before that, I was just a child. My family went whizzing up the elevator. I pressed my hands on the glass of the observation towers and looked down. My knees trembled, my bowels quivered. I was small and the world was big.

Now the whole thing is burning, smashed, torn, twisted.

I think of friends who work in the city. I dial numbers, talking to some, leaving messages for others. On any other day, I might be jealous of the lives they had—big paychecks, expense accounts, and catered lunches. But now I'm sitting in my car while they're running for cover.

I pull in to the train station around 10:15 A.M. I first approach two women sitting next to an ATM machine. As I remember, they are Long Island women; jeans and T-shirts, long painted nails, a bit of gold jewelry. They tell me about their trip on the train; they made it as far as Jamaica, Queens, before being turned back. They could see the smoke rising from the city. "Horrible." "So sad." "So much smoke." Now they sat, waiting on the westbound platform, as if they could still get into the city, as if the world were normal still.

With no trains running westbound, I walk over the footbridge to the eastbound track. I hear on the radio that people are walking over the Brooklyn Bridge from lower Manhattan to get to the Long Island Railroad station in Brooklyn. Slowly, the trains begin to roll in, the first one around noon. As the day wears on, each train is loaded with grief; the passengers are more stunned, more soot-covered, like worn, dusty cowboys dressed in Brooks Brothers and Ann Taylor. On the platform, people mingle in clusters, new friends bonded by terror; others stand alone, staring absently across the empty tracks. The sun harsh, mocking.

Shyness is a horrible affliction for a reporter, but not unusual among journalists. On many other reporting stints I practice a particular form of self-hypnosis, living outside myself, shutting out the doubts, enthusiastic, extroverted. But this day was different. I was still uneasy, but it was words, not people, that scared me:

"As the first plane hit, I was talking to a guy on the 105th floor. The phone just clicked."

"I saw shoes all over the place."

"The debris was just chasing us. It was dropping like flies."

"A friend saw a woman crushed by the debris, right outside the first building."

"I saw at least twelve people jump."

My notes from that afternoon are as chaotic, incomplete, and confusing as the day itself. The notes have a particular, irregular rhythm, like the beat of a drummer trying to keep up with the rest of the band. I burned a lot of excellent material, some heart-wrenching, compelling stuff.

At midafternoon, I approach two men sitting on the curb, talking. I ask to speak with them. I sit down in the street, legs crossed, pad in my lap, gravel uncomfortable beneath me. They had never met before they stood on the train together. Yet the two strangers trade stories like old war buddies (the concrete jungle, streets awash in powder, flames, body parts, running, everything crashing down).

One of the men is British, a veteran of London's IRA bombings, he says. He approaches catastrophe with the sad, sober realism of those to whom tragedy and terror are a way of life. He led his co-workers out of their John Street office, two blocks from the WTC, toward the East River.

"It was like walking in snow," he says.

The other guy is in his mid-thirties, a father. He fiddles with his

A Fireman's Son

gold wedding ring as he tells his story of narrow escape, the type of tale that has now grown tired, told too many times by too many. All the while he has a stunned "what the fuck?" expression on his face. When all was said and done, I have the uneasy feeling that he knew someone who died that day.

Looking back, I was numb, floating. Putting on a happy face. *I get what you're going through. Tell me your story.* I felt like I had to have all the answers, the weathered reporter swallowing it all whole. It got better as I talked to more people, but I still operated outside of myself, never stopping to think, to grieve, to shout out loud.

Six o'clock. The light now softer, sideways, I struggle to put it all together. *What does this all mean? What do people want to know? What on earth should I write about?*

I walk to my car, pull a parking ticket off the windshield, and head home.

The men in my family are firefighters. My grandfather worked at Engine Company 263 in Astoria, Queens; my dad at Engine 238 in Greenpoint, Brooklyn. My dad retired two years ago, got a big gold ring and a shiny plaque. I hadn't spent much time at the firehouse since I was in my early teens.

I remember being very young and riding in our car to firehouse Christmas parties. My parents, two sisters, and I would weave along the Long Island Expressway, past the green lawns of the suburbs to the industrial landscape of Brooklyn, one exit before Manhattan's Midtown Tunnel. I was frightened and fascinated by what I saw. The towering billboards. Steam billowing from the manhole covers. *If the streets themselves smoked, they sure needed firefighters in Brooklyn!*

The parties were wonderful. We climbed on the trucks, our party clothes stained with grease, our hands smelling like gasoline. Larry, a young firefighter, walked around with a Kermit the Frog puppet that popped out of a cardboard box. In his even younger days, Larry was known as Larry "the Crazy in the Upper Deck" for his antics at Jets games. He had an enormous curly wig. He would moon the crowd, his ass cheeks alternately painted in Jet green and white. To a little kid from the suburbs, Larry was very cool.

When I was about twelve, I went to the firehouse with two friends. We hung out with "the boys," guys with nicknames like "Spot," "Beefy," and "Flapper." We checked out the *Playboy* in the bathroom (multiple trips) and hung around. Finally, the bell rang, all of the men swinging into action. They leapt into their uniforms, black and yellow like bees. We rode in the truck to an auto fire, sitting on the firefighters' laps, undoubtedly in violation of a million safety codes. We watched as they doused the small fire in a big, glass-strewn parking lot.

Before September 11, I never really considered the danger that my father faced on the job. To me, the firehouse was a playhouse for grown-ups. A pool table, a stack of movies and porno magazines. A fridge full of junk food. All your friends under one roof.

Dad, who rarely talked about his work, was infrequently inside a burning building the last fifteen or so years of his career. He was the "chauffeur," driving the big red truck. The only on-the-job injuries my dad suffered were a broken finger in a car accident and a burn on his ass after backing into a hot radiator in an apartment building. There were no narrow escapes, perilous rescues on tall ladders, and breathless searches through thick, poisonous smoke. In my experience, being a firefighter was as dangerous as putting on your socks with the lights off.

On September 11, twenty-seven years of repressed fear flooded into my head. I see the pictures of the dead firefighters, those dreadful mug shots. Then I see myself, twenty years ago, with a dead father in black and white. I see him in a stairwell as a building rumbles, crumbling with unforgiving force. I can picture the look in his eye. What was it like in those darkened stairwells? What is the last thing you feel: anger, sadness, regret? Do you feel pain? I'd

A Fireman's Son

like to think it was beautiful, like in movies, when the gates open and the light shines in.

Dad's old firehouse lost one member, small by comparison. My dad didn't know the man terribly well, but he went to the wake. He grieved with his old friends. For Christmas, he gave everyone in our family a T-shirt commemorating the man's death. My dad has amassed a pile of these things over the years. All cotton with iron-on letters, a blue collar monument. It's an odd feeling wearing the shirt: *should I sleep in it, work in it, keep it in the drawer?* But wearing it is the idea, I guess, like "We're sorry, buddy, but we'll take you to our bars and our bedrooms and our kids baseball games. Anywhere you want to go."

I've never seen my father cry. Not before September 11, not after. I suppose it's against the firefighter's code. But I'm sure that the tremendous loss burns him deeply. Firefighters are a hardy breed— as best as I can tell, they really believe their work is fairly ordinary. Most days, it probably is, but when the flames are licking at the top of a hundred-story building, they run inside with hard hat and a hose. That kind of bravery—and optimism—astounds me. I think my dad might get that now.

After September 11, I wanted to write a story about firefighters. *A journalist, the son of a firefighter, an editor's dream!* I hoped to find some greater meaning in it all, some consolation for all the death and destruction. But one of the most important lessons I've learned as a journalist is that ambiguity is your friend, and that if you're seeking a definitive answer, you're asking the wrong questions. In reality, I couldn't tell you how I felt about it, let alone distill the emotions of an entire fire department, with their fallen brothers still buried in rubble. I never wrote the story.

I haven't talked much about all this with my dad. I suppose I'm uncomfortable exposing us both to that sort of emotion. I do what I can. Today, he is down with a cold. I go outside and shovel the ice from our driveway as he naps on the couch. *Scrape, scrape, scrape.*

Chipping away at the ice, I look west at a far-off plane leaving a white trail, twin plumes of smoke. I look back at our house, where my dad is stirring.

I went to Ground Zero a couple of weeks ago to shoot some film for a class. Up close, the scene looks harsher, more impersonal. The metal is orange and rusty. The trucks move deliberately, American flags wave in the wind.

The tourists have invaded the area. It's a particularly American scene. Cameras slung around necks, hot dogs in hand, heads covered in FDNY hats. I hate myself for being among such vulgar people. *Get a picture of me and Johnny in front of the worker with the gas mask, honey!* I was no better. I stood there and kept filming, got some good shots.

These are the types of things I think about when I'm there: about the sorry spectacle, the stench of burning flesh, the crushing of bones, the agony. I don't think about Osama bin Laden. I don't think about George Bush. I think about humans blown to bits. I think about the hopelessness of it all.

The world seems so immense to me now, like I'm in kindergarten and running my hands across a spinning globe. For all the bonding against terrorism, I feel more distant from the rest of the world than ever before. Walking through Penn Station to the subway, I am suspicious of everyone, nonchalantly eyeing shopping bags and backpacks. I see National Guardsmen in camouflage, standing next to a man serving popcorn into big paper cones. I feel myself being blown against the wall by an explosion, popcorn, camouflage, and people flying in a concussive burst.

I wonder what we can do stop the death, the bombs, the groups of people stewing in hate. I wonder about the passion and anger it takes to fly a plane into a building. I fight against thinking that we are complicit in this. Were we were content to play deaf while the world barked their vituperations? Whatever the answer, I can't resolve our self-indulgence with the killing of three thousand inno-cent people who were just going about their lives, sitting down to their morning coffee.

The Friday after the attacks, we had a touchy-feely session at school to talk about dealing with trauma victims and how to handle the trauma ourselves. Two hundred aspiring journalists packed into an auditorium at Columbia University. I don't remember anything specific, but I do remember feeling cold, detached.

Through all this crap, I haven't allowed myself to cry. I'm a little uncomfortable about denying myself that great new national pas-time. Truth is, I haven't allowed myself to open that door (*Hello, pain and misery here, anyone home?*). I'm scared about the scars I might discover. Maybe I'll freak out, never to write again. Maybe I won't have all the answers.

Then again, maybe that is the answer.

Creating September 12

By Benjamin Wallace-Wells—*Philadelphia Inquirer*

Television captured the images: planes disappearing into towers, survivors spilling out from under wreckage, firemen racing to the scene. For out-of-town reporters like BENJAMIN WALLACE-WELLS, a metro reporter at the Philadelphia Inquirer, *the challenge of covering terrorism centered on conveying the grief of the survivors. That sense of responsibility drove Wallace-Wells to chronicle Christina Parris's search through the human carnage of the city morgue for an identifiable part of her husband's body. He also told the story of Peter Fink, a lawyer. Caught in a cloud of blinding debris, Fink crashed into a parked car and couldn't tell up from down.*

Wallace-Wells, now twenty-three, was raised in the Inwood and Spuyten Duyvil sections of New York City. A 2000 graduate of Dartmouth College, he had worked at the Inquirer *for only nine months when he was assigned to cover Ground Zero.*

In the middle of the afternoon, September 11, 2001, I cut off my interviews and slipped into a friend's apartment on 19th Street to send my notes back to Philadelphia. I paced around three small, white rooms, chewing on white bread and sipping tap water.

I watched my friend Megan carrying a small glass of water around the apartment with her. Now it was on the coffee table. By the kitchen toaster. Tottering on a bathroom sink. She never took a drink.

I sat down at her laptop. Marveled at how slender it was. Looked through the door—these cushy white rooms splashed with color: discarded parkas, cell phones, suit jackets. I noticed all the inconsequential things.

A small girl I'd never met before came in, a rookie bond trader. She'd heard I was working on a story about the events of the day, and told me a detail I ought to include. Two blocks away, she'd seen eight or nine men standing in a bunch. They'd all watched while another man kicked a big Arab man, again, and again, as he slumped on a stoop. The crowd looked on approvingly. An even mix of blacks and whites, it was a perverse moment of simultaneous racial harmony and antipathy.

"People shouldn't do that," she said, twice. Her voice clicked and stuttered. The day had dried and twisted her vocal chords to the point of nonfunctionality. I pictured the twisted stalk of a squash.

People shouldn't do that. Of course. But when I e-mailed my notes to my editor, I left that story out. No way to verify it, I told myself.

But I had another reason, too. An hour earlier I had walked past the bright-colored awnings of a group of Indian restaurants on Lexington in the East twenties. Pakistani cab drivers, plainly frightened, cowered inside. I imagined charging those men, swinging wildly. Imagined pounding a cabbie's head against his car's bright yellow hood, and scarring his face with my teeth—because I knew of no more violent way to do it.

This was one of the many ways I experienced September 11. And as a journalist, it was one of the ways my readers did, too.

I graduated from Dartmouth College in September, 2000, twenty-one years old, with little to offer beyond a belly full of ambition and the ability to affect a sustained sneer. I had edited a journal in college, the *Dartmouth Review*, for which I had written mostly essays—political, literary, whatever—in which I used someone else's reporting as a jumping-off point, as an excuse to write what I thought about the world.

I took the job as a reporter for the *Philadelphia Inquirer* in January of 2001, equipped, for my first few months, with that same arrogance. I thought of newspaper stories as essays whose subject (and to a certain extent form) was dictated by the news. I thought that if I were smart enough to give some additional context to stories, to understand what was really going on in behind all the official talk and countertalk, I might be able to contribute something worthwhile. I thought I might be able to phrase the terms in which people understood the world, and force readers to consider their own constructs a little more deeply.

My efforts to communicate that sort of deeper understanding from New York were restricted, at least a little bit, by my role: I was a feed-man. There were five or six of us there, depending on the day, and we were each paired with a reporter in Philadelphia. We sent in our quotes, observations, and thoughts about how the articles ought to be directed and they fashioned a story. But early

Creating September 12

in the afternoon on September 11, as I first began to think through the ways in which I might tell the story, I felt the real power of my role. I couldn't write the story, true, but I held the information pursestrings—everything that was going in the story ran through me. By picking which quotes, observations, and details to send in, I could shape the story—I could choose an implicit narrative that, because the writer had little other information to use, could become the explicit narrative. In Megan's apartment that afternoon, feeling like I was watching the city dissolve around me, I was, perversely, excited. Alone among the people I knew in New York, I could do something with all of this. I could take this overwhelming raw mess and wrench it into something you could use to begin understanding.

My notes seemed to form a ready narrative, like liquid taking the shape of its container. That container had three essential phases: shock, bedlam, and surreal calm. In the morning, with lower Manhattan still clotted with victims and ruins, I was in midtown and interviewing anyone I could find. The event seemed far away to people there—a curiosity, a morning's entertainment and conversation piece. There was a man named Peter Taylor, jogging home to make sure his dog had survived the terrorist attacks all right. A Jamaican immigrant named Colin Biglew, working the door at an apartment building, who said the United States, for all its well-muscled international might, had gotten a little too cocky; we were getting our national comeuppance. All the familiar New York cadences, inhabiting the gray area between petty and perverse.

Then as I made my way downtown, I saw the victims walking up Third Avenue, covered in chalky dust, in thick, regular lines, like soldiers in paintings of the revolutionary war. In midtown, the survivors were the only people in the streets who didn't look out-of-their minds frantic. Instead, they just looked dead. By the early afternoon, that distinction would collapse. Everybody in New York would look dead.

But watching the victims move North, I began to understand how huge, exactly, this story was. I began to feel an invigorating pulse in my head: not horror, or despair, but the simple thrilling thought that this was the story of a lifetime, and I was right in the middle of it.

I was, after all, lucky. I didn't have to sit and be shocked. I had to do something.

What I tried to do that day, tried to do each of the days I was in New York, was to produce something worth the depth and fact of the victims' experience. I spent three days beating the city's withered bushes for stories, looking to forge some coherent narrative. To take this ugly, horrific mess of razed buildings and a stunned and cowed eight million-strong city and give readers in Philadelphia something to seize on, a way of understanding how people were experiencing things in New York. To provide an emotional map of the local topography of despair and hope.

By those standards, I spent my three days in New York shipping failures back to Philadelphia.

Stories usually develop in the cadences of punctuated equilibrium: instances of epiphany when your entire conception of the issues and the article changes, in one moment. But there are only a few of these dynamic moments with each story, because they are narrow. At most you're writing about an issue or two, a few characters, providing a little bit of background.

But the story didn't fit these neat journalistic constructs. It was too big and wild-haired, too self-contradictory and too tender to shape into pat dichotomies, conflicts, or policies. And so every narrative I tried to establish, each of the contexts I tried to convey, seemed way too thin to communicate any real sense of the event.

This burden fell a little more heavily on those of us who were writing for readers outside of the New York, New Jersey, and Connecticut area, who hadn't experienced the attack firsthand, who mostly didn't know the dead or the grieving. For media outlets in

Creating September 12

New York, it was enough to be uncensored channels for the phenomenon, to convey the visceral experience of September 11 and its aftermath. For the rest of us, we had to tell a story—how did New York change so much in the space of a single camera frame? How was it refusing to change? Who are the heroes? What is the nature of this heroism? What is the nature of villainy? While I tried to answer these questions, the people I talked to in New York were struggling with the same questions, but not just on paper. They were living it.

But we tried. I tried. I went back to my friend's apartment, looked back at this colossal mess of reportage and tried to come up with something to do about it.

On September 11, I sent back a narrative saturated with the concept of bedlam—the manic, confused energy of the morning and the odd ways in which that settled down in the afternoon.

The most powerful image that first day was something a man named Steven Fink told me, a lawyer from Long Island whom I ran into just south of Union Square. He was covered in chalky dust and he was stopping people on the street to tell them what he had seen, heard, felt. Volunteering intimacy.

"I saw the first tower begin to collapse, and I started to run. I looked back, within two, three seconds the smoke was completely engulfing me. It wasn't like a smoke you get from a bonfire. It was so thick, so dark, so black, you literally couldn't see as far as the tip of your nose. It was like someone had duct taped your eyes shut.

"So people started panicking, and running. But you didn't know what was going on, you didn't know where anything was coming from. You didn't know where danger was, you didn't know where safety was. And you also couldn't see more than an inch or two in front of your face. So people were running into buildings, running into each other, running into cars. The drivers were trying to get out of there too, so some of them were still driving. I was lucky. I just ran into a parked car. At least I think it was parked."

Steven Fink kept using the word "bedlam." He meant, quite literally, that no one knew which way was up.

While I had been making my way to Steven Fink, interviewing people I ran into, I saw this unimaginable chaos, translated north.

The police had been routed to deal with the collapse, and in the early afternoon, traffic was being conducted by gray-shirted cadets from the New York Police Academy and men and women in light blue shirts and pinnies, from the Police Auxiliary. At 34th and Third I had seen cars and trucks ignoring their commands, refusing to turn when told and clogging up intersections. Ambulances blew their horns impotently, stuck in midtown traffic. Crowds crossed the streets, making it nearly impossible for any vehicles or rescue workers to get through. The officers blew their whistles, adding to the general noise.

And I had talked to people who had been down at the World Trade Center, whose experiences echoed Fink's.

Parts of the story were so ugly you wished they had just been borrowed from fiction.

"There were people jumping out of the windows. I didn't want to look. I knew the bodies were going to be piling up, and I didn't want to look." This from Marjorie Cano, who worked as a sales assistant three blocks away.

Some did look.

"I saw the plane crash, and I knew I didn't have very long until everything started falling down," said Brian Kelly, who worked as an investment banker in the World Financial Center, for CIBC Oppenheimer. "I ran outside and dove between this car and the building. I could see people get hit by falling debris, falling beams. I saw people getting their heads split open. I saw people getting their backs crushed."

But the South part of Manhattan Island wasn't a simple zone of bedlam. Some parts were perversely functional, perversely calm.

"What was crazy was that we saw the first building at the World

Creating September 12

Trade Center go up in smoke, and we didn't really know what to do," said Megan Cummins, a twenty-three-year old trader at the Lehman Brothers offices at 3 World Financial Center. "Then they came on the intercom and told us to stay put. They said it wouldn't affect us at all. And people were walking around telling each other it was going to be OK, and it seemed surreal. It didn't seem like it was really happening. The phone rang, and I could see this enormous fireball, but I was thinking, should I take this call, should I make this trade? The attitude was like business will go on. Then I called my boyfriend in Providence and he was watching on CNN, and he said, another plane just hit the second building, get out of there. Everybody pretty much left at the same time, but it was eerie. Everybody was very polite, and moving quietly out of the door. Then when we were outside we literally saw the World Trade Center collapse, and it looked like it was coming right at us. Everyone I know got out in time, but if anyone was paying attention to the intercom, maybe they wouldn't have."

She paused.

"I saw people jumping off the World Trade Center, off of the highest places. There was debris falling too, and if you watched the debris it seemed to float in the air. The people didn't seem to float. They just dropped, much more heavily."

I sent all of this, and I also sent back some details of a walk I took after six o'clock, when it was still warm and light out and my notes were safely stored in a Philadelphia mainframe and it seemed plausible, in some corners of Manhattan, that nothing out of the ordinary had happened.

The cars were all off the streets by 7 P.M. Though I could always hear a siren going, somewhere in the distance, the streets I was walking along were very quiet. In Washington Square Park I counted nine couples walking, arm in arm. I saw a really remarkable number of people walking their dogs. Two dealers offered me drugs: "Smokes, my man, smokes?" The familiar seedy cadences. Business as usual.

I walked along Astor Place, and a man walked past me, talking to himself: "McDonald's is south," he muttered.

At the time, that seemed to me as emblematic of the afternoon as Steven Fink's blind ash storm was emblematic of the morning. New York City, however disoriented and distraught, was trying to find a new normality in all of this. McDonald's, thankfully, was still south.

I walked further. People crowded along Canal, Franklin, Leonard Streets, where the police had established a perimeter with a long, single line of metal barriers.

I saw a camouflaged Humvee driving along 23rd Street, carrying soldiers in fatigues. No one blinked. I saw a long line of fire trucks drive in along Canal, with emblems of suburban companies—Setauket, Centerreach. Two young men walked out into the middle of the street to photograph them. A hefty battalion of police and court officers gave directions. Crowds were moving quietly and efficiently, moving on.

I sent these impressions, observations, and reactions back to Philadelphia. Fused with the thoughts and ideas of editors, they made their way into print. I had constructed a neat day: the chaotic morning dissipating into the afternoon's surreal calm, with people struggling to find some way to live normally again while their city bore all the marks of an occupying force. And I had constructed this day through the eyes of people who had experienced it.

I had made a series of calls back to Philadelphia, one from the back room of a closed Häagen-Dazs, and had been shuffled from one person to another—writers, editors.

What was I supposed to be doing, I asked Bettinita Harris, Diane Mastrull, Mike Topel, Ralph Vigoda—as if they had a template. Details, they said. The wires are drowning in information. Get us a few images that will really stick.

But I wanted to do a little more than that. If what the paper was trying to do, at least in part, was convey a sense of what was really going on in New York, then I knew—me, and not Ralph or Diane or Bettinita or Mike. So when I sent my feeds back to Philadelphia, I didn't just try for those gold-ring images. I tried also to frame a range of reactions, thoughts, and emotions.

But I missed a lot, too. In trying to extract some coherent narrative, and in sticking, for quotes, to the articulate few, I think I missed the way most of the city experienced it: with a subarticulate array of powerful emotions, with a sense of an unprecedented event that was no more fully formed than a red blinking light in their heads.

I spent much of the next morning seeking some volunteered metaphor: I asked people what it was like to be there, what did it sound like, what did it smell like, what did it look like?

But originality failed my sources. To a person, they responded in terms of seen-on-screen fantasies: *What did it look like?*

You know the movie *Independence Day?* It looked like that.
What did it feel like?

The footage from war-torn countries? Bosnia. It feels like that.

I e-mailed these quotes in but I missed the confusion that produced them. It didn't look *like* anything. What kind of metaphor do you use to describe hell? It's like itself.

Reporters are taught to seek out the human side of stories, to find how ordinary people are coping with enormous events, to find details that confirm that what matters is not what happens to us but how we deal with it. To seek out the lyrical orchid at the city dump. But in this story the orchids mattered less than the dump around them.

Even so we look for the firefighters. We talk about how people give at least the appearance of normality. We seek isolated expressions of courage, of bravery, of personal nobility and human-sized tragedy.

I gave the story a brain and missed a big part of its belly. Television did a better job not only of conveying what it was like to be at

Ground Zero but duplicating the experience. That clip of the second plane crashing into its appointed tower, the subsequent fireball progressing through one floor, looped over and over, made my narratives and thematic shifts of the day feel limp, shallow, and not too meaningful.

I had been at Newport with my girlfriend Suzanne the weekend of September 8, sick of work after a sweaty summer and set to gorge myself on feel. We listened happily to bad music played live, tromped through those gilded nineteenth-century mansions, and walked along cliffs watching the sea. Then, on the afternoon of September 10, we drove back to New York. I slept at her place on 66th Street Monday night, and had just left to go back to Philadelphia when the planes hit.

So I was still wearing flip-flops and beach shorts when Mohammed Atta et al., dressed far more gravely, crashed the planes into the towers, and I wore those silly clothes the whole day. I walked thirteen miles. By the end of the day, I had big blisters all over my feet—fat red discs of open skin. On Tuesday night, after that awful day, neither Suzanne nor I could sleep, so, too freaked out to even kiss, we just lay there parallel in bed, staring silently at the dark ceiling. I slept, eventually, but when I did it was fitfully. I believed, absolutely, that I would quit journalism as soon as I was done with this story. Go to law school or something. I was dogged by the idea that I was here, faced with the story of a lifetime, and I was somehow not communicating it fully enough. I was seriously fucking it up.

When I woke up on September 12, I was determined to do better. To get closer to some fundamental truth about the event, to convey how New Yorkers were really experiencing all of this. Nearly everyone I ran into on September 11 already knew of someone they knew who had perished, and I wanted to write that story. How was the city of New York finding itself, at a moment when it was at once loving more intensely than it ever had, and missing so many thousands of people it had loved.

September 11, freakily enough, was something we'd all seen before—in *Independence Day*, in the footage from Bosnia. But those stories always moved rapidly on, and away. To a fictional Oval Office, or to a real-life tribunal. This was one story that stayed, and so we had the chance to cover what felt like new ground. We might be able to write about the ways real people reacted when thrown into the most awful fantasy. We had the chance to create September 12.

I called Mike Topel, who had settled in at the national desk amid a nervous flurry of editorial assistants, at eight that morning. They'd managed to get a couple more reporters across the Hudson early that morning, he told me, and now my reporting could be a little more particular and directed. Everything I'd turned in the previous day, he'd told me, had been used—the wires were demanding quotes, and so even what the *Inquirer*'s reporters didn't use got sent out to papers around America.

Today, we decided, I should go to Bellevue, where they'd set up a registry for relatives and friends of the missing to come in and add names to the awful, morbid list that was accumulating. I was to record the stories of missing friends, lovers, brothers, and sisters.

Most other news organizations in America seemed to have more or less the same idea. When I got to Bellevue's gates, it was covered with cameras and microphones as thickly as the Eagles' locker room after a loss. The reporters seemed to outnumber the subjects.

This was from Christina Paris.

"My husband is George Paris. He works for Cantor Fitzgerald on the 101st floor in World Trade Center One.

"When I saw the reports on TV, I was just in shock. I was just hoping he'd got down the stairs. I don't think I had a single other thought, or emotion.

"I'm hopeful. I've heard that they're still finding bodies, alive bodies, people who got buried under the wreckage and are still alive. I've also heard of people who were very high up, some higher than him even, who are still alive. It's easy to get discouraged but I'm hopeful.

"We only got married in June. This is crazy. We were happy newlyweds.

"I want to get a sense of closure. Even if the news is bad, I want to know. I've been asking people at the hospital if they have any unidentified bodies. I want to go through and see if he's among them."

The image of this wife from Queens picking through hundreds of shards of bodies, looking for a recognizable fragment: a nose perhaps, or the way an elbow connected to an arm, stayed with me for a very long time.

This was from a man named Parkinson Small, who had incredibly precise diction, considering the circumstances. His girlfriend ("What I regret most is I had one thing I wanted to ask her, but I never got around to") was probably dead.

"I didn't know at first that she was in the World Trade Center that day. But then calls kept coming in. Throughout the day I kept trying to contact her on her cell phone, and I kept not being able to. The anxiety was just building.

"We've been going through these radical ups and downs. One minute you're sure she's all right, she's somewhere else. The next you're absolutely resigned to losing her. And there's no more reason to believe one than the other.

"I'm tired of waiting, either way. It's not someone coming home two hours late. It's knowing they may never come home again.

"It's kind of nice being out here, actually. It's kind of like collective sharing of the pain, and the experience. When I was staying in the house, it was just getting oppressive, making me feel so closed off. I had to get out here."

I interviewed dozens of these people; got rejected by dozens more.

On September 11 the city's mood and the ways in which the city was understanding what had happened to it had seemed remarkably

Creating September 12

fluid, journalistic ground for the staking. It seemed possible that someone could say something that no one else had.

On September 12 I had lost this sense of originality. As dramatic as these stories were, they seemed already to fit into patterns. There was a certain set of feelings expressed by people who had lost loved ones. There was another meta-narrative used by people who were at the registry to look for victims who had only been distant friends. Rescue workers had certain stock phrases. Ditto for the thousands of people who lined up to donate blood. I felt like I was living a TV news program, cycling through the most obvious, pat reactions, devoid of context or contradiction.

These narratives were already being expressed. On the news programs that looped constantly between the same four relevant sites in New York. On the newswires, happily buzzing with stories. On the radio stations.

It was impossible that everyone had experienced those twenty-four hours in such similar ways. There had to be something different and new to say about all this. Some things that people were going through, that weren't yet being said. I simply wasn't finding them.

So as the first day's bedlam began to settle, I was taking part in something that was resembling a morality tale, a public narrative of people overcoming, of those orchids popping through the debris.

I saw dozens of businesses with OPEN signs, amended in black Magic Marker: "Like New York, We Will Not Be Intimidated!"

The grand narrative had its appointed heroes: the firemen, the rescue workers, the blood givers.

It also had its villains: a vaguely appointed band of rogues, probably based somewhere slightly west of Jerusalem.

Nearly everyone I talked to that second day, no matter how potent their personal grief, wanted to weigh in on these heroes and villains, let me know what they thought of it all.

This from Michelangelo Reyes, a surgical technologist in

Bellevue who had spent the night waiting for patients who never arrived:

"What I can't understand about this whole thing is how heartless whoever did this was. How cruel. To want to kill so many innocent people, just kill them. How could you do that? It's not human. How could you do a thing like that?"

This from Michelle Ticknor, a twenty-eight-year old artist manager who was donating blood:

"I can't say enough about the firefighters, the rescue workers. The heart they're showing. It really made me think that maybe we could do something about all this, that we could fight back, a little bit."

And from Parkinson Small:

"What really got to me was those shots on CNN of those people in Palestine cheering the news. Did you see that? That was so inhuman. How could you cheer something like this, all this suffering? That really got to me. That really got to me."

On Tuesday afternoon, I had run into a man named Shlomo Mantz, a thirty-two-year-old paralegal carrying a sign on which he'd written: "*Hundreds are Hurt!* " The sign went on to advise that concerned citizens contact their representatives in Washington, to urge them to "fight terrorism." Mantz told me he was originally from Philadelphia, and considers himself a Zionist.

"I've been walking around the city, and I've seen people looking incredibly lackadaisical, nonchalant," Mantz said. "I wanted to remind everyone what happened here today, to make immediate, to make it something they couldn't avoid."

But I didn't send much of what Mantz said back to Philadelphia. Reporters get all sorts of extraneous junk. Interview schoolteachers about a new social studies program and end up hearing about the tyranny of standardized tests. Talk to locals about the Amish community in their town, and suddenly you're in a conversation about the disincentives the Pennsylvania tax code gives to small business owners to expand. The world is full of closet theorists, amateur

Creating September 12

wonks, and information hounds. More often than not, a reporter's job is to listen patiently, ignore opinions, and focus on the subject's own experience.

But this story was different. Because that endless theorizing and politicizing was really an attempt to find some heroes and villains, and the attempt to find heroes and villains was really about finding meaning in unprecedented disorder. When I tried to sanitize the story, to expunge opinion in favor of experience, I missed a crucial part of the way people struggled through the event.

But the assigning of heroism and villainy had become public domain—we had the firefighters on television, the long lines of blood givers, the politicos coming and going on the cable channels, talking of Bin Laden and "evildoers." Critics charged that the overwhelming real-time weight of that communicated narrative obscured important parts of the story.

People like twenty-four-year-old Michael Cartier, who had walked over the Queensboro Bridge from Jackson Heights, looking for some evidence of his brother.

"I turn on the TV and all I see is you guys talking about the firefighters and the EMS workers and the policemen. Well what about the victims? What about the victims' families?

"My brother James was working on the high floors of the World Trade Center. We talked to him on his cell phone right after the first explosion hit, and we haven't heard from him since. We call the numbers they tell you to call, and all we get are busy signals.

"We've walked over the 59th Street Bridge five times now, come into the city to try to find him. And no one can tell us anything. Nobody knows what's going on. All we hear about is the firemen, and the policemen. What about us?"

And when I looked around, I had to agree. It wasn't as if the victims' families were being undercovered, exactly, but it did feel like the media had become Rudy Giuliani's personal PR machine. Rather than strictly reporting what happened, we were making ourselves useful as a sort of psychological buttress, overreporting the stories of the valiant firefighters and tireless mayors to reassure a shaky nation that everything would turn out all right.

At two in the afternoon, I was outside Bellevue speaking with doctors and people who had lost their family members, a security guard, acting a little self-important, invited me to a press conference inside.

The press conference turned out to be given by George Pataki, the Governor of New York. At 6'5", he's a really big, energetic man, but he looked worn and slumped at the podium and his voice barely qualified as a whisper. The cameramen yelled at him to speak up, he apologized quickly, and made his voice a little louder.

"That long line of people around Cabrini [Medical Center] waiting to donate blood says more about New York than any bomb."

Perhaps it did. But for all the public good of blood donation, some people I talked to knew better: most of it was not for the victims.

"We had four people stay overnight with us in the OR," said Reyes, the surgical technician at Bellevue. "I was expecting hundreds, maybe thousands. This is the city's main trauma center. You know what that tells me? That tells me they're all dead."

And that was probably the most powerful narrative that emerged, on Wednesday, September 12, the oppressively grim understanding of exactly how many people had been killed.

The sheer size of the event should have prompted me to report it in a different way. What was relevant about this story weren't the dramatic personal anecdotes, the ones that departed from the norm, but the ones that articulated the norms. I spent the day resenting my own notes for their eternal repetition. But the pat narratives into which everybody seemed to be lapsing were not made derivative by their universality but were redeemed by it. I spent these days looking for the story that would shock *Inquirer* readers. I wanted to give them something different and better than what they saw on the Web, or local channel 3, 6, or 10. But the conventional story was the

Creating September 12

better one—the more derivative, the more worthwhile. The very fact of its repetition affirmed its validity.

I consider myself a New Yorker, adamantly. I was born here, grew up in Inwood and the Bronx until I went to college in 1996. Most of my friends moved back here after graduation, and I knew people who had died in the World Trade Center. I also knew people who had worked in those towers and survived. Some of my best friends lived in Battery Park City, and had been forced out by the dust and the stench. They were scattered around the city, crashing on friendly couches. A week earlier we had gone up onto the roof of a friend's Chambers Street apartment, taken in the matchless view of lower Manhattan, the Hudson, and Jersey City. From our angle there, my girlfriend pointed out, you could only see one of the World Trade's Center's towers: it blocked out its twin.

My girlfriend lived on East 66th Street, my parents lived in the Bronx. So every night, after spending twelve hours reporting the story, I went home and lived it. I'm not sure which experience was more wearing.

We went out to dinner with friends every night, and though we were worn, we went out for drinks afterward. Nobody wanted to go home alone. We ate at bad, crowded Mexican restaurants with overburdened waitstaffs. Went to dark, slimy bars that ought to have been playing lousy music, but lacked the energy. And though these places all looked full—crowded with bankers and consultants, thin-shouldered men wearing white shirts and dark ties—there was none of the city's usual boisterous rumble. The social city felt muted and unsteady. No one laughed. People didn't talk to strangers in the bars, just themselves. Mostly we talked about what we'd seen on TV that day.

I saw my father. He worked three blocks from the World Trade Center, a fact that hadn't occurred to me until about six hours after the attacks. He said he was the guy in his office who told everyone to go back to work, there was nothing to see. We shared a grim little chuckle.

On Wednesday night, though, my girlfriend and I finally shut off the television. We shut off the radio. Stopped talking about the news, the survivors I'd seen. For an evening, we managed to forget.

If I had woken up on Wednesday morning with a heady sense of purpose—that I was going to find something raw and real—I woke up on Thursday feeling decidedly more worn, and less directed. The editors sounded pleased over the phone—"This is going to get you a fantastic next job," Mike Topel told me. I wasn't so sure about the quality. Mostly I just wanted to do my job.

I spent Thursday working on a story around Canal Street, where police barricades blocked everyone without local addresses. My assignment was to identify the ways in which life was and was not getting back to normal in New York. I was advised to think about the particular groups of people who could return to ordinary life and those who could not.

So I tried to find small stories of recovered normality.

"Last night I finally had to turn off my television," said Jens Lund, a twenty-seven-year-old bartender from Copenhagen who lives on Thompson Street. "I shut off the radio, too, and just put on some music. You have to get away. If you just sit there watching television, you go crazy."

Bill Holahan lives in Brooklyn Heights, right across the East River from the World Trade Center.

"For two days I sat at my window with the television on and watched this huge, dark cloud of smoke, the debris, drifting up the river, drifting down the river," he told me. "Today I watched it evaporate, up and away. It felt like this city's soul had been released."

I interviewed Cornelia Schall, a documentary producer originally from Germany, in a playground, where she was watching her children play.

Creating September 12

"For a while it felt like you couldn't get away from it. Because it's all everyone's thinking about, all everyone's talking about, so you have to talk about it. But at some point—and for me, I think it happened yesterday—you realize that the kids have to be fed. The kids have to be clothed. And that sort of brings you back to life. There are all the little things that always need doing, and maybe having kids makes you realize it faster, but I think everyone is starting to realize this—these things still need to be done."

What I saw bore out what these people said.

Schools were open. So were theaters, bars, and restaurants. I walked by a yoga class at West 16th Street. When I walked along the East River esplanade in the evening, it was clotted thick with joggers in their regular running gear.

The New York families I spoke with on Wednesday felt as if they literally could not wrench themselves away from the tragedy. They spent their days walking through damaged streets, and their nights riveted to televisions showing shots of those same streets, talking to friends who could think of nothing else. Now, they were forcing themselves to look away.

But there were some who couldn't avert their eyes so easily, some whose small narratives of recovered normality were set against a backdrop of absurdly grand aberration. I tracked down those people, too.

People like Susan Kramer, whose dining room windows faced the physical truth of that monstrosity.

"I look at the Twin Towers every day," Kramer said. "I don't think, after this, I'll be able to look downtown again without thinking of this."

People like Syed Huda, who was going through a period of sustained emotional trauma.

"It's the first day of school and I took my son in and I'm waiting for him the whole day [outside the school]," Huda said to me.

"It's not a normal day. I'm scared. Being Muslims, we are victims twice. We were victims of the attack, too. And now we are victims again. We get threatening phone calls from people, telling us they will kill us. We called the police and they said they had been dealing with complaints like ours all day. My wife wears the traditional dress, and she is very visibly Muslim. She has not left the house, because we are very afraid of what might happen to her. It is not right that we have to live like this. I sleep maybe five, ten minutes, then I get up again. I can't sleep through the night. My son is eleven and he is sleeping in the room with my wife and me. I went out once yesterday, once today. My wife does not go out at all. I don't know when life will return to normal again. When the World Trade Center was bombed in '93, it took a very long time."

Maybe what I sent in on Thursday—this simple story of the people who were getting back to normal again and the people who couldn't—was a little pat, a little easy. But that was fine by me. Like the rest of the city, I was really tired.

Late that night, after I got off of work, I walked down Sutton Place, a quiet street cushy with wealth. There's a landing at the base of the street with a small park, where you can step up to a rail that overlooks the East River. There was a helicopter flying loud circles over lower Manhattan, spraying the area with a searchlight. I saw lights from police cars flashing on Roosevelt Island, in the middle of the waterway. I heard sirens from a long line of police cars and motorcycles racing down the East River drive.

Three men stood next to me on that landing on Thursday night, with cameras. They took photos of the helicopters, of the motorcycles, of the police cars. But they also took photographs of things that, out of the context of this week's events, would have looked very mundane. Bridges and apartment buildings that were standing untouched. People sitting in the park. The dips and heaves of the current.

I understood why. New York had changed forever. So what remained of the old New York, the permanent New York, felt more valuable than ever.

Creating September 12

They told me on Thursday night that the shift was changing. Six new reporters would move into New York on Friday morning to take our spots. But the editors didn't demand that I report back to Philadelphia immediately. "Stay loose, Ben," Bettinita Harris said. "Take some time off."

That weekend, we went away. We got together a dozen or so friends and met at Suzanne's family's house in Connecticut. Got obliteratingly drunk, over and over again. Swam naked in the pool at midnight. Laughed. Tried to find some romance in our own emotional desperation. Succeeded only in getting some physical distance from New York.

On Monday I drove back to Philadelphia, and for the first time felt the familiar, giddy bubbling of ambition and pride in my veins, the sense that I had done something worthwhile.

And if I failed at finding some coherent narrative, maybe that was OK. Maybe what was important was not what I produced but simply that I was there at all.

I also began to feel incredibly fortunate. How could I have experienced this all if I had to stay in Philadelphia, unable to get through the clogged phone lines, forced to sleep each night alone in my bedroom in Manayunk?

When things settled down, when I forced myself back into the routines of my job, going to the school board meetings and sorting through story tips from wackos, I came down from that high, began to think of my time in New York in more muted tones.

I hadn't made an unqualified success of it. The job, after all, was not just to print quotes and details but to tell a story, and all the stories I tried to tell were too thin in some way, or too derivative or too played out. But it hadn't been a total bust either. The quotes and details I'd gotten were pretty good, even if context and structure were hard to come by.

But when I'd been successful it hadn't been because of my brain, hadn't been because of any context or sneer or order I'd imposed. It had been because I'd trusted myself to simply listen. "A reporter's first act has to be one of sympathy," Phillip Dixon, then the *Inquirer's* managing editor, told me once. When I'd been successful, it had been.

As I was trying to put this essay together, in early January, I was driving back from a reporting jaunt in Chester County, Pennsylvania, listening to WMMR—where radio Means More Rock. A fellow called up, and said he'd read a newspaper article about a song Neil Young had written commemorating the heroes of Flight 93, the plane that crashed in a field in western Pennsylvania sometime around the moment I was talking to Steven Fink, on 19th Street. The song was called "Let's Roll," which is what a passenger said to an AirFon operator, just before he burst into the cockpit with other passengers, forcibly downing the plane.

The DJ played "Let's Roll." It was really terrible. But after the song ended he said: "That was the flight which some people say would have crashed into the Capital, or the White House. Can you imagine what would have happened then?"

I lost it. Pulled over to the side of the road, on Darlington Street in West Chester, PA, and for the first time I flat-out sobbed. That weird half crying where your torso shakes and you can taste the salt of the tears in your mouth and feel them tingling in your eyes but they're not big or numerous enough to tumble out of your ducts, down your cheeks. Maybe I sobbed because I could imagine, more or less exactly, what would have happened if that plane had hit the Capital. Because I had seen something very much like it, up close.

I have had a much more difficult time writing this essay than I thought I would. The problem isn't only that I've been emotionally overwhelmed by memories of September 11, 12, and 13. The bigger problem has been that in the face of all this material, it's hard to know what to say. Criticizing and blaming seems not only crass but irrelevant. My problem was sort of like Neil Young's: you want very

Creating September 12

badly to say something wise and piercing, but you fall pretty quickly into platitudes.

But beyond the platitudes, I am left with one of journalism's real gifts: the privilege of experience. I saw it all, for three days. My memories don't need to rely on someone else's observation, analysis, metaphor. In just about every relevant way, I was there.

Out of the Blue

By Alexander Epstein—*Stuyvesant Standard*

Reporting for a high school paper often means aggressively pursuing every nugget of news. On September 11, Stuyvesant Standard *reporter ALEXANDER EPSTEIN, seventeen, watched the biggest story of his lifetime unfold from the eighth floor window of Stuyvesant High School, just blocks away from the World Trade Center. The budding journalist urged his peers to stay away from windows and prayed for his family members, some of whom worked near the towers. Thousands of students eventually evacuated the school as lights flickered and adult supervision dissipated. It would be a month before the student body returned and the* Standard *resumed publication. In the meantime, Epstein recorded his experiences here with the eyes of a reporter, witness, and survivor.*

Epstein, a senior, is opinions editor for the Stuyvesant Standard, *where he has written about the 2001 mayoral campaign and the Florida teenager who flew a plane into a Tampa skyscraper. He has also written columns for the* Spectator, *another Stuyvesant paper. A Midwood, Brooklyn native, Epstein's Russian-American parents moved to the suburbs of Long Island when he was four. In 1996 his family returned to Brooklyn to live in Bay Ridge, where they remain.*

At 8:30 A.M. on Tuesday, September 11, 2001, I was looking forward to several developments in New York City politics, particularly the Democratic mayoral primary. The big question was "Who will face off against Mike Bloomberg in the race for City Hall?" This was an electoral crossroads that could decide the fate of Republican candidate Bloomberg, whom I supported. In fact, I had just enthusiastically backed him as the opinions editor of the *Stuyvesant Standard*, one of Stuyvesant High School's newspapers. Since Stuyvesant students often lean left, I wondered how my peers would receive this endorsement. Although Bloomberg, a former Democrat, was arguably not far to the right of his opponent, Mark Green, it is surprising how many Stuy students flinch from the mention of "Republican." I do not consider myself staunchly Republican either. However, I am often confounded by the logic of liberals and by the decidedly utopian sentiments of their adolescent supporters.

The day promised to be fairly humdrum, even forgettable. Sitting in a first-row seat in room 829 and listening to a typical research physics lesson, I was jotting down notes and looking forward to my new classes. I had been grappling with the program office for three days to eliminate a pair of blank periods in my daily schedule. The efforts had paid off, and the useless ninety-minute gap would not plague my semester with intolerably long school-days. Maybe when I'm older and working overtime, an 8:00 to 3:40 day will become the nostalgic highlight of my bygone high school era, but now it was simply a pain. For students looking out from the lecture-style eighth-floor physics room, the cloudless sky was a brilliant azure, and four blocks away the Twin Towers of the World Trade Center dominated the urban horizon.

At 8:45, I heard the rumble of a jet passing nearby. Then came a single, deafening boom. Car alarms were triggered, and I felt the school tremble; my pen rolled back and forth haphazardly across my desk. Peering out the window, I didn't see anything unusual—the top shades were lowered, blocking my view of the top of the towers.

"A sonic boom?" I suggested. My friend Arcady, sitting at the next desk and immersed in his Palm Pilot, disagreed, pointing out that we heard the plane before the boom. Furthermore, planes are prohibited from flying at supersonic speeds over the city.

"Maybe a plane crashed into a building," I theorized.

"Ladies and gentlemen," Mr. Blaufarb, the assistant principal, solemnly reported over the PA, "at 8:45 this morning, a light plane crashed into the World Trade Center." We rushed toward the windows. The teacher stopped midsentence, and I felt goose bumps. My erstwhile joke had been realized on an unimaginable scale.

My classmates climbed onto the radiators, pulling up the shades to reveal a vista straight out of an action movie. Outside, a cavalcade of fire engines raced toward the World Trade Center, like red blood cells streaming through an artery. This was no "light plane." A two-hundred-foot crater billowed noxious smoke from the top floors of Tower One. Nonetheless, we tacitly understood this to be a mishap caused by some extraordinary technical fault. *What else could it be?*

At a few minutes past 9 A.M. I heard another explosion, though fainter. Immediately, large metallic pieces rained down from two-thirds of the way up Tower Two; then more plumes of smoke. Two airplanes had now crashed into adjacent buildings, within fifteen minutes of each other, on a clear autumn day. *Now this was suspicious*—and I was running out of excuses. We set the classroom

Out of the Blue

television (there's a wall-mounted TV in each Stuy classroom) to NY1, the local news channel, to see what the hell was going on. They showed the footage of the second explosion, shot from afar; then they zoomed in to show the massive fireball up close. "Oh my God!" became the phrase of the day. Our jaws dropped to the floor when the commentator reported that the planes had exhibited "deliberate behavior" and reeked of terrorism. The Metropolitan Transportation Authority had shut down buses and subways. The city had closed all river crossings. Stuyvesant students had become sitting ducks.

Toward the end of the second period I set out to find the best vantage point in the building: the tenth floor. It was breathtaking, to say the least, gazing down West Street from the drafting room. *If I only had my camera...* At this time, my sense of duty to the *Standard* competed with a far more important consideration, as a suddenly sensible question occurred to me: if the towers toppled, would they reach Stuyvesant? The *Standard* would not cross my mind again for hours. I eyeballed the angle of elevation to the World Trade Center to come up with a hasty trigonometric estimate, but before I could finish my calculation, a teacher directed me to leave. (Incidentally, the North Tower would have fallen at least two-hundred feet short of the school if it had fallen over on its side, and would have almost certainly broken into parts before it reached us, anyway).

In American History, Mr. Sandler hesitantly offered a lesson before gathering from our countenances that we were disoriented to the point of distraction. We tried to turn on the television, but there was no reception. As I sat there, in the second-floor classroom, I listened for clues in the dialogues around me. I also noticed that electric clocks don't "tick." Some students claimed to have seen people falling from the towers; I was relieved to have been spared that sight. Random and unrelated thoughts floated through my mind, and my anxiety plateaued.

Ten A.M. was hardly the time to relax. The lights in the room flickered forebodingly, and a deathly silence overcame the class.

"Look!" one student in the back screamed, pointing outside the window. We all faced south, like sunflowers, and beheld an irregular darkness composed of specter-like shadows descending heavily through the growing cloud of ash and smoke. Dozens of flashing fire engines, not to mention the pedestrian bridge linking the World Trade and World Financial Centers, were in the path of this inexorable darkness tumbling down like a firework. *What had fallen?* I couldn't imagine that the tower had collapsed, and some suggested that different parts—that is, the top or the side—of the building had come down. Meanwhile, semi-intelligible announcements made over the PA proved less than enlightening. I gathered that the administration was convening in the conference room, presumably to come up with a "plan."

The collapse forced me to gather my wits. I warned the teacher—long before the principal did—that we should stay away from the windows. As a precaution, I slipped out of the room and stood in the hallway. Students everywhere consoled and embraced each other, while others wept alone. I dared not ask why. The atmosphere began to unsettle me, too. *Was my family affected?* That's when it struck me that my brother Eric, an architect at Gruzen Samton, 90 West Street, was even closer to the World Trade Center than I. *Was Eric in the office? Was he alive?* These questions aggravated me. I prayed—it was all I could do.

Homeroom began, so I walked up to room 427. With some difficulty, Mr. Lostal took attendance above the din. I fiddled with the TV but couldn't get any signal. I don't remember what anyone said to me, but I do remember the homeroom teacher, Mr. Lostal (with his distinctive Majorcan accent), the loudspeaker, and I importuning everyone to get away from the windows—this room was on the south side, just like the first two. At this point, everyone with cell phones, including Mr. Lostal, found that they could not get dial tones. We were trapped in Manhattan, and couldn't even communicate! Announcements on the PA reassured us that "the building is the safest place to be right now." Ominously, a list of names was read. I assumed the worst—that the relatives of victims were being listed—and took heed of every name. After what seemed an eternity the speaker revealed that the names referred to unaccounted-for pupils. At 10:20 the principal informed us that homeroom was "extended indefinitely." So much for my new schedule—and perhaps for so much more.

While others in the room stubbornly stood near the windows and gazed outside, I remained on the interior, near the doors, in case something flew in. *What were they thinking?* If any debris came hurtling toward the school, at least there was a chance I could flee to the inner hallways. In the past, whether it was climbing Breakneck Ridge or preparing a term paper, I had always found careful planning to be critical. Accordingly, I now visualized the school building in my mind, searching my mental blueprint for the safest nook. The second and third floors, situated in the widest part of the building and farthest from outside walls, seemed to promise the most protection. But my effort became moot when the administration ordered an evacuation. After a few organizational glitches, we entered the west staircase. The elevators and escalators had stopped running after the power disruption.

On the next-to-last flight of crowded stairs down to the first floor, it happened again, at about 10:30. The lights dimmed and flickered warningly. I told those around me that the second tower must have fallen, but they were too numbed to listen. The floor rumbled briefly, as if in confirmation. Indeed, this flickering system was beginning to resemble a terrestrial thunderstorm, where the flickering corresponded to lightning bolts, and was followed by thunderous tremors.

Unlike the fire drills of the past, this real evacuation was neither calm nor organized. Instead of leaving through different exits, all thirty-five hundred of us funneled out a single passage. And before that came the main lobby, perhaps the scariest moment of the entire morning. Looking at the seldom-used north exit, I saw daylight. Glancing back, I saw the grand Chambers Street entrance and the mezzanine windows and only darkness beyond. The stately, marble-clad lobby, carved out between the theater, swimming pool, and the Chambers Street entrance hall, became murkier still. Police and firefighters goaded us on, further crowding the lobby, which was already packed in sardine fashion. (Normally, this vast vestibule on the first floor is quite empty; sometimes a couple of students can be seen there after school practicing dances). About five to ten minutes later, I passed Mr. Blaufarb, who was shouting something along the lines of, "Walk up West to Canal Street!" By then, I had found, and soon lost, many familiar faces in the stagnant river of students.

I passed the bottleneck of the exodus at around 10:45. Here rescue workers with stretchers cut through the swarm, and I got my first hint of the deathly stench that would plague the city long afterward. On my left was the familiar West Side Bikeway, now our avenue of escape. On the right was the towering blur of ash, smoke, and asbestos—or worse—emanating from the site where the World Trade Center had stood just minutes ago.

After starting up the riverside path, many of us glancing back every several steps, our journeys homeward diverged—just as they would on any other short school day. But now, no matter where we went, everyone was going to take a good hike. Well, maybe not *everyone*. As I marched north, I noticed that very few teachers were visible. I tried walking slower, only passing a few more, none accompanying students. *Where were the teachers, counselors, or administrators who were supposed to lead us to safety?* In the subsequent months, I informally interviewed several Stuyvesant teachers about 9/11, and found that they also noticed how chaotic and progressively less coordinated the evacuation had been.

I kept walking, looking for fellow students to join. I frequently gaped back at the pillar of smoke enshrouding all of downtown. At one point I took a mental picture of a road sign that read "South / World Trade Center" under an arrow pointing ahead; no such place any longer existed. I also cast my sight up. The attacks came from the sky, after all, and if they were to hit New York again, we would find ourselves in the open on the shore of the Hudson River. It wasn't long before I heard the Pentagon had been hit; then rumors that Los Angeles and myriad other places were targeted. In this light, I think my paranoia was justified. The perpetrators, whoever they were, had planned a comprehensive and devastating strike on many fronts.

Like most of my compatriots, an early concern was calling home to my parents in Brooklyn, both to inform them that I was OK, and to inquire about relatives who might have been in Manhattan that morning. My efforts were frustrated. The pay phones lacked dial tones, and everybody's cellular phone was dead. By now there were just six of us, half lost because street signs were few and far between. Finally, one kid's mobile phone got through the overloaded networks to my parents' number. I was able to reassure my mother, and learned that my brother had not gone to Manhattan that morning. In fact, Eric had seen the second plane collide while on the F train viaduct at Smith-9th Street station, and immediately returned home, without leaving Brooklyn. It was the answer to my prayers.

The midday hours of September 11 were a critical time. We needed to stay informed, make phone calls, plan travel arrangements—if possible—and find physical shelter. Fortunately, Cindy, a member of our expedition, could provide those resources at a nearby location, and was generous enough to share them. At 14th Street, we diverged from the erratic northward flow of Stuyvesant students and cut crosstown.

It isn't often that clichéd expressions like "out of the blue" are given new meaning. But this was one of those extraordinary times; we could tell which passersby "knew about it" by the way they would anxiously glance skyward, looking out for the "next plane."

I figured that any other hijacked plane would have to head for the Empire State Building, another major landmark, and another easy target. Thus 14th Street was strategically ideal—a couple of miles from the WTC and a minimum of one mile from the Empire State Building. Nonetheless, I remember scaring the wits out of myself and the rest of the group when I spotted an ambiguous object flying high in the air. It turned out to be a plastic bag riding the wind.

Continuing east along 14th, I suggested that we make a stop to buy beverages when I saw a discount store on the corner with inexpensive spring water. On a nearby corner, we found that the payphone would only work for collect calls. A city bus covered with a thick layer of gray ash passed by. Looking down every avenue, I beheld the ever-growing cloud from the WTC site engulfing all the buildings in its path. I noted that the fifty-four-story Woolworth Building foregrounded the collapse and that the cloud was still at least three times taller. And wider. Meanwhile, I mentally plotted different routes to Brooklyn: buses, trains, ferries, even walking the bridge. Every subway station entrance was cordoned off by police.

It was now 12:30 P.M. On the East Side, we entered Cindy's small but cozy apartment and turned on the television (only channel 2 worked) to understand what was going on. We gaped at the new footage. Ernie Anastos and Dana Tyler were covering updates from Mayor Giuliani and announcements by the Department of Transportation as they happened. Although there were still no adults with us—Cindy's parents were apparently at work—we were now in relative safety and began to settle down. The place was homey and casual. Shirts hung on a rod extending between the foyer and the kitchen were drying. An upright piano nearly hidden by books and bric-a-brac occupied a corner of the living room, which had a window facing the courtyard.

Cindy allowed us to use the phone, so it was constantly either dialing or ringing. We couldn't access the MTA website. Since its hotline was perpetually busy, our only link to transportation

Out of the Blue

updates was television. Among the staff of the *Stuyvesant Standard*, furious brainstorming, debate, and research had always characterized our editorial meetings. Perhaps that's why I now felt strangely at home, as if I were at a press conference amid fellow reporters, or maybe preparing for a blitz of interviews.

Even at the young age of sixteen, I had learned to look at the world objectively, or at least to observe it without panicking. At about half past three, I thought I had my "scoop," as certain subway lines began reopening on a limited-service basis. I made backup plans to walk with someone across the Manhattan Bridge and have my brother pick us up. Allen Lew, Joseph's father, was also coming. Thus, I wasn't sure whether to take a restored train, walk over the reportedly open bridge, or continue to sojourn until the arrival of Mr. Lew, the first authority figure I would see since I left Stuyvesant. I figured the longer I waited, the better informed I'd be about the options, and maybe I wouldn't have to trek home alone.

At about 3:50 Channel Two announced that most of the letter lines, or the B division of the subway, were operating. Finally, the road home was clear. Bidding farewell to Cindy, our generous hostess, I set off for the W train. On the subway, the other riders seemed unusually civil, weary and subdued. Crawling over the Manhattan Bridge, we were afforded one more view of the heart-rending downtown panorama. The train rarely topped 5 mph, but it eventually brought me to my home station: 77th Street, Bay Ridge, Brooklyn. Incredulous that I was again walking down my familiar street, I trudged two blocks home.

Over the next four months, Stuyvesant students endured two and a half weeks of school at the rival Brooklyn Technical High School, overcame another two weeks of major subway diversions, inhaled the lingering stench of downtown Manhattan, and faced unprecedented security restrictions at school. In school, however, no more Bush jokes could be heard in the halls. Instead, intelligent discussions took place in every social studies class, all the English classes, and in health class; even my math teacher encouraged us to share our feelings. A few inveterate leftists in my American history class brazenly insisted that our foreign policy had virtually justified the attacks. However, the vast majority of us—including Mr. Sandler—dismissed this hogwash. Most students wanted the mutually congruous goals of long-term peace and swift, adamant justice.

By no means has it been easy for the Stuyvesant community in the wake of 9/11, but we are no less resilient than the rest of New York. Normalcy, or some semblance thereof, is visible on the horizon. On October 9 the Stuyvesant community regained its Chambers Street campus. Being back in lower Manhattan did not feel entirely normal, though. Dignitaries, donations, and media flooded Stuyvesant, and giant posters from all over the globe expressed sympathy and compatriotism on every wall.

After the return to our regular building, the *Stuyvesant Standard* reorganized and resumed normal operation. "Before 8:46 [on September 11]," wrote then-managing editor Daniel Egers, "many of us worried about getting a program change, about surviving five months with the teacher that just does not seem 'right.' After 8:46: We worried about loved ones who work in the vicinity of the World Trade Center . . . about seeing our friends and family again. Worried about bombs and bomb scares and bomb threats and airplanes turned into bombs and bombs on airplanes. Our thinking after 8:46 became muddled."

When a teenager in Tampa, Florida, effortlessly took off and rammed his plane into a skyscraper, even the respected Civil Air Patrol came under scrutiny. "What are the prospects of a Charles Bishop copycat flying down the Hudson River and slamming a Cessna training plane into Stuyvesant?" I asked in the January 30, 2002 *Standard*.

Rufino Mendoza, the chief financial officer of the *Standard*, predicted in the December 21, 2001 issue, "Europe and Asia will be affected by the recession to a lesser extent [than the U.S.]. The

Out of the Blue

more consistent growth of Europe, exemplified by the symmetrical British monetary policy, does not experience the greater ebbs and flows of a more laissez-faire economy."

Also in December, the *Standard* broke the story on the board of education's unanimous resolution to have all schools pledge allegiance. The ethics of this decision were passionately debated in a Point-Counterpoint opinions feature. The newspaper kept tabs on national and global issues—the war abroad and the new economy—and the opinions section ran the gamut from defeatist liberal criticism to rightist war hawking.

On November 6, Michael Bloomberg won the mayoral election by a relative landslide. I smiled, recalling my fervent editorial endorsement in the *Stuyvesant Standard*. Today, I realize that this memory has already begun fading.

Following my return home from Manhattan on September 11, I had a similar epiphany. At first I was immensely grateful that my family and relatives had come out of it unscathed. Then emotions of joy, relief, and contentment were joined by fear, and also by what President Bush has called a "quiet, unyielding anger." But I also realized that unless I were to do something soon, my memory of that fateful day would become hazier and hazier, until it would escape my grasp altogether. So I sat before my computer in my room to write this essay. I vowed to record as faithfully as I could my observations, thoughts, and recollections. Granted, I wasn't the best reporter on that grim day. But I felt I could only do justice to the events by capturing them in words. I feel that this account is basically accurate and complete. As a witness and journalist, I have an obligation to objectively report the catastrophe. But as a survivor, I also feel a personal compulsion to forever immortalize it, both for myself and for others, so that we will never forget.

40 Hours in Hell

By Katherine Eban Finkelstein—*New York Times*

No one made provisions for reporters when the Twin Towers collapsed. At Ground Zero, KATHERINE EBAN FINKELSTEIN of the New York Times *tried to get the whole story. Along the way, she scavenged for notepads, manufactured makeshift bathroom facilities, and found a creative way to phone in her story after her cell phone died. For forty hours she slept on chairs exposed to the elements, rode in jam-packed ambulances, and fled buildings on the verge of collapse. Even months later, Finkelstein can see the dark, chaos-filled sky falling on her. She feels the sharp fiber-dust prickling her skin.*

Finkelstein, thirty-five, was a metro reporter for the New York Times, *where she covered the Manhattan State Supreme Court until that morning. After September 11 she worked as part of the Ground Zero investigative team covering terrorists, anthrax, and detainees. She is now writing under the byline Katherine Eban at New York City's newest broadsheet, the* New York Sun.

Reprinted by permission of American Journalism Review

The morning of September 11 began like any other for me. I went to the gym for a workout, had plans for breakfast with my apartment mate. And though I cover Manhattan courts for the *New York Times*, my assignment that day was to cover New York's primary election at Staten Island nursing homes, where the residents had lost their in-house voting booths.

I had no idea that soon I would be at the heart of the biggest story of my life. I would be at the base of the World Trade Center when it collapsed, killing thousands. And after narrowly surviving and briefly leaving the epicenter of the tragedy, I would work my way back through numerous security cordons. By the time I left around 1 A.M. Thursday, I had spent forty hours on the scene, the last twenty-eight at Ground Zero, for hours the only correspondent there.

At 8:45 A.M., I first saw the top floors of one tower flaming from the windows of my gym at Chelsea Piers at 18th Street and the West Side Highway. A clutch of people standing there had seen the first plane strike.

I left the gym and broke into a half run toward my apartment, where I called the desk and was told, "Go down there." It was 9 A.M.

I put on jeans, a T-shirt, and comfortable shoes (no socks), grabbed a small backpack, a notepad, two pens, my pager, my cell phone, and a charger. My apartment mate, Tracy, who was watching the news, suddenly cried out, "Something hit another tower." No subways, I figured. I'd ride my bike. Down Seventh

Avenue, I slipped through traffic that was being diverted by the police at almost every intersection.

The closer I got, the bigger the story seemed. Outside St. Vincent's Hospital at 12th Street, some fifteen nurses in scrubs stood on the sidewalk with gurneys, waiting for casualties, their gazes fixed on the flames downtown. Emergency vehicles roared past me, sirens whining. At each corner, crowds of commuters stood transfixed, staring at the towers.

Seventh Avenue became Varick Street and still I rode lower, people scattering haphazardly as the building spit and crackled. Papers, thousands of them, fluttered through the air. A plainclothes police officer, his shield around his neck, stopped me.

"Press."

"I don't care," he said. "Get out of the way."

I hopped off my bike, wheeled it to a side street, and locked it to a scaffolding, about a block and a half from the World Trade Center. The air was thick with acrid smoke, the heat palpable.

"Where are the victims?" I asked two police officers as ambulances screamed up Church Street. One officer pointed east, away from the trade center buildings. I ran, then went south one block and saw them: A line of employees wet from sprinkler systems and fire hoses streamed from the buildings as firefighters tried desperately to keep them moving so they didn't block the streets.

I began to interview. The workers came from floors low and high, recounting the plane hits in rage, fear, and shock. I tried calling the desk on my cell phone. No signal. Long lines snaked from each pay phone and police were clearing the streets.

It was 9:50 A.M. when I finally got through. Behind me people were screaming. I think *I* was screaming. I was spelling names, barking quotes to someone taking dictation. It seemed the situation was getting worse, not better.

I turned again and plunged into the crowd, noting now that workers exiting the buildings were bloody, one man with red trails down his face, blood-spattered newspapers on the ground, women hysterical.

I fought against the tide of employees, past one rescue command center and down to the entrance of the north tower, where the dust and paper storm felt thicker. I was feet from the door through which employees were being evacuated. The sunlight was gone, the air thick with ash. People waiting to leave were backed up the stairwell in what looked like an endless line.

It is hard now to say what I heard or saw first. A low and ominous rumble, in a split second turning into a roar. A vast black cloud forming at the top of the south tower, then sinking quickly as though the building were made of fabric, not steel. The orderly effort to evacuate people splintering as people broke from the door and raced past me.

A man shouted into a walkie-talkie. People yelled out, "It's going to go." As the building collapsed, black funnels of debris raced toward us, about to overtake us. I turned east and barreled up a side street, the lethal column of debris at my back.

This cannot be real, I thought for a nanosecond, arms pumping, legs flying. I am running for my life up a street I have known all my life, being chased by a building. It's like a demented Bruce Willis movie.

"Let's go, let's go," an FBI man screamed from the mouth of a subway entrance. Two cops hurtled in. I leapt in after them and almost fell down the stairs as the pulverized building thundered over me.

I am being buried alive. It was black and debris kept pouring in. A man called out, "My ankle is broken. Someone help me." He screamed as more people fell in from the street and tripped over him, then tumbled down the stairs with a thud. My mouth, eyes, and ears were filled with dust.

I heard the two officers: "I'm here. Are you?"

"I'm here."

"Yo."

I was holding someone's arm, that of the FBI man. "Can you help me?" I asked, not even knowing why. He was in a desperate crouch, his other arm over his head.

As the blackness subsided into a murky dust, the FBI man bolted for the exit. I headed deeper into the subway. The two officers and I met by a turnstile and embraced in an awkward circle. They were from the Board of Education and had come to evactuate the schools.

I pulled out my notepad but had lost my pen. One of the officers took a dust-covered pen from this shirt pocket and extended it. "Keep it," he said. I barely wrote anything except their names: Sgts. Peter Calise and Norbert Davidson.

Our skin was caked with sharp, stinging dust; a bucket of it was in my hair. My eyes blinked out from a hood of ash. And then a man staggered down the stairs with a woman slung over his shoulder. She was covered with blood, her clothing tattered. She looked dead.

"Come on," said Davidson, and took my hand.

We went up the stairs and emerged into a completely brown world. The air was thick, the streets gone under inches of debris and soot, windows blown out, people staggering. Some poured into a nearby bank. Others screamed to avoid the plate glass or anything that might blow.

Clutching Davidson's hand, I turned the corner and saw a miraculous sight: New York University Downtown Hospital, as welcome as a Red Cross tent in a war zone, I imagined.

The floors inside were streaked with blood. Dust swam in the air. Hospital workers were handing out water, asking people to remove dust-coated clothing. Lines for the pay phones stretched down the hall. My skin was burning. Volunteers were passing out moistened gauze, and I wiped my face with a piece of it.

I wandered the hall and interviewed two investment bankers,

who said they'd left the building and saw people jumping, clawing at the air.

Suddenly, we heard screams and more people surged in through the lobby doors. It was 10:30 A.M. The north tower had just collapsed. The Pentagon, too, had been hit, someone said.

And that is the first time all morning that I actually grasped the story: We were under a terrorist attack.

I must have been in shock. As I drifted through the hall, people began asking whether I needed medical attention. I was trying to follow a changing line of thought about the morning's events.

I wanted to leave lower Manhattan. Someone announced the bridge was open. The skies were safe. But were they? I wandered to the hospital steps and heard a nurse say, "Oh, my God. They're bringing in the children." She wept as a stroller appeared. Another nurse embraced her.

Finally, I managed to call my boyfriend, Ken, and arranged to meet him on Grand Street, in Chinatown, at his architecture office.

Outside, lower Manhattan looked like something from *War of the Worlds*. Brown snowdrifts covered the streets. Stunned police officers roved outside City Hall. SWAT teams with automatic weapons stood on the steps of every courthouse.

And as I walked, people offered me medical help. Others offered me blessings.

Ken's colleagues fell silent as I entered his office, an emblem of a changed world. In the bathroom, I threw out my T-shirt and washed my hair in the sink with liquid soap. As Ken used soapy paper towels to scrub my back, he too felt the stinging fibers of insulation creep over his skin. He gave me his undershirt.

Then I called the desk and filed my notes, despite audible chaos as editors struggled to dispatch their cops and courts and City Hall reporters to cover a war. I was coughing up dark phlegm. Then we went outside to a coffee shop and actually ordered lunch, drinking coffee and splitting a turkey club sandwich as waves of dusty people walked past us, leaving downtown.

Lunch lasted only minutes. The desk paged me again, this time to report on the activity at local churches.

Wandering back toward the security barrier that had been set up along Canal Street, I realized that, by leaving, I had probably locked myself out of the story.

Why hadn't I stayed at the hospital? I had wanted some coffee, some food. A wash. A hug. But now I was turned away from two checkpoints and feared that I wouldn't get back in. At a third checkpoint, I showed my press pass and got the officer there to smile. He let me through.

A few blocks down was a new sign taped to a lamppost, "Please join us in prayer," directing people to a mission and shelter diagonally across from the courthouse where I worked every day. Inside the chapel, some people were praying. In the basement, homeless men watched CNN, staring rapt at the images of mayhem and terror still unfolding, live.

It was about 2 P.M. I filed more notes, then walked farther south to the federal courthouse at Foley Square. A makeshift triage center had formed there, organized by no one and staffed by anyone. Air Force medics visting town, medical residents, and ambulance corps volunteers were scattered around the fountain there, waiting for casualties or a call to Ground Zero.

Burn dressing, gauze, defibrillators, and oxygen pumps were strewn on the sidewalk. Seeing my notepad, a man trying to organize this mess said, "Follow me and make a list of all the supplies these people need."

He began striding around the fountain as I scribbled behind him. "Can you get me ambu bags?" a nurse asked.

"I can't get you anything," I said. "I'm a journalist. But I'm making a list."

40 Hours in Hell

Then a call came out for ambulances: they were wanted and needed at Ground Zero. As medics scrambled for ambulances, I called the desk and was told to go down if I could.

I approached what looked like the motliest crew: a group of guys with Hatzolah, the Jewish volunteer ambulance corps, mixed in with stragglers. "Can I get a ride?"

"We have no room, we're packed."

"*New York Times*. I'll squeeze, stand, sit anywhere."

"OK." One of the medics offered a hand. We were fourteen in the ambulance. The driver took off with the doors still open and we jolted against the sides. I tripped over a rolling oxygen tank.

Our convoy ground to a halt as a medic peering out the window said, "It's fire. A building's fully engaged."

Someone opened the doors. I climbed over a stretcher, shearing my jeans at the knees. There was another skyscraper, completely aflame: Building Seven of the World Trade Center complex.

The police directed us to another triage site, this one in the outdoor plaza of the Salomon Smith Barney building at Greenwich and North Moore Streets. Stretchers for casualties were lined up beneath handwritten signs—critical, noncritical, morgue—taped on the building's marble pillars.

A *Times* photographer, Nicole Bengiveno, saw me and we hugged. As I called in more notes, building seven came down in a shower of dust, and I loped behind an ambulance. The crowd oohed as though at some strange civic display.

A group of volunteer medics soon assembled to head down, and I slipped among them, my press pass tucked beneath my shirt. As police led us through, firefighters were everywhere, napping on the West Side Highway, clustered by company. We kept moving downtown, through checkpoints where some in my group waved medical credentials. No journalists in sight.

We arrived at the lobby of Stuyvesant High School, just blocks from the site. Rescue workers, firefighters, and trauma surgeons in

251

scrubs shuttled into the lobby, which had been turned into an operating theater lit with emergency generators. IV bags hung from the school lockers.

It was about 6 P.M. My cell phone was dead. I couldn't charge my pone because the building's electricity was off. And there were only four pay phones in the lobby, which stopped working one by one. But I waited, managed to file more notes, then went up to the school cafeteria, where someone had opened up cans of food and was serving cold corn, cold spinach, and frozen pizzas.

I ate with an Air Force reservist named Tim; he'd been in town for a conference. We looked north up the West Side Highway, where emergency vehicles stretched for miles.

As the wait for casualties continued, Tim and I walked outside to the overpass, looking out on smoke, flames, and rescue vehicles. The weather had been beautiful, a gorgeous day in late summer now dissolved into soot.

By 8:30 P.M., with no casualties still, our trauma center was disbanded. Tim gave me his stethoscope and tattered medical security pass and went home. I borrowed a cell phone and called the desk. Did they want me to try and go lower still? A bristly cordon of police officers had closed off all access to the disaster site. But a volunteer firefighter who had no credentials either offered to try to help me get farther south.

We turned west on Chambers Street and walked intently past a row of firefighters to Battery Park. It was entirely dark. The power was out. No streetlights. We passed a cop and kept walking down to Vesey Street and took a left, sharing a moment of oddly casual conversation about my work for the *Times*. And then we were there.

Only Gustave Dore's drawings of Dante's Inferno looked anything like it at all. Streams of water crisscrossing giant shards of building, metal piercing through smoke, skeletal crews in the intersection with tools as tragically inadequate as single fire hoses against smoldering rubble heaps seven stories high.

There were no journalists here. There seemed even to be few firefighters. A throng was just up the street, waiting for word to come help. But what help might that be? A single easel sat on the street, with aerial photographs of the building site to help the rescuers navigate.

"Come on," said my guide as he strode through the soaked debris of glass, paper, mud, and ash. I moved cautiously behind him. What might I do with one almost-filled notepad, no socks, and a dead cell phone, in the midst of this catastrophe?

"I want to call the desk," I said, pointing toward an intact building being used as home base by the rescuers. It was the American Express Building on Vesey Street, right across from the downed towers.

The lobby was a hub of shattered glass, klieg lights, and men tramping in and out. That morning, as the first tower fell, fast-thinking cops shot out the lobby's plate glass windows and those who dove through them survived. Inside, the lobby was strewn with garbage. The emergency lights threw off eerie shadows.

Remarkably, one police officer there was a longtime source of mine. He quietly gave me a tour.

To the right of the lobby, a narrow hall lined with folding tables served as a temporary morgue. The floor was streaked with blood, as sixteen charred bodies with no identifying clothing had just been moved out into a refrigerated truck.

The bathrooms, "a little gross," he said, were on the seond floor. There was no running water or electricity. The working telephone, also on the second floor, had no local service.

I walked up the escalator and there was the phone, sitting on a marble reception desk by a vase of flowers. I dialed 9 and then the desk. Nothing. A 1-800 calling card. "It only calls long distance, like to New Jersey," said a passing firefighter.

Who did I know where? Seattle? California? My sister lived in Philadelphia. She'd just moved and I didn't have her number. I got 215 area code information, but she was unlisted. I tried calling the California bureau of the *Times*. No answer.

The Washington bureau. I called 202 information and got through. Someone answered the phone and transferred me to New York. I dumped more notes and, after some arduous explanation, the desk arranged for a clerk to stay all night in the Washington office to transfer me.

I was out of notepads. It was getting cold. I needed to go to the bathroom. I ventured over to the bathrooms that had been used—without flushing—by firefighters all day. The smell was prohibitive. But on the floor was a trampled American Express Security jacket. I picked it up, grabbed some napkins from a nearby desk and went in search of a more remote restroom.

On the fifth floor, I was wending my way in the dark along a corridor when I saw a flashlight beam: two female rescue workers looking for the same thing. We found a toilet—a little less terrible—in the back of a women's locker room. We took turns, holding the flashlight for each other. On the way down, I opened a supply closet in an empty office and pulled out several notepads stamped "Lehman Brothers." A woman was asleep on the floor.

On the second floor, my firefighter said, "There's a better view," and walked me around the corner. From here we saw directly into the collapsed walkway, a mass of impenetrable steel. A bulldozer was crunching into it, bite by bite, revealing the grilles of buried fire trucks. The way to it was studded with treacherous humps of debris. And on a nearby flagpole, a tattered American flag flapped pathetically. Two firefighters slept on the stairs below me.

I picked my way down the stairs, through deep puddles in the lobby. Outside a man in an NYPD community affairs jacket was standing there, staring into a snow of falling ash. Normally, he would have been assigned to chase me away. But where would he chase me to? There were few policies left intact and almost no one to enforce them.

I stood next to him and introduced myself. He was John Costigan, a retired police officer who'd driven in from Long Island with boxes of bottled water donated by local supermarkets. "I'm looking around thinking, 'Where do you start?'" he said. "The world changed today."

The world had changed. Or ended. I wasn't sure which or whether there was any difference between the two. Welders now stood at the bottom of the flagpole, gnawing at it with their power tools.

I wandered around the American Express building to a side door that led to the temporary morgue. A curtain was now drawn across the bloody hallway, a police officer stationed outside, as though guarding the dead from any further outrage.

A Bellevue Hospital Center truck was parked outside, orange bags stacked in the truck bed. As I peered inside, a man behind me said by way of explanation, "body parts." He was a volunteer undertaker who'd been working all night in his rumpled suit and respirator mask.

"You move some things, you find some parts," he said grimly. "A little here, a little there."

Hours had slipped by. It was 1 A.M. I had been either standing or running since 9 A.M. the morning before. My legs were tired. I was cold.

I had wandered back toward the front entrance of the American Express building to file my notes when I saw another *Times* reporter, David Barstow, who'd arrived wearing a business suit. I led him to the phone and was calling the Washington bureau when a cop, the new night guy in charge, asked, "Who are you?"

"*New York Times.*"

"Get out."

I tried moral indignation. "You know, I've been here from the beginning. I was nearly buried this morning. And my paper needs people down here."

"Get out."

"It's cold out there. Do you have a blanket?" I asked.

"No."

Out I shuffled, with no way to call my desk and nowhere to sleep. Barstow headed into the rubble. Outside, firefighters sat in upholstered office chairs in the street, watching as their colleagues battled the fires, red, smoky smudges across the nighttime sky.

I knocked on the door of an ambulance and asked if I could sleep in the back of the truck for an hour. No. "If casualties come, I need to move out," the driver explained, suggesting the Embassy Suites, a hotel on the corner that was dark and looked a world away.

I walked slowly west on Vesey Street to canvas my options. Between Ground Zero and the hotel sat an abandoned Mexican restaurant, beer bottles still on the table, doors open. Could I sleep there in the dark, invisible to rescuer workers and potentially in danger from falling buildings or even ordinary crime? It was still New York, after all.

I continued down a few doors. The street got darker, emptier, more remote. This wouldn't work at all. By dawn, just these few yards away, I'd be locked out permanently with no way to get back.

Already, there was a cop posted halfway down the block who hadn't been there when I'd set out. "You can't get back in," she said.

"But I just walked past here."

"I have orders. No one gets through."

"Look," I said, gesturing to David Barstow, who was now seated in an office chair, also wearing one of the globe-blue American Express Security jackets, "he's my colleague."

The woman scowled. "I'm not supposed to," she said and shrugged. I continued on. Obviously there was no leaving. I wandered toward the band of firefighters and put two office chairs together. I was freezing. For warmth, I used a strip of gauze to wrap one foot and a trampled towel to wrap the other, then curled up and slept.

40 Hours in Hell

I awoke in the predawn an hour or so later, when volunteers began bringing supplies. It was time to improve my situation, especially if I was going to stay another night.

It had been ten hours since I'd last gone to the bathroom. I awoke my volunteer firefighter, who was slumbering in a chair beside me, and asked him to help me reattempt the American Express building. We got inside and at the supply table I washed my eyes with saline, stocked up on paper towels and Handi Wipes, then walked up the escalator.

Slivers of natural light now cut into the building. A small corporate art space lay down the marble corridor, where a cart of art objects had been abandoned. Below me, I saw an atrium, an elegant cafeteria, and the curtain hanging in front of the temporary morgue.

An unlocked and elegant florist shop, flowers intact, sat at the back of the hall, the personal effects of the owner still lying near the cash register. I walked in. In a small, dark back office was a large trashcan filled with flower stalks and petals. This would do very well for a personal toilet, I figured, grateful for a moment of privacy.

Outside, the sun had risen on another devastating day.

Boxes of supplies went by. I grabbed a fleece blanket, a package of socks, a toothbrush and washcloth and stood on West Street with the blanket over my shoulders, brushing my teeth using bottled water, then wiping my face with the washcloth.

An official from the medical examiner's office went by and gave me the morning's count: twenty-one body bags and four bags of parts, though he added angrily, "If you get a thumb, is that a part? I feel like going home and going to sleep, and maybe in the morning all this will be gone."

More rescue workers had come with the light: men in those lunar-looking hazmat suits, K-9 units with their dogs, in military uniforms from many divisions, parajumpers with equipment strapped around their legs. Men everywhere, alive and dead.

I need to charge my telephone. A Verizon truck was parked on the corner of Vesey and West Streets, and the guys inside had hoisted an American flag to the top of their truck antenna.

I poked my head inside. Did they have a wall plug where I could charge my phone? No problem.

I climbed in and sat on a big spool of phone cable, the blanket wrapped around me as my phone charged. I fell instantly asleep and woke up when one of the guys brought me a plastic container of fruit cup.

Outside, the morning was hot and glorious. It was time to gather my thoughts and notes, write something coherent, and call it in. The desk said they wanted it all. I gave them everything I could gather, from the parajumper unit—eighteen of them—who'd ended up sleeping on a yacht, to the K-9 rescue worker who'd driven through the night, fifteen hours from Halifax, Nova Scotia, with his body-sniffing dog.

I wanted to be closer still. Carrying a shovel, I worked my way to the heart of the rescue effort, the crumpled walkway, and stood amid the local steelworkers and carpenters. Lalji Salassie, a carpenter who said he'd helped construct each of the World Trade Center buildings, looked on in anger. "It's like somebody destroyed my work," he said.

A group of doctors in the street were washing out rescue workers' eyes with saline. I asked where they were from.

"Sloan-Kettering," said Dr. Rafael Barrerra. They were cancer doctors. I instantly thought of my best friend, Karen Avenoso, a journalist with the *Boston Globe* who'd died of cancer three years ago. She'd covered TWA Flight 800. Months later, she'd been diagnosed with cancer and died after a ten-month fight.

She should have been covering this, and I suspected that, somewhere amid the crowd, she was here. These doctors, who'd tried to save her from cancer and who came down to treat the five thousand people now feared dead or trapped beneath this rubble, were reduced to rinsing out people's eyes. My heart slipped into the craters of the buildings. I wept beneath my mask and plastic goggles for all the world's loss. The tears kept coming.

Back at the truck, I filed a long rescue insert, then revisited the flower shop. I was exhausted and disheartened and wanted to be home. Bruises had formed on my legs,. My lungs hurt. And I was increasingly nervous about reports that other buildings were on the verge of collapse.

Barstow was watching the rescue efforts from a tenth floor balcony of the American Express Building. I was hoping the *Times* could get someone else down here to relieve us but was bracing for a night in the Verizon truck. I was sitting on the spool of cable at 5 P.M. talking on the phone to my boyfriend, when I saw people running past the truck. "Oh shit," I yelled, disconnecting the phone. "Run, run," people screamed. I leapt out and raced up West Street, ducking behind a fire truck as people slowed.

Rumors were whipping up the street: that the winter garden was going to collapse further; that the American Express Building was coming down. My legs were trembling so much I could barely stand up from this repeat of yesterday morning's dread.

Slowly, I drifted back, and in the Verizon truck, one of the men said, "You know, you really should get out of here. They just designated this a building collapse zone, eight blocks in all directions."

I didn't need to ask where the center of the zone was: We were parked in it. I called the desk and got an editor on the phone, asking, "What do you think about the fact that I am now in what has been designated a building collapse zone?"

"I think that Richard Pérez-Peña is writing that story," he said. "I'll transfer you."

He was not heartless, just distracted. We all were. I wanted to leave, but not until someone else able to stay for the long haul replaced me. By then, my phone was ringing with calls from family members, wanting to know when I would leave. They were scared. I was too. There were all sorts of possible hazards: falling buildings, leaking gas mains and the air, putrid and filled with dangerous dusts.

The evacuation plan if a building did fall was primitive at best. "If you see these guys run, then run," said one firefighter.

The next eight hours passed in a blur: I visited the flower shop, shuttled through the debris, watched the procession of orange bags, changed face masks, drank more water, and sat in exhaustion, then got up and did it again.

At about 10:30 P.M., the desk said they were launching another reporter, C. J. Chivers, to try to replace me. He had a security pass from One Police Plaza and they thought he could slip through.

I was in the Verizon truck on my spool of cable when he arrived; a more welcome sight it would be hard to imagine. He'd even brought me a cup of coffee. I gave him the tour, then left him my blanket, the cell phone charger, and a neon New Jersey Transit vest. I took my American Express jacket and carpenter's hat and walked up the West Side Highway, past emergency vehicles lit up like Christmas.

It was early Thursday. And though more than forty hours had passed since I first hopped on my bicycle, the terrible story had just begun.

This Is America

By Rob Walker—*Slate*

ROB WALKER, a Slate *magazine columnist, describes the powerlessness of watching the news of September 11 from his New Orleans office. Searching for a way to make a positive contribution the next day, he filed a column speculating about what would happen when the stock markets reopened. Because he lived in New York for eight years, he took the attacks on the World Trade Center especially personally. Although the liberal Walker had opposed Operation Desert Storm, he found himself sympathetic to the American military strikes in Afghanistan. While he does not believe the world changed fundamentally on September 11, he is reluctant to see it return to normal.*

Walker, now thirty-three, is a former editor at the New York Times Magazine. *He has previously worked as an editor at* Money *and* Fortune *magazines. More of Walker's writings can be found at www.robwalker.net.*

Hey, bro, you see that shit on TV?" I'm walking the dog, over by Bayou St. John, in my New Orleans neighborhood. It's a residential area, and the streets are empty at this time of the morning. A guy rides by on his bike. He says: "Hey, bro, you see that shit on TV?" He pronounces "bro" as "bruh." I look at him. I think I've seen this guy—young white guy, brown hair, soft features—working at the Whole Foods. He's exactly the sort of person your subconscious plucks out of nowhere to give a pivotal role in a dream. Anyway, I don't know what he's talking about. My dog is a chow, was there something else on the local news about a violent chow attacking somebody? I say: "No, man." He says: "Two planes just hit the World Trade Center." He's past me already, going wherever he's going, as he adds, "It's fucked up."

It's fucked up. I have the TV in my office on now. One of the World Trade Center towers seems not to be there. I am imagining what it will be like, the next time I'm in New York, to see just one of the World Trade Center towers standing there. But there's so much smoke, maybe it's in the smoke somewhere. The second tower falls as I'm watching, and weirdly the TV people don't seem to notice immediately, one of them is babbling about something, and when that person finishes, another one says, "I think the second tower just collapsed."

I write an online column on the subject of American money culture, and somewhere around this time I send e-mail to my editors asking them to spike the story that I filed the day before but was

This Is America

due to go up early this morning. It's a limp effort about Bush and the stock markets. It's no longer appropriate.

"This is America." People keep saying that—declaring it, sort of—on television on September 11, and the next day. The man in the street says: This is America. The witnesses say the same thing. What do they mean?

It took several weeks for me to recall that I could not remember anything about the experience of being in New York when the WTC was bombed in 1993. I have no memory of it at all. In 1993 I was working on Fifth Avenue, just below 14th Street. I have a vivid memory of going home from work early the year before when the Rodney King riots were happening in L.A. and people thought (for a few hours) that something similar might go on in New York. At that time I was working in midtown, and the office pretty much cleared out by midafternoon. The subways were weird and tense. That I remember.

And I remember very distinctly an essay in the *New York Times* by Herbert Muschamp that must have appeared not long after the Trade Center bombing. This piece made a big impression on me, and I wrote some notes about it in a journal I was sort of keeping at the time. (There's nothing in that journal about the bombing itself.) The thing that struck me was Muschamp's line "Exploding buildings are this community's landmarks." Not churches, not castles, not banks—the things that at various times in human history have been the tallest buildings, the one everyone in the village could see from his or her window. Now, he wrote, the tallest building is the building that's exploding.

My office has a window that faces a quiet street of houses, but there was nothing happening there. Or maybe there was, but I was looking through the window of my television set at the building that was exploding—over and over again—and I was looking at the window of my computer monitor, trying to learn why.

Rob Walker

• • •

My journal entry from 1993 about the Muschamp article contains no useful insights, just a summation that I no longer trust. But I'll look for a copy of the article later. I'm watching that bloom of fire as a plane strikes the second tower. I'm watching as the TV people locate new footage, new angles of the planes hitting—one, then the other. I'm watching the buildings fall, one, then the other. I'm watching as the networks show again the original live footage with the original stunned voice-overs. The one I'll likely always remember includes some correspondent reacting as it becomes clear that the second plane has hit. "What is going *on?*" this guy says, and he sounds helpless.

I think the thing that will be hard to hold on to is just how helpless we felt there for a moment. Or at least how helpless I felt. For these hours, maybe less time than that—when the news was: one plane hits, another plane hits, a plane has hit the Pentagon, a plane has crashed in Pennyslvania—for this stretch, it felt like it could, conceivably, go on all day. That it just wouldn't stop. One by one planes would come down from the sky and smash into buildings and kill as many people as possible. Maybe things would begin to explode (remember that on that first day there were any number of false reports and hoaxes and bomb threats that did not materialize), maybe a fucking nuclear bomb would go off. Who knew? Who knew what would happen next? And how could any of this be happening at all? What is going *on?* This is America.

Another thing people said, again and again, on television and in casual conversation, is that everything has changed. But here I'd like to pause to mention *The Hitchhiker's Guide to the Galaxy*, the science fiction humor book. One of the lovely conceits of the universe that Douglas Adams imagined was something called The Total Perspective Vortex—being tossed into this was a horrific and mind-bending experience, because the result was a complete

This Is America

understanding of one's own insignificance—"an invisible dot on an invisible dot."

Watching those towers fall had a similar effect. Nothing else seemed particularly important. Certainly not my work, which generally consists of making smart-ass remarks about the stock market and so forth. I assume that while this feeling was not just a reaction to the awful suffering—we knew that day that it was thousands of lives, though we did not know how many thousands, and I remember TV newspeople more than once citing the statistic that fifty thousand people work in the tower, although that figure seemed unlikely and close to irresponsible even as it was being spoken. Anyway, the Total Perspective feeling must have been a reaction not just to the fact of all that suffering, but to the fact that our knowledge of it was universal and simultaneous. It's rare, to say the least, that we all look out the same window at once—but when it happens, we know it. You couldn't watch the horror without thinking of *everyone* watching the horror. That's what made it distinct from, say, reading a newspaper story about famine somewhere. There's always suffering, and we always know it, but usually we know it in a way that's easy to minimize. Maybe we don't even make it to the end of the famine article—we know how it turns out, and we're late for the movie, or whatever. In this instance it was not possible to minimize. Total Perspective.

I went to the grocery store. All morning I'd done nothing but watch the images over and over. And the fact is I had no food for lunch. So I went to Winn-Dixie.

At Winn-Dixie, everything was normal. Early afternoon on a weekday, the size of the crowd seemed about average. At our nearby Winn-Dixie, the customer base is overwhelmingly working-class black, and that was the case on September 11. I overheard roughly the same amount of incidental chatter as always, and on strictly mundane topics. I heard no one talking about the Trade Towers, the Pentagon, terrorists, any of it. I thought it was weird then, and I think it's even weirder looking back on it. Maybe people were talking about it in all parts of the store except the ones I happened to be in. Maybe to the customers at my Winn-Dixie, this seemed like a matter of concern to rich white Yankees, many miles distant. I have no idea. I bought my things—whatever they were—and I went home.

When the United States launched Desert Storm, I was living in Dallas and working for an alternative newspaper. I opposed the military action. I had no doubts that it was wrong, that its justifications were thin and misguided. I registered with some organization in Washington as a conscientious objector in the event of a draft, and in fact wrote a piece for my newspaper about ways to "dodge" a draft, which at the time was much discussed. I also remember Operation Just Cause, (or "Just 'Cos" as I liked to call it), the U.S. action in Panama to capture Manuel Noriega, news of which broke while I was in an electronics store; it was on all the TVs. Anyway, the Gulf War seemed of a piece with that operation—a brutish demonstration of America's ability to throw its weight all over the world, picking and choosing targets for one reason, but stating another.

What's different this time is that the United States was actually attacked. The threat wasn't abstract at all. Putting aside whatever feelings I might have had—what feelings I had—about an animal desire to "hit back," it seemed to me that a military response was inescapable. To have done nothing would have been to show weakness that would inflate the power of this group that was vocal in its desire to wreak havoc on the United States.

This was a new feeling. Later the bombing started in Afghanistan and I followed along in the newspapers, the Web sites, the television window in the bedroom. I read the arguments in the magazines, listened to them on the radio, engaged in them via e-mail with friends. I had my reservations, but by and large I sided with the overseers of this war. Possibly because what was happening was different, justifiable in a way those earlier campaigns were not. Possibly because I'm just older, and changing.

I did no work on September 11. I watched television. My nod to work is that for long stretches I watched CNBC. (The magazine I write for immediately switched gears and didn't particularly need any copy from me.) There was Maria Bartiromo, typically unflappable as she barked out the latest dope from the trading floor of the New York Stock Exchange, where she was usually buffeted by the sea of scurrying bodies. She was out on the floor this morning, too, but today you could actually *see* the floor, as she was the only human being in the shot. She'd been out on Wall Street when downtown Manhattan was physically rocked by the jets that slammed into the towers. She told what she'd seen, in an unfamiliarly demonstrative way, her Brooklyn accent, normally wrestled to the ground, coming through clearly.

Ron Insana appeared, speaking from Rockefeller Center; he, too, had been on Wall Street when the drama unfolded—and had a dust-covered blue blazer to prove it. It also appeared as if there was perhaps a layer of dust on his head, but that may have been a function of the lighting. An hour later he popped up again on NBC, where he shared his firsthand observations with Tom Brokaw. He was still wearing the dusty blazer, though it was by now about 1 P.M. in New York. Was he going to wear it all day? Should I file something about CNBC's coverage? The idea of Insana trooping around from studio to studio covered with ash could be played for a laugh, couldn't it?

No. Nothing could be played for laughs. If the television adaptation of *The Hitchhiker's Guide* had been scheduled to run on the night of Tuesday, September 11, it would have been canceled. The news ran wall-to-wall; there weren't even any ads. Actually, I distinctly remember turning on the television on Saturday, September 15, seeing an ad, and feeling joy and relief: Normalcy.

• • •

I felt I needed to file something. On Wednesday I wrote a piece dealing with the most obvious question on my "beat": What will happen when the markets open. It was a bad piece, but again I felt a *need* to file. In a sense I was relieved that I could write *something* that was related to Topic A. I was relieved not to be an entertainment or fashion reporter. Still, I have a tendency to go for cheap laughs in my column, because people respond well to cheap laughs. I couldn't do that at the moment. Nothing could be played for laughs. They kept saying on television that everything had changed forever, humor had changed forever, irony had died. My column sort of concluded with a note of who-cares-about-stocks-anyway-at-a-time-like-this, and it was surprisingly well received. I'd spent the last five years thinking about and writing about American Money Culture. Was this the end of that?

Online, there were a lot of pictures of tiny bodies falling from the Trade Center towers. Little shapes. Human bodies. Later I read a story from the *Washington Post*, in which a reporter sat and talked with a radical in Pakistan, sympathetic to Osama bin Laden, bellicosely proclaiming that the attacks were justified, that the people in those towers were complicit in evil. The reporter had a copy of *Time* magazine and showed the radical some of the pictures. The explosion. The ashy aftermath. And one of those pictures I'm talking about. "What is that?" the radical asked. "Is it a bird?"

"No," the reporter said, "it's a person. It's a person leaping from the high floors of the tower, dozens and dozens of stories above the ground."

Even this radical closed his eyes. Even he, if only for a second, felt horror and grief. *That's good.*

I did have an odd desire to go to New York after September 11, or maybe not so odd. I wanted to see the aftermath for myself. By the

This Is America

aftermath what I mostly mean is the physical rubble of Ground Zero. The smell. The "missing" posters all over downtown. I lived in the West Village, and I gather that for a day or two I would have had to show ID to get around below 14th Street. I wanted to see the empty restaurants, and streets, the backdrop for a crisscross of personal memories.

I chalk up a good part of this feeling to a desire to be "in on it." To be "part of the thing."

Someone asked me if I wished I'd been at my old job, at the *New York Times Magazine*. That hadn't occurred to me. The answer was no. It's true that this would have put me mentally closer to the action, in a sense, as I'm sure my old colleagues were consumed with "the thing," and obligated to deal with it. My online column turned out to offer almost precisely the professional outlet I wanted. Money culture issues—the stock market, the curious idea of spending as a patriotic act—hovered on the outskirts of Topic A, and held my interest. I also have a great deal of control over the worldview of my column; the problem with being at the *Times* would have been the obligation to deal with all of this through someone else's worldview. I know how to make magazine stories work, I understand the prism of the magazine. I was not interested in that prism, which has a tendency to flatten out everything, to bend everything into focus in exactly the same way. I knew what the stories and the angles would be, and I didn't want any part of that. It was a relief.

And I can't even say that I wish I still lived in New York. I just wanted to see it again. The thing about New York is that any given corner is always the same, but you find yourself at that corner as many different people. A person with a different job, a different ambition, a different lover, a different set of memories. I was many people, the corner was always the corner.

On this issue of "being in on it," there is something else I need to say. Some weeks after the attack, I read a story called "Why Didn't I Know Anyone Who Died on September 11?" I hated this story. I hated it because it was dishonest. It consisted of some very unsurprising math—probabilties and degrees of separation and all that. Well, no shit. Five or six thousand people, a city of 8 million, a country of 290 million, no fucking shit that it's unlikely most people would directly know anyone killed. What the story should have been called was, "I Wish I Knew Someone Who Died On September 11," because that's what really inspires the question of "Why Didn't I?"

I lived in New York City for eight years. I left a year and a half ago but have visited six times during that period. My last visit was in late August, passing through on the way to a wedding upstate. In Hell's Kitchen, discombobulated as I often am when I'm in Manhattan now, I wheeled around and found the towers as directional markers. I spent most of my twenties in New York, and I feel deeply connected to the place. I know, literally, hundreds of people there. I was worried about whether anyone I knew might have died in the towers, but only for a relatively brief moment. When I heard that no one from the *Wall Street Journal* (located next door) was killed, or anyone I knew at TheStreet.com (also nearby) or the couple of people I know who live in the immediate vicinity of the World Trade Center, then I was more or less certain that the only way someone I know could have been killed would be the result of a wild coincidence—for some reason they just happened to be in the wrong place at the worst possible time.

Obviously I checked in with people anyway. Not frantically, but steadily. I found if they were OK, and if their friends, loved ones, acquaintances were okay. The answers were almost all affirmative. An old colleague was due for an interview in the building that morning but had overslept. His interviewee, and various other familiar sources of his, were dead. A fellow exNew Yorker here in New Orleans lost one of her closest friends, who was a pastry chef

This Is America

at Windows on the World. A friend whose wife used to make use of the studio space within the towers that a special city program made available to artists told me one person, a sculptor, was working in the building that morning and presumed dead; my friend thought there should be a show of work by artists who had used the space, on the theme of a view that no longer existed.

Most people, though, knew no one in the buildings, and many expressed a kind of feeling of surprise or good fortune at this. I think what they really felt was closer to guilt. Or at least partly guilt. The other part is they felt a desire for a more direct connection to this thing, a desire to share more directly in the grief. But forget what they felt—I'm describing what I felt.

I never actually wept, but on several occasions I felt the desire to. I'm hardwired not to shed tears, so it takes something fairly extreme to bring them out. I felt it the afternoon of September 11 as I listened to an interview on MSNBC with a guy who had been in one tower with his wife when the other was struck. He'd been told the tower they were in was safe, had not been hit—it still seemed like a horrible accident at that moment—and he and his wife went in different directions within the building. He had gotten out, and now here he was on television, breaking down in front of us, begging viewers who might have seen his wife to contact him. I choked up and wondered why they didn't have the mercy to get this man off television. I choked up reading about the travails of *Wall Street Journal* managing editor Peter Kann on the day of the attacks, and the emotional moment when other top editors there, who feared he'd been killed, heard from him by telephone. I also choked up, oddly enough, looking at a line-drawing map in the *New York Times*, showing the area that had been leveled. Something about all those familiar street names . . .

And I choked up on Monday night, September 17, during David Letterman's monologue on his first post-attack show.

But the tears never came, maybe because they would have seemed hollow. There's been a storybook quality to my life, or maybe I should say there's been a storybook quality to the American narrative over the course of my life. Every time something has seemed bad, there has been an incredibly happy ending. I was born at the end of 1968, a year of discontent, uncertainty, riots, and protests not just all over the United States but from Mexico City to Paris. Some of my earliest memories are of the jittery Jimmy Carter years, the energy crisis, hostages in Iran. It seemed bad. It all worked out. Reagan meant a kind of confrontational stance with the USSR, and the seemingly authentic threat of nuclear war. The Evil Empire fell while I was in college. I graduated at a bleak economic moment, reading stories that my generation would be the first not to surpass its parents' standard of living. Instead, the economy exploded, and I've never had the slightest problem finding work. By the time I was twenty-eight or so I was making more money than I ever thought I'd make in my life, and today I live in a house that's nicer than the comfortable one I grew up in. Things just seemed to work out.

What did people mean when they kept saying, over and over, This is America?

This is America, and we will not be cowed?

This is America, and we are strong and we are not afraid?

This is America, and this can't happen here?

This is America, and they told me I was safe?

This is America and we live in a special bubble in which all is always well?

This is America, and someone is fucking up the storyline?

David Alger was a money manager. He specialized in momentum investing, making a massive number of trades in his funds to ride hot stocks while they were hot. He was not a long-term guy. It's one

This Is America

philosophy of money. When I worked at *Fortune* I edited a piece about him, and I followed his career afterward because I found his high-risk style fascinating.

He died in the World Trade Center on September 11.

The pastry chef I mentioned before was named Heather. She was my age, thirty-two. From Honolulu. I have here the mini-obituary that the *New York Times* ran about her, on September 15. There's a picture of her smiling and wearing sunglasses. The friends of mine in New Orleans who knew her traveled to Hawaii for the services. They tell me she was a smoker.

I still have this obituary, and I believe that September 15 was the first day that the *Times* began running these thumbnail sketches of lives lost in the World Trade Center. There are twenty on the page. I look at this feature almost every day, and now the *Times* tends to put about fifteen on a page. At one point I figured that at the pace the *Times* was going it would take more than a year to run these little sketches of everyone who died. David Alger's sketch finally appeared in late November. Perhaps I'll save it, along with Heather's.

Why? Why am I saving the obituary of a woman I never met? Why am I still reading these things every day? Or at the very least scanning them?

I look at this page every day because I am looking, with trepidation but also some other feeling that I'd rather not articulate, for a familiar face, a familiar name. I have not given up.

I can't quite bring myself to discard Heather's obituary because it is the most authentic connection I have. I can say with complete honesty that I wish I had met her, and that I badly wish she had not been killed. I badly wish I could meet her still. And when I work through that set of feelings, it makes my relief authentic. And my grief, as well. It makes me understand that while I don't have a clear connection to this tragedy that would perhaps bring a clarity to my grief, and that would make the reasons for my grief more visible, more *justifiable*, I understand that I don't care whether the motives for my grief are clear or justified—I know what my motives are, and what my grief is.

The thing about September 11, the day, the way that day felt, that I would like to remember, was the possibility that the happy story line was over. Even a few months on it sounds ridiculous to say any of this, but, again, in that moment anything seemed possible. That the explosions would keep coming. That they would get bigger. That foreigners would be rounded up. Armed guards everywhere. The economy reimagined completely. Maybe even the president assassinated, governmental chaos. That morning, it seemed that all bets were off. The storybook was full of lies.

No wonder I wanted to weep! And yet . . . the story has always worked out. Wouldn't it work out again? Isn't life a movie, and by the next reel we'll be seeing the glimmers of hope that will show us the way to another happy ending? Won't I still be able to live in my happy house, and take a nice vacation now and then, and enjoy music and wine and Letterman?

If I had known someone who died in the World Trade Center, it would have pushed all these questions to one side. I would have felt a direct link to tragedy and catalyst for grief that needed no explanation. Something direct would have been more cathartic than all this abstraction. Something real and authentic. A person into whose eyes I had looked. I think that this was the animating desire behind the idiotic rumination over "why didn't I know anyone there?" On those rare occasions when we're all looking out the same window on the same thing at the same time, it happens, for most of us, over an enormous distance, both physically and emotionally. *Is it real?* We want to rush into the town square and see. We want to be a part of it. Authentically and unambiguously connected to it. It is a big and special thing, and to touch it would be special. It would make me special and real. It would underscore that fundamental idea: I exist.

This Is America

● ● ●

All of this is not so bad as it sounds. I'm making it sound like callous solipsism. But that's not really what I mean. In fact what I mean is that what I was reaching for was a negation of solipsism—the more direct the connection I could have to the tragedy, the better, for the simple reason that it would make the empathy more powerful, the event even more undeniable and unforgettable. There was a lot of talk of getting back to normal, and I'm sure I wanted that too, but in a way I didn't ever want to get back to normal. Despite the insistence that this thing had changed us all forever, what I was afraid of was that, actually, it hadn't.

I never believed that, for example, humor had changed forever. To those who said that we would never laugh the same way again, I had a two-word response: *Hogan's Heroes.* A sitcom set in a German prison camp. If there can be sitcoms at all after the Holocaust and the atom bomb, then anything is possible. Within weeks, Letterman dropped the "cold opening" to his show, and within months was telling Osama bin Laden jokes. Still, that period when nothing was funny, when one after another the late-night hosts went on the air and agonized at the futility of their enterprise, it was an extraordinary thing. It was a brief time of Total Perspective, and awful.

John Gray, writing in the *New Statesman*, proclaimed in the wake of September 11: "The dozen years between the fall of the Berlin Wall and the assault on the Twin Towers will be remembered as an era of delusion." Those same dozen years also happen to encompass my adult life. Since he more or less articulates what I, and a lot of people, I think, felt at that moment, you can see why the attacks, and what their aftermath might mean, was not an abstract matter. What did it mean if the fabric of my entire adult life—all that business about things working out—were a naive fiction?

On the other hand, I read Gray's comments in the December issue of *Harper's*, on a day when I'd already digested various articles about people showing up at shopping malls at three in the morning

275

for a chance to buy cheap televisions at after-Thanksgiving sales. Television was thick with ads again. My column in *Slate* had resumed a good deal of its traditional smart-alecky tone. Photographs of women in bikinis on the cover of magazines had been replaced by photographs of women in stars-and-stripes bikinis.

This is America. If we live in fear (people said) our enemies win. But if we go back to what we were (others mused), then maybe our enemies were right about us. So this bizarre ritual of looking at Heather's picture, of reconsidering over and over my tenuous connection to David Alger, these things are a way of resisting that powerful call to get back to normal and be exactly what I was before. Because that, really, is the last thing I want.

From the Pentagon

**By Sandra Jontz as told to
Timothy Stewart-Winter and Rebecca Hanover
—European and Pacific *Stars and Stripes***

SANDRA JONTZ of the military's daily paper for overseas service-members, European and Pacific Stars and Stripes, *was one of the few reporters to make it to the site of the Pentagon crash. Watching CNN's coverage of the World Trade Center attacks from her Pentagon office, she felt the vibrations of American Airlines Flight 77 as it slammed into the western edge of the building, just one wedge away. Ignoring orders to evacuate the building, Jontz slipped into the building's center court-yard to get the story. As burn patients trickled out, she put aside her notebook and tended to their wounds. Over the next fifteen hours, she treated victims and firefighters and occasionally called her editor to dic-tate notes.*

Jontz, thirty-two, grew up in a military family. Her American father is a retired Navy Chief Petty Officer who met her Italian mother more than thirty-five years ago while stationed in Sigonella, Italy. After grad-uating from George Mason University in Fairfax, Virginia, in 1992, she worked for two daily Virginia newspapers. In 2000 she joined the mil-itary publication for overseas servicemembers, Stars and Stripes, *as its Pentagon and Capitol Hill correspondent. Jontz's essay describes the conflicting loyalties she faced as a reporter, Pentagon employee, and emergency medical technician.*

The day began normally. I awoke at 6:30 and slugged it to work, which entails standing in line to be taken to the office by a carpool—an extreme solution to D.C.'s chronic traffic problems. At 8:15 A.M., I arrived at the Pentagon's E-ring on the second floor, one wedge away from the one that would be attacked. I had just returned the week before from five weeks in Bosnia and was looking forward to getting back into the swing of things on my Pentagon and Capitol Hill beats.

I write for *European and Pacific Stars and Stripes*, the military's newspaper for overseas service members, and cover the Navy, Marine Corps, Capitol Hill, and the military education system. I also cover the military health-care system, called TRICARE, which is made a bit easier since I'm a certified emergency medical technician.

I was in the midst of responding to my backlog of e-mails when my editor called shortly after nine o'clock: "Turn on CNN," he barked. "Something happened at the World Trade Center. I want you to cover it." I needed information, but didn't know how I would get it. The mayor's office in New York had to be in chaos. And with all hell breaking loose, nobody would take a call from *Stars and Stripes*. I needed a game plan.

I wanted to call my cousin, Roberta Mazzarino, who works in the Financial District, a couple of blocks from the World Trade Center. I planned to ask whether she had heard the attack, felt it, seen it and whether she was OK. Then I heard the thud. It shook the ceiling-high partitions in the inner office of our press division.

From the Pentagon

Have I lost my mind? Am I sympathizing with the World Trade Center victims? Is this what they felt? I asked a colleague, "Did you hear and feel that?"

"Yeah. You?"

Almost immediately Pentagon employees ran through the halls. "Evacuate the building! There's been an explosion!" *From what? A car bomb? Are we under attack?* Nobody suspected a plane had crashed into the building.

Lisa Burgess, a colleague and close friend, was walking in the Pentagon toward the subway system on route to the National Transportation and Safety Board in Washington, D.C., to cover the investigation into the New York crash when the Pentagon plane hit. She rushed back to our office and found us safe but frantic. I couldn't find my cell phone and was searching for it as Pentagon employees barked: "Get out of the building! Get out of the building!" Nonetheless, I collected a notebook, tape recorder, and briefcase and found my cell phone to dial my editor in D.C. at his office in the National Press Building on 14th Street. I told him we were being evacuated.

Lisa and I tried to figure how we would cover whatever had happened. Instead of evacuating, we made our way toward the center courtyard, where we could see smoke billowing from one side of the building. The central courtyard, what used to be called Ground Zero before the World Trade Center collapse, was filled with patients and medical experts from the Pentagon clinic. As an EMT, I'd dealt with accidents before, but I'd never seen so many people so severely burned. In Fredericksburg, Virginia, (where I am a volunteer member of its rescue squad), most of our calls are medical—people suffering from heart attacks, difficulty breathing, allergic reactions. Apart from the occasional car accident, I don't see too many trauma patients. Still, I am a certified EMT—with enough training to be useful. I asked a woman clad in a white lab coat, with an air of being in charge, "What can I do?"

Sandra Jontz

Although I was no longer thinking about how to get my story, I knew in the back of my head that I had a dual function. I would help now and retain information to dictate to my editor later. I don't know if it was the decision a good journalist would make but I decided not to take notes or conduct any interviews.

Lisa has been covering the military for more than eleven years and consequently also has some medical training. We attended to patients. A few had black soot on their noses and mouths, but were breathing fine and didn't exhibit external burns. Others had skin just melting off their bodies. I tried to help patients as quickly as I could so I could move on to others.

I assisted a medic putting an IV into a patient. I held down the patient's arm to stabilize it. Another patient had blood on the upper part of his shirt. I worried he might have a sucking chest wound, a potentially fatal wound in which air enters the lungs through the chest instead of through one's nose or mouth. I put my ungloved hand over his chest to keep air from entering his lungs through his chest. When Lisa handed me trauma shears, I cut open his shirt to find no wound. The cut on his chin that had bled onto his shirt.

As rumors about the plane crash circulated, other scares arose. I was tending to a severely burned patient when people started shouting, "Hurry up. Another plane inbound, another plane inbound. We've gotta get out of here!" It was terrifying. We were trapped in the center courtyard, unable to escape without reentering a building that might be attacked at any time.

We loaded the casualties onto little vehicles that look like golf carts with no covering. Normally, these four-wheelers roam the Pentagon's hallways, but now they ferried victims to the building's perimeter.

After treating patients, I joined others looking for fire extinguishers. We planned to fight the source of the smoke pouring out of Corridors Three and Four. When we got there guards barred the way. "Everybody get out of the center courtyard," they ordered, now that there were not more patients. Then they escorted us underneath a bridge and out to the nascent command center in front of the crash site.

Outside the Pentagon we saw light poles strewn across the field. The plane had clipped them. We could visualize its path. It must have been so low that people who had been in the cars on Route 27, a major roadway passing next to the Pentagon, could have almost reached up and touched it as it passed. I saw a Department of Transportation camera that monitors traffic backups pointed toward the crash site. But I haven't seen any video from it yet.

Everyone was barking orders. The Pentagon is concentrated with leaders, policy makers, and higher-ups who all wanted to take command. They were all shouting:

"Come ten feet in."

"No, go ten feet back."

"Come in front of the guardrail."

"No, stand behind the guardrail."

Eventually, doctors arrived and took over. "This is where we need to set up triage."

We shuttled stretchers, IVs, gauze, long boards, and trauma shears to the field directly in front of the crash site. Nobody came out of the building. Then it hit me. *My God, they're dead! The survivors have already escaped.* It was between 11 A.M. and noon. Military fighters buzzed overhead. When one passed, the crowd would shout, "Whoo-hoo! The good guys!"

I worried about my friends and family, but couldn't get through to anyone but my editor—and then only every fifteenth try. I dictated mental notes to him and lent my phone to people trying to reach family in California and Florida.

The response to the situation was classic military: fast and extremely organized. The Red Cross arrived immediately and handed out drinks. People in the Pentagon broke open soda machines and passed around cans of Coke and juice. Medical experts identified us by taping duct tape to our arms with our level of certification written on them (CPR training, IV proficient, basic skills). Later they gave me a blue clinic vest to indicate I was medical personnel. Emergency responders set up an immediate critical care tent for "the walking wounded" and a communications center in the field in front of the crash site. Other people closed down Route 27. They brought in a Bobcat (a tiny bulldozer) and somebody with a jack hammer to demolish the Jersey walls that divide the highway. Urban Search and Rescue teams from Fairfax County, Virginia, and Montgomery County, Maryland, began their work of shoring up the building and sending in rescue workers to recover victims. This within three hours of the attack.

At two o'clock in the afternoon I started interviewing people. I felt good about it. I never disguised myself as a medical person. Instead, I carried my notepad visibly and made it clear I was a reporter. Some people didn't want to talk—and I didn't bother them twice. But many did. One man knew his fiancée's new office had been hit, because he remembered seeing the helipad from her office window—the helipad now littered with debris from the crash. A former marine had run from the Navy Annex, a military building about half a mile away, when he heard about the crash. At the Pentagon he helped a woman crawl through a window. She was severely burned. Her eyes had melted, he described.

Even as a reporter in Bosnia and Herzegovina, I had never seen anything like this. I arrived after the war. One day I watched as forensic anthropologists unearthed a mass grave containing about fifty bodies. The smell was unimaginable, revolting. It sounds disrespectful, but it's not. But those people had been buried for years. They had died in a war that had ended. And, equally important, I had felt no immediate threat to my life. Even when I had gone on patrol with several peacekeepers in the Republic of Serbska, the Serb-controlled region.

At three o'clock, I finally reached my mom by cell phone. She

From the Pentagon

cried. We both cried. She had sent me an e-mail, but mistyped the address. What luck. The misaddressed e-mails get routed to Victoria Coleman, our computer server manager, who read the subject line "Are you OK," and decided to respond. "Your daughter has been in contact with her editor. She's trying to get in touch with you but can't, but know that she's fine."

I stayed at the site until early evening, when it became clear there wouldn't be any more patients. After that I was assigned to a triage bus for firefighters still fighting the stubborn blaze. I treated them for heat exhaustion—taking their blood pressure, making sure they were hydrated, and giving them cool rags for their heads.

At one-thirty in the morning I walked about a quarter mile to a nearby intersection not blocked off by security. Lisa picked me up at a traffic light and we went to her house. Once there, she asked, "You want anything?"

"A beer!" We each had a bottle and went to sleep.

At seven the next morning we were back at the site. Lisa went into the building to cover it from the pressroom. Somebody suggested I use my blue clinic vest and duct tape armband to reenter the crash site. I didn't. It would have been deceitful. I'm an EMT, and the emergency was over. Instead, I went to the media staging area at the Citgo gas station half a mile away. There we had periodic access to heads of the Federal Emergency Management Agency, urban search and rescue units, firefighters, police, FBI, and Pentagon officials.

I interviewed the heads of the Urban Search and Rescue teams and passersby. A stringer photographed people setting up memorials and vigil sites (my camera was still in the Pentagon). I profiled a woman waiting for her husband to come out. Her family and friends sat with her, waiting.

Wednesday night, I saw my parents for the first time since the attack. They picked me up at the Springfield metro stop, about fifteen minutes from where they live. At their house, I was finally able to reach my cousin Roberta in New York. She was terrified. She had seen the second plane crash into the World Trade Center. We were both angry and relieved. I cried like a big baby. "Oh, my God! I'm home! I'm safe! I'm alive!" Roberta took it badly. I felt awful. She's from Italy and wanted to forget about her work and studies in New York and just go back.

I worked from the Citgo gas station for two days, taking notes, writing articles longhand, and dictating them to my editor by cell phone (my laptop was in the office). It was onerous, but got the story out.

The deadlines were unremitting. *Stars and Stripes* comes out in Europe and the Pacific. Both editions are printed overseas and have their own time zone-specific deadlines: 1 in the afternoon for Europe, and 10 P.M. for the Pacific.

I was proud to cover the Pentagon and the friends and families of the victims because other media were overlooking the Pentagon and conflating 9/11 with the World Trade Center. At the Olympics, for example, New York was on display: their police officers, firefighters. I wanted to interject, "Hey, don't forget the other victims!" What about the 185 people who died at the Pentagon and who were on that plane. Their families are forever changed too. As are the families of the victims of United Flight 93, which crashed outside Somerset, Pennsylvania, before it could fly into another building.

We worked six days a week that first month and a half. Then, on October 7, we went to war. Driving to work that day I was leery. *Will they retaliate? Hit the Pentagon again? Somewhere else?* It was the first time since the attacks that I was hesitant about going into the Pentagon, which already had been a target once.

But now the Pentagon was much more secure. MPs with M-16s stand outside the doors. National Guardsmen and Military Police check IDs and badges, often manually. The parking lot was barricaded to keep cars or trucks loaded with bombs from parking near the

From the Pentagon

building, though they recently moved the perimeter in a bit to open up parking.

At the same time, the military is communicating more. The formerly biweekly press briefings now occur almost daily. Donald Rumsfeld, the Secretary of Defense, joined by the chairman of the Joint Chiefs of Staff, Gen. Richard Myers, attend many of them instead of sending other press officers.

Despite all this new press-related activity at the Pentagon, I hear less and less about the attacks. For a while, Pentagon officials held monthly anniversary observances: one, two, three. That has stopped. After October 7, we started focusing on the operations—Enduring Freedom, Noble Eagle. Now it's returned to business as usual. It really has. Even the war at times becomes secondary to the news of the defense budget, which is a perennial huge story for our readers, especially when writing about salaries and benefits.

My feelings about my job haven't changed. I've always wanted to be a reporter and still do. I didn't plan to be a military reporter, but now that I am one I love it! I would love to go to Afghanistan or the Philippines. I'm not scared. It's where I want to be. Unfortunately, *Stars and Stripes* already has reporters in the Pacific and European theater, making it cheaper to send them instead of us. Lisa and I keep champing at the bits. We want to cover a war. Be war correspondents. My parents pray daily for the opposite. Though my dad spent thirty years in the navy, and a stint in Vietnam, he doesn't want me near a war zone. My mom is just being a mom.

I just got back from covering the detainees in Guantanamo Bay. I wanted to be there to cover it fairly and objectively. I was among the first reporters in the fleet hospital. As I stood fifteen feet away from some of the detainees (they wouldn't let us closer) I didn't feel hate or anger. I needed to be removed from those feelings. And I didn't know who I was looking at. *Did that man lying on the hospital gurney actually shoot at U.S. forces? Did he know about the plot?* All the prisoners looked so young. I can't imagine they were very highly placed in the Al Qaeda network. The Defense Department isn't telling us much about the detainees. They don't want the other side to know who we've got.

The foreign press has been calling foul a lot. Our service members are living in worse conditions in Afghanistan than are the detainees living in Guantanamo Bay. Our servicemen are cold and haven't showered in months. All to make sure we're safe. God love them! I've watched their daily exercises and know how grueling their training is. It's ten times worse during war. I am very proud to cover the military. It's why I go to work every day despite the uncertainty.

Facing the Fear

By Chris Williams
—Columbia Graduate School of Journalism

September 11 represented both the most important and most disturbing story that many journalists would ever cover. CHRIS WILLIAMS of the Columbia Graduate School of Journalism saw both sides at once. He interviewed a woman who had been in the World Trade Center mall at 8:00 A.M. to buy her kids a stuffed animal. He also spoke to a man who had sent a subordinate to a meeting in the WTC in his stead.

The crisis and subsequent interviews triggered a crisis of conscience. Williams was proud of the stories he produced (reproduced here), but disturbed by the ease with which he subordinated his helping instincts to pursue his journalistic mission. He wondered whether journalists inherently exploit their subjects. By the end of the dreadful week, he didn't know if he still wanted to pursue journalism, afraid of the reporter he would become. But with the help of his journalism professor, Sig Gissler, and Mary Gissler, a former nurse and compassionate woman who is married to Professor Gissler, Williams redoubled his commitment to his work.

Williams, twenty-five, is a native of Virginia Beach, Virginia. Before enrolling at Columbia's Graduate School of Journalism, he wrote for a small alternative weekly in Virginia Beach about rave scenes, teenage driving, and mayoral races.

Homesick

I was planning to sleep in on Tuesday.

I had a meeting scheduled for 1 P.M., but no morning classes. Tuesday is always a reporting day. I was covering the Williamsburg and Greenpoint beat in Brooklyn.

At 9 A.M. there was a knock at the door. It was Muneeza, one of my suite-mates, telling me to turn on the television. I sat on my bed watching smoke pour out of one of the Twin Towers. As we wondered what was happening, the news anchors reported a flash and an explosion from the other tower. Another plane had hit.

There goes the neighborhood story. I immediately called my professor, Sig Gissler. Busy. He was no doubt on the phone with one of my classmates from Reporting and Writing One, the core course in the fall semester at the Columbia University Graduate School of Journalism. Gissler ran his class much like an editor would a newsroom. The former editor of the *Milwaukee Journal*, Gissler was a reporter at heart and there was little doubt as to what his instructions would be when I did reach him.

As I scrambled to wash up and change my clothes, I heard something about the Pentagon. A plane had now crashed into it as well.

"What the hell is happening?" I asked aloud to no one in particular.

The phone rang. Gissler.

"Get as far down there as you can and see what you can see," he instructed. "And be careful."

So much for the curriculum. Everything we thought we'd be

Facing the Fear

covering this year as students at Columbia, a school where you spend more time reporting on the streets of New York than sitting in a classroom, had just gone up in smoke. Our new beat: the biggest news story in the world.

Sitting in the lecture hall during the August orientation, I had listened to an endless parade of speakers tell us what was in store for us in the coming months. "Come September, you'll feel as though you were shot out of a cannon," we were told.

No shit.

Muneeza and I raced out of our apartment building, fueled by urgency and chocolate-chip granola bars.

Jen Chen, another friend and classmate, met us outside. The scene on 109th Street and Broadway was chaotic. All the trains were down and people lined either side of the street hailing cabs and even thumbing rides.

As Jen tried to flag a taxi, I tried to collect my thoughts. *What the hell is happening?* I just couldn't get my brain wrapped around this thing. *What am I doing?* I had confidence in my reporting and writing skills, sure. But I was still an "entry level" journalist. I had barely two years of experience at a small weekly paper in Virginia covering things like the local rave scene, teen driving, and the Virginia Beach mayor's race. Mere trivia by comparison. *There's no way I'm ready for this level of reporting.* With a growing feeling of self-doubt, I hopped in a cab and headed downtown.

We sat in stunned silence as the reports came over the radio. The first tower had collapsed. The second building had fallen as well. *How could these massive landmarks be gone?*

The cab dropped us at Charles Street and 9th Avenue, about twenty blocks from the scene. People ran east and north as we headed south and west—into them. Every type of vehicle you could think of with lights and sirens flew by, something always coming at thirty-second intervals. Ash and dust billowed off their tails like smoke screens from James Bond's BMW.

Rumors were out of control. One woman stopped us and said another plane had crashed into Camp David. Another said a fourth plane had been shot down over Pennsylvania. I tried my best to scribble down everything, being careful to make notes separating rumors, of which there plenty, from facts, of which there were few.

We stopped near a police barricade to catch our breath three blocks from the World Trade Center. I tried to call my family in Virginia, but cell lines were jammed. People came in and out of a small clothing store on Duane Street. The store's manager, Rhea O'brien, let us use the phones. We sat in the store's converted basement office, watching the news coverage on television and talking to a visibly shaken Rhea. She had been in the World Trade Center mall at 8:00 A.M. to buy a stuffed animal for one of her kids.

"I really just want to go home," she told us. "I just want my children and I want to go home."

Me too, Rhea. I'm ready to get the hell out of here myself.

I walked outside, again trying to pull my thoughts—and myself—together. I had never felt more homesick. I sat on the store's steps while Jen and Muneeza placed calls, and doubts about this whole journalism gig crept in. I was smack in the middle of the biggest story I'd probably ever cover, and suddenly I wanted no part. I considered telling my friends to go on without me.

But then I saw a parade of determined-looking men and women march up Duane Street toward the police barricade. Led by federal agents in FBI windbreakers, they included doctors, nurses, construction workers, and other citizens offering their services. Suddenly, I was ashamed of even thinking of running away. When Muneeza and Jen came out, I suggested we follow them. Not having recognized the earliest signs of the bipolar mood swings that would fill the next few days, I jogged up the street with my friends.

From union workers in tank tops and hard hats to yuppies in khakis and polo shirts, the diversity of volunteers was impressive. Some talked of once serving their countries in wartime, of being

Facing the Fear

prepared to do so again. As the crowd grew, self-appointed leaders emerged. The prerequisites: a big mouth and strong vocal chords.

Leaders passed out sign-up sheets of scrap paper instructing volunteers to write down their names and what skills they had to offer, as well as emergency contact information just in case. Police and FBI agents fought to control this rapidly growing and increasingly impatient crowd, shouting at everyone to move onto the sidewalk and out of the street so emergency vehicles could have access. Moments later a convoy of nine New Jersey ambulances and fire trucks rumbled through the streets. The crowd cheered.

I sat on the sidewalk among the volunteers with my friends from the journalism school. Three others had now joined us: James Brown, Dave Phillips, and their roommate, a law student named John Hirsch. As we exchanged stories and talked about all we had seen that morning, the doctors, nurses, and engineers were called in and the crowd of volunteers began to shrink. Soon only the construction workers and the average citizens looking to help with search and rescue remained. And the journalists. Sitting duck-duck-goose style on the concrete just a block away from chaos is an odd venue to have an ethics debate, but I had to pose the question that had been bothering me since we began following the volunteers.

"Guys," I asked, "are we going in as journalists or volunteers?"

Some, who didn't have specific story assignments from their professors, were ready to strap on the dust masks and head into the rubble. Others argued that we needed to be removed from the situation, keeping an emotional distance so we could report on what was happening around us.

I was torn. I did have an assignment, but how in God's name do you distance yourself from your subject at a time like this?

Our discussion was interrupted by a search and rescue mission. The entire crowd moved forward, and we went with them, marching up Greenwich Street toward the site. I stood next to John, someone I knew who wasn't a reporter, who was headed in there with one purpose—to help people. I just couldn't see holding a notebook and pen, writing about people trying to dig out survivors and not lending a hand. It felt wrong. It felt inhumane. Another volunteer handed me a facemask. I strapped it on while millions of butterflies fluttered around my insides.

At the police line, an officer on guard stopped everyone. The fire from 5 World Trade Center was too big and the smoke was getting too close. Some construction workers argued with the police, saying they were ready to work, but it was no use. Four blocks from the site, we would go no further.

"It's going to be hours," the officer announced.

The volunteers argued as the six of us turned away. But I couldn't help but feel an incredible wave of relief wash over me. There was no way in hell that I was ready to go in there. And, of course, the relief was seasoned with guilt because I was off the hook.

After that, we became reporters again. Sitting down for two hours had given us time to consider what had happened. Now that we were up and moving again, the adrenaline was pumping and the sense of detachment kicked in.

We spent the rest of the afternoon as journalists: Walking the streets, gathering quotes, trying to find an angle. As students, we wouldn't write stories leading with two planes crashing into the World Trade Center. We would be writing sidebars. I scribbled down everything I could, filling my notebook, still not sure where I was headed.

By the end of the day we were wiped. I was stressed out because I still didn't know if I had a story. Muneeza and Jen looked over the map to find our way home. I switched on a portable AM radio to hear the latest news. The President of the United States was about to speak.

Sitting on the curb next to a blue police barricade a few blocks from the disaster with orange-red road flares as the only source of light, I listened to George W. Bush talk about the lost mothers, daughters, fathers, and sons. Suddenly, my feelings of homesickness came rushing back. I wanted very desperately to go home. Not just home to my apartment on the upper West Side, but to Virginia Beach and my family. Away from all this madness, suffering, and death.

When I made it back a little after 11 P.M. I called my mom in Virginia Beach, and my girlfriend in South Carolina. I cried. I cried because the magnitude of what had happened was finally settling in. And I cried because I was no longer sure that journalism, something I had previously expected to have a successful, enjoyable career in, was what I wanted to pursue. The day had changed everything. I didn't want to be that detached, emotionally distant journalist that I had seen myself becoming at certain times of the day. I knew I could never be like that. I wanted to be more involved. I wanted to help. But did that mean I would be limiting how successful I could be in this business? The question knocked around my head all night.

But before this doubt-inducing insomnia, I dried my eyes and began to write. I wrote about the volunteers, everyday people who offered their skills. I wrote about Rhea O'brien offering her phones and tears. I wrote about Tom Perron, a registered nurse who had just finished a graveyard shift at the hospital when he turned on his television and realized his day was just beginning.

I filed the story sometime around 1 A.M. and crawled into bed.

Eager Rescuers Mark Time on Edge of Ruins
September 12, 2001

When registered nurse Tom Perron finished his eight-hour graveyard shift at Columbia Presbyterian Medical Center, he thought it was time to relax. Then he switched on the television and realized his day was just beginning.

Perron was one of the many people who offered their time and talents in downtown Manhattan on Tuesday to help the victims of the World Trade Center attack. Perron was stationed at the triage center on Beach and Greenwich streets, where he helped prepare for casualties.

"We've spent most of the day just getting organized and setting up trauma slots in noncritical areas," Perron said, dressed in blue medical scrubs with a green bandanna covering his head. "We're prepared here for hundreds of patients."

But by 9:30 P.M., they had seen only three patients, the worst of whom had to be treated for a knee abrasion he received when running to safety when the first of the two towers collapsed. The reason, Perron said, is that the rescuers were bringing people out very slowly.

"They lost several hundred rescuers when the first building came down," said Dr. Marino Tavarez of Wyckoff Heights Medical Center, in charge of the volunteer triage. "They have to move hundreds of tons to get people out of there. They have to move the World Trade Center."

Tavarez said rescue efforts were more hampered by the collapse of World Trade Center buildings 5 and 7.

"Unfortunately if it had just been the first two collapses, we would've been able to get more people out sooner," Tavarez said. "But with the other two coming, they literally had to wait for the fires to burn them down."

Earlier in the day on North Moore and Greenwich streets, just a block away from the triage center on Greenwich Street, hundreds of labor union workers and others just wanting to help crowded the street corner. Those wishing to volunteer for search and rescue teams were asked to be sure to have identification or to write their names and emergency contact information down on a piece of paper and keep it in their pockets.

While laborers offered their tools and hands, Rhea O'Brien offered her phones. Volunteers trying to reach friends and family members to update them on their whereabouts and find out the

Facing the Fear

latest news from those watching at home on television were welcomed into the Working Class, a clothing store at 168 Duane Street where O'Brien was doing what she could to help while trying to cope with the day's events.

"I really just want to go home," O'Brien said. "I just want my children and I want to go home."

O'Brien was inside the World Trade Center just fifteen minutes before the first plane crashed into the building. She was shopping at the Warner Brothers Store for a stuffed animal for one of her children.

"It just blows your mind," O'Brien said. "No matter how much you think you're prepared for things. That's why I kiss my kids every day. Every day."

Guilty Pleasures

The next day began with another early phone call to Professor Gissler. Today he was teaming me up with Alexandra Polier, another classmate. I woke Alex with a call.

Alex, twenty-four, had even less journalism experience than I did. She comes from a New York public relations background and had also worked as a press secretary on Capitol Hill. But her enthusiasm became contagious as we chased down our story.

Gissler had given us a tip about a Wall Street executive who was supposed to be at a conference at the Windows On The World restaurant at the top of the World Trade Center on the morning of September 11, but decided to send a colleague and friend in his place. Through her old public relations contacts, Alex knew of a few people who were also supposed to be in the building, but had overslept.

We raced around midtown, and the same feeling of detachment that I'd had yesterday was coming back even stronger. I'm almost ashamed to admit it, but it was fun. Alex was almost giddy. If she was feeling guilty about her excitement, she didn't show it.

When we arrived at our interview with our executive, the

enthusiasm was drained from my body. The mood there was solemn. The executive had obviously had little sleep. His office was now a command center dedicated to finding his friend.

During the interview, he was understandably emotional. Listening to him talk, I found myself fighting my own tears and losing focus. I had trouble keeping track of the questions I wanted to ask, and started wondering if I had any right in the first place.

But Alex didn't flinch. She asked him point-blank if he felt any guilt or responsibility for sending his friend to this conference when he was the one who was supposed to be there.

He paused. I couldn't even look at him and pretended to scribble something in my notebook. Who were we to ask him such an insensitive question at a time like this? I felt like a parasite. We were exploiting him. It's not like we were reporting for the *New York Times*, for God's sake. Essentially we were students working on a homework assignment. And Alex was asking if he felt guilty about sending his friend to his death. I felt ill.

But instead of showing us the door like he should have, he just gave a sad smile.

"It's like I'm the lucky guy who switched seats at the last minute and didn't get on the doomed airplane," he said.

We thanked him for his time, wished him luck, and headed out to finish reporting before the approaching 6 P.M. deadline. After filing our story, Alex suggested we go out and get some food and beer to "celebrate."

I cringed at her choice of words. But I understood how she felt. It had been a rough couple of days, and we had accomplished something. But over our dinner of Mexican food and Brooklyn Lager, the guilt returned. While I was running around reporting I was fine. But once I sat down and caught my breath, I saw the bigger picture. My self-doubt would start creeping back in.

Alex's giddiness didn't help. She was clearly having a blast. What bothered me was that I was too. Aside from that one interview,

Facing the Fear

chasing this story all over town was a great experience. The pressure of writing the story on deadline was exhilarating. But as soon as I stopped and caught my breath, I realized I'd become a mosquito that had sucked the blood out of its sources.

As one friend put it, this was a horrific event, not some fortunate bit of happenstance. Even Gissler—who always refers to us as reporters and never as students—once said that the Columbia Journalism School press pass I wore on a chain around my neck, plus $1.50, would get me a ride on the subway. What right did I have to make Ground Zero my own personal learning lab?

I went home that night feeling like I needed to go to confession.

Running Late and Dodging Death
September 13, 2001
(with Alexandra Polier)

A missed meeting and alarm-clock snooze buttons saved three New Yorkers who might have perished Tuesday if they had followed through with their day's plans.

Late for work, Adrian Sisser, twenty-five, had just left his West Village apartment and headed for the subway station at Houston Street, when he heard jet noise passing overhead. Moments later, he saw the first of two passenger jets crash into the World Trade Center. Sisser worked at Lehman Brothers on the fortieth floor of One World Trade Center. He stood in shock watching the surreal picture of what was to be his destination set ablaze.

"You imagine it's not really happening," Sisser said.

When the second plane hit, Sisser was brought back to reality and ran to his apartment and up to the roof to watch the scene unfold. Wednesday morning, he sat on a friend's couch feeling lucky to be alive.

Sisser's friend Darren Valente sat with him. A software developer with Marsh Putnam Mercer, an insurance brokerage firm with offices on floors ninety-five through one hundred at One

World Trade Center, Valente worked on the ninety-sixth floor, one of the floors struck by the airplane. Fortunately, Valente keeps tech hours.

"It's part of the technology culture nowadays to start late and work late," said twenty-five-year-old Valente, who usually gets to work at 9:30 A.M. "Most people think our age group in this industry are slackers, but it worked in my favor yesterday."

On Tuesday morning, however, Valente had planned to get up early to go to the gym, which would have gotten him into the office before 9 A.M., he said. As luck would have it, he overslept. When the first plane struck the World Trade Center, Valente was in the shower. When he heard the news, Valente immediately picked up the phone to get in touch with friends and coworkers who were part of his approximately ninety-person software development group.

"There were a few people in my group, including my boss and two of my friends who were known for going in notoriously early," Valente said. "I called the hotline number on the Web site and they weren't on the survivor list. I'm assuming they're dead."

A late-afternoon conference call with his company revealed that of the sixty-seven members of Valente's group who reported to work Tuesday, about ten or twelve remained unaccounted for, he said.

Ten flights up from Valente's office, the Waters 2001 Financial Technology Congress, a conference that included high-ranking executives from companies like Compaq, Merrill Lynch, JP Morgan Chase, Reuters and others, was under way with an estimated two hundred in attendance. One senior executive from a Wall Street firm, who wished to remain anonymous, was slated to attend the conference, but sent someone else in his place. He has yet to be accounted for.

"It's like I'm the lucky guy who switched seats at the last minute and didn't get on the doomed airplane," he said.

Facing the Fear

He and other colleagues have created an informal network collaborating with others through phones and e-mail, looking for missing coworkers. At one point while speaking with reporters, the executive ran to his desk to read an e-mail message from a survivor writing to let everyone know he had made it out of the building alive.

"I only knew a couple people at the conference," he said, "but when you get into the six degrees of separation, yeah, we all know someone who knows someone who worked there."

For these three survivors, the magnitude of Tuesday's catastrophe has not yet sunk in.

"My first priority right now is to find my colleague," the executive said. "The emotions aren't coming into it right now. All I'm focused on is finding my friend."

Yesterday afternoon, Valente said the scene in his neighborhood was eerie.

"Everyone on the street had the same blank stare, not really knowing what was going on," he said.

"We lost a fundamental sense of security we had in this country yesterday," the executive said.

"Before, we were worried about street crime. Now we have to worry about guided missiles in the form of airplanes."

Resolution and Reaffirmation

We were given the rest of the week off from reporting. I took the break as a chance to sleep off the dark circles that had formed under my eyes since September 11. I avoided television whenever possible, though if I stayed away too long I'd get antsy, switch it on and cycle through news channels to make sure I wasn't missing anything. I didn't realize until later that the anxiousness I felt, that craving to be plugged into what was going on, would help me sort out my own inner conflicts about my job.

I had class on Saturday morning. Normally, I firmly believe that weekend classes are an evil institution that must be destroyed. This time it got me out of doing a story I had no desire to write.

Gissler was looking for someone to cover the funeral of Father Mychal Judge, the beloved New York firefighter and chaplain. Judge perished when he was hit by falling debris at Ground Zero after he took off his helmet to administer last rites.

Was it an important and compelling story that needed to be told? Of course. Just not by me. I'd had enough experience in covering grief and misery that week, thanks.

I breathed a quiet, selfish sigh of relief when Gissler's wife, Mary, answered the phone and said he'd assigned the story to another student. Mrs. G. also said that after four days of being cooped up in the office and at home, Gissler was now venturing out to Ground Zero to survey the scene for himself, his reporter instincts finally boiling over.

She then asked how I was feeling. I spent the next half hour posing all my dilemmas: What was the point of this job? Was I serving any purpose by going down there and observing and running my mouth instead of volunteering my services? And what right did I have to be there anyway? Should I feel guilty about using this tragedy as a means to get clips and build up my portfolio? Was I adding to these people's pain by prodding them for personal information and making them talk about their missing friends and family? *Am I a parasite?*

I felt bad dumping all that on Mrs. G., but it felt good to get it out. Aside from an e-mail to my old undergrad adviser, I hadn't talked to anyone about any of this. Luckily, she didn't freak out. As a former nurse in a cancer unit, she's had a lot of experience dealing with grief.

She also assured me that I was not, in fact, a parasite, which is always nice for a reporter to hear.

"In many cases," she offered, "it actually helps for victims to talk about their experience. So by just being there for them and listening

Facing the Fear

to their stories about their loved ones, you're doing them a service. You're helping them heal. You'll find many of them are thankful to have someone let them talk."

This journalist-as-counselor idea had never occurred to me. I'm often worried about people thinking the worst when it comes to journalists, so I'm usually focused on projecting sincerity to convince my sources that I have the best intentions. I've always thought that when someone is talking to me for a story, they're doing me a favor, not the other way around.

But now I think of that weak smile from the Wall Street executive as he spoke of his missing friend, and how warmly he treated us when he was so clearly heartbroken. I realize that it was probably the first time he had taken a break to sit down to talk about his feelings. Maybe it helped him a little by opening that pressure release valve just a notch, the same way talking to Mrs. G. helped me.

When I got home that afternoon, waiting for me was an e-mail from Kathy Merlock Jackson, my undergraduate adviser at Virginia Wesleyan College.

She said she'd thought of me the night before as she watched Dan Rather on *The Late Show with David Letterman*. "How can one respond to a disaster as both a journalist and a human being? The very fact that you address the question shows your depth of thought and commitment. I'm proud of you."

That meant a lot coming from Kathy, a trusted and respected friend. Plus, she compared me to Dan Rather, so there's hope for my metaphor and simile writing skills yet.

I was starting to feel better again. I turned on the television to see if there had been any new developments. The remote wasn't the only thing that clicked.

I suddenly remembered something one of our professors, Stephen Isaacs, said during Friday's class. The question was whether journalists were providing a worthwhile service by reporting on the human stories at Ground Zero. Perhaps, it was suggested, it would be more helpful for us to put down the pen and notebook and join the volunteers. It was the same question our little group had debated September 11, just a few blocks away from the disaster area.

"I'm not a doctor," Isaacs said. "I'm not trained in medicine or for search and rescue. I'm a journalist."

We were filling an important need—the need for information. It's one of the basic purposes of journalism. It was same reason I couldn't help but turn on the television even when I tired of seeing the horrific images replayed over and over again. I had to know about the latest developments. People craved news, and journalists were the only ones who could provide it to them in a fair, accurate, and detailed manner. Are we at war? Will we be attacked again? Who's responsible for this? Will we strike back?

We needed people with the skills to clearly explain what had happened and why. But we also desired the human stories. By focusing on one person's story, that Wall Street executive trying to find his friend while fighting the growing realization that he's lost, it helped us all grasp the magnitude of what happened.

As hokey as it sounds, journalism is a noble calling. The work that rose from the ashes of September 11 is proof of that. It was a rebirth of public service journalism. I realize now that in my own small way, I was a part of that.

On Monday, Gissler began class with a moment of silence. We shared our stories and tears. Mrs. G. joined us to offer her advice and fudge brownies. We took a short lunch break halfway through the session, and when we came back, the tears were gone. It was time to go back to work. I pitched a story about the disaster memorabilia that seemed to hit the streets almost immediately. T-shirts with images of the Twin Towers with a stars and stripes backdrop and slogans like "I Survived September 11," and "Evil Will Be Punished" were being peddled by vendors in Times Square.

When class was over, I headed down to Broadway and 42nd Street and did my job.

Facing the Fear

Flag-Waving Vendors Get Back to Business
September 19, 2001

Jose Soto, dressed in a camouflage U.S. Army jacket and khaki shorts, knelt to light a candle in the median on Broadway and 44th Street in Times Square. Then he stood, holding a white T-shirt on a hanger in one hand and a white ski cap with the American flag embroidered on it in the other. "Five dollars, three dollars, five dollars, three dollars," Soto called out to those passing the roadside memorial of photographs, flowers, poems and children's drawings for the victims of last week's attack on the World Trade Center.

Perhaps responding to the call from America's leaders to return to business as usual, street vendors in Times Square were doing just that this week, stocked with an assortment of World Trade Center memorabilia. Some sold framed photographs of the Twin Towers before they were removed from the New York skyline by a pair of hijacked commercial jets. "I Love NY" T-shirts flew off the shelves at two dollars each. Other T-shirts had images of the World Trade Center with a backdrop of a waving U.S. flag and messages like "America Under Attack—I Can't Believe I Made It Out!"

Most of the people buying the merchandise have been tourists, vendors said. The motives vary. Some buyers say they want to own a piece of history, something that will prove that they were here during the attacks. Some see wearing T-shirts like those being sold as another way to patriotism. Vendors gave many of the same reasons for selling the merchandise.

"A lot of people, when they see these pictures, they cry," said Lanawang Thinley, thirty-one, who has a stand on the corner of Broadway and West 45th Street selling framed black-and-white photographs of New York City.

"I can't sell any other pictures except for the Twin Towers," Thinley said.

Despite the lack of interest in the rest of his photos, Thinley said that enough people are buying the World Trade Center pictures to more than make up for it.

"In a normal day, I make $150 to $200," Thinley said, "but now, I'm making $1,000 to $2,000 in a day."

Across the street from Thinley's stand, another table was covered with a pile of white T-shirts. Three young men assisted customers, while their supervisor, forty-seven-year-old Guy Bazelais, handled the money transactions. A handwritten sign posted above the table read "WTC Shirts $4."

One shirt that has caused a stir is white with a U.S. flag in the background and an image of a smoking World Trade Center, Bazelais said. The words "I Survived The Attack" are written at the top.

"Last night I was surrounded by cops upset about the shirts," Bazelais said. "I took them off the shelf. I think they're right. I don't want to cash in on people's emotions."

The shirts, however, were back on the shelf Tuesday.

"I'm just trying to get rid of them now," Bazelais said, raising his voice when asked why he would continue selling shirts that some people found offensive. "After these are gone, that's it. I'm not going to mess with them no more. Look, man, I've fought for this country. If I had the ability to go into battle for America, I would. I was in a construction accident and out of work for three months, so I can't fight and I don't have any money to donate, but I'm going to donate my blood."

When asked what he thought about the shirts Bazelais was selling, a police sergeant standing with three other police officers said: "We normally don't give our opinions or comment on things like this." He declined to give his full name.

Behind the police building in the middle of Times Square, Soto, forty-three, and his partner Norma Gonzalez were still selling T-shirts and other memorabilia near the memorial.

While Soto continued to push his items on people looking at the memorial, Gonzalez, forty-six, stood to one side dressed in a white

Facing the Fear

T-shirt with the words "Evil Will Be Punished" written over an image of a waving U.S. flag. Another shirt was draped over her back with the sleeves tied around her neck like a scarf. The shirt had a similar design to the one she wore, only the words "God Bless America" were written over the flag. Around her neck she wore a pewter U.S. flag pendant, along with a dozen red, white, and blue pens.

"This is actually my first day out here," Gonzalez said, holding a garbage bag full of T-shirts. "Jose's been out here since Wednesday. He brought me out today to show me the ropes. He's the salesman."

Soto held up the hat he wore over his hand like a sock puppet, followed by the T-shirt.

"Three dollars, five dollars," he said, his voice going up and down like a seesaw.

"He's good," Gonzalez said.

Gonzalez admitted that she and Soto saw a chance to make some money, but that it wasn't their primary motive.

"We just like seeing everyone from all over—different countries, different parts of the world—wearing this stuff and showing their American pride," she said.

"Hey, Norm," Soto said. "Put one of those pens around my neck."

Soto, a U.S. Army veteran, said he saw nothing wrong with peddling memorabilia right next to a memorial.

"Hey man, what's more American than this?" he said. "This is the American way of life. This is what we do."

As the digital image of the U.S. flag waved on the ABC Studios screen overhead, overlapped by a large television screen broadcasting a commercial for dishwashing detergent, Soto wandered over to another small group of people viewing the memorial.

"What do we want? Peace!" Soto said. "We don't want war! It costs too much money! This guy knows what I'm talking about! Five dollars—three dollars—five dollars—three dollars."

Camaraderie and Sorrow

By Abby Tegnelia—*New York*

ABBY TEGNELIA of New York *magazine and Amie Parnes covered September 11 as a team. Friends since their days at the University of Miami, they joined the same prayer circle, saw the same bloodied American Express business card, and realized, in unison, that few had survived the raging inferno and the collapse of the towers. Two days later, Tegnelia received one of her first reporting assignments: interview the grieving people holding missing posters at Bellevue Hospital. Struggling with her own raw emotions, she interviewed the victims' loved ones. The captions she wrote appeared in the magazine's photo grid of victims.*

Tegnelia, twenty-five, joined New York *magazine in November 2000 as a reporter. She has previously interned for the* Washington Times, *freelanced for the* Miami Herald, *and reported for Reuters. She graduated from the University of Miami in May 1999 and finished her master's degree in journalism at the Columbia Graduate School of Journalism one year later. Her story explores the reportorial power of camaraderie.*

I got out of bed at 9:00 A.M. and flipped on the TV. Groggy and alone, I listened to an NY1 announcer frantically describe the second crash. I was calm and half asleep, but the images and sounds on the TV were chaotic. I mulled over the idea of a terrorist attack, not understanding that people had been killed. I could think only that something big was happening right here, in my city. I ran to the roof of my East Village apartment. Outside, everything was quiet. A thick, black mass of smoke poured from the towers and covered the eastern skyline, but it seemed flat and unmoving, like a painting. It was monstrous but horribly beautiful. Back downstairs, my roommate, Amie Parnes, also a reporter, was watching TV. She yelled at me for not waking her. My mind was racing and my heart pounding. Amie told me I was crazy to think of going to the office and that I had to go there with her and start interviewing. I was itching to go, but as an entry-level reporter at *New York* magazine, it was unlikely I would cover something so large.

But the subways soon closed, so I knew most of my coworkers couldn't get to the office. It was difficult to accept that something so catastrophic had happened that I couldn't easily get to work. We threw on clothes and flip-flops and then watched the first tower crumble on CNN. Amie and I ran upstairs, but at first glance nothing looked out of place. Then I noticed that only one tower was standing. And then Amie saw it. The smoke was so thick that it stayed in the form of the first tower, as if the massive building was still there.

Abby Tegnelia

This is when I finally grasped the enormity of the situation. After three tries, I got through to my mom in Albuquerque, and she told me she'd been calling me for an hour. I had no idea the phones weren't working, but she told me that friends had been calling her to see if I was OK. I realized millions of people were glued to their TVs, watching what I was staring at from my roof. Amie flipped off the TV on the way out, cutting off the footage of the first tower's collapse, the last TV image I saw until Thursday night, when it was mistakenly reported that a group of police officers was found in the rubble.

We headed down Second Avenue. Standing near Third Street, Amie and I were struck by how quiet our usually noisy neighborhood was. I questioned a man walking alone up the street, while Amie wrote down what he said. The survivor's words trailed off, and he walked away, shaking his head and looking toward the clear sky as he moved in the opposite direction of the towers. We realized that the second tower was falling, too far away for us to hear the crumbling tons of concrete. Everything happened quickly. A taxi, the only vehicle on the road, slowly pulled over, and storeowners stepped outside to look up into the sky. We all looked up in awe, even though we couldn't see the tower. When I have nightmares about covering these events, I don't see images of the inferno or desperate souls jumping to their deaths. It's that moment of deafening silence that jerks me awake. To console one another, Amie and I started whispering. I had already trusted her to help me decide to ditch work and not hibernate at home with CNN, and I knew I could count on her for the other help I needed.

After the second collapse, we started running toward the crash site. We are both obsessive reporters, and we had to get as close as we could to the towers. Crossing Houston Street, more than a mile from World Trade, we were surprised to find ourselves already moving against thousands of zombies walking north. It was chaos, but I started reporting as if on autopilot, approaching people to ask

Camaraderie and Sorrow

them what they'd seen. One of the first people, Amanda Allen, was only twenty-two, two years younger than me. She and her friend, Virginia Zepeda, assistant bank examiners for the Federal Reserve, walked me through the evacuation of their Maiden Lane office building. They told me that as they walked through Chinatown, they turned around to see people jumping, some hand-in-hand, from the highest floors. My heart beat rapidly, and I felt like I was moving in slow motion as I told Amie. This woman had seen it with her own eyes, and Amie was my witness to her words.

Amanda pulled out a bloody business card she had found amid the exploding papers after the towers collapsed. The man on the card, Manny Garcia, worked for American Express Corporate Services on the ninety-fourth floor of the first tower. "He's gone, gone to heaven," she told me. During any other event, those words would've seemed melodramatic.

Making our way down Bowery, we passed a mission, and two men grabbed our hands to form a prayer circle. We gently resisted, but they held tightly. *We're just reporters*, I felt like saying, but I couldn't speak. *Maybe someone who just fled that horror needs to pray with you.* The words didn't come out, and I don't think anyone would've listened anyway. We'd been walking south, and we were gripping notebooks, so they knew who we were. One of the men started to pray. "Almighty God, we ask you to weigh down your mighty hand," he rumbled toward the sky, as people trudged by, rubbing our shoulders, sobbing. At first, it was infuriating, being forced to stand still like that for so long, unable to take notes. But then I started to think about what I was getting myself into. As journalists, we're usually an outside presence, recording other people's feelings. But that morning, people were trying to help me. I realized that by going down to the scene of so much carnage, I had become part of this story, and I would eventually need consolation, like everyone else.

Many of the survivors wanted to talk to us, eager to tell someone, anyone, about what they had seen. I wondered what it was like to survive something alongside a cubicle mate, a coworker. Some walked alone. Covered in ash, many didn't want to talk. We interviewed two soot-covered men wearing bow ties. They told us about being engulfed by the cloud of smoke as the towers fell. They said they'd gone inside the first synagogue they passed to pray for help. They were older than many of the people in the streets, and as they walked off to go home, a young man approached. He said that the towers had been built in the 1960s and therefore contained asbestos. It was released in the soot when the buildings exploded. A few people stopped to listen, and soon several groups of strangers were chatting about asbestos. We believed it of course, because after those towers crumbled we'd have believed anything. It was strange to see New Yorkers chatting with random people in the streets. I noticed camaraderie all day long.

A man named Rick Puerto told me about firemen racing up stairwells as everyone fled down. "I looked them in the eye as they passed me," said Puerto, who escaped from the eighty-first floor of the first tower, one of the highest evacuated floors. "I got three blocks away, turned back, and saw the building crumble to the ground." He knew those firemen perished. The scope of this disaster was so unimaginable that it closed off the island and canceled ordinary life. But those firemen stuck to their duty. They hadn't looked back like the rest of us.

At about 11:30, after reaching Spring Street, we turned around for home, so Amie could call in her notes to the *Boston Globe*. Our third roommate, Jessica Yurocko, a Lehman Brothers employee who worked across the street from the World Trade Center in the World Financial Center, was sitting in our living room with several coworkers. The boss of one of the guys had been in the lobby of the first tower when the plane hit. "He said this huge fireball shot out from the elevator well," he told us, struggling to find the words to describe people being engulfed by a moving wall of jet-fuel. "People

Camaraderie and Sorrow

were running, on fire." Maybe the burn victims were written about, but it would be months till I would hear about them again. It took a brilliant photo essay in the *Times* to illustrate how badly scorched people were. The brief captions said that most of victims were undergoing intense physical therapy to learn to walk again.

We left, this time for St. Vincent's Hospital with our neighbor, Sam Lubell, a freelance photographer and reporter, in tow. It was about 1 P.M., and the sun was blazing. The crowds were thick with people hoping to donate blood, but by that time the banks were full. Everyone stuck around, eager to find some way to help and begging the volunteers for something to do. One woman stood alone in a roped-off area, holding a clipboard with a list of the injured. I was standing nearby when a man came running up. He gave his sister's name and office floor number, one of the highest floors of one of the towers. The woman shook her head. The man ran off to check another list somewhere else. He remained hopeful, but I felt like I had just witnessed him learning about the loss of his sister. I interviewed a doctor on his way home. "They have a whole room full of doctors standing around with nothing to do," he said. "No patients are coming here. We don't know if that's because they don't exist, or because they can't get here." No ambulances drove up with their sirens wailing; no stretchers were unloaded. We headed down Sixth Avenue.

At about 4 P.M., we stopped at a fire station at King Street, which houses Engine 24 and Ladder 5. An ash-covered pickup truck was parked in front, with a smashed-in windshield and broken windshield wiper sticking straight out. No one could say who had driven it up there or how the damage was done. "It's a war zone down there," said firefighter Frank McCutchen, forty-four. "I saw at least forty cars on fire. Now I'm here talking to the wives. You have to give them hope." He was solid as a rock with broad shoulders and a defiant stance. He had worked all morning but hadn't found any survivors. "No one's been inside the collapsed building yet—it's an inferno," said fireman Tom Staubitser. "We go toward the fire to extinguish it in a normal situation," he said, as if repeating what he'd learned in training. "No one expected the buildings to go down the way they did." His eyes were bloodshot. "They're waiting for their shift, so they can go look for their brothers," he said, pointing to a handful of firefighters fidgeting nearby. A few relatives paced back and forth. "My husband just started," a woman said. She was the first person I saw crying.

Amie went home to call in more notes, and Sam and I headed south. At Canal Street, people used Starbucks paper cups to scoop up dust. The ash covered every building and vehicle like a fine layer of snow. We still believed that the soot had asbestos, and we were horrified by the thought that people were collecting the stuff as a souvenir. I was not ready for New York to start getting back to normal, for onlookers to gawk or find pieces of the disaster to take with them. Down by West Broadway and Franklin, about ten blocks from the towers, we found an exit point. Everyone coming from Ground Zero was exhausted. One volunteer, Troy Nightingale told us about sneaking past checkpoints in order to help. I'd been observing the damage from the outside, and in talking to him, a civilian like me, I wondered what it would've been like to have gotten in. "What's left of the buildings looks like dinosaur bones," he said. "The ruins are on fire, surrounding buildings are on fire. I passed out pitchers of water and helped clear roadways. Everything's very orderly until the barriers stop. Then everything's chaotic."

On Wednesday, I reported to work as if it were an ordinary business day. The subways were running, and the weather was still clear and sunny. I was still in shock, and I wondered what I needed to accept before I could cry. I wanted to be with my family and friends. My ears rang, and I couldn't shake that dreamy feeling, as if what I had observed the previous day was happening to someone else. The hours ticked slowly by, but I was glad I had something to keep me busy. Someone in the office had a copy of the *Times*, but I couldn't

Camaraderie and Sorrow

read more than a sentence or two of each story. I'll never forget the photographs that ran in that edition, especially the blur of a picture of the gaping hole in one of the towers before it fell. I didn't even see the people at first, but when I noticed the ghosts peering out from inside, I felt a wave of nausea.

I typed up my notes and emailed them to my editors. I got some good feedback, which made me proud. A lot of people asked me why I rushed toward the unfolding tragedy. I always want to be where the action is. I wouldn't have gone without a reporter's notebook; I've never been the type to gawk at a car accident on the side of the road. But I am addicted to people's stories, especially ones such as I heard on September 11. There was so much going on, and I was one more person to jot down experiences that wouldn't have been recorded and shared without me.

At our midtown office, notes kept pouring in, from our on-staff reporters, from freelancers. People depicted scenes on rooftops, at mosques, in the crowds of survivors. Less than half of our main writers had made it downtown. Many were stuck in Brooklyn after the subways closed; some were scared. My editors had been on the phones, trying to get as many people near Ground Zero as possible. They didn't know I was there until I e-mailed them my notes. Later that day, I had to fact-check our theater and book listings. It was the day after a national tragedy, and I had to call publicists to double-check show times, even though most shows had been canceled. We were all reeling from September 11, but we still had to finish the back half of our magazine. The ad-free September 11 front half would be written over the next two days.

That night, Amie was evacuated from the N/R train, just as it pulled up to the Empire State Building stop. Fire marshals swarmed in, yelling, "Go go go!" As she ran, she called me from her cell. She was crying and screaming and telling me every detail. Still in reporter mode, she said a marshal scooped up a toddler and ran with him, as the mother screamed, "Where's my baby?" We got cut off, and about half an hour later she came home. It had been a false alarm, but enough to shake us all up again. She had met another woman as they ran, so we walked her to the Path station, so she could go home to New Jersey. We were given dust masks to guard our noses from the foggy stench that hung in the air. Not one vehicle drove by. It felt like a war zone. Back home, our apartment felt really hot. But we couldn't turn on the air conditioner, because the acrid, burning smell it pumped in was worse than the heat.

By Thursday, the subways were closed for security reasons. I guess there had been other bomb threats. I put on sneakers and a T-shirt to go to work, and I walked up to 14th Street to catch a bus. It was so slow that I got out and walked. Midmorning, I was sent down to Bellevue Hospital to interview people holding "missing" posters. It was one of my first official reporting assignments. Aside from the "longest week" runner put together from all the reporters' interviews, there was very little room in the September 11 issue. So I was ecstatic at the opportunity to contribute. I knew the next few hours were going to be heart-wrenching, but I was going stir-crazy at the office. Filled with nervous energy, I ran most of the way from 49th Street and Madison to 27th Street and First Avenue. With my Gap T-shirt, ponytail, and no makeup, the photographer must've thought I looked twelve. My assignment was to write captions for his portrait grid. I was to interview people, then he would swoop in to photograph.

The scene in front of the hospital was a media circus, where the stars weren't looking for publicity, but a missing person. Everyone was desperate to get on TV, hoping that someone would see their pictures and reunite them with their missing relative or friend. They were less eager to talk to me, since our photos wouldn't run till the next week.

The veteran photographer was impatient, but I stood on the outskirts and watched the scene for a few minutes before talking to anyone. Emotions were raw, and the last thing I wanted to do was descend on a potential subject during an inappropriate time. He

Camaraderie and Sorrow

snapped at me to hurry up. I was mad at him for being so insensitive, and my feelings startled me. It was the first time in three days I'd felt anger. One of the first people I interviewed was Enrique Vidal, who was looking for his daughter, Joanna. My heart skipped a beat when he showed me her picture. She looked like me. She was a young, smiling brunette, dressed up for a party. Enrique was soft-spoken, and he told me Joanna had called him after the first crash from Windows on the World, where she had helped set up a conference. "Whatever happens, Daddy, I love you," the twenty-six-year-old had told him. Her "portrait" was one of the first ones published in the *New York Times*, on September 27. Enrique had told the *Times* reporter the same anecdote he told me.

Ingrid Smith was looking for her brother-in-law, Wade Green. She kept repeating, "We need him home." She was speaking forcefully, as if she was trying to convince us how important he was so that we could give him back. Eneida Lugo was searching for her brother, Daniel. He was a security guard in the lobby of the first tower. He'd called his wife after the crashes to say that he was OK, and that he'd leave his post when everyone was evacuated. Nadine Aoun, twenty-six, and Theresa Safi, twenty-four, were looking for three friends from childhood, all of whom worked on the 104th floor of Tower One. I hadn't even cried yet, but I realized I was starting to crack when I choked down a painful sob. Someone was giving out bottles of water, so I grabbed one and guzzled it.

Carmen Barreto was looking for her son, Benito Valentin, a travel agent for American Express Corporate Services, the same small office where the owner of that bloody business card I'd held on Tuesday had worked. By that time, I knew that their floor took a direct hit. The scene suddenly played in my mind, and I could picture two young coworkers at their cubicles, together, as the plane came crashing through the walls. Many at Bellevue were looking for Cantor Fitzgerald employees. I had to get them to spell the name for me, since I had never heard of the firm.

Abby Tegnelia

At one point, I was interviewing a husband and wife with their daughter, and as I was writing down their answers, I began to repeat the exact same questions I'd just asked. They looked at me quizzically. It took me more than a minute to realize I wasn't making sense. Normally, I would just laugh something like that off. But it was the first time I had made a blatant mistake, and it jarred me into recognizing the emotional toll the last days had taken on me. The woman touched my hand. "This is hard on all of us," she said.

The next day, the photos came back, and I wrote the captions. The portrait of Alisa Schindler, thirty-one, really stood out. Her eyes were glistening. She was looking for her friend, Charles Lucania, thirty-five, a striking guy, always surrounded by children. Later, when I would walk around the shrines in Union Square, I would stare at his picture. My editor, Rob Levine, is a jokester, and he had been trying to keep spirits up around the office. But when he was editing my stuff, he got visibly choked up. When we finished, I noticed that my byline wasn't there. "You want your name on this?" he asked. I felt the assignment was more of an obituary than a news story. I felt more responsibility to the victims and their families than to the reader. For most of these people, it would be the only time they'd ever be in a magazine. It was my responsibility to get everything right, and I wanted my sources to be able to quickly find me.

At the end of the day on September 11, Amie and I shared our notes. It's a common practice when a large story is breaking, since reporters can't be everywhere at once. After years of helping each other with our work, as well as teaming up years ago for stories for the University of Miami newspaper, we trusted each other completely. My Amanda Allen interview appeared in the *Boston Globe*, and one of Amie's interviews, of a mysterious woman named Julie Davis, appeared in *New York*. Julie had seemed disoriented and paranoid and refused to give Amie a phone number where she could be reached. She told her she had escaped from the eighty-second floor of Tower Two amid a frenzy of people. A later report

316

Camaraderie and Sorrow

by *USA Today* described only four people escaping from between the seventy-eighth and eighty-fourth floors, surrounded by smoke and fire. Maybe Julie got the floor wrong, or maybe she left as soon as the first tower was hit, and did not show up in *USA Today*'s list of survivors who made it out after the second plane hit.

A man claiming to be an FBI agent called about a month after the attacks, looking for information about Julie Davis. His sister had worked on the eighty-second floor and perished in the attacks. He said his family was searching for clues about how she died and wanted to talk to Judy. He had searched and could not find her, but he said that any information about her looks or her accent would help. I wrote down all of his information on yellow Post-It notes. Those notes stayed on my desk for more than a month. I mentioned the conversation to an editor, who told me that if the man were really an FBI agent, he would've been able to locate Julie on his own.

On Thursday night, I got home a little after ten, knowing that most of my work was done. I turned on the TV. It was the night that a prank call had convinced rescue workers that a group of buried police officers were still alive. Fox News was airing the search live. I sat in front of the TV and sobbed. Sitting Indian-style on the floor, I stared at the screen, silently and impatiently waiting for new developments. When Sam's roommate came in and picked a fight with Amie, I jumped up from the floor and physically pushed him out the front door, screaming at the top of my lungs. Sam came in and sat with me for a while, and Amie joined me later. I believed that there were living people with cell phones buried in that collapse and waiting to be rescued. At around midnight, I went to bed, only because I hoped that when I woke up there would be a new group of saved people.

Living with Fear

By Amie Parnes—*Boston Globe*

AMIE PARNES awoke that Tuesday morning in her East Village apartment to the screams of her roommate, Abby Tegnelia, who was watching the towers burn on CNN. The pair shelved their assignments for the day and headed south. As the towers collapsed before her, Parnes interviewed survivors, victims' families, and other observers. She captured Julie Davis's story for the Boston Globe. *Davis escaped from high in one of the towers after seeing firefighters rush past her. She described how on the way down she met a man whose colleague had been sucked out a window. The next night, after a dinner with a friend, Parnes had to evacuate the subway under the Empire State Building and sprint twenty blocks south due to a bomb threat.*

Parnes, twenty-five, is a freelance writer who splits her time between New York and Florida. Her work appears regularly in the New York Times, *the* London Independent, *and the* Boston Globe, *where she covered the Elian Gonzalez custody battle and the 2000 presidential election debacle. Today, she is at work covering the much-anticipated 2004 Florida governor's race between Jeb Bush and, if she survives the Democratic primary, Janet Reno.*

I was coming back to New York from a day of job interviews at the *Philadelphia Inquirer*, on an Amtrak train, and my mind wandered as we rushed closer and closer. *I don't want to leave New York for this job, I just moved here*. My fantasy of living among its lively streets had become my reality.

I stared at the World Trade Center, because they were the only city buildings I could see from that distance.

Almost there, almost there. They comforted me and drew me closer to the city I craved .

My mind wandered to other things, like paying rent, meeting a friend for dinner, why the man in my life hadn't called that day. I kept staring at the Trade Center. I thought about how my world would change if the *Inquirer* offered me this job.

A sandy-haired guy about my age, sitting alone, turned around looking for some company, his green eyes peeping through the crack between the patterned cloth chairs.

"It's amazing we can see them all the way from here," he ventured, pointing to the buildings.

"I know," I replied, trying to end the conversation there. I wanted to go back to my ruminations. I looked at the powerful buildings some more, and then I closed my eyes and tried to sleep away my day and the talkative guy in front.

I woke up sixteen hours later to the same buildings, except this time they were on fire. International terrorism had hit only two miles from my new apartment in the East Village. My roommate, Abby, pointed at the television, "Look."

"*Both?* "

Abby nodded.

My cell phone rang. "Amie!" screamed my friend Tali, who was one block from the Trade Center. "I saw everything! We had to evacuate our building in the middle of a meeting."

I didn't comprehend it and at the time it didn't seem like a big deal. Abby continued packing her lunch for work. Though the buildings were on fire, I assumed they would be extinguished in no time. I never imagined smoke would emanate from the site, months later.

I don't think we really understood what was unfolding, but we knew this was a story.

Fire engines raced south outside our apartment on Second Avenue, sirens blaring. I peeked out the window, watching them, one after the other. Many of those "heroes" would never return.

I grabbed my cell phone, and we ran to our roof to see for ourselves that yes, this was real. There they were. Two powerful buildings that all of a sudden seemed powerless.

I'd say it looked surreal, but it would be an understatement. This was worse than any nightmare, worse than any horror flick.

By this time, rooftops were full of the curious, the nervous.

More fire trucks sped by. The sounds of sirens horrified us. They still do.

Staring at the fiery building from the roof, I called the *Boston Globe*, where I had freelanced from Florida continuously for about a year (I still lived about half the month in Florida in order to write some off-the-wall, only-in-Florida kinds of stories) and told them I was in New York. My editor, Dean Inouye, the deputy national editor, wasn't in the office yet, so I dialed the main number in a hurried frenzy.

"I'm in New York," I repeated to countless employees. "How

Living with Fear

can I help?" I could see the fires in the buildings had quickly spread downward. And while I was on hold, Abby asked me if I thought our third roommate Jessica was OK. She worked in the World Financial Center, a building adjacent to the World Trade Center.

I hoped so.

I was transferred from the national desk, to the city desk, to countless unfamiliar voices, and repeatedly left on hold. Finally, I reached Martin Baron, the executive editor.

"You're in New York! OK, get down there. Get down there and call us with what you have."

That's when I panicked.

Stumbling on words and thoughts, I ran downstairs, to get my camera. When I returned, our neighbor Sam Lubell (a freelance journalist) had joined us.

I had taken five pictures of the burning buildings from the roof when the south tower disappeared. We ran inside and saw close-ups of the building crumbling on TV.

I threw on a T-shirt, a pair of jeans, and running sneakers. Abby thought she should go to work at *New York* magazine. I reminded her of college at the University of Miami, of how we were a team, the stories we had written for our college newspaper, the *Miami Hurricane*, and how we could do it all over again. We should go report the hell out of this story, I said.

She agreed.

I grabbed a used notebook and began interviewing people the second we reached the streets. We found people who had been there, had seen the planes hit the buildings, had witnessed rescue efforts, had seen people jumping one hundred floors to their deaths. Some had been pelted by body parts, fingers, toes.

"Excuse me," I said as I approached one woman. "I'm a reporter with the *Boston Globe*."

Sure enough, she had been evacuated from her office in the financial district.

Wiping her eyes, she told us that the destruction was worse than an Arnold Schwarzenegger movie. She rambled. She needed to tell her story, to talk to someone.

We thanked her and continued south. Thousands of emergency workers streamed by and New Yorkers bolted in the opposite direction.

Fights broke out over the crowded pay phones. People were desperate to reassure loved ones.

We passed blank-faced businessmen. Ties loosened, jackets on their arms, beads of sweat dripping down their foreheads and cheeks. They looked as if they had just run a marathon.

"Excuse me, I'm a reporter . . ."

"No thank you," they said in what could be interpreted as disgust.

But a twenty-eight-year-old man who had escaped from the seventy-second floor of the north tower stopped us to talk. Eyes bulging and forehead creasing, he told us how he had raced down the stairs, thinking his life was over.

"When I reached the plaza, it was like a war zone," he explained. "FBI agents were rushing past me, firefighters were pushing me aside. I thought it was all over. I thought my life was about to end." He could barely utter his name before he walked away.

Many people held cell phones to their ears. "Yes, honey, I'm OK. Don't worry. We made it out." Others cursed, angry that they couldn't get through. Abby and I recorded their comments. It provided what we in the news biz call *color*.

"I can't get through!!" Another woman, convinced her husband was dead, screamed. "What if he's dead! What if he's gone! This is it. This is the end of the world!"

Then, quiet. All of a sudden, everything stopped. The streets went dead silent. Conversations halted. No honking. Drivers pulled over. People just stopped and looked south. The second tower had fallen. I put my arm around Abby. We continued walking, passing

Living with Fear

men covered in soot and women short of breath, their faces pale. We stopped to interview them.

One woman had managed to salvage a business card from the paperwork flying out of the collapsing buildings. She handed it to us. It had small drops of blood on it and belonged to Manny Garcia of American Express Corporate Services on the ninety-fourth floor of the north tower. She believed the man to be buried beneath the rubble.

"I want to keep it as a memento."

She quickly snatched the card back, afraid I intended to keep it. And I did—but only for my story.

Instead, I copied down the information on the card onto my notebook, including this: "the card has drops of blood."

Abby and I looked at each other. "Poor guy."

We walked closely together. I asked Abby if she thought there had been a bigger story in our lifetime. She shook her head.

At the Miami *New York Times* bureau, I had covered what I thought were huge stories. The 2000 presidential election. I was there when federal marshals raided a home to physically remove Elian Gonzalez. Cuban community members threw lawn chairs and water bottles at us. I was temporarily blinded by tear gas thrown by police and I briefly thought that Miami might just fall into the Atlantic during all the rioting madness. I called the man I look up to the most in all of the journalism business, my mentor, Rick Bragg, the *New York Times* Pulitzer Prize winner, and tried to read him my notes for the main story he was writing about the raid and the rioting and I told him I thought I might be blind. He laughed. "Junior, dab some water in your eyes and just keep moving," he advised in his Southern twang. Rick, whom I admired because no one writes anything better, told me this story, this big story, would be good for my resume. "Parnes," he told me one day kind of like a loving drill sergeant, "There are not too many twenty-three-year-olds who get to do what you do, so take your experiences and run with them."

Half a year later, I covered the Florida election of pregnant chads. At the time, *New York Times* Washington reporter Don Van Natta Jr. told me, "This, kiddo, will probably be the biggest story of our time."

But this was different. The attack. The collapse. The murder. It really was the biggest story of our time.

Most of the morning, I walked the streets of downtown New York with Abby taking notes. I wrote down how beautiful the sapphire sky looked that day and how it contrasted with the black smoke and the smell of burning rubber in the air.

Fifty-year-old men cried, holding on to each other's black pinstriped jackets. Strangers hugged and asked each other that comforting question: "You all right?" Churches opened their chapels, and people formed prayer circles. "We ask you for your guidance and love, good Lord," two men intoned. "Weigh down your mighty hand."

Dumbfounded police officers handed out bottles of Poland Spring.

My notebook filled up.

I tried to use my cell phone to contact the *Globe* and dictate my notes, but, like everyone else, I couldn't get a signal. I waited in line for a pay phone, but grew impatient. Surely Dean needed this material now.

I decided to turn back and use our home phone to feed my quotes to Boston. Abby walked with me. My mind always races when I report a story. Now, my brain was in overdrive.

Would my editor like what I had? Did I forget to ask a particular question? Did I interview the right people? Did I have enough color? I reached Dean at the Globe's national desk. He was remarkably calm. He asked if I could e-mail him my notes, and I told him I would try but that there were no guarantees I would get a dial tone.

I typed up my notes: I wrote about a twenty-five-year-old man, Rick Puerto, who had escaped from the Bank of America office on

Living with Fear

the eighty-first floor of the south tower. "The whole building shook and people were hysterically screaming," he said, his eyes red and watery. "I grabbed my cell phone, called my fiancée, and I just starting running for the stairs. I knew we were in trouble when the FBI agents were running for the door." As he left the building, firefighters rushed by on the way up the stairs to rescue stranded workers. A few minutes later, he looked back and saw his building crumble. "What a weird feeling that was."

After I finished typing, Abby and I headed down to St. Vincent's Hospital in Greenwich Village to speak to more survivors. Our neighbor Sam wanted to donate blood and photograph the scene. The three of us walked in silence, staring at a group of women gathered in the middle of the street hugging.

"Noooooooooo! Noooooooooo," they screamed.

Abby thought we should let them grieve in peace, but I approached them anyway. One of the women shooed me away.

More people lingered in front of the hospital. On an outside wall, victims' relatives had plastered colored copies of photos of their loved ones.

"WE NEED YOUR HELP!" many read, and below those words were pictures of daughters, brothers, fiancées, mothers, friends in happier times at birthday parties, ski trips to Colorado, weddings.

Countless people approached a woman with a clipboard asking her if so-and-so had been admitted. One thirty-something man pushed through the crowd to ask if his sister was being held there. He could barely speak and spelled his sister's name through tears.

She looked on the list of the admitted, of the safe. "No, It doesn't look like she's here."

"Are you sure?"

"Yes, unfortunately."

He walked away, head slumped down.

I followed and asked if I could interview him. He asked if I worked for the hospital. I told him I was a reporter. He just shook his head and walked away.

Abby was listening to a doctor speak about the inactivity at the hospital. She called me over, but I wasn't interested. I needed a more personal story and spent the rest of that afternoon looking for it.

As I left midafternoon to file some more notes to Dean, I spotted two women crying.

"You are so lucky to have escaped," one said.

I asked if she had fled the Trade Center.

"Yes," she said, her hands and voice trembling. We walked down Fifth Avenue, and she told me her story. She was at the Trade Center that morning dropping off a friend's cell phone when the second plane hit. "The coffee I had in my hand spilled all over my skirt," she told me.

She had known that something big had happened, and panicked. She heard screams of "Oh my God" and "Get out!" and ran for the stairs. She spoke of a man who had just seen his colleagues get sucked out the window. Minutes later, he was unconscious in the stairwell.

"I was thinking we were doomed," she continued. "Dozens and dozens of firefighters were running past us, telling us to stay calm and keep moving. I remember looking into their eyes, thinking how brave they were. Now I bet they're all gone."

As she struggled down the stairs, she couldn't tell which floor they were on or how much farther she had to go. "Random strangers kept patting me on the back and putting their arms around me." Finally she made it out. "I thought we would have severe burns, but I never thought the entire building would collapse. Nothing makes sense to me today." She cried for half an hour and felt lucky to be alive. At one point during the interview, she paused to ask me for a hug.

Miraculously, my cell phone rang. It was Dean asking if I had

Living with Fear

any survivor stories. I told him I had the perfect one. I came home to type up my final interview with Julie Davis. I e-mailed it to Dean just as the sun set. A few minutes later, he called back with fact-checking questions. Ten minutes later, my day was done—at least my workday. I had seventeen messages on my cell phone from concerned friends. "I know wherever danger is, there you are," said one. I spent the next few hours returning calls, informing everyone that I was still with them. I tried my best to keep my mind off that day. I even drank a beer, and I hate beer.

By nightfall, when I'd finally had time to ponder what had happened, I broke down.

Abby and Jessica had fallen asleep long ago. Tears drenched my pillow and the images of the buildings dropping replayed in my mind. *What was next?* I asked myself over and over. *Would the city be around tomorrow?* I had never been so frightened.

I picked up the phone and called my best friend, Craig, in Florida. I had spoken to him earlier, telling him I was OK, but I retracted those statements.

I cried for ten minutes, largely unintelligible. I needed that familiar voice. I told him I was scared, afraid to fall asleep.

We stayed on the phone for hours. I cried myself dry.

The next day, I hit the streets on an assignment for the *New York Times*, which owns the *Boston Globe*. An editor asked me to write a little profile about how business in the garment district had been affected by the attacks.

I left my apartment and walked south of 14th Street. Police barricades had blocked all the traffic. It was as if everyone were in hiding, afraid to come out. The brave souls who did walk around wore surgical masks. The subways were running but on alternate routes, and few headed downtown. Most stores were shut, and I was irritated that I couldn't find a copy of the *Times* anywhere.

I spent most of the day interviewing garment workers. I felt funny. Abby called it walking outside of herself. I definitely was not all there.

The day passed quickly, and I went home to try to take a nap. I had closed my eyes for two minutes when I was awakened by my friend Tali asking to meet for dinner. Afterward, I hopped on the subway home. I was making funny faces at a little boy on the subway, when our train pulled into the 34th Street stop near Penn Station. A dozen out-of-breath police officers stormed the station yelling, "GO! GO! GO!" Our train was being evacuated.

"What's happening!" I yelled, racing down 34th Street across the street from the famed Macy's.

No one answered. "Just keep running!"

I couldn't run well in my wooden platform shoes, and one officer screamed out that I wasn't going fast enough.

U.S. Marshals arrived and ran alongside us. They led us away from the Empire State Building. We ran in and out of stores and hotel lobbies. The marshals appeared as confused as we were.

"Keep running!" Policemen shouted like coaches on the sidelines.

My legs trembled. My ponytail came lose. I started crying. The last time everything had been wrong, Abby had been by my side. Now, I was alone. I grabbed my cell phone and called her.

I wailed when she answered. "There's a bomb threat or something going down at the Empire State building! They're making us run."

She knew what was happening. She had been watching it on CNN. She told me to stay calm and keep going. Sounds of breaking glass crashed behind us (I still don't know why), causing everyone to sprint faster. I lagged.

"Abby! What if I die!" I cried, slurring my words.

Then the line went dead. I kept running, turning south on Sixth Avenue hauling past 30th Street, and then 29th, past delis and storefronts. A few storeowners came out to see what the commotion was about. As I ran, I noticed a girl around my age next to me. She

Living with Fear

looked over and smiled. Her knee was bleeding. She was limping. In the panic, a man had pushed her out of his way.

"Are you alone?" she asked.

"Yes."

"Me too." Her face was red from running, and with tears in her green eyes, she looked as frightened as I felt.

"Well, I guess we have each other."

We ran together to 18th Street and Sixth Avenue. A policewoman told us we were in the clear. She offered us bottles of Evian, which we declined.

The girl told me that she had just come from meeting a friend for dinner. He had escaped the Trade Center, and had recounted his harrowing tale.

"It was sort of a celebration. We toasted to life." Then she laughed. "Ironic, isn't it?"

She needed to get back to Hoboken, but was frightened to take the PATH train through the tunnel. I convinced her to walk to my apartment and stay until we knew it was safe. Her knee bled more. I told her we would fix her up at my place.

The city, as if it had been under curfew, was quiet and dark. The roads downtown were closed to traffic. The 60-degree air was thick. We coughed, suffocated by the stench.

Almost everyone we passed wore a surgical mask, and one guy stopped to point us in the direction of an apartment doorman who was handing them out. It felt funny to walk the streets with a mask over my face, but I did anyway. Who knew what was in the air?

Mask over my mouth, I told the girl I didn't feel safe in the city, and it was not because of armed robbery or drug busts or organized crime. This was a whole new fear. The city I had once loved and admired now horrified me. It was as if the attacks were forcing me to give up my enthrallment with this lit-up city of skyscrapers and intrigue. She nodded. Back at the apartment, Abby and Sam and some other friends were waiting for me.

"We were so worried" Abby hugged me. "Well, at least you're home now."

And it was true. I was home, and despite the fact that this horrible burning smell hung in my room for months, home was New York. They say that home goes far beyond four walls, and I can't agree more. I had started a life here before terrorists touched it, and New York was where my friends and family were. I had uncles and aunts that settled here years ago, and my mom, wanting to be close to me, had followed me and settled in New Jersey. This mystical city can inspire many fantasies and I had dreamed those dreams for months and years at a time. And now, even with this horrific disaster, New York was my reality. I slept, that night, for the first time in forty-eight hours.

The next day, I got up and wrote my little story about the garment district for the *Times*. I wrote a business piece about a man selling "We shall overcome" T-Shirts. He told me it was the best way to make a dollar. I submitted it early and took the rest of the day off.

That night, Sam and I snuck into Ground Zero, past dozens of national guardsmen and checkpoints. It was our city. We had to see it.

And we did. Now I have my own mental images of the wrecked skeletal side of the building that stood alone under what looked like stadium lighting. I can still see a soot-covered Wall Street, and the tired eyes on the faces of firefighters and policemen near the scene. I can conjure an evacuated gym, its lights and televisions still on. A man, a volunteer worker, rushes us away, fearful that there might be something poisonous in the air. But most of all I can see New York. And I'm still there, right in the midst of it.

One City, Many Worlds

By Carla Sapsford
—Columbia Graduate School of Journalism

CARLA SAPSFORD of the Columbia Graduate School of Journalism felt uncomfortable with the idea of advancing her career on the tragedy. She worried about the effects of the ubiquitous displays of patriotism on Arab-Americans. As a result, she spent the days after the attack on an unrelated story, and never directly covered the events of September 11. Instead, she focused on the aftermath: chartered jets for the wealthy, layoffs that moderate- and low-income workers could ill afford, immigrants eager to join the armed forces, and a renewed sense of mission among New York's unofficial supplementary police force: the Guardian Angels.

With roots in Washington and Florida, Sapsford, thirty, is the author of the guidebook Sexy New York 2000, *and her reporting has been published in newspapers throughout the West and South. A graduate of Wellesley College, she has worked at the State Department, the White House, and for an international development nonprofit.*

The morning of September 11 found me at home getting ready for work, listening to WFUV on the radio. A mellow song ended and the morning host announced an unconfirmed report of a plane hitting the Trade Center. Initially, I thought the pilot was just another nut. I had begun to stop being surprised by all that happened here. I flipped to New York One (a local television news channel). Confused anchors intelligently opened the phones to joggers and other witnesses. The second plane hit. It couldn't be an accident. Although I am a student at Columbia's School of Journalism, it did not occur to me once to scramble downtown to cover the disaster.

The year before I had temped at a law firm on the eighty-ninth floor of the south tower. I knew the sick feeling I had felt in the pit of my stomach as the building swayed six feet to and fro in rough winds. I used to get vertigo just standing at a window and looking down. I tried to imagine the shaking from the impact, but I assumed the building had fail-safe evacuation procedures. It did not occur to me that thousands had gone up in smoke.

I am of the *Die Hard* generation, and this time there was no Bruce Willis to scale the sleek building and carry off the victims. For once the television talking heads were at a loss. Their loss of composure made me uncomfortable. So I went to work at the *Columbia Journalism Review*, a trade magazine on West 116th Street. On the way, the first tower fell. I didn't know and was confused when NBC announced on the office television that the first tower

One City, Many Words

was no more. Half the office had left by the time I arrived. I still thought things must be better than they looked. Everyone always picks themselves up in this city, no matter what. And, I'm sorry to say, I also felt distance from everything that was happening—it's awful to say, but I had three jobs to go to and stories to report for class. I initially tried to work, but soon left when it became clear nothing would be happening for quite some time.

My coworkers helped put my emotions in perspective. The baby boomers were horrified, nauseated. Someone on the top floor of the building showed me the smoke billowing all the way from downtown (over 130 blocks south of us). I started to realize this was a big deal and that I wouldn't wake up the next day and it would be gone. I had a feeling of déjà vu, the same sinking feeling I had gotten when I interned for the State Department's Refugee Programs during the Haitian and Rwandan refugee crises. Then, I was in shock that no one did anything when people were being massacred. Now, I was in shock for two days because of the proximity of the disaster and the helplessness that most people felt.

My jobs at Forstmann Little, a venture capital shop, at the magazine, and as a teaching assistant at Columbia were all called off for the week. I watched television constantly and became a spectator. I just felt. Many newly arrived students at the Columbia School of Journalism were sent by their professors down to Ground Zero to cover the story. I was revolted. There was no way I was going to interview chalk-like people covered in devastation. I didn't want to speak with frantic families—*What if I traumatized them more? What if I cried during an interview?*—and I didn't want to chronicle this day. I was unprepared.

Instead, I walked around my neighborhood near Columbia, on the West Side of Manhattan between 106th Street and the Cathedral of St. John the Divine on 110th. People freaked out at the sight of buses careening down quiet streets with no one in them. The cathedral tolled its bells mournfully, consistently. Students lined up outside St. Luke's Hospital to donate blood. The city felt like a war front.

Desperate missing posters appeared near my neighborhood. On September 14, my recent ex-boyfriend, Hector, told me not to worry. He was from Spain, he explained, where those Basque separatist types are always blowing up something or somebody. "You'll get used to it," he said dismissively. That didn't make me feel any better. I had studied and worked in countries in crisis. But that stuff was supposed to happen over there. Not here. I felt stupid, naive, and angry. I was changing in unexpected ways.

The rhetoric and the flags pissed me off and saddened me. Most people weren't looking at why this happened. Although I love my country with an intensity that has only been strengthened by living abroad, I do not wear that love on my sleeve. I felt that people weren't asking themselves the reflective questions, like why so many people around the world hate us. Instead, they accepted official explanations for the government's responses (and lack thereof).

I was also upset that my immediate journalistic future would be consumed by the aftershocks of death. *Was I too sensitive?* I didn't want to participate in what many called "the story of the century." It's not how I wanted to get ahead. I imagined the chaos reigning in newsrooms across the city. As a journalism student, I had the luxury to not become a domestic war correspondent because I picked and chose my stories. I didn't approach Ground Zero until Sunday, September 17, and then went to Union Square to see the memorials. Plenty of journalists have covered this story well, and I felt too tender to tread on it.

Since September 11, my reporting has become more sober and humbled. I can't stomach fluffy stories about strip joints or S&M theme restaurants anymore. People's internal lives are what interest me, as do their reactions to the frictions in their lives. I am interested in covering those who aren't traditionally covered by the mainstream media, often people who don't speak English perfectly.

One City, Many Words

I am not a great writer—I know my limitations. But I am good at identifying overlooked angles. Growing up in neighborhoods where being a white girl made me a minority gave me a sense of being on the outside looking in. I can't say I will always want to report the so-called "hard" stories, but that has been my mood of late. New York has changed and so have I.

So here's what I did:

The Hitler in All of Us
September 13, 2001

This title comes from Elizabeth Kubler-Ross, a psychiatrist famous for work on children, grief, and healing. Her point was, if Hitler hadn't been abused as a kid, he might have become his village mailman instead of the mass murderer he was. So this essay is my way of saying, the capacity for evil lurks in everyone. No one can say, "I'm good, you're evil," as if life were as simple as all that. We could all kill, wound, if put in the right circumstances. I wrote this essay on the idea of subjective evil after a particularly upsetting evening of television. The lack of reflection about why this awful thing occurred and about how Americans are seen abroad disturbed me.

People who grow up in poverty all over the world see the U.S. as a scapegoat. Our foreign policy hasn't helped this image much. Working and traveling internationally, I have heard much that troubled me: Americans trample others' cultures; we are arrogant; we use people; and we binge on our supremacy. I wrote this piece to say we are reaping some of what we have sown. To say, it doesn't take a monster to kill. All this talk of evil has turned our political debates into cartoonish parodies of good and bad. "We good, you bad."

No doubt, Americans were violated, assaulted, victimized. I cried and cried. But we don't have a monopoly on suffering. I sent this piece to an editor I had worked with who said it had already been done and needed extensive reworking. I agreed, but felt better for writing it.

This story, if it had been published, would have been controversial. I am a proud American, but am sometimes ashamed of how my country behaves abroad. The piece reflected these split emotions. I see my job as a writer as not to please readers, but to provoke them to see old problems anew. A friend compares my methods to those of a "sniper," who hits people in a vulnerable spot. This is not a bad thing, thought it doesn't always make me popular.

The Empire Strikes Back
September 28, 2001

I cowrote this television story for a class, about a public service announcement filming to promote Broadway. Over fifty divas and divos assembled behind the TKTS ticket office in Times Square for one electric hour. Broadway turned out to support its own. Matthew Broderick, Molly Ringwald, Nathan Lane, Brooke Shields, Glenn Close, Alan Alda, and Bernadette Peters all sang "New York, New York," in an advertisement that aired all over the tristate area. My Columbia Journalism School partner climbed aboard the public relations firm bus while I watched the rest of the equipment from the McDonald's across the street. The stars were elated, a group of sunflowers beaming back at the sun. They joked, laughed, and clowned around. The costumed participants included Beauty from *Beauty and the Beast*, a clean-cut stripper in a cop uniform from *The Full Monty*, and Bernadette Peters in fishnet stockings. My partner filmed.

Although many shows were struggling, most Broadway standbys were in no danger. The stars saw job number one as entertaining a blue city. They laughed, they sang. I felt more depressed. Life rolled on. The big business that is Broadway made money. The stars seemed unaffected by the shadows in their midst. We went back to school, cut and edited the tape, packaging it as a

One City, Many Words

story about divergent casts coming together and mingling their egos and star power.

Who Wants to Be an American?
September 30, 2001

This story was about immigrants' patriotism. I had not expected their outpouring of feeling. Rescue workers literally wore their patriotism on their sleeves, but one of the most patriotic New Yorkers I encountered was my Dominican greengrocer. Immigrants have a hard life in this city and face many indignities. Many work crazy long hours for little pay. I expected them to be subdued about our ongoing terrorism fight. I was wrong on all counts. I got this idea when I overhead my Dominican greengrocer say he wanted to volunteer for the Army to fight these guys. He slammed his fist into his hand, exuding righteous anger. I was an ambivalent lifelong American unwilling to fight. And here was someone who had been here for about fifteen years who was willing to put his life on the line for this country. My grandfathers—second- and third-generation Americans—felt like this. They were ready to defend our borders.

I developed this story while being profiled by CBS' *The Morning Show* on Sunday morning. They wanted to film me (young journalist type) interviewing people for my school articles and so my interviewee was profiled as well. Even the seasoned reporter, Martha Teichner, was surprised. I felt like a clueless white girl, when many Dominicans, and other recent immigrants, told me: This is my flag too. This is my home. And this is my country.

Thousands of people had recently signed up for military service. It reminded me of family lore of my patriotic ancestors fighting in the Revolutionary War, the Civil War, the First and Second World Wars, and Vietnam. I could understand some of their zeal (except for Vietnam) for fighting in more innocent times, but I had expected a more informed public to be cynical about the use of military force. My family is mostly Anglo-Saxon Protestant, with some Irish, Scotch, Dutch, and Native American thrown into the mix. This story was an example where I just should have known better. I had a cousin who used to be an Army Ranger. But friends I knew who joined up did so to pay off student loans, not for patriotic reasons.

This story was a lesson in humility. I never know how a story will turn out when I start. The stories hold the power. I believe this country has betrayed many of its citizens, but others don't. I grew up in a succession of trailer parks, was raised on and off food stamps and welfare, and have seen the devastating fallout from drugs, gangs, and alcohol in my schools. But today, I am relatively privileged. It affects my news judgment for the worse sometimes.

Skeleton Crews
October 11, 2001

Let them eat cake: the restaurant industry gets served a bitter pill and the workers most affected can least afford to lay idle. This television story for class revolved around the downturn in the restaurant industry and a charity event for the Windows on the World restaurant's employees' families (called Windows of Hope). My partner and I interviewed participating restaurant owners. The event was held one month after the towers fell. Each participating restaurant donated 10 percent of their profits from dinner that evening toward the relatives of the restaurant employees (the Windows of Hope Fund).

When I tried to pitch the story to newspapers, they told me, "We already covered the restaurant angle." Nonetheless we dutifully still interviewed the restaurant managers at Tavern on the Green, Sardi's, the Four Seasons, and the Monkey Bar. They discussed how well they treated their own workers. One claimed that his workers were very close, "like a tribe." The managers were no doubt sincere, but the fact was that they had unhesitatingly laid off members of

One City, Many Words

their tribes for as many as four weeks while the restaurant industry rocked and reeled.

Many laid-off workers were immigrants without a safety net, living one up against another in crowded apartments. These are the silent majority of restaurant workers, and there seemed to be little their restaurant union could do. The approximately 250 Windows on the World workers not on duty that day lost their jobs instantly. Their union tried to farm them out but there was just no work. Tourists and the expense account set were hibernating. This was another downer story for me.

Subway Strikes
October 20, 2001

The evil empire, for many, lurked below this city. Thousands of New Yorkers took buses and cabs rather than ride the subway, for weeks. This television story for class was about people's fears. It wasn't one I was initially interested in; it didn't resonate personally. I've gone skydiving and survived several car crashes, so I don't feel especially unsafe in the subway. But my partner felt trepidation whenever she entered the subway. It reminded her, she explained, of that nutty Japanese cult that poison gassed the Tokyo subway, the Aum Shinryoko. With reports of crop dusters and other schemes to chemically mass-exterminate Americans running rampant, she was freaked. We filmed people in the subway, waiting in the stations, and coming in and out of the entrance. A few were terrified but most said, what the hell, they couldn't live in fear. Some would have taken cabs if they could have afforded it.

We interviewed a psychologist from Mt. Sinai Hospital. She had observed that general anxiety was running high among her clients, and that riding the subway was even more anxiety-producing for many. Her pregnant daughter, for example, refused to ride the rails.

Straphangers said that unexplained delays had increased markedly since September 11. The Metropolitan Transit Authority didn't explain what was going on, and they felt anxious. Unexplained events took on a sinister cast. Teens and seniors seemed to have the least fear. Both trusted the mayor to handle the threat. Nonetheless, filming people riding the subway wearing gas masks was unnerving. This was the first story since September 11 I felt any distance from. It was a welcome relief. We giggled at babies wearing little cloth gas masks, and overall we had fun.

The Poor Pay More
October 21, 2001

Service without a smile: service workers in New York know they are expendable. These last months they got further proof. This print story for class detailed underemployment among the working class employed in service industries who largely run New York City. The story's genesis was a car service I took home four nights a week from my job at Forstmann Little, a venture capital firm. To non-New Yorkers, a chauffered car trip home is an extravagance, but in New York City it is standard for people in corporate offices to get a free ride. It is dangerous to take the subway to some neighborhoods late at night (or used to be, anyway). I traveled nightly from the GM Building on Central Park South and Fifth Avenue to my neighborhood on West 106th Street. I noticed that cars from Charge and Ride, my car service company, arrived more quickly after September 11. Most of their limousine drivers (they aren't really limousines, but that's what they are called here) are Pakistani or Indian. Other companies are predominantly Latino or East Asian. One night I asked a driver why so many cars were available. "How's business?"

The Pakistani driver, who didn't want his name used, became overcome with emotion. His command of English was middling, but he was eloquent. He made a motion like a hand pulling bread from his mouth. "Bin Laden," he said, "killed those people in the towers. But he also kill me by taking the bread out of the mouth of me and my children." The driver was quitting the business because the limo licenses and insurance premiums were beyond his means. He planned to pump gas for minimum wage. "At least I know I make fifty dollars a day," he said.

Based on this one story, I interviewed other drivers. They told similar stories. Many Latino drivers were sticking it out. They had to work twice the hours to get the same number of jobs. One dispatcher was annoyed that her bored limo drivers goofed off on the radio and were telling dirty jokes in Spanish.

I also interviewed restaurant owners and managers. Luxury service jobs, like car drivers, maids, waiters, and so on, employ about 75,000 people in this city. Companies who used to spend lavishly on entertaining and car services, like Lehman Brothers, Merrill Lynch, American Express, and Goldman Sachs, had all cut back drastically. Hotels had laid off 3,400 people. When I first came to New York I worked at Goldman Sachs for a year to pay my way until I could get into grad school. My friends who still worked there told me how bad things had gotten. I concluded that when the economy gets bad, the service workers are the first to suffer. Most of them are immigrants who can ill afford the gap in income. I felt like I had a decent story, but didn't have the time to flesh it out. Then the *New York Times* wrote about it a few weeks later, so I felt like my instincts were improving.

Fitzgerald and Fitzgerald
October 27, 2001

"The Irish mafia," some Latinos called the police and firefighters. I wrote about the resentment these Latinos felt about what they perceived to be the disproportionate attention and support given to the largely Irish firefighters and policemen. "Hey, we hurt too," they were saying. "We bleed like you do."

I watched more Spanish newscasts. Having had a Spanish boyfriend helped my comprehension and I occasionally conducted interviews in Spanish. My Spanish isn't fluent, but competent. The TV reporters on Spanish-language channels like Univision and *Telemundo*'s evening *Noticias a las Once* (The News at Eleven) always found a Latino voice with a perspective on the night's story. Outside of these TV channels and the local Spanish-language papers *Hoy* and *El Diario-La Prensa*, losses to the Latino janitors and service workers were largely overlooked. The English-language coverage focused on emergency personnel, but Latinos died too, doing their duty. Reading a Spanish newspaper and then reading the *New York Post* or the *New York Times* was like glimpsing two separate universes. Do we live in the same city? Yes and no.

One woman I interviewed called this the Fitzgerald and Fitzgerald phenomenon. White reporters, she implied, interview white people. Another explanation that I heard from Latino service organizations was that many families of Latino victims were undocumented immigrants afraid of being deported. The mainstream media covered this, but not very well I think.

This issue resurfaced when American Flight 587 to Santo Domingo crashed in Rockaway, Queens. Many families felt that the attention paid their families was abysmal compared to those of the terrorist attacks. Where was all that money the white relatives had received within days? The crash was incredibly traumatic for the Dominican community, but the story faded as reporters focused on the largely Irish Belle Harbor neighborhood. Many firefighters and cops had grown up there. Fitzgerald again.

Angel-Eye View
November 9, 2001

Patrolling the subway is assumed by many to be the purview of the metro police, but there is a shadow security force that sees itself as a necessary part of the city's safety. Derided by many, appreciated by others, the Guardian Angels have been a sometimes goofy fixture in

One City, Many Words

the subways and streets of New York for twenty-three years. This television segment examined the Guardian Angels' take on security after September 11. It was a tie-in to my television piece concerning people afraid to ride the subway. The Angels, a hot media subject in the 1970s, had faded from view in the 1990s as crime in New York City fell. Many found their presence in subways and neighborhoods unnecessary. They disagreed, seeing themselves as a supplemental policing force, filling gaps that the city's police system could not.

My partner and I interviewed the last original remaining leader of the Angels, Arnaldo Salinas. He was nicknamed Number Thirteen after the thirteen original members. Like the other members, he had been recruited by his boss while working at a McDonald's in the South Bronx. They had initially called themselves the "Magnificent Thirteen" and had been a sanitation committee. Later, their focus switched to crime prevention. Their original leader, Curtis Sliwa, is now a radio personality in New York on WABC. I knew them only as the red satin-jacketed and-bereted men who occasionally stood at the end of my subway car, arms akimbo.

Salinas described a renewed sense of mission and had noted a rise in appreciation for the Angels' presence in the city's subways and streets. The Angels now carried little gas masks in their pockets along with first-aid stuff. People, he claimed, felt safer with the Angels around. Number Thirteen had seen it all. He had been stabbed and otherwise assaulted numerous times by what the *New York Post* would call "thugs."

As we talked the radio crackled in and out. Thirteen was constantly communicating between the headquarters office near Times Square and volunteers patrolling various neighborhoods all over the city. The Angels were like warriors on a holy mission although that isn't how they would describe themselves. They had lost one major contributor to the organization on September 11 and felt personally attacked. I didn't understand their copycat militaristic culture, but found them interesting. That they were paid little or nothing illuminated their level of commitment. And, in the end, bad news is always good news for somebody. Like the army, they were getting new recruits all the time.

The Thrill Is Back
November 10, 2001

Just when Gary Condit got dull, the story of the century arrived. Suffering, for many, is diverting. This story followed members of the moneyed class, who I felt viewed terrorism as another opportunity to demonstrate charitable and patriotic impulses. Dozens of charity auction invitations passed my desk after September 11. Most included a sorrowful note about the terrible event and their intention to donate a portion of their profits to the September 11th Fund.

I also noticed that society dames wearing red, white, and blue filled the society pages and glossy magazines. Magazine covers featured babes in American flag bikinis. I see these as the reactions of people largely insulated from the mess, who see it all as an exciting game. To the über-rich, losing millions in their portfolios is depressing but not financially fatal. I remember one friend describing a socialite coworker who just kept saying petulantly, "It's just so saaaaaaaad." Give me a break. My piece could have been called, "Cry Me a River." So my professor interpreted this piece as a rant against the rich, and I gutted it accordingly.

I eventually killed a similar piece about rich New Yorkers moving out of the city and into their weekend houses. The ladies who lunch took their kids to the suburbs rather than face the city's daily annoyances and perils. The working husbands often had to stay behind during the week. Brokers in Bronxville, New Jersey, and Long Island told me that real estate queries from New Yorkers newly interested in the suburban lifestyle were on the rise. I once had a coworker who commuted to the Hamptons in the summer while his wife and kids stayed there full-time. It sounded

One City, Many Words

like a nice arrangement to me, if you could afford it. But also a funny kind of marriage.

What was true, and not my jaded opinion, was that in November President Bush agreed to let the travel industry use a speech of his to promote tourism. Spend, spend, spend, was the message. "Fly, and enjoy life," he intoned. "Take your families, and enjoy life." This spot was aired 1,035 times to the tune of $10 million.

I noticed that members of the moneyed classes complained about the waits at commercial airports. Many started flying out of private airports like Teterboro in New Jersey. Terrorism is just so inconvenient. For most New Yorkers, "enjoying life" and flying to Barbados for the weekend isn't really an option even in the best of times. Changing jobs, habits, or hobbies is an unaffordable luxury for many struggling to raise kids on a diminished income.

At the time I was reporting this, Mike Bloomberg was running for mayor. The thought of getting a billionaire mayor just tickled me pink: New York would be, in the coming months, exposing its super-rich to super scrutiny.

Who Ministers unto the Ministers?
December 1, 2001

The city's ministers and other religious leaders were seen as rocks supporting the collective grief of the city after the attacks. They oversaw countless funerals and eulogies. I explored the personal costs of this bravery, the cracks in the armor of these pillars. This story focused on how the city's ministers, rabbis, and mullahs dealt with the outpouring of grief in their communities. I was raised Baptist and nondenominational Protestant, but don't go to church much anymore. I initially had a sense that religious leaders were under siege when I heard reports of parishioners sitting shiva in morgues, volunteer pastors ministering at Ground Zero, and priests convening three funerals a day in some parishes. This story was born out of this hunch.

Carla Sapsford

I am a counselor's daughter. I know counselors burn out if they don't take care of themselves, and these counselors were under immense stress. I always enjoy interviewing men and women of the cloth. Their perspective is often practical and philosophical. The head rabbi at the Board of Rabbis (Doniel Kramer) revealed that the city had to contend both with changes in burial procedures and with congregations of Holocaust survivors reminded of attacks against their shtetls and cities in Europe many years ago. Congregations, he related, had stepped up and supported their rabbis and each other in ways they hadn't done before. Jews all over the city, he continued, opened up their houses for visitors.

One seminarian said Union Theological Seminary, one of the most liberal in the country, was asking thorny theological questions, such as how does one serve oneself and God at the same time? How to take time off when everyone was asking for your solace night and day?

The Lutheran Counseling Service in Long Island said that many marriages of pastors were on the verge of breakdown. Wives of pastors, explained the head counselor, felt like the mistress and not the wife. Husbands spent less and less time at home. What about the wives' needs?

A Nation of Islam mullah said that black Muslims in particular have known oppression and that they as a group are better prepared to deal with this crisis. His group is fairly controversial here, but afforded a counterview to the feeling that all religious leaders were reeling under the collective weight of need in their communities.

This was my favorite story. It covered the very real problems men and women of God faced in their mundane lives when they came home at night. I converted this piece from a television piece that I had done with a partner into a radio piece, and wrote a new script for it. It ran on March 23, 2002, on WFUV at Fordham University's public radio station.

• • •

One City, Many Words

Cops Are Hot
December 8, 2001

Hunks are in again. Who cares if they know how to peel an artichoke or wear Armani? This story was about the romanticizing of blue-collar workers. In *People* and other fluffy magazines, cops, firemen, and other brawny rescue worker types were being profiled with and without their shirts. *USA Today* ran a story about white collar women lusting after men they would have ground beneath their Manolo Blahnik heels six months before. To see that emergency workers' attractiveness quota has skyrocketed, one need only frequent working class bars. I had seen the phenomenon amongst Jersey friends. "Cops are hot," they say, and actively scope them out in clubs. They're socially acceptable too, it seems. Women can bring them home to mama now.

A few years ago I co-wrote a guidebook called *Sexy New York 2000*, then coedited the next year's edition. I saw plenty of New Yorkers slumming it in S&M and voyeur clubs with names like "Hellfire," "The Vault," and "The Noose." "Hogs and Heifers"—the bar that inspired *Coyote Ugly*—attracted Hollywood and frat boy types looking to ditch their bras and underwear in public. This type of story bored me by the end of the book. But here was a real story about people (at least briefly) changing their social habits. The fireman fetish abounded. In the end, I suspect that many of these ladies will tire of their heroes and return to their own kind to mate. For lifelong New Yorkers, the sudden escalation in the status of the police and firemen is dizzying.

I shied away from the lascivious aspects of the story. I heard one radio interview from a rescue worker kitchen in which the male interviewer kept asking, "What about reports of women using this volunteer kitchen duty as a way to meet men?" Who cares. Just some reporter's fantasy about women flinging themselves at the feet of scruffy blue-collar workers. That didn't interest me. What did was the turnabout in class status.

Carla Sapsford

A friend did go for the jugular, and pursued a story of the fireman's association annual beefcake calendar. It had been canceled out of respect, but the relatives of the pictured firemen (many now dead) said the show should go on. It was for a good cause. The calendar was released, and sold like hotcakes. My friend got a prominent byline on the Marketplace section of the *Wall Street Journal*, with a picture of a gleaming fireman astride the Wall Street bull. I am fascinated by these kinds of stories, but feel a little cheap doing them. I hesitate to perpetuate stereotypes of women as fickle gold diggers of any type. But this was a valid trend, so there was the story.

Parting Words
New York is a fascinating testing ground for a reporter. The whole world is here, and everyone really does have a story. I haven't mastered the art of storytelling, but with so many opportunities to practice I feel blessed to be here. Life may be more challenging since September. It's certainly more nuanced and yet simple. Many reporters want to chronicle this period for posterity. Future generations, they argue, will read our words with wonder. Maybe. It doesn't feel especially portentous to me, writing and reporting on life as it's playing out day to day. I see normal people being tested in extraordinary ways. It makes for exciting reporting. And exciting living. Thank you for sharing your stories with us, New York.

Witness to Catastrophe

By Michael Howerton—*Stamford Advocate*

With more than twenty-five hundred metropolitan New York residents killed in a single day, journalists fanned out across the area to undertake the grim task of interviewing their families and loved ones. MICHAEL HOWERTON of the Stamford Advocate *interviewed Donna Hughes on September 13. The next week, Howerton spoke to Beverly Eckert. Both women had lost husbands. Eckert's husband, Sean Rooney, had called from the 105th floor of the World Trade Center as smoke permeated his office. Howerton describes confronting the disaster, and how that effort helped him see both the privileges and shortfalls of his profession more clearly.*

A California native who moved to New York to attend the Columbia Graduate School of Journalism, Howerton, twenty-eight, earned his degree in 1999. He then joined the Stamford Advocate, *where he now covers education.*

I I heard a whirling about me followed by a deep loud boom a few blocks away. Walking a few yards south, I saw a smoking void in the upper floor of one of the Twin Towers. The top of the building was surrounded by what looked like a million pieces of confetti glistening in the sun. Flames circled the area of impact and strips of the tower hung down like paper streamers. I thought a bomb had exploded and my mind conjured up images of the 1993 blast. I relaxed when people described a plane. *A plane in trouble smacking into the tallest thing around?* In the wonder of the moment, I guess it seemed plausible.

I watched the flames and smoke as the sidewalk filled with people. I could not grasp the situation. *Were people injured?* The reality of many deaths should have been immediately clear, but I could not comprehend it. About ten minutes later, again the buzz of a too-low airplane, again the boom, again smoke, fire, and shimmering debris. People screamed and I felt my fear grow as I realized we were under attack.

The World Trade Center towers dominated the New York City skyline for the three years I've lived in the city, but they have never been real to me. I was never in them and seldom around them. A few years ago, I had gazed up the towers' endless vertical line into the night sky. But I never knew the buildings, never knew anyone who worked there. They had seemed cold and uninteresting to me. Standing on the sidewalk that Tuesday morning I couldn't help but think how the office towers, ripped open and spilling their contents

Witness to Catastrophe

into the sky, looked like a giant piñata. In their last hour of life, the towers, suddenly fragile and wounded, shed their impenetrability and became beautiful.

Police suddenly filled the streets. They ordered us to leave lower Manhattan. I felt the thrill of danger hearing their shouts. But how to get home to my apartment, near 125th Street, about 150 blocks away. I tried to call Mary, my fiancée, who was working uptown at Columbia University, but my cell phone was jammed. Sirens filled the streets. The subways seemed an unwise option. I began walking, mapping my long trip home, then stopped. I was a reporter. The realization came as a shock and a relief. With a role to play, I felt freed from helplessness, fear, and danger. I reached into my shoulder bag to make sure a notebook was there. The feel of the pages and spiral binding calmed me. I could avoid being a victim by becoming an observer of victims. I asked a man next to me to tell me about what he had seen.

Sirens and shouts filled the streets, but the city felt still, spooky and sad. I had never felt so relieved to be scribbling in a reporter's notebook, a task I have repeated thousands of times at school board meetings, crime scenes, and community events. But here the notebook gave me buoyancy. I channeled my anxiety and fear into my reporting. A surge of adrenaline propelled me from one interview to the next as we all moved uptown.

Looking back I am ashamed at my giddiness as I scribbled. People were scared; people were dead, and I was excited to be among it, to see it, as a witness and a reporter. Maybe this is part of the pathology of being a reporter, this wanting to be where most people wouldn't, wanting to see what most would turn from. It's a game. A reporter has the privilege to feel included, but not consumed by events. It makes sense to me now that part of my exhileration that morning was a defense against realizing the horror. As a reporter I could at least have the illusion of control and usefulness.

I came to Kenmare Street just before 10 A.M. There I saw Sam

Crawford slumped on a bench in front of a grocery store as people streamed past. I asked him if I could talk with him about what had happened. He nodded and I knelt down to be level with him when I heard yet another boom, louder than the first two, followed by shouting. Assuming another plane had crashed, I looked at Crawford, but he made no move to rise. He buried his head in his hands. I rushed to the corner to see what was happening and saw smoke rising where the burning tower had been. I came back to Crawford and told him one of the towers had just collapsed. He nodded.

He told me he saw the second plane hit from his office on the thirty-seventh floor of World Trade Center Seven. He watched people in the doomed office towers panicking with no way of escape. How to articulate such a senario? "There is something horrible about watching people trapped like that," Crawford told me. I asked him where he was heading. "I'm slowly walking home," he said. "I need to let my wife know I'm OK."

On the corner of Houston and Broadway a woman sobbed in the arms of a friend. She kept repeating, "I'm so scared, I'm so scared, I'm so confused." She had been in the World Trade Center plaza, under the towers buying peaches when the plane slammed into the building above her. She had run north away from the explosion and falling debris until she came across her friend.

As I crossed Houston Street and walked north through Greenwich Village the city seemed more recognizable. People bought food from street vendors. A village nail salon had a few customers. At St. Vincent's Hospital on Seventh Avenue a woman was holding a large handwritten sign reading, "WE NEED BLOOD." In my bewilderment it seemed an amazing coincidence. I thought they might have better luck another day, since everyone was bound to be distracted by the day's events. I was a full block past before I realized the sign was a response to the attacks.

By late afternoon the subways were back in service and I reluctantly boarded the 1 train at 34th Street to my stop at 125th. The

Witness to Catastrophe

train riders were sullen, whispering when they talked. A woman wondered aloud how easy it would be to leave a bomb under a seat. My stomach lurched. The next morning, with thousands presumed dead, I headed downtown on the subway to see the collapsed buildings and report on the rescue efforts. The day after was harder. The impact of what happened had begun to set in. Only devastation remained. A woman in the subway car was crying. The rest of the car was silent. No one moved or spoke. At Times Square, a man asked whether the Q was an express, then corrected himself. "It doesn't matter," he said. "Today nothing matters."

Ash fell on my notebook as I waited at the Canal Street checkpoint. Police, only allowing local residents with proper identification past, turned me away. I walked west for a few blocks until I saw a few people duck into a parking lot. Following, I found an open gate to an alley onto Sixth Avenue. I walked through soot-covered TriBeCa, terrified at how easy it was to evade the barricades. I watched residents carry belongings away from their damaged apartments. My notebook gradually filled with tales of fear and disaster.

On Thursday my editor asked me to return to Stamford. I left with mixed feelings. I was reluctant to separate myself from the scene, but I also was relieved to get away from the pall. I drove the thirty miles, past hundreds of American flags freshly taped to car windows and hung from houses. It would be in Connecticut where I would come to better understand the scope and devastation of the disaster. By Thursday, the paper identified about twenty-five people from the area missing in the attacks. They were mostly family men, commuting to the city for financial services firms. The paper, over the next few weeks, would be focused on telling the story of their deaths. Terrorists attacked lower Manhattan, but much of the pain spread quickly to the suburbs. Hundreds of homes on tree-lined streets in New Jersey, Westchester County, and Connecticut were suddenly in mourning.

I called Donna Hughes, an elementary school teacher whose

husband was missing, but got no answer. Thursday afternoon, I drove to her house on a quiet Stamford street. A paper American flag, which the newspaper included as an insert the day before, was taped to the door of the modest ranch-style house. I sat in my car and tried to rationalize knocking on her door. I had a cell phone next to me. I picked it up to call her, then put it down again. She would be less likely to refuse an interview in person, I thought. I knocked on the door and was flooded with dread when a young girl opened it. Standing a few feet behind her daughter, Donna Hughes invited me in. She told her daughter to play outside and offered me a chair. For the next hour and a half she talked about her husband, Paul. He left just after 6 A.M. each morning to catch the Metro North train to his job as data systems manager on the ninety-seventh floor of World Trade Center One.

Unlike many family members of victims, Donna was not holding on to hope that her husband was alive. Paul would have turned thirty-nine on that Friday, three days after the attacks. "I know he's gone," she said in her cramped living room, blinds drawn. Television and radio did not intrude on the stillness of the house. Donna said she was thinking about her ten-year-old daughter, Amanda, and how Paul's death will affect her life. As she talked, I could hear Amanda playing outside with a friend.

Donna said she felt like a war widow with a husband missing in action. It struck me later as a more apt analogy than it did at the time. Whoever drove those planes into the World Trade Center did so as an attack on the symbol of American commerce. Paul Hughes, as a middle class father with a long commute to his midlevel corporate job, was a foot solider of sorts in that American army. Donna spent her days on the phone with other wives trading worries until she couldn't stand it. Like Donna, the mourning spouses were almost all wives. Ninety men and six women from Connecticut were missing in the attack. The list of the missing was a snapshot of a particular business culture, which was in this case mostly affluent,

Witness to Catastrophe

familied, white, and male. The demographics seemed an antiquated image of the corporate world, but evidently a remnant of it thrives among Connecticut commuters working for financial service firms in Manhattan.

As I drove away from the home, Amanda played in the yard, balancing on the raised curb, trying to walk its length without falling.

Knocking unannounced on the door of a house in mourning and writing quotes from a grieving family are among the stock tasks of a newspaper reporter. This is an image that I think usually makes the public's skin crawl about the media: the eagerness to exploit sorrow, the forced intimacy with victims, the transparent compassion. I have sat in these darkened living rooms too many times. I understand the suspicion of these encounters; they are exploitive. The reporter is asking them to expose themselves at their most vulnerable, to talk about their grief before they have processed their loss. They risk a lot in agreeing to participate in what can only seem an abbreviated and garish rendering of their emotions. But the stories are also useful for the family, who generally want to talk and serve the memory of their loved one. The stories are popular with readers, who want the insight into suffering, even as they disapprove of the instrusion. They are also good for me as the reporter. I benefit from the tragedy by being the one who gets to tell the story. I get to sit next to horror, examine it up close, but not be crushed by it.

The desire to sit in those houses is a mix of curiosity, fear, and ego. If I can get close enough to study misfortune and calamity, to record the texture and measure the pain, maybe I can inoculate myself from its reach. By being close to the target, I could surely avoid the next strike. It was as if by withstanding the heat from the fire I could prove my toughness, and by watching the victims, learn how not be burned.

The following week I visited Beverly Eckert. She led me to the patio in the back of her house. I heard children's laughter and shouts from the nursery school next door. She told me her story of the morning her husband died. He was on the 105th floor of the second tower, trapped and suffering from the smoke when he called her for the last time. As she told me about her morning, I lost my composure. My shaking hand made it difficult to write. I focused on my notebook as her words appeared in black ink by my hand. As long as I could transfer each word she spoke to the page, I could control the wave of emotion I felt welling up. Her story, like all the stories, was too terrible. We sat silently. As tears coated my cheeks, she offered me tissues and hugged me. I told her I was sorry, ashamed that she should think of comforting me. I was embarrassed of my tears; crying was not professional. Yet in her company I finally felt the stress and sadness of the past week.

I left her house and sat in my car at the end of her block. What was the value, I wondered, of offering these morbid, voyeuristic tales of horrible death? My job seemed ghoulish, feeding on corpses and destruction. I wrote the article anyway, sickened by my joy over writing a good story. Over the next few weeks I wrote stories about others who had lost fathers, husbands, and brothers in the attacks. I visited Donna Hughes's class and tagged along as Beverly Eckert took her husband's golf clubs and shoes around the course for a ceremonial game. I felt my focus and purpose as a reporter tighten around this event, the same event that had unfastened so many of the lives I wrote about. I gradually returned to writing local school stories, which I had neglected as long as I could. Municipal elections were a few weeks away. I could barely muster the energy to cover the school board race. I resented the return of everyday activities and assignments, not only for their seeming lack of importance, but also for the loss of prestige I felt in turning my attention to them.

Looking back, I not only had been a reporter, but also a scared bystander, close to, but not in, harm's way. I needed to hear the accounts of others to recognize that this had also happened to me. My fear on September 11 was unrecognizable to me. I had never before been scared in that way and I couldn't immediately make sense of how I felt. In the following weeks, as I wrote and heard stories about the attacks, I began to understand my emotions. My story of the attacks became clear only after I heard the stories of others. It was as if I had to hear it to feel it.

At the end of October, the families of those killed in the New York attacks were invited to a memorial at Ground Zero. One of the widows gave me her pass, declining to visit the place her husband died. On October 28, I rode the subway to Chambers Street, trying to guess which of the other riders were heading to the same event.

On the street, I was ushered through a gate alongside the twisted steel debris that was once the World Trade Center. I joined the crowd of people staring at the still smoking wreckage. The devastating sight was not the crumpled and torn buildings. It was the thousands of people, family and friends of the dead, crowded against the destroyed offices.

As we waited for the service to begin, I saw no other reporters in the crowd. The press had been directed to a media pen on the other side of a barricade. I listened to people around me sharing stories about where their loved ones had been when they died. I began to panic. I was worried someone would ask me about my story. Everyone was there, packed shoulder to shoulder, for someone they had lost; I was there for myself. I also felt a debt to the woman who had given me her pass to be there in her stead. I felt a certain responsibility to represent her and honor her husband's memory. I never told anyone I was a family member of a victim, but with the badge I wore, people could only assume I was.

I didn't take out my notebook, knowing it would have exposed me as a fraud. The magic it had possessed on September 11, setting me apart, now felt appalling. I moved to the edge of the crowd, interviewing people as discreetly as I could, not for their benefit, but mine.

Digging through the Rubble

By Heidi Singer—*Staten Island Advance*

Reporting on lower Manhattan's fractured cityscape after September 11 often meant navigating unfamiliar moral ground. Following the attacks, HEIDI SINGER of the Staten Island Advance, *the last local daily newspaper in New York City, visited the home of a grieving family and abandoned colleagues to dash through the rubble near Ground Zero in search of violent slogans and body parts. In retrospect, she realized she had traversed uncomfortable terrain. Yet in the process she gained a deeper and more complex understanding of journalistic ethics.*

Singer, thirty-one, covers city hall for the Advance, *where she has worked for four years. After graduating from the University of Toronto with a major in English in 1993, the Canadian-born Singer hitchhiked through Eastern Europe, settling in Tokyo and London for long stretches. She then went on to earn a master's degree in political communications from San Francisco State University and work at a small paper in upstate New York. In 1999 Singer won a certificate of merit from the Deadline Club, the New York City chapter of the Society of Professional Journalists, for two articles exploring the treatment of the violently mentally ill. Singer is a Brooklyn resident.*

I arrive by foot after it's all over, with lower Manhattan already a calm, lifeless netherworld. From the Brooklyn Bridge, the swirl of ash is more disorienting than traumatic, having blown away the ambling tourists and rushing secretaries, and the flyers hawking cheap lunch specials. I'm alone in a silent snowstorm, leaving fresh prints in the white dust as I trudge west toward the crime.

A couple blocks away, white haze suddenly gives way to a familiar scene of fiery activity: a jumble of shouts, the shrill caw of ambulances backing up. Blue police barricades sculpt an abstract enormity into clean, digestible lines of order.

I know what to do. Pulling out my notepad, I hang press tags around my neck and turn to a group of firefighters just emerged from the wreckage, peeling off hot layers and dousing their skin with plastic cups of water. I start looking for Staten Islanders, but a distracted firefighter waves me away with a gruff, "Not now."

A familiar stress twists in my stomach: I need to do my job, and I don't want to be a pest. But this time, it's tempered by ignorance because I don't realize how many of his friends must be dead. Besides, there are worse offenders, like the asshole photographer who stole a firefighter's jacket and tried to sneak behind police lines. Now, he's sitting in handcuffs against the wall. A firefighter tells me the story, tossing out a contemptuous *"of course"* as he walks off.

Idiot. We watch cops hauling the imposter off. But I doubt I'm the only one with mixed feelings. *What if I worked for a more cutthroat newspaper? Under pressure from an editor squirming behind his desk, egging me on to outmaneuver the competition?*

On that day, when numb shock clashed with the feverish excitement of being alive, I relied on my instincts. In that free-for-all first moment, when everyone got the same shot at the story, I didn't realize the toughest part was building painfully in the background of my mind. I never talked about it, but I think I became dimly aware that I was feeling my way through a changed moral landscape. Propelling myself forward on nervous energy, I didn't stop much to think. But my conscience came back to me. It came out in my stories, my nightmares, and in the memories I couldn't get out of my head.

There was such a surreal, dreamlike quality that first week, when everything had been jolted out of place, and anything was possible. The story came automatically: the material was everyone and everywhere and the news hole was bottomless. Telling it seemed like the easy part.

"The buckets are all over the ground and a couple thousand people are stampeding over them," I wrote after being caught in a mass panic attack during a September 13 visit to Ground Zero. "It's the most terrifying moment of my life by far. I trip over a bucket and I know a thousand people are behind me, not planning to stop.

"How far away is safe? A block? Five blocks? The stampede ends at Nassau Street, where a police officer collapses from a heart attack. Someone screams for an ambulance. I see sergeant's stripes as they rip open his shirt."

I've been a reporter for five years, long enough to rub away the glamour from the famous and newsworthy, but not long enough to erase another kind of thrill. On that first weekend after the attacks, I confidently stepped over the velvet rope and into a mosque in a Middle Eastern neighborhood of Brooklyn. Although female, I boldly poked into men's prayer rooms, joined a group of frightened, angry Arabs confronting a police officer on the sidewalk.

Digging through the Rubble

I knew a journalist who could disappear into his role so well that people confided their racism to him, forgetting he was black. What enormous freedom. In this case, pen, pad, and dangling press tags were my entrée into the mind of a woman who was glad the attacks had happened.

She was veiled and sweating from the heat. She wore her glee openly, and as she talked, I came to see that this was the culmination of a building fury—an ending, for her, not a beginning. She wouldn't give her name, but was happy to tell me, the anonymous, objective reporter, that not everyone in New York was shocked and horrified. I was proud that people trusted me to be the objective recipient of dangerous thoughts, but it was also chilling. Did they really think I had no emotions? It was a burden to carry her voice in my head.

I dragged my burden into a dinner party in Williamsburg that night, where a group of friends gathered to console each other with food and candlelight. A guest angrily condemned U.S. foreign policy in the Middle East, saying the attack was justified. Normally I might have listened politely, but not that night. I felt the room go cold and silent as, my voice shaking angrily, I dared her to remove her veil of political correctness and reveal herself as the ideological partner of that hateful, gloating woman in front of the mosque, to follow the logical conclusion of her argument—that she was glad for the attacks. Of course, she didn't mean it that way, and probably neither did the other woman. Ideology had won out over humanity in their minds, and I couldn't understand why.

Part of my anger came from exhausted frustration. I felt powerless to describe some of the horrific images I'd seen: Rescue workers on that first night battling smoking steel beams with hastily bought garden shovels, their labels still attached. The haggard face of an old woman who knew her son was dead. If anyone had seen those things, I was sure, they wouldn't even hint that the attacks were justified. So maybe, despite the endlessly looping cartoon images of planes hitting buildings, this woman at the dinner table and the one at the mosque hadn't seen what I saw.

Could I have written anything that would make those dinner guests feel the tragedy as naked and raw as I was seeing it, stripped away from history and politics just in those first few days? It's always a struggle translating images into equally powerful words, but I never tried harder than in that week. So it's maybe not a surprise that I strained and chafed at the boundaries of convention, and at times good taste. A couple of times, I think I broke through them.

I'd covered fires, building collapses, and natural disasters. Death by suicide, homicide, disease, and accident. They all have their own peculiar rules and procedures. The suicide: Call the family once. If they shout obscenities at you and hang up, wait fifteen seconds and call again, gritting your teeth and digging your nails into your palm. The murder: Sneak up to the detectives' room on the second floor of the police precinct. Or even better: Wait outside in the biting night air, in the stench of the nearby Fresh Kills landfill, hoping the neighbor will invite you inside to spill dirt on the cop who shot his wife, then turned the gun on himself. Later, find yourself at his kitchen table, peering out at the Halloween ghosts and goblins swaying in the dead couple's front yard, as you listen to incriminating gossip you can never print. Register a vague sense of guilt as you leave, notebook crammed full of juicy hearsay.

This time, the stakes were higher. The tragedy was worse, and I was a part of the story, the buffer of objective listener torn away. I think that's why my sense of protocol was in disarray two nights later, after sneaking into Ground Zero with a Red Cross volunteer to shovel debris on the pile.

That was the night we were caught in a stampede, after a worker saw rubble crumbling off a building. Riding back to Staten Island on the ferry, we sprawled out on the back deck, facing the shrinking, smoking city, and let the warm night wind pull some of the dust out of our hair. When I got home, I washed my clothes in

Digging through the Rubble

hot water, scrubbed the ash out from under my nails, and let myself absorb the shock from fearing I would die.

Days later, I recognized the restless, letdown feeling of not having gone far enough, leaving too early, without enough compelling material. I was also uncomfortably aware I had gone too far.

I became conscious of my conscience in short bursts of remembered ambition: I'd hoped to find a body part sticking out of the rubble because it would make great copy. When half-burned papers floated down at us from an inky sky, I was frustrated because the sheets were impersonal payroll ledgers. I'd abandoned my coworkers to zigzag back through side streets, searching for a particularly violent slogan that someone finger-scribbled into the dust. I remember the way they looked at me. *Was I being a good reporter? A crass voyeur?*

I'd faced an even tougher test the previous day: a victim's family. On September 12, I sat in the living room of Domenica Giovinazzo, mother of Martin, thirty-four, listening to the pathetic white lies her relatives concocted to keep her spirits up. The family allowed me to record her family's pain because of some vague hope that as a reporter I possessed special string-pulling powers that would help uncover her son unconscious in some faraway hospital.

I climbed the stairs to the porch of the house where the dead man had grown up. The screen door opened into a hallway, which took me into a small living room crammed with couches and relatives. Haggard faces looked up at me expectantly. They assumed I was there to help. I shrank into a corner couch, embarrassed. This wasn't what they expected.

I wrote that the TV was an endlessly droning soundtrack to their suffering. Listened to someone observing aloud to the dead man's mother that a backhoe on TV was clearing rubble "nice and easy." Noted that from the comfort of his studio, the newscaster carelessly slipped and said there was no hope for the missing. But my silence made them uncomfortable. I couldn't help noticing they were drifting into the kitchen. I was silent ostensibly because the best reporters know when to shut their mouths and listen, but really I couldn't think of anything to say.

Then this scene unfolded in front of my open notebook, and I scribbled it down:

> Martin Sr., who has been sitting silently by himself, seemingly dozing, suddenly opens his eyes. "I lost another son."
> "Don't say that," Damino gently chastises. "Martin, you never know. It's like you've buried him."
> "I lost a son," he repeats. "Twenty-five years ago. He was in an auto accident."
> In the bedroom is a photograph of Dominick, who died at 17, a fresh red rose rolled up and tucked into the frame. "This world is coming to an end," says Damino.

Martin is Mrs. Giovinazzo's husband. Nick Damino is her brother-in-law. Their words were heart-wrenching, but they also became a quietly harsh and violent burden. They dug deeper into my emotions than any of the horrific images I saw and recorded in my notebook. Part of the reason was the strange mixture of pride and guilt. I pictured the words and image of that sad, quiet old man making people put down the newspaper and cry. It wasn't an action-movie shocker that left you numb, but a horribly intimate family snapshot. I felt a rush. I had captured something important.

But I still don't know whether I exploited the situation, wrote down things too personal for the world to see. Was the family aware that I would wade so deeply into their pain? How rationally could one expect the Giovinazzos to be thinking that day? I felt the stress then but I didn't stop to think too hard that night. I had a story to write and I was exhausted. Journalistic convention probably would tell me to leave when I sensed they didn't want me anymore. But I didn't. A few days later, when I confronted the women at the mosque and party, I would more fully understand why.

Digging through the Rubble

I suspect that for reporters, the numbness lasted longer than for our audience. There was a lot to temper our mourning: the exhaustion of sixteen-hour workdays, our professional duty to listen with detached objectivity. Of course I allowed my emotions to show and I allowed myself to shake my head and commiserate. But I was still expected to evaluate the information coldly: Can I verify the anecdote about the man flying past a window still strapped to his airplane seat? Could readers take one more story about a firefighter who closed his eyes and hugged the wall through two explosions and lived to tell about it?

When it came, the pain sneaked up in odd ways. Driving down Hylan Boulevard, the main strip of Staten Island, that first Friday night, past clusters of whooping teenage girls shaking their flags at traffic in almost celebratory fervor. Then later, glimpsing the flashing lights of an ambulance speeding past me down an empty highway in the direction of lower Manhattan, noiseless as if to spare exhausted people some small measure of new sadness. After three days of rubbing my face in tragedy, the sadness was sinking in.

They were running the city out of a pier on the upper West Side, and that's where I landed a week after the attacks. I sat at a long table and fought over telephone jacks with reporters from around the world, but mostly waited around. Rudy Giuliani showed up twice a day for press briefings, along with many celebrities and world leaders; only the major ones turned heads. Still, I was a million miles from the story, at least the one that mattered. I paced around the room and ate too much of the junk food put out by sympathetic Red Cross volunteers. I felt benched.

With time to think, I realized the trauma had surfaced in my writing—the quotes I chose, the passages I lingered over . . . which meant mistakes, awkwardness, and overdone descriptions glared off the page for an audience of thousands.

I was exhausted and overwrought in that first week, and wrote things that make me wince even now.

Heidi Singer

"These are the images we fear we'll remember for the rest of our lives," I typed shortly after my mosque visit, in an introduction to a collection of vignettes. It was melodramatic and embarrassing. But recently I was in the audience during a talk by Rick Bragg, the legendary and aptly named *New York Times* reporter who's been known to overwrite. Bragg told us to go easy on our September 11 work because even if you went too far, at least you didn't cheat anybody.

I didn't cheat anybody. I overwrote, searched for a limb, and possibly added to a mother's suffering. But somehow I still didn't cheat anybody. That's probably the most comforting thing I heard about my work as a journalist during the World Trade Center attacks. Even though someone who knew nothing about my work said it, he understood what I wanted most to get right.

Role Play

By Lauren Wolfe
—Columbia Graduate School of Journalism

During the chaos of September 11, journalists had little time to consult with editors or professors about the nature of their roles. For student reporters like LAUREN WOLFE, navigating this complicated web of ethical and professional challenges was particularly wrenching. After two frustrating days stuck in Brooklyn, from where she could see the smoldering ruins from her bedroom window, she traveled to Ground Zero. Planning to help clear rubble, she discovered that she could be most useful interviewing and photographing anyone wearing a hard hat or a uniform. She watched more experienced print and television journalists set up shots of buildings on the verge of collapse, and delicately interview firefighters knee deep in human carnage.

Overwhelmed by the suffering and loss of it all, Wolfe couldn't even look at her notes and photographs when she got home. She was inspired to write by a redheaded woman she met on the subway who had managed to provide therapeutic massages to rescue workers despite being repeatedly turned away by city and federal officials. Wolfe wrote about the contributions of volunteers like David Cole, a sculptor who joined a group of ironworkers for six eighteen-hour shifts to sort clothes and deliver supplies. Like Wolfe, the volunteers had forged their own crucial roles without official recognition.

Wolfe, twenty-seven, is a full-time editor at Architecture *magazine and a part-time student at the Columbia Graduate School of Journalism. Her work has appeared in the* New York Times *and the* Hartford Courant. *She has worked at the Peggy Guggenheim Collection in Venice and at the Metropolitan Museum of Art in New York. She currently works for the Associated Press in Rome.*

As I came up the stairs of the Delancey subway station on Thursday, September 13, the streets looked dusted as if for fingerprints. The scuffs of shoe tracks and tire marks were still distinct. It was quiet. Oversized rides of the aborted San Gennaro festival in Little Italy sat empty, covered in a fine layer of silt, and only one corner restaurant had old, dyed-blond people at an outdoor table, speaking in low tones. At the Canal Street barrier, I asked an officer if press could pass. He waved me through. After the soft sounds of people talking at the borderline, the path toward Ground Zero was silent, except for the hum of emergency trucks whirring past. I stopped to buy batteries for a camera and a pen at a Chinese-run stationery store where I was the only customer and where the workaday smile of the woman ringing me up was startling. A block or so later, two police officers gave me a surgical mask for the dust; until then, I'd occasionally covered my mouth with a red silk scarf. I now tied it to the black strap of my bag. It's still there.

A CNN cameraman named Mad Dog and I spent a few hours standing on the corner of Greenwich and Duane streets, a few blocks from the smoke. We talked about the gourmet meat sandwiches being handed out and what war zones he'd worked in. In spurts we ran to the other side of the street, when the men in fatigues shouted that the building we'd been watching all afternoon might finally fall. Otherwise, we huddled on a corner with other reporters and volunteers who had passed the border, and with touristy types

Role Play

wearing flag pins. (It was only two days after the attack, but flag pins and T-shirts were already on the market.) I tried talking to Mad Dog through my mask, but it was too hot and too hard to do, so it bobbed on and off:

Me (mask down): "So, is this like anything you've ever seen before?"

Mad Dog (no mask): "I've been in Rwanda, Sarajevo, Kuwait, Kosovo, and this isn't like nothing I'd seen there. The trucks remind me a little of Sarajevo, though."

Me (mask up): "Lots of trucks?"

Mad Dog wore long khaki shorts loaded with hanging pockets weighted with film canisters and metal tools. His reporter's vest had more pockets and a sewn-on label with his name, like army identification. Under it was a Hawaiian-style shirt. Mad Dog's legs looked like they'd scrambled more than once when snipers fired in his direction, or had climbed a lot of trees and scaffolding to get the shots he needed—strong, kind of dirty legs. I grabbed him a turkey sandwich from a cart with food and bottles of water of every size, most warm. He let me look through his camera's eye. To our left Russian priests in full black gear (tall hats, long cloaks) waved incense and chanted. A couple of army guys walked over to them, which prompted all the bored photographers to jump to, as the uniforms together made a more interesting shot than the building in front of us that still refused to fall. (Its windows were blown out and the shape looked buckled, I thought, but maybe that was what it had always looked like.) A young, short woman with frizzy hair and a clipboard walked up to Mad Dog and told him they couldn't get a power feed, and that no one could. She was his CNN producer, not much older than me. They prattled about what NBC was doing, where a good shot might be.

I lost Mad Dog for a couple of hours when I walked over to West Broadway. On the two-block walk, I saw three doctors in green scrubs with "Ear, Nose, and Throat" written on masking tape patched across their shirtfronts walking out of Ground Zero, sort of stunned looking. I asked them who they'd treated, what they'd seen. "Nobody," one man said. "It's eerie. It's silent." I nodded and they kept walking.

All day I had been told to move out of the way of passing trucks (flat-bedded ones leaving the site with crushed police cars on top of them, or vans carrying K-9 dogs heading in the opposite direction). In that still moment when the doctors left, I found myself alone at the barriers to the debris, staring back uptown, aware of my own discomfort in the scene. It was an oddly palpable feeling of incomprehension: Who was I to be there? What would I do next? I was not sure whether to head back over to Greenwich to try to find Mad Dog. But I knew he and his producer were setting up around the area with a feed to make. I saw them on and off from a distance after that. Each time I got close enough, I lingered, not sure how to help, wanting to be useful. They laughed occasionally, and like the hundred other reporters on the street, didn't do much. We all waited.

That Thursday I went to Ground Zero to do physical work: carry boxes, a piece of bent metal, whatever. I wanted to use my hands to move things. But the men in uniforms wouldn't let me do this. I was only allowed to talk, interview, and eventually write. Unsure if it would help anyone, I lulled myself anyway into a false sense of importance under the pretext that it was something I could do. And in those days of helplessness, I did it vengefully. I spoke to ironworkers and doctors and steamfitters and residents who couldn't get in their buildings to save their cats. I spoke with air force sergeants and with a twenty-three-year-old army private who boasted that he hadn't slept in two days. And I felt conflicted and small because hour after hour I watched firemen drag themselves past me and let other reporters speak to them.

But how to help? I was a student; I couldn't report breaking news—every experienced reporter in the metropolitan area was

Role Play

loose in the city—but I did have the time to take in information and deal with it considerately. I could speak to experts and meet with people for long interviews, repeatedly. I could try to understand my role in a time and place when people heard personal calls to action whenever a fire engine's siren rang out again. On the eleventh I didn't know this. Then I just felt powerless. (I circled my apartment for two days: making phone calls to my family in Manhattan, sensing the borough—separated by a body of water—had become as distant as another planet; listened to the radio; stared at the searchlights on the city's skyline from my bedroom window; felt pained and numb and unable to process anything, at all times simultaneously.) And even on the thirteenth, I still expected my body to carry rubble with its hands, with its strength, not stories with its eyes and ears. That resignification of meaning would happen later, when the environment didn't seem so new and suddenly extreme.

Upon reaching West Broadway, I joined fifty or so press people herded behind sidewalk barricades by army officers so emergency vehicles could pass. I fell in next to an ABC News convoy and reporters from the *Daily News*, APTV, the Newark *Star-Ledger*, and other media organizations. It seemed they were waiting for information or instruction; Diane Sawyer materialized at one point for a briefing. ABC had a run-the-show appearance, selectively choosing its interviews, mostly passing on the doctors and area residents revolving through. The TV people treated the firemen like dessert, rushing them with tentative requests to speak with them on air. Many of us hung back. The firemen were the most roughed up—approaching them felt like devouring them, as if reporters' insensitivity could be more dangerous than the physical smoke and sharp steel of Ground Zero. Interviews were sorts of flybys. As people came out, photographers shot them—it felt like that to me, literally shooting them—and writers asked them questions.

Lauren Wolfe

Between the standing, choosing of granola bar flavors from boxes left on the curb, and general milling around, a young CBS reporter did a brief interview in front of a group of fellow reporters that confronted the ambiguity of the job we were all doing. Two firemen, a father and son, agreed to speak with her on their way out. They stood at the curb of West Broadway, as a crowd of journalists gathered around, hushed.

"Um, I'm not going to ask you how you *feel*," she said.

The two men focused on the middle distance and answered her questions. They did not offer how they felt. It was clear from the weight of their equipment and the slouch of their bodies and the soot on their faces that they did not have the energy. And she didn't ask.

After the firemen walked off and the reporters re-nested behind the barricades, I told the CBS reporter that what she'd said seemed appropriate. "No," she told me, "I felt ridiculous. I didn't know what to say." But to me, on a hot, ashy, shocking day, not asking felt right.

I left the frozen zone at dusk. Heading uptown a few steps at a time, I encountered Al Baker, a *New York Times* reporter who had spoken to my first class at Columbia, Reporting/Writing I. He'd told us how he got his Pulitzer for reporting on the 1996 crash of TWA Flight 800 into the Long Island Sound. On that summer Saturday, Al had told us about climbing fences in suburban Long Island, gaining the Coast Guard's trust, and being taken out on trawlers. He had made his way through barricades and past police, and managed to stay at the site of the disaster, reporting, when no one else did, for days. When I saw him that Thursday, Al was mid-sentence, trying to talk his way to the center of Ground Zero.

In the chaos of the aftermath, decisions about who could be useful at the site were briskly made, and strangely distinguished. (A press pass from Columbia had granted me passage downtown, while volunteer construction workers were told to wait with their shovels at the borderline. Volunteers and reporters generally determined their own usefulness and whether they needed to work at

Role Play

the site, though the people "in charge" repeatedly made arbitrary gate-keeping decisions.) Al scanned the length of Greenwich Avenue and the smoking heap of buildings at its terminus. He was frustrated as he spoke to a man in a hard hat. "You have to get me in there," he said. "I'm recording history." An hour earlier, Al had walked right up to Ground Zero's closest barricade and watched as a group of yellow-T-shirted Scientologists emerged from the rubble, where they had done a kind of counseling that entailed mentally leading workers out of their surroundings in order to refocus them on the task at hand. Al was dumbfounded. "But you let the Scientologists in there!" he told an officer. "Well," the man replied, "they have a purpose." As he recounted the incident, the two of us waggled our heads at each other in disbelief that roles could be so unclear, decisions so convoluted. I mentioned that people carrying water were allowed in. "Yeah, sure, do that," the hard-hatted man offered. But Al didn't sneak his way in. He chose to not represent himself as anything other than a reporter, which seemed important enough to him.

Al and I talked for about an hour after that, a few blocks away from the press ghetto. He told me about plugging in his laptop at the house of a nearby shopkeeper to send in his reports, and we stared downtown together, not knowing each other really, but comfortable for a minute to stand together in a place where the unthinkable had happened, and where we, as journalists, were trying to make sense of it. He told me I was doing a good job. I told him I had to get to class—my magazine-writing workshop—but that it was hard to leave the site when there was so much to report. We were silent for a few minutes. The sun was low, and the dust was still heavy. I watched as he looked toward Ground Zero, clearly tired, but still planning his entry. He wasn't going to leave. I didn't know if I would either. It was a jolt when I decided in my sweaty, exhausted state that I should get to class—that even though I wanted to stay, work, *do* something, staying there was not going to change or help anything right then. I was not yet a reporter with a bureau to feed.

Considering it from a few months' temporal distance, it seems that the writing quickly had to address issues that most reporters had never had to face—death, mostly—and local reporters were like war correspondents at a still-unsafe scene, where people they'd known may have died. Those days felt unsafe not only at Ground Zero, but also in the city in general. More terrorism seemed likely. (My office at *Architecture* magazine, where I am the copy editor, was evacuated on October 12, because of an anthrax "scare." Announcements over the loudspeakers told us not to leave the building. Many of us left anyway. When we got outside, I lingered around the entrance among police, trying to hear what was going on, while hundreds of employees stood behind impromptu tape barricades. The cops told me to "get the hell away from the building." But, I protested, the announcements were still telling people to stay *in* the building. It turned out we'd actually been terrorized by our own profession: the "anthrax" was actually pulverized foam packing in a shipment of books.)

With this change in daily preoccupations and subject matter came a change in the tone of news: more urgent, more readily emotional, more expansive. All my journalism school education seemed useful as a new reporter, but also suddenly a little prehistoric. As an American, and especially as a New Yorker, there could be no objectivity on terrorism—it was everywhere outside and inside of us. And after those first few days in New York, going to Ground Zero became only a small part of the story. Frank Rich wrote in the November 14, 2001 *New York Times*:

> Suddenly even print seemed essential again, especially for a story whose intricacies beyond Ground Zero required on-site foreign reporters who knew what they were talking about

Role Play

and could provide subtle calibrations that cannot be encapsulated in headlines or talking-head bombast.

It was a fine affirmation of my newly chosen profession. Now I just had to learn some subtle calibrations.

Despite my newfound hunger for news reporting, back at school I was enrolled in a magazine-writing workshop that reflected my earlier interest in long-form writing. For it, I had a three-thousand-word piece due in mid-October. In preparation for our own feature, each week our professor, Bruce Porter, gave us exercises that came from an old *Newsweek* file, most from the late 1960s. He had handed them to every class he'd taught for the past decade: old dossiers about a mother-hen type in Chicago who fed and clothed people from the streets, or the rise of the San Franciscan Chinatown gangs in rebellious "flared, white trousers." We were supposed to write a story based on these dusty facts gathered before we were born. When asked what topics we would like to cover for our own pieces, I considered dropping out of school. I couldn't imagine writing about anything but what had just happened, yet writing about that seemed ridiculously untouchable. Files, class, school—it all seemed pointless. My day job, ludicrous. All I could do was not eat and not sleep and read the newspapers and listen to WNYC and read online news. For weeks. I couldn't write a word about the tragedy. I had (and have) somewhere in my apartment notebooks scribbled with interviews and recorded sounds, all unread and unmoved since being dropped off after the last day they were used.

Eventually, the collective blare of news reports and analyses woke me. By keeping the public informed as the news moved in widening concentric circles every day, reporters helped that news make sense in a time when little did. Every story I thought of ended up being covered in one format or more. (Reporting on Ground Zero also meant contending with thousands of angles and hundreds of other working journalists scooping them.) These reporters were the people I wanted to be like; this was the thing I wanted to do, and needed to know I could.

In smoky downtown Brooklyn on September 11, I'd made my way from a stalled N train to the promenade across the water from the Financial District. There, I'd filled steno notebooks with what had been said ("Have mercy, Jesus. Have mercy on our souls") and what the smell had been like (burned-out fluorescent bulbs). Between scribblings I would touch my hair and think how stiff it felt with plastics and pulverized glass in it; the wind coated us from the northwest, often blowing ash into our mouths. I hadn't known how to write and still live: life had never felt so insecure, and thus so intense; the need for purpose had overwhelmed me, but so had the pain. (This is the only city I've ever called home. I grew up just outside it, and moved here with my family while in high school. My mother is from the Bronx, and my father is from Brooklyn, and their parents are from the lower East Side and Eastern Europe before that . . .) Each time I recorded a quote from someone, I lived their feelings a little bit more—the anxiety of the woman in the red suit on the bench next to me whose sister was in the Trade Center that morning; the nervous excitement of the loud man who had seen "two hundred people" in the first plane as it glided low across the water. I was less frightened, busier, when I wrote. (Reporting revealed itself to be a shield and a weapon at the same time. A sense of being occupied and productive and thereby protected.)

Later, I wondered about the trauma involved in journalism. I saw horrible scenes, smelled terrible, cloying odors that resurfaced later in my mind. For months, sirens would stop me mid-block while I fumbled for something to hold on to, and, like so many New Yorkers, couldn't hear a plane overhead without tracking its path and gauging its height. Two friends of mine had died in front of me—a new fireman I hardly knew but had danced with at parties, and a college friend, a dancer I'd performed with, who was

Role Play

only in New York for a conference at Windows on the World that morning—and I had a feeling this would be true while I was watching the buildings sparkle with exploding glass. When a person told me about their brother, sister, or friend who was probably dying across the water from us, I had to make a decision: Write it down? If not, it would never live on paper the same way if I tried to recall it later; I'd learned that from years of recording scenes for my personal journals. But I also felt ghoulish, like a photographer who chooses to make a picture of a dying man he might have helped. (*Record, record, record it.*) I finally asked Professor Porter if I might write a long piece about an aspect of what had happened. "Of course, of course," he said.

A redhead with a hard hat on the F train finally inspired my piece. She held a white hat covered with signatures of the men—firemen, police officers, ironworkers—she'd massaged. Around her neck hung a respirator, and near the shoulder of her sweatshirt was pinned a red World Trade Center Emergency badge. She scanned the passengers that night "to see if they had dust on their boots, or a pass, to see if they understand." She had snuck into Ground Zero, lacking the recognized qualifications to be there. I later learned that others had done the same. These volunteers were told "no," but pushed into Ground Zero anyway. Like me, they entered with no plan and didn't know which of their skills would be valuable. They never backed down. This handful of people found the means to remain in the frozen zone by camouflaging themselves as "legitimate" workers, skipping barricades, or joining vague relief groups, like a downtown organization that previously worked to aid homeless children. They didn't care what officials said; their need to help trumped regulations.

I both understood and was mystified by these volunteers. Each person "did something" for slightly different reasons; whether someone explained that she wanted to be a hero, be of assistance somehow, or just simply see the place, each individual described

377

tangled, complicated desires. Beforehand, many were not already aware that they would react in this way. I interviewed psychologists and "ordinary" people, and located a variety of psychological reasons for people's tendencies toward action/inaction (previous exposure to trauma, feelings of satisfaction in their careers or family life, a desire to identify with recognized heroes like firefighters). At the time of the events, people were just acting or not acting, seemingly unaware of their own decisions. I certainly did not understand why my body kept finding its way to Ground Zero, into cop cars, and across a table from an aid worker, though it is clearer to me now why I'd chosen this topic and to confront these uncomfortable ideas: My own abilities and usefulness were too foggy, and the choice I'd recently made to be a reporter was being tested in an acute moment. At the time all I had were questions. *Was it enough to write about things? Why were we approaching this brutal work zombielike, as if there were no alternative?* There was. Be like most New Yorkers: volunteer in small ways; do nothing at all; give blood, or money, not a week sleeping amid the destruction on ash-covered floors. (Some people approached Ground Zero, were rebuffed, and then retreated.) But these volunteers persisted despite barricades both physical and mental. Veronica Mosey, the woman on the F train, an employee of Seagram's by day and a comedian at night, spent a week in an army-issue tent at Ground Zero massaging workers. David Cole, a sculptor from Providence, Rhode Island, took a bus down to New York and joined a gang of ironworkers who kindly tucked him into the center of their group and snuck him into Ground Zero. For six days, Cole sorted clothes—sweatshirts, clean T-shirts, socks—and, when supplies were bottlenecking, drove a golf cart past the barricades to ferry alternative loads of water and respirators. He worked eighteen-hour days, and slept on the floor of a nearby chapel. When I spoke to him, he asked a question of himself that probes the fine curves of what the media and anyone who wasn't moving steel with their own hands has to consider: "Was it 'disaster tourism'?"

Role Play

I have further questions as a reporter: What are our motivations, and are we actually helping? What, exactly, is "disaster journalism"? The coverage of a disaster? Or a kind of drive-by writing?

A couple of months before September 11, I spent eight hours on a Saturday night in the car of two Lower East Side cops patrolling their regular beat. Officers Sal Tudisco and Joe Guardino talked to me about their exhaustion as the motor ran on the corner of First Avenue and Houston Street. When the music got good they'd flick an internal car light from white to red, red to white. It was a cop-car disco. "Sometimes I get out and do the 'Running Man' at red lights," Guardino told me. Named "Officers of the Month" for having pulled a jumper off a bridge, they liked having their 8 x 10 pictures up on the wall of the stationhouse's dark room, and proudly sent visitors to view them alongside the candy machines and crime pin maps. I rode with them again just a few weeks into October. This time around, my ride was more subdued—less superheroing and dancing. Grayer, quieter. They hadn't slept in weeks. Their shifts ran from 3 P.M. to 7 A.M. or worse. They talked less about themselves this time, mostly in exhausted quips, and more about what they called "the bravery of all New Yorkers."

Tudisco and Guardino had agreed to talk on the condition that I jump in while they were on a shift. Joe, it turned out, had been massaged by Veronica Mosey. She'd remembered only Joe—one of only four cops I knew—from the guys at the 7th Precinct. In that car, five weeks after the fact, Joe said he'd met her, but never got a massage from her. It didn't matter. He and Sal wanted to talk about their lengthy hours at the site and the efforts of New Yorkers who cheered them on and helped out. The city was coming together just as it was unraveling, and in that car I saw how these cops, who just a couple of months before were talking about how hard it was for them to get any respect in the neighborhood, were as proud of their city's citizens as its citizens were proud of them.

They didn't care about my angle of cops interacting with the "volunteers" they were working to keep out of the area. But I thought it was a story that covered the whole strangeness of people undifferentiating themselves in a crisis. Everyone I spoke to, including Tudisco and Guardino, wanted to tell me about the role they had played in this massive event. And each story was different. And in that cop car, I really knew that all these stories from all these different kinds of people needed to be made sense of, and that I could find my role through doing this, through writing down and interpreting. Now it became a matter of figuring out what was worth telling, and then how, exactly, to tell it.

The Lost

By Jennifer Smith—*Newsday*

Armed with only a telephone and a list of names, JENNIFER SMITH spent five months summoning the ghosts of the victims of September 11 for "The Lost" section of Newsday's *Long Island edition. The resulting stories were refracted images shaped from the memories of those left behind—an anguished father's words on his just-grown son, a widow's halting recollection of a time when her family was whole. Smith, twenty-eight, never met the people whose grief she probed in countless phone interviews. Yet over the course of a thirty-minute call her role might shift from media telemarketer to counselor, interrogator, and even therapist. A first-time obituary writer who wrote more than seventy profiles for "The Lost," she found the process both curiously anonymous and intensely personal.*

Raised in the San Francisco Bay Area, Smith graduated from the University of California at Santa Cruz, and began her journalism career as a fact-checker for LA Weekly *in 1998. She moved to New York in August of 2000 to attend the Columbia Graduate School of Journalism. After graduating in May 2001 and winning the 2001 Baker Prize for Magazine Journalism for a story about the life and hard times of a band of alternative circus performers, she decided to stay in the city. Smith spent last summer as an intern on the national desk at* Newsday, *the fifth-largest metropolitan daily in the country.*

My first day of raising the dead found me somewhat at a loss.

There I sat at a borrowed computer at *Newsday*. Just two months ago I had been a summer intern for the Long Island daily's national desk, on the other side of the newsroom. Back then it had been what my jaded editors dryly termed a slow news summer, one whose dubious highlights included wild speculation about Chandra Levy's disappearance and breathless updates on the spate of shark attacks along the East Coast.

Now it was late October, one and a half months after the terrorist attacks on the World Trade Center and the Pentagon. No one was complaining about the lack of hard news to cover—not the national desk, certainly not the foreign desk, and not the Long Island desk, where I sat staring at the phone I knew I would soon have to pick up and dial.

On one side of me lay a copy of that day's paper, folded open to expose "The Lost," a special section dedicated to profiles of those who died in the attacks on the World Trade Center. I had just been hired on as a freelancer whose exclusive assignment was to write as many of these profiles as possible over the next two months.

Propped up on my keyboard were a handful of e-mails, from families who had sent death announcements into the paper, that Ben Weller, the editor of the Long Island desk, passed on to me. "It shouldn't be too hard," he told me by way of instruction. "At least these people want to talk to us."

The Lost

That was of singularly little comfort. Nervous, I took the phone off the hook and listened to the dial tone while I mentally rehearsed what I would say to whoever picked up on the other end. "Hi, this is Jennifer Smith, calling from *Newsday*. I'm trying to reach the family of [insert name here, pause]. I'm sorry to bother you at what I'm sure is a difficult time, but I'd like to write a profile of your [spouse/child/sibling] for the paper. Is now a good time to talk?"

As good a time as any, I supposed. I can't imagine it's ever a good time to share your feelings with a stranger about losing a loved one in a national catastrophe.

The insistent ring of the phone jolted from me from sleep on the morning of September 11. I lay in the guest bedroom of the house in Studio City, California, where Justin, my boyfriend, grew up. It was barely light out, just after 6 A.M., on the day of my flight back to New York.

It was supposed to be our last day in Los Angeles. We met here two and half years before. I moved to Hollywood from the San Francisco Bay Area, where I'd grown up, gone to college, and proceeded to stagnate in a series of aimless entry-level jobs after getting a degree in history at UC Santa Cruz in 1995. I had come here with a vague idea of working in journalism, under the theory that a change in surroundings and social life would kick-start my nascent career. It did, although not as quickly as I might have hoped. I fact-checked at *LA Weekly*, an alternative news and arts weekly, for a year and wrote some freelance news stories. Soon after Justin and I were introduced by mutual friends and began dating, I moved on to a job as an editorial assistant at the *Los Angeles Business Journal*, a small but respected weekly paper.

He and I fell in love. Our romance progressed wonderfully, but I was increasingly unhappy at work. I felt stuck in entry-level limbo, but didn't know where to go next. Casting around for a solution, I applied to the graduate journalism programs at Columbia

University and UC Berkeley in the fall of 1999. I got into both programs, and after much agonizing, decided to make the move to New York. Justin, a surfer who made movies for love and Web sites for money, stayed in Santa Monica. Neither of us was happy.

Lonely, I loathed New York at first. It was dirty and humid, my apartment was a dark hole, and I couldn't afford most of the cultural niceties, like tickets to plays, that New Yorkers use to justify living in such conditions. But as I lived and reported and drank my way through the city I developed a stealthy fondness for it, almost despite myself.

New York was a hassle—where else does a trip to the post office consume the greater part of a morning?—but New Yorkers were fascinating. The odd hours of free time in my grad student schedule I used for endless rambling walks through the park, up and down the avenues, out in Jackson Heights, Queens, where I was reporting for school. I became hooked on the street life, on the infinite variety of bars and restaurants and neighborhoods. And, my God, the convenience. Vast consoles of ATMs, trains running all night, Duane Reade drugstores on seemingly every block.

By summertime, returning to California seemed, well, a little dull. What if I got bored? My relationship with Justin had survived ten months of graduate school and an additional summer apart while I interned at *Newsday*. Now twenty-eight, an aspiring journalist fresh out of grad school and deeply, massively in debt, I had persuaded him to swap his life in Southern California for a year in New York. Our packed bags stood by the bed, ready for the 11:00 A.M. plane trip that would mark the beginning of our new life together.

I could hear Justin on the phone in the kitchen, his voice first groggy, then agitated. The call was from his father, a veteran TV news cameraman who lived nearby. Justin switched on the TV in the kitchen. "Jenny, get out of bed," he called.

"What's going on?" I asked, fumbling for my glasses.

The Lost

"Just come in here," he said, a note of grim panic in his voice.

I walked out of the bedroom, my mind thick with sleep. What I saw on the small TV set in the kitchen woke me up in a hurry. Black smoke billowed from the twin towers of the World Trade Center. I had no idea what was going on.

No flights left that day, or the next.

We came back into New York three days later, on a red-eye that arrived early Saturday morning. Our pilot made a slow swoop over lower Manhattan on his way to JFK, giving us a clear shot of the smoking holes where the World Trade Center once stood. The city sparkled in the autumn light. Justin leaned as close to the window as he could, capturing the approach on his digital video camera. I scrunched around him, craning my neck for a glimpse of what I didn't want to look at but had to see. I felt sick.

Later, in line for the ladies' room at the terminal, I saw a woman burst into tears. She dabbed at her eyes, blew her nose, but the tears kept coursing down her reddened face. No one had to ask her what was wrong.

I was equally rattled by what had happened to my adopted city. Watching the story unfold on cable from the sun-drenched safety of Southern California, I thought the collapse of the towers and the subsequent state of undeclared war seemed like a bizarre nightmare, a Hollywood movie proposal come hideously to life. At one point Justin and I had all three TVs in the house going simultaneously, calling out to each other from different rooms, "turn on NBC," or "CNN's got a number of how many were in the building." We waited, tense, for a news development that would make sense of the whole thing. It didn't come.

Restless from days of enforced passivity, I felt an overwhelming urge to get back to New York. But once I got there I didn't know what to do. Part of me just wanted to cocoon in my cozy apartment in Brooklyn, averting my eyes from the hazy columns that still drifted up into the sky over lower Manhattan. But the guilty journalist in me knew that this was the biggest story since, well, since anything I could remember in my twenty-eight years. I was unemployed and sending out resumes, and freelance reporters would no doubt be in demand. Somewhat reluctantly, I let my old editors at *Newsday* and at *LA Weekly* know I was in New York and available for assignments.

Still, my first weekend home it was all I could do to walk around Union Square. Over the past few days it had morphed into a sort of makeshift shrine made up of dollar-store candles and fliers begging for information about people who had worked in the Twin Towers. I picked my way through the clumps of people, vaguely repulsed by the numbers of people wielding pocket cameras and video cameras. My reaction didn't make much sense—after all, I was there gawking at it all like the rest—but the relentless documentation of the moment seemed somehow vastly inappropriate to me. The missing themselves presided over it all, flashing incongruously cheerful grins from photos snapped at the high points of lives— weddings, birthday dinners, graduations.

Soon after, I rode the subway down to Broadway and Nassau, the closest you could then get to Ground Zero without proper press credentials. It was close enough. My stomach knotted and clenched as I walked out of the station and shuffled past what little of the wreckage was visible. I lacked the heart and nerve to lie my way into the rescue site in search of a scoop, and found myself curiously blank of story ideas in the weeks that followed.

Newsday's offer came about a month and a half after my return to New York. It was my first real opportunity to cover the aftermath of the September 11 attacks, aside from some reporting on Red Cross relief efforts for *LA Weekly*. Financial difficulties had turned dire—I was temping as a receptionist in a real estate agency when I got the call—so I jumped at the chance to return to journalism,

The Lost

regardless of the circumstances. Now I sat back in the newsroom in Long Island, trying to ready myself to cover an event that had scared and depressed me like nothing else in my experience as a reporter or as a citizen.

The goal of "The Lost" was simple. We would tell the story of every person who died on September 11 until we ran out of families who would talk to us.

Initially, reporters pulled names and phone numbers off the flyers that plastered Manhattan in the wake of the tragedy. By the time I came on board, the reporters assigned to the project had it down to a semi-science. They worked off two ever-changing master lists: the names of the dead and missing whom we had yet to write about, and the names of those whom we had already covered. The list was compiled from AP wire reports and other sources, such as requests for profiles by victims' families, which we processed and wrote as they came up.

Most of the entries at least listed the person's age. Some had an employer or town of residence as well. As a regional daily, our first priority was to write about people from Long Island. After that, reporters basically picked which names they wanted to pursue at random, tracking down relatives and coworkers as best they could from the information provided.

At an average of 250 words, most profiles were short (a similar project at the *New York Times*, called "Portraits of Grief," allowed about 150 words per subject). A maximum of three stories per day, usually those that were particularly moving, were given a more generous 500 or so words in which to detail the shapes and contours of lives cut short. Whatever the word count, the challenge was to tell each story in a way that elevated it beyond the standard obituary catalog of milestone dates and survivors.

Given my complete lack of experience with writing about dead people, deviating from the standard template didn't pose any particular problem. I was quite possibly the only intern at *Newsday* that summer who had never written an obituary for the paper. In the absence of a conveniently located national calamity—say, a plane crash off the Long Island coast—my time on the national desk had been devoted to covering less dramatic stories. These I mostly reported by phone: a historical recreation of the Pony Express rider route, an in-depth look at California's new drug laws, an update on the long-abandoned Boston Strangler case.

Nor had I done even the most elementary cops or courts stories, which would at least have trained me in the fine art of barging in on people who want to be left alone and coaxing them to answer difficult questions. My previous journalism experience had been heavy on public policy and business, but light on tragedy. During my year at Columbia I had avoided death stories whenever possible. The closest I came was a mock obituary of the fallen televangelist Jimmy Swaggart, written for a classroom drill on deadline writing.

So I came to the assignment fresh—blank really—both on a professional and a personal level. I didn't know anyone who died as a result of the September 11 attacks. I have never lost a parent or a lover. The deaths that have touched me—grandparents and family friends who succumbed to age and/or terminal illness—while difficult, were at least expected and left the fabric of my daily life intact.

Luckily for me, I have what the author Michael Chabon called "a catastrophic imagination." It's the type of deep-seated paranoia that leads me to assume my loved ones are in constant danger of being snatched from me by forces over which I have no control: a swerving city bus, for instance, or a knife wielded by an overzealous mugger. It's not the healthiest trait, but it comes in handy when I'm interviewing the bereaved.

I don't know what it's like to kiss a spouse good-bye in the morning and then watch the office building where he or she worked crumble to dust on TV. But my dubious talent for conjuring up the worst-case scenario can help me at least try to imagine

The Lost

what it might be like. Unfortunately, it's not a skill that vanishes after the conclusion of an interview.

Sometimes the profiles strike you where you live. One young woman whom I wrote about was just twenty-four, a would-be artist and graduate of the Pratt Institute. She worked a day job as an administrative assistant in the towers to pay the rent while she tried to break into the New York art scene. She lived with her boyfriend, a filmmaker who supported himself by editing corporate videos for Lehman Bros. They were young and hopeful and just barely able to afford their small apartment in Fort Greene, Brooklyn.

The parallels between their situation and my own were unmistakable. I'm a struggling writer who works office jobs in between assignments. Justin has a documentary film under his belt but makes ends meet by working in new media, or at least he did back when such jobs were available. Like them, we are living together and building the first part of what we assume is a future together.

But then again, nearly everyone I wrote about was on the verge of something—retirement, marriage, buying a home. Men died days before their wives gave birth; one young woman died while seven months pregnant. The young artist I profiled was going to give notice at her job that Friday, an irony not lost on her grieving boyfriend. September 11 was replete with such "if onlys."

My natural pessimism, as much a part of me as my eye color, already told me that my future plans could be derailed at any time by random chance. My work on "The Lost" provided daily confirmation of that fact.

Writing these obituaries day in and day out didn't seem all that much easier for more experienced reporters. Novice or veteran, we were all grappling with the same emotional issues. If interviewing people about September 11 made us relive that day all over again, what must pushing the reset button do for the victims' families whom we prodded to talk?

Jennifer Smith

That shifting mix of guilt and shyness made the few interviews I conducted feel awkward, even though the families had contacted us, not the other way around. But that was nothing compared to the process I came to call "stalking" the families of the missing. As time went by, more and more families had their phone numbers blocked to elude the media. That didn't matter, logistically speaking, since *Newsday*'s research librarians could ferret old phone numbers out from voter registration records or using Autotrack, a paid information service that tracked people through past billing addresses, yielding unlisted numbers, names and contact information for their relatives, and even car registration records.

The hardest part was actually getting someone on the phone. Some days I'd spend entire afternoons leaving carefully solicitous messages on answering machines and then calling back repeatedly, hoping to catch a resident before the machine picked up. The whole process made me feel like a journalistic telemarketer whose sales commission depended on two things: the degree of detail I could pry of out reluctant victims' families and the volume of confessions I could extract in a day and repackage, complete with art, for the following day's paper.

Some people were eager to talk, even thanked me for writing the piece. Others were at least civil when declining my offer of a profile. Many never responded to my overtures at all.

I found it hard to blame them. It's bad enough to lose a loved one without having your personal tragedy turned into fodder for a media feeding frenzy. If I were in their shoes, I wouldn't want to talk to me. Not unless I was given a pretty convincing argument.

So the only way to get started on each day of invading families' private pain was to remind myself exactly why I was doing it. Yes, I needed the money, and yes, I wanted to be reporting on the biggest news event of this year, or even the previous decade. But there was something at the heart of it that mattered more: making sure that each person was not forgotten.

The Lost

Unlike a story about a car crash victim or a more ordinary murder, the fact of how these people died was curiously beside the point. There was a terrible unanimity to everyone's story. All the victims died in more or less the same way on the same day. What made each person's tale unique was not which floor of the World Trade Center they worked on or why they were there, but how they lived their individual lives.

The only problem was, I hadn't anticipated how hard it would be to pinpoint what made one person different from the next.

After two weeks on the job, I found myself wanting to outlaw a handful of phrases: "Family came first." "She was so full of life." "An avid Yankees/Mets fan." "His smile lit up a room." They kept coming up again and again, as if each of my interview subjects was reading off a press release handed out en masse to the families of World Trade Center victims.

Getting the details that truly made each story worth telling was like emotional teeth pulling. So I developed a repertoire of questions for my interview subjects. "What was _____ like as a child?" "How did you two meet?" And, "is there anything else you'd like to tell me?" This last one was taught me by a fellow reporter who is wise in the ways of phone interviews, and it works like a charm if you've established enough of a rapport over the phone—just stay quiet, and your interviewee will often rush in to to fill the conversational space.

Sometimes it worked wonderfully. The family and friends of Balewa Blackman, a junior accountant at Cantor Fitzgerald, gave me such a good idea of what he was like that my profile practically wrote itself. He heard "music in the most prosaic of noises. One time, the twenty-six-year-old hip-hop enthusiast from East Flatbush, Brooklyn, even recorded the sound of a pan dripping water into a sink. He recorded it and created a beat, the rhythmic base for a rap song." Blackman's mother told me my favorite anecdote, a story about her son charming a group of strangers at his boss's wedding last August. Balewa sat next to a bashful cousin of the groom. "Within minutes, the two were chatting like old friends—much to the amazement of the other relatives. Asked who he was, Blackman, who was black, pointed to the groom, who was white. 'I'm his illegitimate brother,' he said with a straight face. Upon meeting the groom's mother, he exclaimed, 'You must be Mom!'"

Others, such as Maryann Flego, the longtime girlfried of Ed Murphy, a managing partner at Cantor Fitzgerald, didn't have to be pumped at all. She was very forthcoming about his rather unusual interests and told me all about their Los Angeles vacations, where Murphy enjoyed taking tours of celebrity-studded cemeteries like Forest Lawn and once tried to rent the hotel room where comedian John Belushi died. Another time he tried to persuade Flego to brave a blustery snowstorm in order to attend the funeral of a mob figure. Murphy was fascinated by mobsters, she said. He loved how they managed to outwit the authorities, and their loyalty to "the family" struck a chord in a man who was fiercely loyal to his own family and friends.

But sometimes even the most persistent prodding didn't yield results. Judging from the comments of other shell-shocked relatives, many victims appeared to have had no personality traits whatsoever. Stating that someone was "nice" or "a good father/mother/daughter/son," may be true, but it doesn't tell me a lot about what a person was really like. It was especially hard to get a sense of some of the male victims, since they were often described (especially by other men) in the context of sports—what sport they had played in high school, which local pro teams they supported, their devotion to golf.

Absolutes ruled the day. "He always kept in touch with old friends." "She never spoke a harsh word about anybody."

I'm sure that in many cases the people thus described really did feel or act that way, at least some of the time. But a creeping

The Lost

cynicism made me wonder if everyone who died that day had actually been such a saint.

It reminded me of the way my classmates mourned one boy at my high school after he committed suicide in the tenth grade. In life, he had been a quarrelsome loner who picked on those smaller than him. Reinvented with postmortem hindsight, he became everyone's friend.

"We never had a fight," I was often told by the spouse left behind. Never? Not once in a thirty-year marriage? It strained credulity.

Part of the problem was that many of the people I first wrote about seemed cut from the same cloth. Whether they were firefighters, traders, or clerical workers, the victims seemed to be invariably from Long Island or the outer boroughs. They were people from backgrounds not unlike my own, the children of middle- or lower-middle-class upbringings with the usual American Dream-type aspirations: financial and professional success, home ownership, and, eventually, raising a family.

It wasn't that the pool of victims lacked diversity. On September 11 the World Trade Center held white Brooklynites, Bosnian refugees, and Haitian nationals, window washers, secretaries, and managing partners of trading firms. Lives stopped abruptly in every stage of adulthood, people dying in their early twenties all the way up to Albert Joseph, the seventy-nine-year-old maintenance man who finally succumbed to his injuries on January 1 of this year.

But that range wasn't always easy to see from the ground level. If the last three profiles you wrote were about firefighters from Long Island, it became difficult for you to think of anything new to say about firefighters from Long Island. For reporters caught up in the hunt—finding family members who would speak on the record, scrambling to get art, and fighting the usual battle of writing well while filing one to three profiles each day—the full variety of human experience didn't necessarily register.

So after a while I began try and mix it up. Sometimes I would intentionally pick names that sounded foreign or unusual, or focus for a week on covering a specific age group or gender, like very young women or older men who lived in New Jersey.

It became a game: the harder to find a person was, the more interesting their story was likely to be. Still, the more profiles I wrote, the more difficult finding new ways to say the same old things become. It got to the point where I sometimes made a game out of inverting the headlines in each day's "The Lost" section—"Never had a smile on his face." "Her children came last." "Never there for his coworkers." It turned the pages from a list St. Peter might envy into a catalog of dysfunction.

Churning out obituaries on such a large scale brings certain issues to the forefront. When dealing with the deceased, especially those whose death was part of a large-scale national tragedy, it's difficult enough to get people on the phone, let alone to say to a grieving husband or mother, "C'mon, gimme the dirt." How do you report well and accurately without being unnecessarily invasive? When does empathy for a subject skew your objectivity? How do you keep a poignant anecdote from appearing mawkish? And how do you consistently produce profiles that are accurate, interesting, and readable?

Mine sometimes erred on the side of sympathy. Despite my best intentions of remaining objective, I sometimes found myself becoming half interviewer and half counselor, a soothing presence with conflicting motives. On the one hand I genuinely felt sorry for the people I interviewed. But my empathy also had a payoff. Once my interview subjects began to feel comfortable with me they started to disclose more intimate details, the kind that make a chronicle of a life into an interesting read.

People don't necessarily have had to do the most dramatic things to be interesting. Sometimes being a character is enough.

The Lost

Establishing a rapport with family members is crucial to getting them to tell you what someone was really like. For instance, Grace Galante, a young woman I profiled who came from a very traditional Italian family, didn't seem too out of the ordinary. She married young, lived on Staten Island, wanted to have kids. But as I dug further with her brother, Frank Susca, I found out that his little sister—contrary to type—really ran the show, even with his aged immigrant parents. "We used to call her Leona Helmsley," he told me with a laugh. "When it came to family, she didn't mess around. She didn't take any guff from us." Then he related a telling story from when they were kids.

". . . He and Grace decided to play office. Frank, then nine, set up a little work space in a corner of their parents' home in South Brooklyn. He was going to be the boss, he told six-year-old Grace, and she was going to be his secretary. Settling into place, Frank made the appropriate noises simulating a ringing telephone. Grace, all six-year-old secretarial efficiency, answered, 'Boss's office.' So far, so good. Then he asked to speak to the boss. 'Speaking,' Grace replied."

I didn't get that aspect of her personality from interviewing her bereaved husband. That's why I always tried to talk to at least two sources. While a widow may recall her late husband as a church-going accountant with a grave manner, his bowling buddies might remember the deceased as a good old boy with a fondness for beer and off-color jokes. If discrepancies came up between one account and another, my task was to negotiate between the poles and arrive at a tactful approximation of the truth. I didn't want to produce bland pieces filled with platitudes that painted each victim as a pillar of the community, but I didn't want to besmirch someone's memory, either.

But at the end of the day, everything I had to go on was hearsay. The task was complicated by the fact that logistics and the ever-looming pressure of deadline didn't always allow for the luxury of

Jennifer Smith

waiting for people to call back, especially if I had enough material to fill a short piece. A good number of the portraits written by me and by my fellow reporters, both at *Newsday* and at the *New York Times*, quote only one surviving friend or family member.

That troubled me. I wanted to report in the best, most ethical fashion possible, but writing these profiles was different than doing investigative reporting. Personality traits aren't listed on any public documents. Even more concrete facts, like a person's age or how long someone had been working for a company, were not always easy to verify. In the first weeks after the attacks, the list itself of those missing and dead was constantly in flux, and employers struggling to regroup in the wake of September 11 were often slow to respond to media inquiries.

A few people tried to take advantage of the confusion for personal gain or attention. A reporter a few desks away from me kept getting collect calls from an incarcerated man who said his wife had died in the attacks but was unable to provide any sort of detail about where she had worked. Once he had the reporter's ear, he seemed more interested in complaining about the conditions in his jail than in talking about his dear departed. Repeated phone calls yielded no further useful information or contact with other relatives; eventually he was asked not to call again.

One woman I interviewed had originally e-mailed the paper a little paragraph about her father, whom she said was one of those missing on September 11. Over a lengthy phone conversation she told me all about him. She was utterly convincing, grief-stricken but not hysterical, and I took her story in good faith. It was only when I was unable to find her father's name on any published list of the missing and dead that I realized I'd been had: not only had he not worked at the Trade Center, he didn't exist at all.

After a while, the cynicism of the older reporters around me didn't seem so callous. I resolved to temper my sympathy and allowed extra time to corroborate information—can I talk to a close

The Lost

friend of your husband? Did your mother have any longtime coworkers I could speak with who might have memories to share?

But it wasn't always possible to determine the truth. In one case, a woman's live-in boyfriend told me that he and the deceased had gotten married one week before the attacks, a claim her family vigorously disputed. I had enough material to write about her life, but I needed to settle the question of her marital status. Her alleged husband didn't return my calls requesting a copy of the marriage license, a document that the county clerk told me I would be unable to obtain unless I issued a subpoena as part of legal proceedings. When the woman's family stopped returning my calls as well, I ended up having to shelve the piece.

By the end of my two-month soujourn I had developed my own tricks, standards, and practices for writing newsprint headstones. I rarely teared up anymore during interviews, and I'd gotten much better at switching personalities—sympathetic on the phone, but all business efficiency when it came to getting art and tracking down sources. It was easier to write the piece when you thought of it as a story, not a person.

Despite that, emotions held in check got triggered when I least expected it. The sight of an American flag might leave me cold, while a photo of a fellow reporter's offspring could bring up morbid thoughts of what it would be like for that child to suddenly become an orphan.

What I did forty hours a week had a way of leaking over into my home life. It's one thing to write obituaries about people you've never met. It's an entirely different thing when you find yourself thinking about the people you know—the still living—in obituary-speak. My boyfriend, for instance, becomes "an aspiring filmmaker with a passion for surfing." My mother? She's "a twice-divorced native of New Zealand, practical and independent, who raised her two children as a single mother in California's Bay Area."

Neither description is inaccurate. But they feel somehow lacking, just as it must when I ask people to come up with two or three things that define their lost relative. It's like a life-size cardboard cutout of a famous person—all the correct details are there, but the overall effect is two-dimensional, lifeless. When you know someone, when you have loved someone deeply, or perhaps changed their diapers and watched them grow to adulthood, summing up that life as a combination of adjectives, or a list of favorite hobbies, tends to ring a bit hollow.

The thought that lurks below: how would my own obituary read?

The drive home from my office in Melville—conveniently located across the street from the National Cemetery—to my apartment in Williamsburg, on the western edge of Brooklyn, provides ample time for mulling over such things. My morning drive was a sweet, relatively traffic-free forty minutes, a nice restful time where I watched the leaves alongside the Northern State Parkway change color in the autumn sunlight.

But the crawl home took as long as an hour and a half. It was dark by then, the signs alongside the highway the only visuals to break up the tedium.

By December, it seemed that every exit from Route 110 to the Williamsburg Bridge had a story attached to it. I didn't lose anyone in the tragedy, but the cumulative weight of each profile makes it feel sometimes as if I had. I knew about people like Winston Grant, the man from Hempstead whose widow sits alone in her kitchen, limbs stiffened by Parkinson's disease. Before the September 11 attacks, she said, "I could depend on him to be in the house at a certain time each day. Now when 6 o' clock rolls around, my heart just gets really heavy, because I know he's not coming home."

Passing into Queens I remember James Cartier, the Jackson Heights electrician from a family of seven who rarely missed a dinner with his parents, even after moving out of the house. One of his sisters also worked at the World Trade Center. She made it out in time. He didn't. "Pain has a way of taking the prayers right off your lips and you can't speak at all," his father told me. "I'm still stuck in Tower Two with my son . . . as far as I'm concerned, I died with him."

I don't cry often at night. But I'll cry on the way home, alone in my car with my thoughts and the World Trade Center's dead.

Two days before the end of my assignment I was asked to stay on for three more months. I was pleased to have the work, but the thought of writing, say, another sixty or so profiles gave me pause.

On one level, writing for "The Lost" provided a kind of emotional satisfaction I hadn't yet felt in journalism. The job gave me a chance to do narrative writing (at least on a small scale), my favorite kind of work, while gaining valuable experience with the deadlines and pressures of working at a daily newspaper. More importantly, if done well these little stories could become part of a family history—a framed, yellowing testament to the life of someone's son or daughter, clippings stowed away to be shown later to children too young to remember the deceased. It was a way to make a difference, to somehow contribute my skills to helping clean up the mess that had become of my city.

The stories yielded a level of response unlike any other pieces I have written. I fielded a number of calls from readers wanting to contribute money to the college fund for this victim's children, or to send a Christmas gift to the family of another. And nothing can describe how good it feels as a journalist and as a human being to get a call from the mother or husband of someone I wrote about saying, "thank you. You got her. You really got her." Or more simply, from Hyacinth Blackman, mother of Balewa: "It gave me satisfaction."

But two straight months of writing about dead people had also left me tense, grouchy, and depressed. I was snippish with my boyfriend and rarely went into the details of my work with him or other nonreporters.

Jennifer Smith

The work and the long commute had taken an equal toll on my body. My shoulders seemed permanently fused somewhere near my ears, despite sporadic visits to yoga class. A habit of jabbing feverishly at the keyboard while typing interview notes had aggravated what I feared was the start of carpal tunnel syndrome. And I had gained weight—comfort food and alcohol just seemed more appealing options than exercise. I needed to blow off some serious steam.

Worse yet, I feared I was losing my drive to make each story, no matter how short or seemingly pedestrian, something special. I was glad that I had planned to spend the Christmas holidays back in California, with my boyfriend's family. Hopefully the two weeks off would help recharge my batteries, professionally and otherwise.

Back in Southern California for the first time since the attacks, I settled into the same guest room where I had been awakened on September 11. Putting my clothes into the dresser by the bed, I tried to shut my mind as well to thoughts about those who died at the World Trade Center. It was easier here than in New York; fewer people had lost loved ones, and the everyday fact of the rubble was something you saw on the news, not in person. I skimmed over articles about the victims' families or skipped them entirely as I flipped through the *Los Angeles Times* over morning coffee. I just didn't want to get emotionally involved with the news for now.

My mental ostrich ploy worked, for the most part. But lying in bed with my boyfriend one night shortly before Christmas, I found myself trying to blurt out to him all the thoughts I had bottled up, not just over vacation, but over the entire course of the assignment.

"All those families," I said. "It's the holidays, and all those families have to deal with this, thousands of them . . ." I don't know if I articulated what exactly I meant: the phantom ache I felt in sympathy for the relatives of the people I had written about, the weird pang I got when I saw pictures of the Twin Towers, whole, ablaze,

The Lost

or crumbling. I didn't know anyone who died in the attacks, but in a way I did, because I now knew their stories and their families. I broke down to Justin for the first time since September 11, when we had held each other and cried after watching the towers fall to the ground.

On New Year's Day, I awoke from a nightmare in which my mother had died. It was a long dream, chillingly realistic. It opened with her death from complications relating to some nameless surgical procedure and then kept going on and on—past the news of her death, past the funeral. It then charged into that awful territory I had come to know from the many interviews I conducted after September 11: having to tell people over and over that your loved one is dead. The long, drawn-out hurt that never heals completely. The desperate, angry, and unanswered question of why.

I never saw the Twin Towers in that dream, but I felt them there, crouching invisibly over me as I slept. The pall they cast lingers still.

ACKNOWLEDGMENTS

This book would not have been possible without the hard work and patience of all its talented contributors. The editors are grateful for their perseverance, courage, and honesty in facing the challenging journalistic issues raised in the essays.

Matthew Lore, Jamie Jones, Elizabeth White, Michael Grunwald, Sreenath Sreenivasan, Daniel Egers, and Hans Chen helped locate contributors for this book. Valerie Burghar identified Rob Walker's article and arranged for its inclusion. Jennifer Nelson deserves special thanks for her myriad contributions.

Supporters at Thunder's Mouth Press include: Daniel O'Connor, Rebecca Hanover, Emma Hospelhorn, Matt Rinaldi, and Rachel Adler. Timothy Stewart-Winter, Jane Spencer, Howard Erman, Mary Corcoran, and Hans Johnson provided invaluable editing and advice.

PERMISSIONS

Petra Bartosiewicz, "From Nightmares to Redemption," 2002. Printed by permission from the author. • Jennifer Chen, "The Vacation," 2002. Printed by permission from the author. • Peter DeMarco, "Journey to Ground Zero," 2002. Printed by permission from the author. • Alexander Epstein, "Out of the Blue," 2002. Printed by permission from the author. • Beth Fertig, "Listening Back," 2002. Printed by permission from the author. • Katherine Eban Finkelstein, "40 Hours in Hell," American Journalism Review, November 2001, 29-33. Reprinted by permission of American Journalism Review. • Stacy Forster, "As It Became Ground Zero," 2002. Printed by permission from the author. • Jill Gardiner, "A Detoured Commute," 2002. Printed by permission from the author. • David Handschuh, "A Lens on Life and Death," Poynter.org, January 8, 2002, <http://www.poynter.org/ethicsessays/handschuh.htm>. Reprinted by permission from the author. • Christine Haughney, "The Flow of Humanity," 2002. Printed by permission from the author. • Michael Howerton, "Witness to Catastrophe," 2002. Printed by permission from the author. • Sandra Jontz, "From the Pentagon," 2002. Printed by permission from the author. • S. Mitra Kalita, "Seeking Solace in My Notebook," 2002. Printed by permission from the author. • David Paul Kuhn, "All I Hear Is Silence," 2002. Printed by permission from the author. • Matthew J. Malone, "A Fireman's Son," 2002. Printed by permission from the author. • Zlati Meyer, "Start Spreading the News," 2002. Printed by permission from the author. • Heather Nauert, "Have You Seen…?" 2002. Printed by permission from the author. • Amie Parnes, "Living with Fear," 2002. Printed by permission from the author. • Carla Sapsford, "One City, Many Worlds," 2002. Printed by permission from the author. • Cindy Schreiber, "Learning to See," 2002. Printed by permission from the author. • Heidi Singer, "Digging through the Rubble," 2002.

Printed by permission from the author. • Jennifer Smith, "The Lost," 2002. Printed by permission from the author. • Nick Spangler, "Diary of Disaster," 2002. Printed by permission from the author. • Abby Tegnelia, "Camaraderie and Sorrow," 2002. Printed by permission from the author. • Rob Walker, "This Is America," 2002. Printed by permission from the author. • Benjamin Wallace-Wells, "Creating September 12," 2002. Printed by permission from the author. • Chris Williams, "Facing the Fear," 2002. Printed by permission from the author. • Lauren Wolfe, "Role Play," 2002. Printed by permission from the author.